The Conversational Enlightenment

Dedicated
With friendship,
to
Christopher Scott Welser

Parce que c'estoit luy, parce que c'estoit moy.

The Conversational Enlightenment

The Reconception of Rhetoric in Eighteenth-Century Thought

David Randall

EDINBURGH
University Press

Edinburgh University Press is one of the leading university presses in the UK. We publish academic books and journals in our selected subject areas across the humanities and social sciences, combining cutting-edge scholarship with high editorial and production values to produce academic works of lasting importance. For more information visit our website: edinburghuniversitypress.com

Edinburgh University Press Ltd
The Tun – Holyrood Road
12(2f) Jackson's Entry
Edinburgh EH8 8PJ

First published in hardback by Edinburgh University Press 2019

Typeset in 11/13 Adobe Sabon by
IDSUK (DataConnection) Ltd

A CIP record for this book is available from the British Library

ISBN 978 1 4744 4866 6 (hardback)
ISBN 978 1 4744 4867 3 (paperback)
ISBN 978 1 4744 4868 0 (webready PDF)
ISBN 978 1 4744 4869 7 (epub)

Contents

Acknowledgements

I am grateful to more people than I can possibly name – but among them, John Ackerman, Helen R. Andrews, Darin Barney, Michael Bristol, Marshall Brown, Samuel A. Chambers, Brooke Conti, Timothy Costelloe, Brian Cowan, Julie Cumming, Kyle Davis, Samuel Fleischacker, Bryan Garsten, Eugene Garver, John Guillory, Marc Hanvelt, Gerard Hauser, Torrance Kirby, Rita Koganzon, David Kopel, Jacob Levy, James Masschaele, Warren Moore, Kevin Pask, Mark Pennington, Adam Potkay, Ariane Randall, Francis Randall, Laura Randall, Eyvind Ronquist, David Rosen, Elena Russo, Andrew Stevens, Jeff Sypeck, Robert Tittler, William Walker, Ronald Witt, Peter Wong, Paul Yachnin, Leigh Yetter and several anonymous readers for their comments on different portions of the manuscript. I am also grateful to the Social Sciences and Humanities Research Council of Canada, the Making Publics project, and Concordia University for their support while writing it.

Every book I have written has been inconceivable without the love and support of my wife, Laura H. Congleton, for which I am grateful every day, and for which I will always try to make adequate recompense.

I dedicated *The Concept of Conversation* to my son Joshua, saying 'it has never been as important to me as he is'. That is also true of this book.

'Humean Aesthetics and the Rhetorical Public Sphere' was originally published in *Telos* 157: 148–63. © 2011, Telos Press Publishing. All rights reserved. Republished by permission of the copyright holder, and the present publisher, Telos Press. http://www.telospress.com

Introduction

Precis

The rhetoric of conversation remade Enlightenment thought and culture – although the conversationalists of the eighteenth century increasingly forgot that their chit-chat was a mode of rhetoric. Ever less wittingly, they applied a universalised, democratised variant of the old Roman *sermo* (conversation) to the worlds of the schoolhouse and the coffeehouse, to the fine arts and the philosophy of the mind. Conversation informed the *salons* and the eighteenth-century culture of politeness, as well as theories of education and the increasingly egalitarian treatment of women. Virtually every field of aesthetic endeavour became conversationalised, including art, architecture, music, dance and literature. Not all of eighteenth-century culture was conversational, but broad aspects were. Ultimately, the men and women of the Enlightenment applied the concept of conversation to the realm of opinion, and brought forth in *public opinion* the universal conversation in which all humanity discussed all matters of common concern. By c. 1800, *sermo* had become the ruling discourse of the Western world.

In one sense, this triumph of conversation came swiftly. It was only about the middle of the seventeenth century that the *grand siècle* French theoreticians of rhetoric had begun to conceive of conversation rather than oratory as the default mode of rhetoric, and in the next half century this new notion had permeated not much farther in European culture than the *honnête* culture of the French *salons*. The conversational practice of the *grand monde* came to characterise an extraordinarily wide swathe of European and North American culture in the next century, from the philosophy of Shaftesbury to the string quartets of Mozart, from the development of the seminar at Göttingen to Madison's innovations in the theory of public opinion.

In another sense, however, conversation's Enlightenment triumph was the capstone of a meditation on rhetoric stretching back to the ancient world. *Sermo* had originally been an exploration of indefinite topics conducted in the leisure of noble Romans, a complement to inform the oratory of the public world. Italian Renaissance thinkers had turned conversation into a metaphor capable of infinite extension, while Baldassare Castiglione had conversationalised the culture of the court. The French *grand siècle*'s turn to conversation, linked to the *salonnier* and *honnête* variation of court culture, built upon a long intensification of the conversational strand both within the rhetorical tradition in particular and within European thought writ large.

The *salonnier* claim that conversation was capable of usurping the public world, the realm of *oratio* (oratory), which would bear such dramatic fruit in the development of the conception of public opinion, likewise built upon a long history. *Sermo*'s role in the ancient world as the complement of oratory had been transformed in the Renaissance as princely oratory made ever more universalising and compulsive claims to dictate to every aspect of human life. *Sermo* became a refuge, an alternative discourse in essential tension with oratory as it strove to preserve reason from eloquence's compulsions. The conception of *sermo* as refuge from *oratio* led in turn to the more ambitious conception of *sermo* as a possible rival, a superior discourse with which to address the public world – if only it could establish itself. This last ambition had habituated itself in the world of the *salons*. The ensuing spread of conversational public opinion was the capstone of this long transformation in the relationship of *sermo* to *oratio*.

Yet this *salonnier* conversational public opinion was in turn partly supplanted by the more Platonic public opinion of the *philosophes* – and this central drama of the Enlightenment, the combat of the *salonnières* and the *philosophes*, likewise originated in old battles between *sermo* and its rival modes of discourse. Ciceronian *sermo* had always articulated a critique of the inhuman and excessively confident purities of dialectic and Platonic dialogue, and this intellectual critique had acquired sociological trappings in the Renaissance. The Republic of Letters had been born largely as a scholarly variant of *sermo*, but it had slipped towards the assumptions of Platonic dialogue. The *philosophes* inherited the discourse of the Republic, admixed with the new tradition of Baylean critique, and likewise inherited the old *querelle* with the Ciceronian *sermo* of the courts and the *salons*. In the last years before the Revolution, the *philosophes*' Platonising discourse would indeed supplant *salonnier* conversation as the default mode of public opinion in France – but the *sermo* tradition would survive in America as the organising discourse of the Great Republic's constitutional order. The *philosophes*' triumph was in any case narrow in scope: conversation endured as the pattern of much of the Enlightenment's fine arts and philosophy.

The conversational tradition engaged in other rivalries, old and new. The oratorical tradition retained much of its ancient power: conversation's triumph over its old counterpart, such as it was, was partial rather than annihilatory. Edmund Burke did not converse in Parliament, but orated, and the philosophy of David Hume sublimated rhetoric in both its oratorical and its conversational modes. At the same time, conversation faced a new challenge from a discourse of pure reason championed in various modes by Descartes, scientists and Kant. This discourse of pure reason, overlapping significantly with the Platonising discourse of the *philosophes*, rose as had conversation as a redoubt of reason against the claims of oratory – and pure reason's partisans condemned or ignored conversation in good measure because it was so effective a competitor to the mantle of reason.

Conversation's strength against all these rivals lay precisely in its reliance upon a mixture of rhetoric and reason – upon its status as a rhetoric that aimed at truth rather than victory. In an age whose thought inherited from the Renaissance a largely rhetorical matrix, *sermo*'s rhetorical nature made it more familiar, easier to use and ultimately more popular than its rivals of pure reason. Pure reason's reliance on the rational word also inhibited its application to the vast nonverbal realms of human endeavour – the realms of sight, sound and motion. *Sermo*, as *oratio* before it, provided a far more useful model for the fine arts. Then, as against both the discourses of *oratio* and pure reason, *sermo* respected and relied upon a reason rooted in human individuality. Where *oratio* compelled mankind, and pure *ratio* alternately discounted and dissolved the individual, *sermo* called each human being to contribute his unique character to universal discussion. *Sermo*'s strength lay not least in its gentle welcome to all mankind, which contrasted with the twin peremptory demands of *ratio* and *oratio*.

Sermo's strength lay also in its newfound notes of democracy and universality. These qualities had been implicit in the earlier iterations of the conversational tradition – but the Enlightenment variation of conversation, as it emerged from the *salons*, emphasised them ever more strongly. Conversation before, as all rhetoric, ultimately had been a craft – something that could be acquired by some, but not possessed by all. Now it became an attribute, a capacity, of all mankind. This universalisation of *sermo* expressed itself not least in its sublimation into philosophy, as conversational capacity transformed into a quality of the mind – aesthetic in the first instance, but with implications that would affect the realms of epistemology and teleology. The universalisation of *sermo* grounded the cultural and political democratisation of conversation in philosophical first principles. Shaftesbury and Hume provided a foundation for Mozart and Madison.

The full dimensions of the Enlightenment's conversable world have not been drawn before, nor the full extent of its dependence upon the rhetorical tradition of *sermo*, although different subfields of that century's intellectual history have all established the importance of the concept of conversation in their separate domains. This work's first ambition is to establish the ubiquity, and hence the importance, of Enlightenment conversation. Its second goal, however, is to revise those schools of history, philosophy and political theory drawn from the works of Jürgen Habermas, especially his *Structural Transformation of the Public Sphere* (Habermas 1991). Habermas predicates his historical model and his philosophy upon the existence of an Enlightenment public sphere constituted by a quasi-Kantian discourse characteristic of the age. Yet this discourse was at best a rival of Enlightenment conversation – and conversation may indeed have a better claim to be the Enlightenment's characteristic discourse. This book provides the historical grounds for a theoretical revision of the full panoply of Habermasian theory, which will follow in this book's sequel.

From Cicero's *Sermo* to the *Grand Siècle*'s Conversation

All this is the second part of a long story. In this book's predecessor, *The Concept of Conversation*, I depicted the long transformation of conceptions of *sermo* from Roman times to the French *grand siècle* (D. Randall 2018). Briefly, the narrative in that book was as follows.

To begin with, conversation referred narrowly to actual conversations (and their literary simulations), conducted in the leisure time of noblemen, and generally concerned with indefinite philosophical topics only loosely connected to the world of political affairs, which was more properly addressed by oratory. The Greeks and Romans linked together several concepts: *familiarity*; its sometimes-rivalrous complement of *friendship*; the friend's doppelgänger, the *flatterer*; and *conversation*, the mode of speech inquiring after truth that articulated both familiar style and friendship. All these concepts found expression not only in conversation but also in the *letter*, the written analogue of conversation. The Romans in particular also began to emphasise during their Silver Age the concept of *conversatio*, the mutual conduct of mankind. This last concept stood at some intellectual distance from the constellation formed around familiarity, friendship and conversation, but from the beginning it possessed conceptual associations that would allow it to be linked with them more tightly in ensuing centuries.

During the medieval centuries, the concepts of friendship, familiarity and *conversatio* reoriented themselves around the universalising Christian conception of community, while the *sermo* of dialogue began to concern itself with that eminently Christian subject matter, the interiority of the soul. On the other hand, the *ars dictaminis* (art of letter writing) shifted the medieval letter towards the public realm, and thus towards the traditional realm of oratory. Petrarch's rediscovery of classical conversation retained these medieval innovations. The Renaissance variant of conversation that sprang from him would partly slough the theory and practice of its medieval predecessor – but the influence of Christianity and the *ars dictaminis* would endure.

Conversation, both within treatises touching on theories of conversation and in the practice of the literary genre of dialogue, underwent increasingly radical transformation thereafter at the hands of the humanists and their successors. This transformation began with the Renaissance humanists, who intensified the Petrarchan abstraction of conversation-as-metaphor from actual conversation. The changing Renaissance conception of conversation was linked to the simultaneous expansion of oratory's ambitions, which inspired both the use of conversation as a refuge from oratory and, in a revolutionary riposte, the counter-claim that conversation should expand the scope of its subject matter to supplant oratory. The innovative genre of Utopian dialogue provided a climax to this last development, by transforming the old debate as to the *optimus status rei publicae* into a conversation, and thus incorporating the ends of political action within the genre of *sermo*. Finally, in seventeenth-century France, the preceding expansion of conversation culminated in a revolutionary triumph, as conversation replaced oratory as the default mode of rhetoric. These changes collectively set the stage for the centrality of conversation in the intellectual world of early modern Europe.

Conversation in antiquity had been the speech of friends and familiarity – and insofar as friendship motivated conversation as a mode of inquiry, that friendship oriented conversation towards reason and virtue. The Renaissance witnessed a long shift in the conception of friendship, culminating in the thought of Michel de Montaigne, away from an alignment with reason and virtue and towards an alignment with passion and familiarity. This changing conception of friendship brought with it a corresponding change in the conception of conversation, which now also based itself upon passion and familiarity – including in its use as a mode of inquiry. In other words, the expressive aspect of *sermo*, which communicated character in an intimate manner, now became the basis of the philosophical aspect of *sermo*, the inquiry into truth. The communication of intimate, passionate friendship became prerequisite for the search for truth. Furthermore, the development of intimate friendship and the development of friendship with and among women went hand and hand in Renaissance and early modern Europe; together, they came to associate women, as women, with conversation and the inquiry into truth. This association radically differentiated conversation from both oratory and philosophical reason, which remained, respectively, the speech of wrangling and disputatious men.

The humanist project to educate the elite of Western Europe produced as one of its dizzy successes the application of conversation to the speech and behaviour of noblemen at court. This development of the ideal of the courtier took conversation from the leisurely retreat from the ancient political world to the courtly heart of the Renaissance political world. The *salons* of seventeenth-century France further transformed the conversational tradition of the court: in principle, the conversation of the *salons* began quietly to set itself to rival the world of oratory, to address itself to the same worldly subject matter. The Republic of Letters provided an alternate social matrix for *sermo*, scholarly rather than courtly – and one which migrated away from its Ciceronian roots towards the mode of Baylean critique. Where the courtly and scholarly traditions of *sermo* acted as complementary modes during the Renaissance, the increasing scope of *salonnier* conversation and the increasing abandonment of *sermo* by the Republic of Letters set them at odds with one another in the eighteenth century. Both now harboured universalising ambitions, which would set these sibling modes to fierce conflict.

Renaissance humanists classicised their letters so as to approximate the familiar style of *sermo* – but they also inherited the medieval tradition of *ars dictaminis*, which had shifted letters towards the public realm. Humanist letters therefore continued to depart from familiar style in practice – and in Erasmus' theory, he explicitly acknowledged that letter writing was no longer entirely a genre of familiar communication. The Renaissance humanist letter became a mode of communication mediating between conversation and oratory, and firmly oriented towards the public world. One descendant of the humanist letter would be the newspaper – that genre that Habermas took to constitute the public sphere. The newspaper, by way of the news letter, preserved aspects of the style of familiar communication, but, as it shifted in medium towards print, transformed into a distinctly persuasive communication between anonymous correspondents and anonymous recipients. Conversation had shifted in theory to be able to address the public world; the newspaper would be the genre that embodied a familiar conversation, universal and anonymous, that discussed all the subjects of the world.

Conversatio, mutual conduct, had possessed loose affiliations with *sermo* in ancient and medieval times. During the Renaissance, *conversatio* shifted far closer to *sermo* and its constellation of cognate concepts. Most notably, Guazzo elaborated an influential theory of civil conversation in his eponymous late-sixteenth-century dialogue, which reconceived *conversatio* in secular terms as the realm of society and manners intermediate between the *oikos* and the political world. This conception of civil conversation then received a universalising spin from the natural law jurisprudential tradition of Grotius and Pufendorf, transforming it into an amoral disposition towards sociability shared by all humanity. The long parallel tracks of *sermo* and *conversatio* now finally converged: *sermo* became conversation as *conversatio* became sociability. The convergence of *sermo* and *conversatio* made possible the establishment of a causal connection between the two concepts. This connection appeared via *doux commerce*, the application of sociability to the realm of economics: sociability, via the universal exercise of economic self-interest, became the conceptual and historical predicate for conversation – and, as the Enlightenment progressively yoked manners to the civic humanist tradition, the predicate in turn for both virtue and liberty. Sociability thus at last substituted for Platonic love an amoral, entirely human motivation for conversation. By this means, conversation received a coherent grounding in the selfish needs of humanity – the discourse of reason found its base in human passions.

Two quotations from late-seventeenth-century France give a sense of the ambitions – and the remaining limitations – of the concept of conversation, after nearly two millennia of transformations. Madeleine de Scudéry wrote in 'On Conversation' (1680) that

> I think that nothing is precluded; that [conversation] ought to be free and diversified, according to the times, places, and persons with whom we [converse]; and that the secret is to speak always nobly of small things, very simply of great things, and graciously of the subjects of polite [conversation], without transport and affectation. Thus, though the conversation ought always to be both natural and also rational, I must not fail to say, that on some occasions, the sciences themselves may also be brought in with a good grace, and that an agreeable silliness may also find its place, provided it be clever, modest, and courteous. So that, to speak with reason, we may affirm without falsehood that there is nothing that cannot be said in conversation, provided it [is managed with] wit and judgment, and one considers well, where one is, to whom one speaks, and who one is oneself. (Scudéry 2002: 89)

Jean-Baptiste Morvan de Bellegarde likewise wrote in *Réflexions sur ce qui peut plaire ou déplaire dans le commerce du monde* (1688) that

> This is, however, . . . the privilege of conversation: everyone is permitted to say his sentiment, and we must suffer with good grace those who contradict us. It would be an insupportable tyranny to wish to fix the thought of others under one's own opinion. Kings, with all their authority, have no jurisdiction over the sentiments of their peoples, and individuals should not claim to be more absolute than kings. (Bellegarde 1688: 285–6, translated in Gordon 1994: 98–9)

The Concept of Conversation breaks off with those interesting claims, available for further innovation.

The Conversational Enlightenment: An Outline

This book picks up the story where *The Concept of Conversation* left off, and traces the extension of the conception of conversation during the Enlightenment, into (1) European thought and culture generally; (2) the fine arts and letters; (3) philosophy; and (4) the conception of public opinion. In outline, this book's narrative is as follows.

The universalisation of manners and conversation ultimately drew in most aspects of Enlightenment European culture. The spread of *salons* and *salon* culture from Paris throughout Europe provided a fostering social matrix for this universalisation, but three further aspects of this process particularly illustrate this transformation. First, the project of politeness – that particularly British endeavour, oriented after the watershed of the Glorious Revolution towards the people rather than towards the prince – strove to make the now-sovereign people properly mannerly and, in consequence, properly conversational. In the project of politeness, the universalisation of manners and conversation became the democratisation of manners and conversation. Second, the incorporation of women into conversation achieved an Enlightenment culmination, by which women not only became equal partners in conversation but also became, in theory, necessary constituents of manners, of conversation and of the very progress of history. Finally, conversation extended to pedagogical theory, and hence, implicitly, to the education of all mankind. Conversation's expansion from the *salons* to the realms of democratising politeness, women and children exemplified its aspiration to extend itself to all mankind (Chapter 1).

The fine arts and letters – art, architecture, music, dance and poetics – had adopted a rhetorical model during the Renaissance, in the oratorical mode that emphasised moving the passions, seizing the will, and all such features of a fine oration. The shift in the default conception of rhetoric from oratory to conversation during the seventeenth and eighteenth centuries therefore caused, as a corollary, a shift in these various arts towards the model of conversation. The emergence of a conversational aesthetics transformed both the fine arts and poetics, and gave birth to those tight-yoked siblings, the *beaux arts* and the *belles lettres*. The same centuries also saw the culmination of rhetoric's metaphorisation, such that the principles of rhetoric now were applied not only to the genres of the word but also to the several nonverbal genres. Music, art and dance were now taken to persuade in and of themselves, by wordless conversations composed of sound, sight and gesture. Notable exponents of the conversationalised arts include Batteux (aesthetics), Watteau (art), Boffrand (architecture), Haydn (music), Noverre (dance) and Austen (literature) (Chapters 2 and 3).

The universalisation of rhetoric (especially the conversational mode), the transformation of rhetoric and conversation into attributes of natural law and/or a faculty of the mind, and their extension into the realms of aesthetics and taste, led to an interpenetration of rhetoric, conversation and philosophy. Seventeenth- and eighteenth-century philosophers – especially eighteenth-century philosophers in Britain such as Shaftesbury, Hume and Smith – now began to translate rhetorical and conversational concepts into the vocabulary of philosophy. Rhetoric and conversation thus re-emerged within the genre of philosophy, rhetoric's sociological framework rearticulated in the languages of epistemology, morals and aesthetics. In the realm of philosophy, private, inner conversations came to establish both the self and the conscience capable of making autonomous moral judgements, and ultimately created a standard of taste, of judgement, within the strictures of conversational philosophy. This last provided the fundamental basis for conversational philosophy as a whole (Chapter 4).

Conversation, the discourse that united passion with reason, became a universal discourse in the Enlightenment, whose reasonable judgement judged all things. This formation of public opinion occurred in France, drawing directly upon the *salonnier* traditions of conversation, sociability and free judgement upon set topics. Yet in its moment of triumph, this universal conversation of public opinion continued to reflect conversation's old instability. So, just as conversation oscillated between its neighbours of oratory and philosophical dialogue, public opinion oscillated between variations constituted more by oratory – the British example – and more by philosophical dialogue – the public opinion of the *philosophes* and the Physiocrats. In the last generation of the *ancien régime*, the major stream of French thought shifted into the channel of the *philosophes*, and settled upon an imperious version of public opinion, a conversation that assumed sovereignty and command. It was a conversation that thereby had abandoned the old characteristics of *sermo* for a hollow throne.

Yet a minority report of the French Enlightenment, articulated above all by Gabriel Bonnot de Mably and Jacques Peuchet, preserved the conception of public opinion that (as Humean reason submitted itself to the passions) submitted its judgement to the people rather than aspired to command them. This minority report echoed across the Atlantic, to the receptive mind of James Madison, who recapitulated this minority opinion and, translating it into the structure of the American polity, made it an essential component of the new American republic. Madisonian public opinion, submitting itself to Madisonian dispersed prudence, became the keystone of American political practice. Conversational public opinion, a refugee from France, would flourish in the Great Republic – the avatar of the conversational public sphere (Chapter 5).

Scholarly Arguments

This book continues an argument made in *The Concept of Conversation*, of the importance of the history of conversation within the history of rhetoric – and, more precisely, of the importance of the rise of conversation within the rhetorical complex, from marginal component to dominant partner. Indeed, *The Conversational Enlightenment* is the most important part of that argument, for it is the triumph of conversation during the Enlightenment that provides retrospective justification for arguing the importance of *sermo* and its rise within the rhetorical tradition during earlier centuries. *Sermo* mattered in and of itself for both Cicero and Erasmus, and the seventeenth-century ascendancy of *sermo* among French theoreticians of rhetoric likewise has intrinsic interest – but *sermo* and its rise matter most for *sermo*'s Enlightenment apogee, when the consequences of dethroning oratory played out in all the conceptual realms that drew their organising framework from rhetoric. The long history of the rise of *sermo* did not stop with some petty thanedom; king hereafter it became, in that long summer between Louis le Grand and Robespierre. The history of rhetoric cannot be understood without narrating conversation's rise.

This argument that the rise of *sermo* is a fundamental dynamic of the history of rhetoric from the Renaissance to the Enlightenment is bound up with the argument that the history of rhetoric ought to be recast in parallel to the broad framework of early modern European intellectual history Habermas sketches in *The Structural Transformation of the Public Sphere* (Habermas 1991: 1–117) and *Theory and Practice* (Habermas 1973: 41–81). In these two books, Habermas describes the transformations of reason, and its articulation in such genres as the newspaper and such social formations as the *salons* and the Republic of Letters, in terms of processes of universalisation, publicisation and democratisation that would collectively result in a critical-rational public discourse theoretically universal both in its participants and in its subject matter – the public sphere (Habermas 1991: 1–26; Raymond 1999: 111–12, 118). *The Concept of Conversation* provided the first half of this larger historical argument that Habermas' description of the processes (universalisation, publicisation and democratisation) operating in Renaissance and early modern Europe is the proper framework in which to understand the histories of rhetoric and conversation. This book provides the second half of that argument by emphasising the importance of universalisation, publicisation and democratisation to conversation in a variety of fields: (1) in the dynamics that applied conversational capacity to all humanity via the philosophical tradition; (2) in the democratic extension of conversation beyond a male elite via the project of politeness, the incorporation of women into conversational theory and culture, and the extension of conversation to pedagogy; (3) in the development of a universalising conversational aesthetic – what Habermas calls a 'literary public sphere' – in the realm of the fine arts; and (4) in the development of public opinion as a universal conversation, both in its range of participants and in its range of subject matters. Habermas' historical chronology and dynamics apply to the history of conversation – and, more broadly, the history of rhetoric – not least because many elements he takes to articulate the public sphere (the novelistic address to the reader, public opinion) are drawn, somewhat unawares, from that very history. Yet I take it to be no small matter to argue that historians of rhetoric should rightly use Habermas' historical analysis as a framework for their discipline.

Inter alia, this book, in combination with its predecessor, also encourages historians of rhetoric to cross the chronological boundaries between the Renaissance and the Enlightenment more freely. Although this book focuses on the Enlightenment proper, it repeatedly returns to the Renaissance (especially to illustrate the fine-arts transitions from oratorical to conversational modes), by way of demonstrating that the treatment of the history of rhetoric in these two periods can and should be integrated.

This book's presentation of the Enlightenment apogee of conversation also matters for intellectual historians more broadly, because it strengthens enormously the larger argument for the importance of rhetoric. The history of rhetoric is often minimised by non-specialists on the grounds that it fell into severe decline during the Enlightenment, and that there is only antiquarian interest in a movement displaced by the immediate ancestors of modern thought. Yet this decline was more apparent than real – a retrospective imposition by later historians, too credulous of the contemporary polemics that disparaged rhetoric not least by conflating it with oratory. Modern scholars of the history of rhetoric have done much to dispel this Black Legend – but their efforts have had limited success, since they have largely confined their efforts to noting the survival of rhetoric's oratorical mode (e.g., Howell 1971; Warnick 1993; Potkay 1994; McKenna 2011). Recognise Enlightenment conversation as an episode in the long history of *sermo*, however, and you recognise rhetoric as a key constituent of the Enlightenment's intellectual and cultural history – and, in turn, as a key constituent of the Enlightenment's matrix of modern thought.[1] This book and its predecessor invoke the importance of Renaissance and Enlightenment conversation to call upon intellectual historians to recognise the larger importance of the history of rhetoric to European intellectual and cultural history.

A bolder way to put the previous point, and one with implications beyond the realm of intellectual history, is that this book argues the existence of a range of conversational thought so extensive as to constitute a *conversational Enlightenment*.[2] Much historiographical debate turns on characterising the nature of the Enlightenment(s) in Europe, not least for the corollary implications about the proper directions for modern-day intellectual and political endeavour. This book sketches a tradition of Enlightenment thought and culture united by its debt to conversation and rooted in the complementary sociabilities of the *salon* and the culture of politeness – a rival to the Enlightenments defined variously around the thought of Descartes or Bayle, Spinoza or Kant, sketched by figures such as Ernst Cassirer, Peter Gay and Jonathan Israel (Cassirer 1951; Gay 1995; 1996; Israel 2001; 2006; 2011; and see Dijn 2012; Ferrone 2015; La Vopa 2009).[3] This portrait of conversation in the Enlightenment is also meant to depict an Enlightenment *of* conversation, mediating the modes of rhetoric and reason, and in so doing provide a model for the present day. I will return to this last point; but here I wish to emphasise that this book is meant to contribute to the historiographical debate about the nature of the Enlightenment – to be read in conversation with Cassirer, Gay and Israel. Put most polemically, I take any account of the Enlightenment that scants conversation to be insufficient, and any assertion of the primacy of a rival mode of Enlightenment to need to justify that claim against the body of thought and culture amassed here and presented as the constituents of the conversational Enlightenment.

In combination with the continuing innovations in the Enlightenment upon traditional oratorical thought (e.g., D. Randall 2011c; 2016a; 2016b), this conversational Enlightenment may be taken in turn as a component of a larger *rhetorical Enlightenment*. This rhetorical Enlightenment may be conceived of as a phase in the history of rhetoric and an inheritor of Kristeller's Renaissance (Kristeller 1961: 3–23, esp. 11) – democratising, abstracted and universalising innovation upon the rhetorical thought and practices of the Renaissance humanists, whose centre of gravity has shifted very heavily from *oratio* to *sermo*. It may also be conceived of as a phase in the continuing recuperation of the rhetorical heritage of the ancient world;

e.g., the early modern transformation of rhetorical-conversational aesthetics, as we shall see, doubled as an intensifying recovery of and meditation upon the thought of Quintilian. This larger rhetorical Enlightenment is not fully sketched out here, but this account of conversation in the Enlightenment should be taken as a significant preliminary towards establishing the existence and importance of that larger abstraction. It should also be taken as a methodological prompt, encouraging close analyses of the early modern transformations of the diverse elements of rhetoric as a way to deepen our understanding of the genealogy and the nature of different aspects of Enlightenment thought (cf. Colclough 2005: 12–76; Pocock 1985: 37–50; Vivenza 2001: 181–4).

A corollary of this claim is that any account of the Enlightenment ought to include Britain and America at its centre. While I spend substantial time discussing France, and pay some attention to the rest of the continent (especially Germany and Italy), I take my emphasis on Anglo-American culture and thought to have the greatest consequences for its geographical characterisation of the Enlightenment. This book's chapter on society foregrounds a polite culture whose heart lay in England, a changing conception of women framed around the thought of David Hume, John Millar and Hannah More, and a conversational pedagogy put first into widespread practice in England's Dissenting Academies. The chapter on the fine arts is the least British in its material, but it still highlights the aesthetics of Jane Austen, Daniel Defoe, William Hogarth, Jonathan Richardson, Adam Smith, John Weaver and Thomas Whately. The chapter on philosophy centres on the thought of Shaftesbury, Hume, Smith and George Campbell; that on public opinion culminates in the thought of James Madison and Tunis Wortman. To argue the importance of the conversational Enlightenment is to argue the importance, perhaps the centrality, of the Anglo-American Enlightenment. This is not a revolutionary argument at this point in time: scholars of the Enlightenment are aware that their subject was not a landlocked phenomenon (e.g., Gay 1996: 555–68; Porter 2000). But in the continuing argument over how to weigh the different geographic components of the Enlightenment, this book adds its heft in the balance for greater consideration of Britain and America.

A second corollary is in some ways more controversial for its characterisation of the Enlightenment: the emphasis I place not only on aesthetics but also on the histories of the fine arts themselves. While I cannot speak of all scholarly interpretations of the Enlightenment – who can? – it is notable that the history of the fine arts plays a minimal role in Cassirer, Gay and Israel. Neither Cassirer nor Israel incorporates the arts of the Enlightenment into his account, while Gay's swift judgement at the beginning of his brief excursus through the arts of the age is that '[t]here was no distinctive Enlightenment style in the arts' (Gay 1996: 216, 216–48). Indeed, even the more purely verbal field of aesthetics plays its largest role in Cassirer, as a quarter of his book (Cassirer 1951: 275–360), only a sole chapter in Gay (Gay 1996: 249–318), and but glancing mention in Israel's three volumes. If we may also invoke Habermas as a historian of the Enlightenment, his discussion of the cultural aspects of the public sphere is likewise thin – and focused almost exclusively on the written word (Habermas 1991: 29–30, 36–7, 48–51). These scholars almost ignore the fine arts (save Gay, briefly), and (save Cassirer) pay little enough attention to aesthetics.

This book argues that the histories of aesthetics and the fine arts, and the scholarship of the disciplines that have produced these histories, should be central to an account of the Enlightenment. This book invokes the entire field of aesthetics (at least until its reconception by Kant) as part of the conversational philosophy of the Enlightenment. It also takes broad swathes of Enlightenment aesthetic endeavour – art, architecture, music, dance, poetics (the novel) – as articulated by and arguing in themselves a distinctively conversational aesthetic. This invocation of the fine arts is meant to substantiate the importance of the conversational Enlightenment – and to challenge rival arguments that seek to characterise the Enlightenment. What is the tradition of Spinozistic music? How did Bayle contribute to architecture? What is Voltairean portraiture? Kantian ballet? These questions are not idle, but meant to indicate the narrow range of the supposedly revolutionary thought of these iconic figures of rival Enlightenments. The conversational Enlightenment's strength lay not least in its ability to affect and argue within the nonverbal modes of sight, sound and motion. Any rival interpretation of the Enlightenment ought to be able to account for these realms of human endeavour as something more than the décor of philosophic argument.

Indeed, returning up a level of generality, this argument for the importance of the histories of the fine arts is likewise aimed at historians of intellectual history more broadly. I have been struck during my reading by how relatively little impress these historiographies of the fine arts seem to have made in the broader scholarship of intellectual history. The very importance of rhetoric to each of these separate histories, for example, is not (despite the best efforts of Plett and Vickers) as widely known among non-specialists as one would hope. No one can read everything, and disciplines are constituted by their foci and exclusions – yet there is an extraordinary amount of fine scholarship in these fields that could be read productively by scholars of intellectual history, and incorporated into their broader narratives. My practice here is meant to prompt more forays by intellectual historians into these specialised disciplines.

For these scholars of the histories of the fine arts, this book also provides the broad Habermasian framework, as well as a narrative that unifies much of their respective histories along a common transition within a broadly rhetorical framework from an oratorical mode to a conversational mode. It also encourages them to look more frequently to their sister subdisciplines for comparative insight. I think there is some value for all histories of the fine arts in understanding (for example) Watteau, Whately, Mozart, Noverre and Austen as representatives of a common conversational aesthetic; more such exercises in collocation should be fruitful.

This book also continues to argue the importance of women in all aspects of European intellectual history – albeit more by implication than did *Concept of Conversation*. That book argued the importance of conversation as a discourse between women and men, in contradistinction to the explicitly male world of oratory and the implicitly male world of the discourse of pure reason. The rise among all Europeans of the concept of conversation, and cognate concepts, was inseparable from the innovative thought of figures such as Madeleine de Scudéry, Moderata Fonte and Mary Astell.

While this book briefly explores the status of women in the conversational society and culture of the Enlightenment, and analyses the emergence of the *philosophe* conception of public opinion as an exercise in anti-feminine revolt, individual women play a much less prominent role in this book's narrative. The Enlightenment universalisation of conversation may have facilitated a recession of women from conversation's conceptual foreground – though by no means an erasure, as the eighteenth-century conversational tradition still boasted Charlotte von Greiners and Hannah Mores. Yet while I would welcome future research that deepens our knowledge of women's participation in the conversational Enlightenment, my argument here, rather, is that the discourse that recognised women, and was significantly forged by women, became the model for the entire conversational Enlightenment – conversational culture, fine arts and letters, aesthetics, philosophy and public opinion. More polemically, we may put it that this mode of thought became the model for the Enlightenment, full stop, and that the anti-feminine thought of the *philosophes* should be seen as a limited rebellion against the broader Enlightenment conceptually constituted by discourse with women. This reconception places the history of women at the heart of the history of the Enlightenment.

A history of women, I should say. My narrative of the conversational fine arts culminates with Jane Austen – and Austen may be taken as my representative figure of women's conversational Enlightenment (and see Knox-Shaw 2004). But (for example) Olympe de Gouges and Mary Wollstonecraft would seem to have adhered more to the *philosophe* Enlightenment than to the conversational one. My narrative emphasises the importance within women's history of Austen's Enlightenment – the Enlightenment of the Marquise de Lambert, the Bluestockings and Rahel Varnhagen – as against the Enlightenments of de Gouges and Wollstonecraft.

This book is further intended as a component of a theoretical critique and revision of Habermasian theory.[4] While the full argument is intended for a third book, this book sketches a democratised, universalised *sermo* as an alternative to the democratising, universalising Platonic-Kantian discourse that Habermas took to characterise the Enlightenment public sphere. While *Concept of Conversation* provided the long narrative between the ancient world and c. 1700, this book is framed not least to provide an extended parallel and contrast to Habermas' description of the Enlightenment in *Structural Transformation*. My chapters on conversational culture, philosophy and public opinion, and the subsection on conversational poetics, are meant to parallel and contest Habermas' treatment of those subjects. My detailed description of the conversational fine arts as essential components of the Enlightenment's rhetorical public sphere, meanwhile, is intended to demonstrate the superiority of conversation as a theoretical mode in which to understand the Enlightenment, as compared to Habermas' rational discourse and public sphere theory, which are not well equipped to understand the fine arts. It don't mean a thing if it can't take in swing.

I say *rhetorical public sphere*, not *conversational public sphere*. The conception of a rhetorical public sphere is built around the complementary nature of oratory and conversation, but I do not here narrate the parallel transformations in Renaissance and early modern Europe of different modes of *prudence* – the reason of rhetoric in its oratorical mode desiring success rather than truth. These I have narrated in three separate articles, detailing respectively the history of amoralised prudence and *interest* (D. Randall 2011c), the history of economic prudence (D. Randall 2016b) and the history of rhetorical violence (D. Randall 2016a), wherein each of these emerges by the Enlightenment as a component of the oratorical portion of the rhetorical public sphere. These articles, which all turn on a reading of Machiavelli as articulating prudential reasoning rather than calculative or instrumental reasoning, should be taken generally as lurking in the background of this narrative. In particular, the conception of economic interest as prudential rather than (as in Max Weber, Habermas, etc.) as calculative or instrumental lies behind the particular argument that *doux commerce* provides a hinge between oratory and conversation – for economic activity must be taken as prudential for that particular equation to be taken as valid. In sum, the rhetorical public sphere consists of universal, mutual exercises of rhetoric in complementary spheres – of conversation aiming at truth in the social realm, and of oratorical prudence aiming at victory in the political and economic realms. For the lengthier version of this argument, I direct the reader to my articles on prudence and economic prudence – and to the final book of this trilogy, which will contain revised versions of their arguments.

Without belabouring the point excessively here, the concept of the rhetorical public sphere invokes the long intellectual history of innovations upon the Ciceronian conception of *sermo* that is narrated in this book and its predecessor against the narrative of Platonic-*philosophe*-Kantian intellectual history provided by Habermas as the foundation for his characterisation of the public sphere. Where Habermas' narrative points towards a political vision hovering somewhere between the *philosophes* and Kant, mine points rather towards the thought of James Madison – on prudence, on the Second Amendment and on the role of public opinion – and towards the constitutional architecture and practice of the United States of America, as the Enlightenment *exemplum* upon which we should innovate towards the ideal polity. In this rhetorical public sphere, *sermo* is supposed ultimately to defer to *oratio*, not dictate to it, and the discussions of public opinion are supposed to retain the keynote presumption of *sermo*: that the ends we seek are indefinite, and admit of no final resolution. The fundamental goal of the polity is no more – and no less – than to sustain the conditions of conversation.

This rhetorical public sphere may be taken as a rival of the Habermasian public sphere that characterises the Enlightenment equally well – or, more ambitiously, it may be taken as meant to supplant the Habermasian public sphere, because it characterises more accurately the mainstream of Enlightenment thought. I firmly avow the first, minimalist critique; somewhat more cautiously I proffer the second, maximalist critique.

This critique is meant in turn to apply to the penumbra of theoretical writings in philosophy, political theory, critical theory, etc., which draw upon Habermasian theory and have accepted and relied upon his history without demur. Habermasian theory has always stipulated the accuracy of the history he provided by way of ballast – and to revise Habermas' history requires not only Habermas, but also all those successor theorists who have relied upon his work, to see if their theories hold up against this revised intellectual narrative. All such theories ought to account for the critique embodied in this history of conversation. Their transhistorical claims are hollow without historical support.

Yet this conception of the rhetorical public sphere should be taken to support Habermas in the larger theoretical and scholarly battles about the nature of the Enlightenment. Habermas affirms the Enlightenment's power as an emancipatory project; other works, both theoretical and historical, have been read to cast doubt broadly on the Enlightenment's power to forward human liberty (e.g., Bourdieu 1993; Elias 2000; and see Gordon 2002), and narrowly on whether Habermasian icons such as the *salons* actually modelled liberating discourse (Lilti 2015). My historical narrative, and the conception of a rhetorical public sphere that animates it, support Habermas in the largest sense. I take Enlightenment conversation as a rhetorical achievement rather than a rationalising transcendence – I take the historical dynamics of conversation to have contributed greatly to the historical establishment of democracy and liberty, but I would hesitate to claim that conversation is intrinsically democratic and liberating. Lilti, above all, has made it clear that much *salon* conversation was nothing of the sort (Lilti 2015). Withal, I take the Enlightenment more to have fulfilled than to have betrayed its ideals of democracy, universality and liberty – a position I take this book to substantiate by its linked narratives of the conversational Enlightenment's conceptions and cultures of fine arts, philosophy and public opinion. More particularly, I take Habermas' focus on the liberating potentialities of Enlightenment discourse to be absolutely correct – even if I part ways as to the nature of that liberating discourse.

We should note here Goodman's sharply worded review of Lilti's *The World of the Salons* (2015): 'This is a reactionary book whose aim is to restore a traditional interpretation of French history that views the Old Regime as fundamentally corrupt and the Revolution as its necessary sequel' (D. Goodman 2017: 408). To praise the

Enlightenment's practice, it seems, is to damn the French Revolution as a detour to the abattoir; to take Enlightenment discourse as a model is to eschew the still-living urge to approach the heavenly city of the *philosophes* by way of *la rue de la guillotine*. I suspect Goodman is correct that the debates about the nature of the Enlightenment are to a significant extent stalking horses for larger questions about the necessity of the French Revolution and the nature of the project of modernity. In these larger debates, I join with Goodman and Habermas. I share with them a fundamental confidence that the Enlightenment's ideal of mutual, universal and continuing exercises of speech and reason offered and offer the best model for *la vie humaine*. Better the candle to light us to bed than *Madame* the chopper to chop off our heads.

Still, my Enlightenment is not Habermas' – I suspect he would jib at my admiring portrait of the American polity, moulded by yoked Madisonian conceptions of public opinion and prudence, as the true legatee and exemplar of the Enlightenment. More deeply, the Enlightenment I sketch here sidesteps not only Kantian transcendentals but also the atomising philosophical tradition of Hobbes and Locke – traditions which play only a minor role in this narrative. It is an Enlightenment that should appeal to readers dubious about both transcendentals and atomisations – but to repel those readers who incline towards them. *Caveat lector*.

If these scholarly arguments are persuasive, I am beholden to hundreds of previous scholars. My bibliography – lengthy, as it unites several specialised historiographies – catalogues my debts. This book builds particularly upon the works of Keith Michael Baker, Michael Baxandall, Tom Beghin, Peter Borsay, George Buelow, Michel Conan, Timothy Costelloe, Benedetta Craveri, Hugh Davidson, Ann Delehanty, Amanda Dickins, Jane Donawerth, Kevin Dunn, Don Fader, Peter France, Marc Fumaroli, Eugene Garver, Alan Gibson, Natasha Gill, Dena Goodman, Daniel Gordon, J. A. W. Gunn, Marc Hanvelt, Deborah Heller, Wilbur Samuel Howell, Victoria Kahn, Steven Kale, George Kennedy, Warren Kirkendale, Peter Kivy, Lawrence Klein, Paul Kristeller, Antoine Lilti, Deborah Losse, Carolyn Lougee, Maria Rika Maniates, John Martin, Robert Martin, Jon Mee, James Melton, Jennifer Nevile, Edward Nye, Mona Ozouf, Jolanta Pekacz, Heinrich Plett, J. G. A. Pocock, Adam Potkay, Elena Russo, Colleen Sheehan, Christine Smith, Jane Stevens, Nancy Struever, Dabney Townsend, Caroline Van Eck, Brian Vickers, Mary Vidal, Barbara Warnick, Bernard Weinberg, Johnson Wright and, above all, Jürgen Habermas. More than an argument, my book is a continuation of their conversation.

Brief Notes

Some portion of this narrative overlaps with and recapitulates the narrative of the rise of neoclassicism – of those modes associated with chaste Attic oratory. I have tried to follow the strictly conversational rather than the more generically plain and simple, but these narratives cannot be kept entirely distinct. Presumably the parallel rises of conversation and neoclassicism were mutually reinforcing.

This work is largely an intellectual history, although it dips into some surrounding social and cultural history. The first chapter sketches some social and cultural dimensions of the broadening out of the concept of conversation, but the remaining four chapters confine themselves largely to an intellectual history of how the concept of conversation universalised into different modes of Enlightenment thought. Throughout, the history of 'the concept of conversation' is the history of the broadening use in the Enlightenment of conversational style, of conversation as a metaphor, and the social matrices which articulated these aspects of conversation.

The modern conception of conversation crystallised in the French *salons* during the seventeenth century, and spread out during the eighteenth century to ever wider intellectual and cultural domains. The heart of this intellectual history therefore lies in France, although significant portions concern its intellectual neighbour Britain, whose thinkers innovated significantly upon the conversational tradition. The history of the conversational fine arts and public opinion takes place centrally in France, while the history of conversational philosophy is centrally a British history. The history of conversational culture combines English pottery with French pedagogy. The history of the fine arts includes British, Italian and German annexes, and that of public opinion concludes in America, but this is a history of European thought in a Europe defined around elite thinkers on a narrow axis between Edinburgh, London and Paris. I believe this axis is the heart of the Enlightenment's innovations in conversational thought – but the geographical focus should be taken as a prompt for further work, to correct any distortions arising from this intellectual frame.

The great transposition of the meanings of *conversatio* and *sermo* was basically complete by the time this book begins. Save where explicitly indicated, I take 'conversation' to refer primarily to speech (*sermo*) rather than to manners (*conversatio*).

I am aware that *England* and *English* are not synonyms for *Britain* and *British*, and have striven to use the words correctly. I beg the reader's forgiveness for any lapses.

We will now turn to the conversable world.

Notes

1. Some scholars have recognised Enlightenment conversation's roots in *sermo*; e.g., Pujol 2001: 313. Yet I do not think Enlightenment historians as a whole have fully taken on board the implications of that insight.
2. The concept is not original; see L. Klein 2001. To my knowledge, however, this is the first book-length treatment of the subject.
3. I cannot do justice to the enormous scholarly literature on the Enlightenment. Other major works in recent English-language scholarship include Darnton 1995; Hesse 2001; Jacob 1981; 1991; Pocock 1999–2015; Porter and Teich 1981.
4. I am indebted to many previous such critiques and revisions of public sphere theory as it pertains to Enlightenment history, but especially to D. Goodman 1992; Gordon 1992; Jacob 1994; Kale 2002; L. Klein 1993; Landes 1988.

Chapter 1

The Society and Culture of Conversation

Introduction

The universalisation of manners and conversation ultimately drew in most aspects of Enlightenment European culture. In this chapter, I first sketch a history of eighteenth-century *salons*, whose role as social matrix retained considerable importance in fostering eighteenth-century conversational culture. I then discuss three aspects of eighteenth-century society and culture that decisively extended the culture of conversation beyond the *salons*' exclusive guest lists. First, I discuss the project of politeness – that particularly British endeavour, oriented (especially after the watershed of the Glorious Revolution) towards the people rather than to the prince, so as to make the now-sovereign people properly mannerly and, in consequence, properly conversational. In the project of politeness, the universalisation of manners and conversation became the democratisation of manners and conversation. Second, I discuss the culmination of the conceptual incorporation of women into conversation – the Enlightenment transformation by which women not only became equal partners in conversation but also became, in theory, necessary constituents of manners, of conversation and of the very progress of history. Finally, I discuss the extension of conversation to pedagogical theory, and hence, implicitly, to the education of all humanity. Conversation's expansion beyond the *salons* to the realms of democratising politeness, women and children is a rough proxy for its aspiration to extend itself to all mankind.

Salons and Gardens

The proto-*salon* emerged in *cinquecento* Italy and France, but the aristocratic seventeenth-century French *salon* provided the culminating social matrix for the long development of the modern concept of conversation (D. Randall 2018: 142–56). Once formed, this concept – abstracted, universalising, democratising – could and did spread autonomously into different realms of Enlightenment thought. Yet the eighteenth-century *salons* continued to provide important venues for modelling and promoting conversational thought and culture. *Salons* spread from Paris to much of Europe, and their proliferation both registered and promoted the spread of the conversational Enlightenment.

The Parisian *salon*'s *loci classici* were the mixed-sex social gatherings of figures such as Catherine de Vivonne, Marquise de Rambouillet (1588–1665), Madeleine de Scudéry (1607–1701) and Anne Marie Louise d'Orléans, Mademoiselle de Montpensier (1627–93) (Craveri 2005: 27–230; D. Randall 2018: 144).[1] Paul Pellisson's (1624–93) description of conversation in his prefatory 'Discours' to Jean François Sarasin's (1614–54) *Oeuvres* (1656) sketched what would be the preferred discourse of the *salon* down to the Revolution:

> an intimate conversation, free and spontaneous, embellished with playfulness, good humor and civility of *honnêtes gens*, so that the particular character of each would shine through and they would be known and loved. . . . The Proteus of the fable and the chameleon of naturalists will not transform themselves more effortlessly than him. (Pellisson 1656: 13–14, 34, translated in Russo 2007: 38)

Salons championed this ideal of conversational discussion – egalitarian, familiar, devoted to the search for truth, capable of discussing any subject – and delightful, for the *salonniers* allied learning with pleasure (D. Randall 2018: 149–52).

Each *salon* had its own individual style and character, in its discussion as much as in its décor (Craveri 2005: 295; Prendergast 2015: 23–34, 56; cf. Goldgar 1995: 98–114; Tribby 1992). The *salonnière*'s métier consisted in part in fashioning herself to appear, with the old *sprezzatura* of artful artlessness, a hostess who naturally facilitated a sparkling conversation (Craveri 2005: 367–8; Genlis 1825: 171; Lespinasse 1887: 61 [4 May 1771], translated in Craveri 2005: 314). The other part of her art resided in her ability to choose an appropriate mixture of guests. Jean-François Marmontel (1723–99) wrote of Julie de Lespinasse's (1732–76) excellence in both arts:

> She had taken them here and there in society, but so well matched, that when they were there, they found themselves in most perfect harmony, like the strings of an instrument. To follow the comparison, I might say that she played on this instrument with an art that had the features of genius. She seemed to know what sound the string that she was about to touch would produce. I mean to say, she was so well acquainted with our minds and dispositions, that she had but to speak a word to bring them into play. (Marmontel 1827: 10–11; Craveri 2005: 313; and see Craveri 2005: 313–14, 322; Morellet 1812: 87–8, translated in Russo 2007: 315 (note 13))

The *salonnière*'s art of selection was the ability to discern which men, brought together, would kindle one another into the friendly discourse of conversation.

Parisian *salons* continued down to 1789 – and, after the sanguinary pleasures of the Revolution grew stale, revived in the latter days of the Republic, the Empire and the Restoration (Craveri 2005; Hellgouarch'h 2000; Kale 2004). Provincial *salons* sprang up throughout the eighteenth century, in cities including Autun, Avignon, Bordeaux, Dijon, Lyons and Toulouse (Prendergast 2015: 27–32). In Britain, *salons* (often associated with the genteel and intellectual circles of Bluestocking women) spread not only to London but also to Edinburgh in Scotland, Dublin in Ireland, and English provincial towns such as Batheaston and Lichfield (Heller 1998; Prendergast 2015: 45–6, 50, 66–70, 72–3, 78, 80, 84, 88–131, 133, 143, 145, 148).[2] *Salotti* and *conversazioni* sprang up throughout the Italian peninsula, in Bologna, Florence, Genoa, Milan, Naples, Rome, Turin and Venice (Betri and Brambilla 2004: 3–249; Dalton 2009; D'Ezio 2014; Donato 2009; Mori 2000). Even in Spain, where mixed-sex sociability remained strictly limited, *tertulias* appeared by the 1740s (T. Smith 2006: 40–73). In the Netherlands, although Dutch *salon* culture never really bloomed, there were *salons* at Amsterdam and the Hague (Kloek and Mijnhardt 2004: 106). In the 1730s Christina Mariana Ziegler (1695–1760) set up the first German literary *salon* in Leipzig, while in Berlin by the end of the century a handful of *jüdischen salonnières* gathered Jew and Christian to converse momentarily as friendly equals (Hertz 1988; Goozé 2011; Pohl 2006: 143–4; Prendergast 2015: 32). In Copenhagen, three *salons* appeared after 1770 – two German and one Danish (Roos 2009: 164). *Salons* likewise arrived in Austria in the 1770s, quickened by the diplomatic revolution that allied Austria and France (Melton 2001: 216–18). Polish noblewomen hosted politically charged *salons* from the 1730s onward (M. Hunt 2010: 323). In distant Russia, Nikolai Alexandrovich Lvov (1751–1803) hosted his first *salon* in 1779 (Ritzarev 2006: 199). *Salons* formed a thin skein across Europe in the last decades before the Revolution.

The *salon*'s spread was partly a matter of shifting terminology. In *cinquecento* Siena, *veglie* far predated the *salons* (D. Randall 2018: 142–3). Eighteenth-century Germany possessed the company (*Gesellschaft*) and the circle of friends (*Umgang*, *unser Kreis*) (Weckel 2000: 316, 320–1). To some extent, a family of emerging mixed-sex social institutions across the continent adopted *salon* as a common name. Yet the *salon* was also something new – a distinctive French institution, replicating itself across Europe as a natural corollary of the diffusion of French culture in that century when 'the world spoke French' (Fumaroli 2011).

Aristocratic mobility stimulated much of the diffusion of the *salon*. Royalty, aristocrats and other notables from across Europe, and even from America, came to the Paris *salons*; among them were Edward Gibbon (1737–94), David Hume (1711–76), Ferdinando Galiani (1728–87), Benjamin Franklin (1706–90), Princess Ekaterina Romanovna Dashkova (1743–1810) and Stanisław August Poniatowski (1732–98), the future king of Poland (Prendergast 2015: 15, 22). When they returned to their homes, these quondam guests frequently decided to start their own *salons* (e.g., Melton 2007: 274; and note Lilti 2015: 66–7; Prendergast 2015: 16). At the very least they knew how to conduct themselves in a local knock-off of the Paris originals. British figures such as David Garrick (1717–79) and Horace Walpole (1717–97) attended both French and English *salons*; French notables such as Anne-Marie Fiquet du Bocage (1710–1802), Jacques Necker (1732–1804) and Suzanne Curchod Necker (1737–94) likewise attended *salons* in both nations (Prendergast 2015: 49). Personal acquaintance with Paris facilitated the dissemination of the *salon* (and see D'Ezio 2011; Lampron 2011).

The written word also extended *salon* culture. *Salonnières* used letters, considered since ancient times to be a written analogue of conversation, to extend *salon* conversations to distant correspondents (D. Goodman 1994: 136–82; Pohl 2006; D. Randall 2018: 27–30, 166–72). Bluestocking women in England wrote letters profusely; so too in Berlin did the *salonnière* Rahel Varnhagen (1771–1833) (Pohl 2006: 148, 150–1). Such letters came to be written with a public in mind – some to be printed immediately, such as Jean-Jacques

Rousseau's (1712–78) *Letter to d'Alembert* (1758), and others, such as the letters and diaries of Frances Burney (1752–1840) and Rahel Varnhagen, to be collected and published so that the conversation could continue to future generations (Pohl 2006: 140). Eighteenth-century British *salonnières* significantly fashioned their conduct and style upon the models they found in published collections of seventeenth-century French letters, such as those of Marie de Rabutin-Chantal, Marquise de Sévigné (1626–96) (Prendergast 2015: 21, 48–9; and see Pohl 2006: 139–40). *Salons* also played a role in the circulation of manuscripts such as Pierre-Joseph Bernard's (1708–75) *L'Art d'Aimer* (1775) (Prendergast 2015: 20, 59–60). A genteel *Salon* of Letters, constituted by a web of correspondence, set itself up in parallel to the Republic of Letters' more scholarly communications.

Salon culture spread within the broader extension throughout Europe and the American colonies of sociable civil society, manifested in institutions such as the Junto in Philadelphia (Shields 1997: 98), the Women's Society for Natural Knowledge in Middelburg (Jacob and Sturkenboom 2003), the Select Society in Edinburgh (Carr 2014: 45–8), the Royal Economic Society in Spain (T. Smith 2006: 74–107), *musées* in Paris (Lynn 1999), academies in provincial France (Roche 1978) and masonic lodges throughout Europe (Melton 2001: 252–72). These different societies generally forwarded some combination of the overlapping modes of conversation and scholarly dialogue: despite the shift towards *philosophe* tones as the eighteenth century progressed, a hard-and-fast distinction between the two discourses was still more a matter of *philosophe* polemic than of practice by the coming of the Revolution (D. Goodman 1994: 233–80; Russo 2007: 61–72). Within the sociability broadly affiliated with the Republic of Letters (Goldgar 1995), even the proverbially scholarly world of science maintained significant affiliations with *salons*' conversational discourse and culture.[3]

Salon culture spread – and at the heart of European *salon* culture, the very triumph of the Parisian *salon* changed its character. The *salon* had reached its early apogee in the reign of Louis XIV (1638–1715; r. 1643–1715), at a time when the absolutist monarchy claimed, with remarkable effectiveness, linked monopolies of political power, oratorical speech and cultural authority (D. Randall 2018: 142–56). Much of the Republic of Letters during the latter portion of the reign of *le roi soleil*, tinged by Huguenot *ressentiment*, had defined itself in opposition to these absolutist initiatives; so it operated at a relative disadvantage in the French milieu (D. Randall 2018: 160–1). The crystallising *salonnier* formulation c. 1700 of a conception of conversation that could speak on all topics thus combined implicit resistance to the monarchy's maximalising claims with the relative absence of *erudit* rivals. A historical moment of royal power and *philosophe* weakness provided the context for *salon* conversation's claim to be free and universal.

Louis XIV's death decisively altered France's sociocultural balance of power. All the monarchy's varied political, social and cultural monopolisations of authority receded during the regency of Philippe d'Orléans (1674–1723) for Louis XV (1710–74; r. 1715–74) – never to be revived in full. As part of the general revival of aristocratic influence, the *salons*' social and cultural clout expanded to fill the void – not least because the Regent himself was a devotee of *salon* culture (D. Randall 2018: 155–6). Royal esteem increasingly deferred to *salon* judgements: *salonnière* approval now provided great weight in appointments to the Académie Royal (Lilti 2015: 97–100). Courtly conversation acquired the conversational polish of the *salon* (e.g., Lanson 1891: 567–9, translated in Craveri 2005: 367). *Salon* conversation had been conceived as an alternative to the hierarchies, formalities and frivolities that articulated courtly power; now *salon* conversation, in a somewhat Pyrrhic triumph, by acquiring courtly power began to articulate those hierarchies, formalities and frivolities.

At the same time, the end of a generation of war allowed the Republic of Letters to reintegrate itself fully with the French cultural milieu. This return came at a price: *savants* had to accept their status as subordinates within a cultural world defined by *salon* ascendancy (D. Randall 2018: 161–2). The terms of the bargain had already been established under Louis XIV, as *savants* such as Jean Chapelain (1595–1674), Christiaan Huygens (1629–95) and Bernard le Bovier de Fontenelle (1657–1757) pioneered the conversationally learned style by which a *philosophe* might explain astronomy to a marquise (G. Sutton 1995: 41–4, 106–13, 144–57). Now, in the generation after 1715, *savants* generally submitted themselves to the judgements of the *salons* – if only for the patronising patronage that accompanied such submission. Men of letters who could fit into *salon* culture flourished; those unable or unwilling to do so did not (Lilti 2015: 91–132). The conversational style of the *salons* thus extended into a great variety of scholarly realms. Montesquieu (Charles-Louis de Secondat, 1689–1755) wrote conversationally on history in *Considerations on the Causes of the Greatness of the Romans and their Decline* (1734); Francesco Algarotti (1712–64) likewise on science in his *Newtonianism for Ladies* (1737) (Mazzotti 2004; Russo 2007: 167–93). The *savants*' own academies and journals continued, even proliferated (e.g., McClellan 1985). But the *salons* acquired a sufficient hegemony over the world of the *savants*.

Yet the *savants*, transmuted into *philosophes*, never fully accepted *salon* dominance over the learned world. César Chesneau Dumarsais' (1676–1756) *Le philosophe* (1730), which defined the *philosophe* as an *honnête homme*, registered the highwater mark of this fragile amalgamation (Russo 2007: 196). In the ensuing decades, the *philosophes* rebelled with increasing vehemence against *salon* pretensions. Attacks on *salon* style as inappropriate for learned discussions articulated some part of this revolt, as when Voltaire (François-Marie Arouet, 1694–1778) judged Fontenelle critically because he 'talked about science in the same way as Voiture talked of *galanterie* to Mlle Paulet' (Voltaire 1786: 232, translated in Russo 2007: 28; and see Russo 2007: 27–8, 67–8). So too did polemical attacks against the *bel esprit*, that affected doppelgänger of the properly *philosophe* man of letters, whose threatening shadow required anxious denunciation (Russo 2007: 1–2, 8, 43–5, 53–6, 60–9, 72–3, 76). As the century progressed, the *philosophes* directly posed their own authority against the claims of the *salon* – partly in their own name, increasingly in the name of convenient mouthpieces such as *the nation* or *the public* (e.g., Pekacz 1999a: 143–203, esp. 166–88; and see Young 2013). Their claims to authority also relied on reupholstered polemics against feminine judgement in the *salon*: the revolt of the *philosophes* against the *salon* was also a masculine revolt against female authority, in which the *philosophes* increasingly substituted all-male gatherings for the mixed-sex *salons* (D. Goodman 1994: 233–80).[4] The universalising aspiration of the conversational *salons* had provoked from the *philosophes* an equally universalising riposte in favour of their own discourse, society, judgement and authority.

The *philosophe* offensive had some effect. *Salonnières* significantly abandoned the exercise of their own taste as the century proceeded, and adopted instead the role of facilitators of masculine judgements (Hamerton 2002; Harth 1992; Pekacz 1999a; Russo 2001). Yet most *philosophes* who opposed *salon* dominance were themselves *salon* attendees, and frequently the beneficiaries of *salon* patronage. Even Rousseau, that quintessential rebel against *salon* dominance, had participated in the *salon* world. Jean-Baptiste le Rond D'Alembert (1717–83) recommended in his 'Essai sur la société des gens de lettre et des grands' (1753) that *philosophes* limit their time in conversational circles – but the *philosophes* continued to practise the light art of *salon* conversation even when they rejected it in theory as a distraction or a corruption (D'Alembert 1822: 361; Russo 2007: 11, 197–8). Much of the quarrel between the *philosophes* and the *salons* was an internal polemic in a shared intellectual world where *salon* dominance, albeit diminishing, persisted (Russo 2007: 7).

The *philosophe* critique was more than mere polemic. Many *salons*, perhaps most, were indeed loci of triviality, cruel gossip and character assassination, where aristocratic court society made only a faint pretence of egalitarian sociability (Craveri 2005: 327; Lilti 2015). Enlightenment intellectuals clustered in a much-cited handful of *salons*, including those of Anne-Thérèse de Marguenat de Courcelles, Marquise de Lambert (1647–1733), Claudine Alexandrine Guérin de Tencin (1682–1749), Marie de Vichy-Champrond du Deffand (1696–1780), Marie Thérèse Rodet Geoffrin (1699–1777), Paul-Henri Thiry, Baron d'Holbach (1723–89), Julie de Lespinasse and Suzanne Curchod Necker (Craveri 2005: 296; Prendergast 2015: 17). These *salons* indeed possessed an impressive guest list of Enlightenment intellectuals, and they encouraged by publicity and patronage, as much as by the intellectual stimulation of their conversations, the intellectual flourishing of much of the French Enlightenment (D. Goodman 1994; Kors 1976; and see Dalton 2003; Hamerton 2010; Marchal 1991). But if the *salons* of Julie de Lespinasse and the Baron d'Holbach provided one pole of the *salon* world, productively intertwined with the creative core of French Enlightenment thought, another pole lay in the chit-chat of the French court, where conversational style forwarded nothing more than the gossip of *fainéant* courtiers. Only some *salons* enlightened, and only some of the Enlightenment derived in any serious sense from the *salon* milieu.

We should not take the *salon* as the great model for and enabler of the democratic and universalising aspirations of the Enlightenment's conversational world (D. Goodman 1994). Yet neither should we take it as essentially an arena of empty praise, obsequious deferral and the implementation of power (Lilti 2015; Pekacz 1999a; Weckel 2000). Lilti's strong version of the argument that the *salons*, to the extent they existed at all, were essentially a sham of true conversation that merely reinforced the traditional social structures of hierarchy and exclusion (Lilti 2015; and see N. Collins 2006) has already received strong critiques (D. Goodman 2017; Russo 2017) as well as a preliminary factual riposte (Edmondson forthcoming; and see Comsa et al. 2016). The *salon* appears to have had *some* relationship to the larger conversational Enlightenment, if a nuanced one.

How then should we interpret the complicated relationship between *salon* conversations and the conversations of the broader world? It may help if we expand our examination of the *salon* to include the conceptual and social role of the garden. The garden's interstitial position between the *salon* and the larger world both exemplifies and helps explain how conversation drifted beyond the *salon*'s walls.

The image (and probably enough the reality) of the garden had been associated with truth-seeking discourse back to antiquity – the Roman garden in particular an outdoor extension of the noble villa that traditionally provided the venue for *sermo* (Augustine 1937: 61 [23]; Cicero 1988: 37 [1.12.18]; Giesecke 2007: 86–91, 100–9). That imagery linking the garden to (frequently conversational) discourse and inquiry persisted in the Renaissance, and indeed down to the Enlightenment, in works such as Pietro Bembo's (1470–1547) *Gli Asolani* (1505), Thomas More's (1478–1535) *Utopia* (1516), Desiderius Erasmus' (1466–1536) *Convivium religiosum* (*The Godly Feast*) (1522), Justus Lipsius' (1547–1606) *Constantia* (1584), Moderata Fonte's (pseudonym of Modesta Pozzo, 1555–92) *Il merito delle donne* (1592; posthumously published 1600), and Gabriel Bonnot de Mably's (1709–85) *Des droits et des devoirs du citoyen* (1789).[5] But as conversation shifted towards an increasingly tense conceptual relationship with lordly oratory, the image of the garden likewise shifted towards an increasingly tense relationship with the city – a refuge from the tyranny of the world beyond the garden rather than a complement to its civic debates. This imagery persisted down to the Enlightenment: the free speech of the garden contrasted with the unfree speech of the city.[6]

Yet the image and the reality of early modern gardens also transformed in tandem with early modern conversation, for the garden remained a characteristic site of conversation. In art and life, *conversation* in France and *conversatie* in Flanders and Holland were quite often a matter of promenading or other forms of garden sociability (E. Goodman 1982: 250–1, 253, 258).[7] Spacious and secluded gardens also provided what cramped, all-too-public household interiors could not: a site for the intimate conversations of romantic and sexual dalliance, the private revelation of the inner self both in sublimating figure and in starkly literal physicality (Crane 2009).[8]

Naturally, the *salon* had its garden too. Private, aristocratic gardens had flourished in France from the early seventeenth century, imitating royal models. *Salon* conversation therefore alternated naturally between the *ruelles* indoors and the gardens outside. So Madame de Murat (Henriette-Julie de Murat, 1668–1716) on a rural jaunt in 1699, a *salon* alfresco:

> After supper we returned to the gardens: there lovers had the pleasure of speaking together for an hour. . . . After having strolled around like this separately, we joined each other again near a large basin of water whose borders were ornamented with lawns; the conversation became generalized. (Conan 2007: 44; Démoris 1971, cited and translated in Vidal 1992: 91–2)

Madeleine de Scudéry (1607–1701) set many *salonnier* conversations in gardens in her literary works; while Fontenelle's *Conversations on the Plurality of Worlds* (1686) located the astronomical conversation between the *philosophe* and the Marquise in the Marquise's garden (Conan 2005: 333–4; Harth 1992: 123–4).

But as conversation in the *salon* could drift into the garden, so conversation in the garden could drift into the larger world. The French kings had opened the royal gardens of Paris to their subjects, and *salon* conversation in private gardens soon overlapped with the more public conversations of Paris' aristocrats and bourgeois as they promenaded in these nominally royal precincts.[9] *Salon* conversation might be exclusive, but conversations in these royal gardens were more socially diverse, more frequently conducted between strangers, more loose-jointed and open to contradiction, and greater in scale than the *salon* equivalent. Indeed, garden designers began to make longer and wider alleys, to accommodate and attract larger crowds.

The subject matter of these conversations in the royal gardens also drifted from private affairs to public ones, from private gossip about the other publicly promenading figures to public gossip and news-telling – the latter increasingly retailed by *nouvellistes* specialising in various kinds of news. So in Scudéry's *Conversations sur divers sujets* (1680), the first dialogue described Theandre and Cleonte ambling in the Tuileries as gatherings of *peletons*, the hangers-on around the *nouvellistes*, discussed 'the extraordinary merit of the Dauphine' (Scudéry 1680: 2^{r}–4^{r}, cited and translated in Harth 1992: 47). André Morellet (1727–1819) some generations later described a similar slippage of conversation from *salon* to public garden:

> After our dinners at her [Madame Geoffrin's] house, we often went to the Tuileries – d'Alembert, Raynal, Helvetius, Galiani, Marmontel, Thomas, etc. – to meet other friends, to hear the latest news, to criticize the government and to philosophize as we wished. We sat in a circle at the foot of a tree in the central *allée*, abandoning ourselves to a conversation as animated and free as the air we breathed. (Morellet 1988: 97, translated and cited in Chartier 1997: 156–7)

The shift from private conversation to public opinion, geographically embodied in the drift from *salon* to *salon* garden to public garden, partly revealed the *salon*'s limitations. Morellet and his friends left Geoffrin's *salon* in good measure to speak more freely than they could before their hostess. But *salon* and public garden were defined as much by the permeable conceptual and physical boundaries that connected them, which made it possible in the first place for Morellet to conceive of engaging in a public conversation. The *salon* was distinct from the public world, but it was open to it via the garden (Harth 1992: 46–7; Conan 2007: 43–7, 57; and see also Lougee 1976: 70).

This complex relationship by way of the garden – itself iconically halfway between private intimacy and public openness – may stand for the larger relationship of the *salon* to the world of the public. The garden was no longer just a refuge in tense opposition to the city. The *salon* garden was distinct, but not walled off; influential, even when the world it helped create came to be impatient of the limitations of *salon* discourse. The *salon* was not the world, but it was open to the world, and communicated with it – by way of the mediating garden.

Yet the direct participants in *salon* culture, by the most expansive definition, were a tiny proportion of Europeans in the eighteenth century – although a significantly higher proportion of the intellectual, political and social elites of Europe. The *salon* provided an influential model, and it powerfully affected the Enlightenment's intellectual history, but European *salon* culture could not by itself create a conversational world. Even adding the *salon* garden to the tale does not change that overall judgement.

We must turn to the culture of politeness, centred in England rather than in France, to see how the culture of conversation began to slip to the coffeehouses, the everyday courtesies and the material fabric of eighteenth-century life.

The Project of Politeness

The British theorisation of politeness largely derived from the Italian and French innovations upon *sermo* and *conversatio* described in *Concept of Conversation*, but the British context greatly differed. Where in France the absolute monarch monopolised power, in Britain the enduringly loose-jointed polity shifted after the Glorious Revolution of 1688 into one where a free people exercised increasing power, both in fact and in prospect. The realm of conversation now developed as an adjunct of remarkably unrestrained political discourse – a world of functioning oratory, in a mode more enduringly democratic than Europe had seen since the fall from power of the Athenian Assembly. The British theorists, as the French, devoted concentrated attention to the relationship of conversation and manners to the world of power – but the world of power they addressed was one where oratory, and power, were shifting to the multitude as it replaced the monarch in the seat of sovereign power. In France, the project of conversation and manners necessarily addressed itself to making the monarch mannerly and conversational – or at the very least to constraining the scope of the unreformed monarch's will. In Britain, this project rather addressed itself to the sovereign people, and sought to make them *polite* – mannerly, capable of rational conversation, and thus able to rule a virtuous and free government. This project aligned with the universalising dynamic of sociability grounded in natural law, but it received its impetus from the particular political culture that had emerged in Britain after the Glorious Revolution. Universalising sociability made the project of politeness possible; the emergence of a ruling multitude made the project of politeness necessary.

The difference of orientation between France and Britain should not be over-argued: the universalising impulse was scarcely unknown in France, and Britons were not heedless of the dangers of monarchical power. Yet if we consider the late-seventeenth-century writings of Jean-Baptiste Morvan de Bellegarde (1648–1734) and Mary Astell (1666–1731), the monarch is a greater object for Bellegarde than for Astell. So, as we have seen, Bellegarde in *Réflexions sur ce qui peut plaire ou déplaire dans le commerce du monde* (1688):

> This is, however, . . . the privilege of conversation: everyone is permitted to say his sentiment, and we must suffer with good grace those who contradict us. It would be an insupportable tyranny to wish to fix the thought of others under one's own opinion. Kings, with all their authority, have no jurisdiction over the sentiments of their peoples, and individuals should not claim to be more absolute than kings. (Bellegarde 1688: 285–6, translated in Gordon 1994: 98–9)

Contrast this with Mary Astell in *A Serious Proposal to the Ladies for the Advancement of Their True and Greatest Interest* (1697):

> For Human Nature is not willing to own its Ignorance; Truth is so very attractive, there's such a natural agreement between our Minds and it, that we care not to be thought so dull as not to be able to find out by our selves such obvious matters. We shou'd therefore be careful that nothing pass from us which upbraids our Neighbours Ignorance, but study to remove't without appearing to take notice of it, and permit 'em to fancy if they please, that we believe them as Wise and Good as we endeavour to make them. By this we gain their Affections which is the hardest part of our Work, exite their Industry and infuse a new Life into all Generous Tempers, who conclude there's great hopes they may with a little pains attain what others think they Know already, and are asham'd

> to fall short of the good Opinion we have entertain'd of 'em. . . . Now a Modest way of delivering our Sentiments assists us in this, and leaves us at liberty to take either side of the Question as Reason and Riper Consideration shall determine. (Astell 1697: Part II, 185–8)

For Astell, not royal authority, but human nature, chary of imposition of its freedom, was the wilful object that must be wooed to reason, and the enduringly conversational *liberty to take either side of the Question as Reason and Riper Consideration shall determine* now applied also to that same generality. Moreover, such *Human Nature* was also identified with *our Neighbours Ignorance* – with the multitude, not the monarch. Astell here encapsulated the reversed alignment that would characterise the British project of politeness (see also France 1992: 74–96).

This project of politeness in the first place included the inculcation of conversation – it was a register of the interpenetration of the concepts of politeness and conversation that conversation now was taken to foster polite manners as much as the reverse. Late-seventeenth- and eighteenth-century Britain thus saw the publication of an extraordinary number of works both descriptive and prescriptive on the subject of conversation (A. 1683; Bond 1965: I, 429–32, II, 44–6; C. 1673; Constable 1738; Davis 1964: 260–76; Fielding 1972; S. Richardson 1928: 12–16, 55–7, 86–8; Shaftesbury 1999: 29–162; Swift 1957: 87–95, 213–18, 221–2; Temple 1814: III, 541–8; Warren 1983). In the substance of their depictions and recommendations, English discussions of conversation in good measure paralleled or (more usually) echoed their French equivalents; Hurley notes the heavy dependence on continental models of English courtier manuals in the 1660s and 1670s (Hurley 2010: 35–6).

So in the late seventeenth century S. C. praised conversation in *The Art of Complaisance* (1673):

> All the world must acknowledge, that it is Conversation which contributes to render men sociable, and makes up the greatest commerce of our life, so that we may say, that it is impossible to take too much care to render our discourse pleasing and profitable. (C. 1673: 51).

Humphrey Brooke (1617–93) in *The durable legacy* (1681) emphasised conversation's perspicuous revelation of interiority, and the contrast of conversation with the court:

> Let thy conversation be plain and courteous . . . [as opposed to] Statesmen and Courtiers[,] who though they are great exploratiors of other mens hearts, keep their own skreened with the outside of Ceremony,

> and art of obliging: Good men . . . do not hide their hearts in the formality of their carriage and expressions, but intend to be known by them. (Humphrey Brooke 1681: 174; Hurley 2010: 48; and see Saint-Évremond 1700: I, 310)

The British prescription of conversation continued throughout the eighteenth century. Abel Boyer (c. 1667–1729) in *The English Theophrastus* (1702) recycled all the commonplaces on society, conversation, civility and politeness that had resonated through Italy and France since Castiglione's time (Boyer 1702: 103–4, 106–8; Mee 2011: 25; and see Watts 1743: 42). Adam Smith (1723–90) – at least in his early writings – was generally approbatory of the virtues of conversation (Clark 1992; e.g., A. Smith 2002: 399 [7.4.28]), while in his *Lectures on Rhetoric and Belles Lettres* (1762–3) he prescribed a natural, easy, clear and plain style, so as to convey the sentiments by way of sympathy (A. Smith 1985: 25–6 [i.v.56], 55 [i.35–6]). David Hume in *Dialogues Concerning Natural Religion* (1779) recurred to a very old definition of conversation as the discussion of indefinite topics:

> Any question of philosophy, on the other hand, which is so *obscure* and *uncertain*, that human reason can reach no fixed determination with regard to it; if it should be treated at all; seems to lead us naturally into the style of dialogue and conversation. (Hume 2013: 96)

Towards the end of the eighteenth century, Hannah More (1745–1833) wrote in *Strictures on the Modern System of Female Education* (1799) of conversation much as Mary Astell had a century earlier – and, indeed, much as the entire tradition had in describing conversation's genre characteristics: 'Truth and not triumph should be the object' (H. More 1799: 68 [Ch. 14: Conversation]). When (to return to the *locus classicus* of Augustan England) Richard Steele (1672–1729) and Joseph Addison (1672–1719) praised conversation, quite traditionally, as an egalitarian mode of speech, a way to discover truth, a mode of speaking to please all manner of men (where, admittedly, it risked degenerating into empty flattery), and an alternative to the relations of power and powerlessness, they magnified rather than created eighteenth-century England's conversational ideal (Bond 1987: III, 174 (No. 225, 16 September 1710); 1965: IV, 502–5 [No. 557, 21 June 1714]).

Meanwhile, Mary Astell's rhetoric for women, *A Serious Proposal, Part II* (1697), prescribed a clear style appropriate to achieving the goals of conversation, whether in spoken or written communication, and followed the French in redefining proper rhetoric in conversational terms (Astell 1697: Part II, 195–7; and see Drake [?] 1696: 38; Donawerth 1998: 190–8). Charles de Marguetel de Saint-Denis, seigneur de Saint-Évremond (1613–1703), also helped popularise in England the ideal of polite, mixed-sex conversation, and the ideals of sociable *honnêteté* both male and female. So Aemilia, his feminine ideal in 'The Character of a Woman, that is not to be found' (1700):

> In her ordinary Conversation, she says nothing with study, and nothing at a venture; the least Matters discover Attention, and there appears nothing studied in the most serious; her liveliest Discourses cease not to be exact, and her most natural Thoughts are exprest with a delicate Turn. (Saint-Évremond 1700: I, 209; L. Klein 1993: 105–7)

The British concept of conversation preserved the mixed-sex note that explicitly acknowledged women's conversational capacities.

Yet if the substance of the British conversational ideal was traditional, the broadness of its application was not. The sheer intensity of interest in cultivating conversation in eighteenth-century Britain was remarkable: Mee writes that, 'Conversation didn't just happen in eighteenth-century Britain. It was scrutinized, policed, promoted, written about, discussed, and practiced' (Mee 2011: 5–7; and see L. Klein 2001). Moreover, it was no longer intended to be the preserve of a gentle few. In 1740, George Drummond's 'Rules for Conversation' (1740) was composed with an eye to 'comforting success in almost every scene of life' (Drummond 1740, cited in Mee 2011: 6 (note 22); 2011: 6). The multiplication of conversation handbooks in eighteenth-century Britain likewise registered the conversationalising of ever greater swathes of British society (Mee 2011: 5). A telling piece of dialogue by one Mr Sociable in James Wright's (1643–1713) *The Humours, and Conversations of the Town* (1693) provided a fair portrait of how conversation had come to pervade the British scene:

> A pretty regulation of Conversation this, if I mistake not! So that you wou'd reduce the World to that pass, that ev'ry Company shou'd be an Academy, or a *Convivarium Philosophorum*; ha! ha! ha! but I am of much a contrary Opinion; I think that Conversation was ordain'd for the passing away our idle hours with pleasure: Thus far however I'll agree with you, as to grant it shou'd sometimes be consider'd as an improvement, when we endeavour for the converse of Men of Sense and Wit, which may bring us to a habit of talking wittily. (James Wright 1693: 49–50; Shields 1997: 23)

Sociable, contrasting his preference to the solemnity of academic debate, prized the pleasure of a varied company of conversationalists, and was as glad to converse 'in a Lady's Chamber' as in a tavern (James Wright 1693: 50; Shields 1997: 24). Conversation was intended for, and now included as an everyday matter, an ever-increasing number of Mr Sociables.

The most famous locus for this democratising conversation was, of course, the coffeehouse (Cowan 2005: 89–112, 172–5; Fox 2000: 376–9, 401–4; Habermas 1991: 32–3; Mee 2011: 13; Pincus 1995; but see Cowan 2004). Here the people seized leisured conversation from out of the gentle garden and brought it into their realm, the city. And the coffeehouse indeed sprang from the traditional loci of conversation. The coffeehouse, in its cradle in mid-seventeenth-century Oxford and London, was conceived of as a variation on the continental academy – a place for learned and sociable discussion, conversational in form, to complement or rival the university. Restoration and Augustan coffeehouses doubled as quasi-Castiglionean training academies, where one could learn foreign languages, listen to learned lectures, and arrange to be taught to dance, fence or ride. Coffeehouses also had attributes of the *salon* – a site for informal and quasi-egalitarian sociability, in distinct contrast to the hierarchical rigidities of the court. Where the coffeehouse differed from the *salon* was its relative openness to the world at large. On the one hand, this rendered it more broad-based than the *salon* – albeit more masculine, the coffeehouse being entirely too public a place for a lady – not least because even a slenderly endowed gentleman could drop into a coffeehouse without committing himself to the traditional, hierarchical and expensive rituals of aristocratic sociability. On the other hand, this relative openness rendered it vulnerable to ridicule, as merely a vulgar show of gentlemanly civility (Cowan 2005: 90–102, 104, 107, 229, 247–54). Ridicule, however, only registered the success of this democratised, urbanised locus of conversation.

The expansion of coffeehouse conversation also led to its multiplication: there were various coffeehouses for different sets of men, and so coffeehouses drew on the diversity of mankind's subdivisions to produce a diversity of conversations (Mee 2011: 13). At the same time, coffeehouse conversation emphasised the diversity of its participants. John Hill (c. 1714–75) wrote in 1753 to praise this discursive ideal of the coffeehouse, with a reservation as to its failure to live up to that ideal in practice: 'The mixed conversation at Coffee-houses, if it could be restrained within any bounds of order and regularity, would be of the most advantageous kind' (Hill 1753: 15 ['The Inspector. No. 4']; Mee 2011: 3). This ideal of mixed company, reminiscent of that of Stefano Guazzo's (1530–93) *Civile Conversation* (1574), had a more recent British precedent: Isaac Watts (1674–1748) wrote in *The Improvement of the Mind: or, a Supplement to the Art of Logick* (1741) against,

> conversing only with Persons of the same Sentiments. A free and general Conversation with Men of very various Countries and of different Parties, Opinions, and Practices (so far as it may be done safely) is of excellent Use to undeceive us in many wrong Judgments which we may have framed, and to lead us into juster Thoughts. . . . If you happen to be in Company with a *Merchant* or a *Sailor*, a *Farmer* or a *Mechanick*, a *Milk-Maid* or a *Spinster*, *lead them into a Discourse of the Matters of their own peculiar Province or Profession*; for every one knows or should know his own Business best. In this Sense a common Mechanick is wiser than a Philosopher. By this means you may gain some Improvement in Knowledge from every one you meet. (Watts 1743: 125–6; Mee 2011: 71)

The coffeehouses set the tone in eighteenth-century Britain for a multiplicity of conversations diverse in their character and their participants (and see Heller 1998: 68–71, 75–6).

Yet if conversation was spreading among Britons, and becoming both more democratic and diverse, it was not an easy or a natural increase. Addison and Steele admonished in *The Tatler* that, 'even among those who should have more polite Idea's of Things, you see a Set of People who invert the Design of Conversation, and make frequent Mention of ungrateful Subjects' (Bond 1987: III, 172 [No. 225, 16 September 1710]; Mee 2011: 70–1). Improper conversation towards women, the effect of which was to inhibit them from participating in either the conversational or the commercial worlds, was a particular problem (Bond 1965: II, 107–10 [No. 155, 28 August 1711]; Mee 2011: 52–3, and see also 79–80). Conversation decayed all too frequently into disputation or into the declamations of oratory, neither of which was remotely polite (Bellegarde 1707: 138; Theobald 1717: 215 [No. 61]; Mee 2011: 10, 13, 16). Moreover, conversation could also decay into mere courtiership of the modern age; so at any rate was the argument of Jonathan Swift's (1667–1745) *Treatise on Polite Conversation* (1738), as exemplified in the touting prospectus of its appallingly boorish supposed author, Simon Wagstaff (Swift 2013: 267–301; Mee 2011: 56–7). Indeed, Mee points out that the multiplication of conversation handbooks in eighteenth-century England itself registered anxiety that it was all too easy to fall away from conversational speech (Mee 2011: 55–6). The spread of the application of conversation accentuated the need for proper conversation – for conversation moulded according to the canons of politeness.

Politeness, 'the art of pleasing in company', was the the English inheritor of *civil conversation*, of the realm of manners. Here too there had been some linguistic flux: while 'politeness' had related meanings prior to the eighteenth century, it had emerged in its modern sense in the late seventeenth and early eighteenth centuries via translations, adaptations and imitations of continental courtesy books as a derivation of the French *politesse*, itself a term drawn largely from the conversational milieu of the French *salons* (L. Klein 1984–5: 186 (note 1), 189). As late as 1673, Obadiah Walker (1616–99) in *Of education, especially of young gentlemen* gave a Christianising rendition of the concept that preserved the terminology of civility (O. Walker 1673: 212–13 [2.1]; Hurley 2010: 40). In the next two generations, however, *politeness* came into nigh-universal currency. For a rough precis of what it involved, we may look to Addison's prescription in *The Spectator* of easy and informal manners, artfully artless, as against the stiffness of ceremony. 'Conversation [here *manners* rather than *speech*], like the Romish Religion, was so encumbered with Show and Ceremony, that it stood in need of a Reformation to retrench its Superfluities, and restore it to its natural good Sense and Beauty' (Bond 1965: I, 487 [No. 119, 17 July 1711]; Cowan 2005: 102–3). Hume's meditation on civility and conversation in 'Of the Rise and Progress of the Arts and Sciences' (1742) preserved the same essential conception (Hume 1996: III, 136).

The project of politeness aimed at spreading polite manners beyond an exclusive social elite, to an increasingly broad variety of social classes aspiring to politeness' cachet. The project of politeness also operated via a variety of cultural modes, as 'polite learning', 'polite style', 'polite letters' and the 'polite arts' – all of these modes retaining conversation and its virtues as the exemplary model for politeness (D. Goodman 1994: 120–3; L. Klein 1984–5: 189–90, 189 (note 8), 200–3, 205–6, 208; 1994: 4–5, 7–8, 13; 2002; Prostko 1989: 46, 48). To become polite was to become mannerly – and virtuous, for politeness was conceived of as both grounded in virtue and tied to moral improvement. Smith nicely summarised this view in *The Theory of Moral Sentiments* (1759), translated into a historicising mode:

> A polished people being accustomed to give way, in some measure, to the movements of nature, become frank, open, and sincere. Barbarians, on the contrary, being obliged to smother and conceal the appearance of every passion, necessarily acquire the habits of falsehood and dissimulation. (A. Smith 2002: 244 [5.2.11])

This spread of the conception of politeness as a virtue encountered some resistance: the English retained more essential notions of virtue, whether of faith, blood, friendship or sincerity, against which politeness too often appeared as its reflections of hypocrisy, dissimulation, narrowly grasping self-interest, etc. The doppelgänger of the polite gentleman was the dissimulating rogue; thus Richard Head's (c. 1637–86) *Proteus Redivivus: or the Art of Wheedling, or Insinuation, Obtain'd by General Conversation* (1675) (Head 1675; L. Klein 1994: 11–12; 1984–5: 190–8; 2002: 875; Prostko 1989: 44–5). Politeness invited a too-easy intimacy, a familiarity that eroded proper decorum, as well as that excess of mannerliness much satirised in the figure of the fop (Mee 2011: 50; Staves 1982; and see L. Klein 1997a). Moreover, the democratisation of politeness also invited gentlemanly ambivalence because it threatened to efface politeness as a marker of elite identity (Mee 2011: 13–14; Potkay 1994: 59–103; and see Langford 1997). The project of politeness would command broad assent, but always with reservations (and see Langford 2002).

Locations for polite sociability spread throughout England, including London clubs, pump rooms, assembly rooms, theatres, chapels, walks, gardens, squares and circuses (Borsay 1989: 273–4; P. Burke 1993: 117; Mee 2011: 26; Sweet 2002). Commercial culture as a whole became increasingly polite (see also Brewer 1995). Consumption goods were bought as markers and forwarders of politeness; so the sociable drinking of coffee and tea, perhaps on a classicising tea or coffee service provided by Wedgwood pottery. Cutlery, buttons and boxes served a similar function; and these polite goods were housed in equally polite interior décor – the fireplace, for example, that traditional locale of conversation, redesigned with grates and fenders became the acme of ferrous *politesse* (L. Klein 2002: 884–5). Politeness in general emerged as something to which an ever larger number of Englishmen could aspire, not entirely without success. The readership of manuals of polite behaviour became very wide: now they included not only the gentle classes but also would-be ladies and gentlemen, or those simply seeking to understand the polite world out of self-interest or curiosity. Self-improvement societies spread throughout the country. Middle-class Londoners in general, and presumably growing numbers of their peers throughout England, could enter into and participate in the archipelago of genteel sociability (Fawcett 1985; L. Klein 1995: 363, 374–6). The modes of discourse themselves were also to become polite; so, for example, the newspaper now came to be politely coversational both in its style and in its intended function of sparking virtue, politeness and further conversation in its readers (Bond 1965: I, 506 [No. 124, 23 July 1711)], IV, 501 [No. 556, 18 June 1714]; Copley 1995; Mee 2011: 22, 54; but see Copley 1995: 74).

The transformation of male clothing in Enlightenment Britain may be taken as representative of the cultural effects of the expanding culture of politeness. On the one hand, in a sartorial analogue to the conversational tone, male clothing became steadily more informal through the late seventeenth and eighteenth centuries. This informality also eroded the traditional use of male clothing to display an exacting register of hierarchical status, and substituted for it (in another sartorial analogue to conversation) an emphasis on relatively egalitarian and plain clothing, which would culminate in the early-nineteenth-century triumph of Beau Brummel (1778–1840). The democratisation of male clothing was so great that, as the three-piece suit became more common, even servants began to escape livery for the cheap or used suit (L. Klein 1995: 374; Staves 1982: 426–7). Here was both the promise and threat of the democratising culture of politeness: the servant could aspire to dress as his master; the master could be mistaken for his servant (and see Maxwell 2014: 29–45).

The coffeehouses, those places of relatively democratic conversation, were the site of a particularly intense campaign of the project of politeness (Cowan 2005: 225–56; L. Klein 1996). To render them polite was taken to be no small task: Addison and Steele critiqued them in *The Spectator* as the site of '*a barren Superfluity of Words*' rather than of sweet converse (Bond 1965: IV, 187 [No. 476, 5 September 1712]; Mee 2011: 51). Yet while alehouses were irredeemably associated with vulgarity and vice, coffeehouses were perceived of as civilisable, potentially amenable to the aspirations of politeness (Cowan 2005: 105–6). So Addison in *The Spectator*, *inter alia* as he adapted Cicero, aimed to make coffeehouses polite:

> It was said of *Socrates*, that he brought Philosophy down from Heaven, to inhabit among Men; and I shall be ambitious to have it said of me, that I have brought Philosophy out of Closets and Libraries, Schools and Colleges, to dwell in Clubs and Assemblies, at Tea-Tables, and Coffee-Houses. (Bond 1965: I, 44 [No. 10, 12 March 1711]; Cicero 1989: 435 [5.4.10–11]; L. Klein 1994: 36, 42)

In a somewhat less self-congratulatory mode, *The Spectator* described the coffeehouse as already the site of a little platoon of self-controlled and caffeinated Stoics (Bond 1965: I, 210 [No. 49, 26 April 1711]; L. Klein 1996: 49). Both by their own impetus and by the self-important urging of figures such as Addison, spoonfuls of manners were admixed into the coffeehouses – although John Hill wrote as late as 1753 that '[t]he mixed conversation at Coffee-houses' still was not 'restrained within any bounds of order and regularity' (Hill 1753: 15 ['The Inspector. No. 4']; Mee 2011: 3). The project of rendering the coffeehouses polite remained very much a work in progress.

So, of course, did the entire project of politeness. But the aspiration mattered more than the achievement: willy-nilly, all mankind now was meant to be polite, and consequently conversational. The universal capacity for reason, and the universal conversation of public opinion, founded themselves not least on an accumulation of courtesy books, Wedgwood pottery, three-piece suits, and volleys of coffeehouse chat.

La Conversation des Femmes

The project of politeness registered one universalisation; the culmination of the extension of conversation to women registered another. Both the status and the presence of women had been increasing throughout the Renaissance and the seventeenth century. In the eighteenth century, above all in British thought, the theoretical status of women (if hardly yet their social status) within the conversational tradition came to something approaching that of men. Indeed, woman as a category became central to the different strands of that conversational theory, in the theorists' consideration of conversation, politeness, sociability and historical progress itself.

Although this section focuses on women in theory, we should briefly note the British social background to such theorisation. In addition to the growing recognition and practice of the female capacity for friendship and conversation noted in *Concept of Conversation*, women were also entering into sociable relationships in general. The seventeenth-century *salons* of France provided the model for English female sociability: Queen Henrietta Maria (1609–69) imported the new French style of female sociability into England during the 1630s, while Royalist women in exile during the 1640s and 1650s acquired *salonnier* manners that they brought back with them to England after the Restoration (Wahl 1999: 181). British developments thereafter, to the extent that they did not simply reflect persisting French influence, built upon the French model: Madeleine de Scudéry was the godmother of the female efflorescence north of the Channel, for the Bluestocking women of eighteenth-century Britain innovated upon the example of the French *salonnières* (Heller 1998). In sum, the French tradition of polite conversation and civility, and the thematic role of women in conversation and civility – whether as equal participants or merely as the objects by which men rendered themselves polite – was transmitted as the model for the Augustan elaboration of polite discourse among men and women in an ever-increasing range of society (L. Klein 1993: 107–11).

Upon this substantial foundation, the increasingly prominent conception of women in earlier centuries now became one approaching equality. Bernard Mandeville (1670–1733), for example, wrote a dialogue whose Fulvia was as reasonable as her male interlocutors Horatio and Cleomenes (Mandeville 1988: 29–61; Prince 1996: 204–5; Solkin 1993: 14–16). Adam Smith went so far as to note in *Lectures on Rhetoric and Belles Lettres* (1762–3) that 'It is commonly said also that in France and England the conversation of the Ladies is the best standar<d> of Language' (A. Smith 1985: 4 [i.5]; McKenna 2011: 53). Moreover, the age saw a shift towards the feminine in the default gendering of the century's preferred abstractions. Politeness, manners, domesticity, humanity, sensibility – all the conversational virtues were inflected feminine, and the progress of these virtues was considered, for better or worse, a feminisation of the broader culture (Berry 2013: 142; Mee 2011: 10). So Saint-Évremond's model of *honnêteté* in 'The Character of a Woman that is not to be found' (1700) was female:

> I would not look for it ['the Idea of an accomplished Person'] amongst the Men, because there is always wanting in their Commerce, something of that Sweetness which we meet in that of Woman; and I thought it less impossible to find in a Woman the strongest and soundest Reason of Men, than in a Man those Charms and Agreements that are so natural to Women. (Saint-Évremond 1700: I, 213–14)

The image of virtue likewise became more feminine. Hume's feminised personification of virtue in *An Enquiry Concerning the Principles of Morals* (1751), for example, was designed to attract: she embodied the qualities that seduced individuals into sociability and drew them towards participation in society (Hume 1996: IV, 347–8 [*Enquiry Concerning the Principles of Morals*, 9.2]; Dickins 2008: 30). More concretely, *The Tatler* gave to itself, with significance not ultimately lessened by its ironical wit, the chaffing name of 'tittle-tattle' proverbially given to female conversation (Mee 2011: 53). If we recollect that the mirror was the Renaissance image of female self-reflection, it is not idle that the eighteenth century saw newspapers appear with the title of *The Mirror* (Mee 2011: 11). Both female conversation and the image of female self-reflection now were applied to the journals and newspapers themselves, the images of societal self-reflection. Men were now imaging a remarkable amount of their mental map as female – a development we should not overrread, doubtless, but still a remarkable one. In a myriad of ways, perhaps the more telling as a register of the century's zeitgeist for their miscellaneous character, both women and femininity itself were coming to the fore in the culture of the age.

Perhaps most significantly, the theorisation of the role of women was coming to the fore in all the linked conceptions of sociability, politeness, conversation and historical progress. This emergence depended first on the completion of the secularisation of natural law theory. As late as the early Scottish Enlightenment a role remained for God, if only as the inspirer of the will to follow reason. Both Hume and Smith, 'practical atheists' if not avowed ones, shifted to a natural grounding for their philosophy – diachronic, historical and sociological. Smith's variant grounded sociability on a natural, but ungendered, human desire for sympathy, that pertained to the human species as a whole and gave to women no more than a tacit and forgettable role. We will return later to an exploration of how Smith yoked together sympathy, internal conversation and conscience; here we will explore how Hume grounded sociability in the complementary relations between men and women. Hume wrote in *A Treatise of Human Nature* (1738–40):

> But, in order to form society, it is requisite not only that it be advantageous, but also that men be sensible of these advantages; and it is impossible, in their wild uncultivated state, that by study and reflection alone, they should ever be able to attain this knowledge. Most fortunately, therefore, there is conjoined to those necessities, whose remedies are remote and obscure, another necessity, which, having a present and more obvious remedy, may justly be regarded as the first and original principle of human society. This necessity is no other than that natural appetite betwixt the sexes, which unites them together, and preserves their union, till a new tie takes place in their concern for their common offspring. (Hume 1996: II, 250–1 [*Treatise* 3.2.2])

Hugo Grotius (1583–1645) had posited a natural appetite for society, Thomas Hobbes (1588–1679) an agonistic struggle between solitary brutes, Samuel Pufendorf (1632–94) a will to reason – all of these grounded on relations between human beings conceived as fundamentally alike and implicitly as male (Grotius 1738: xviii; Hobbes 1972: 48 [11.6]; Pufendorf 1729: 143 [2.3.20]; D. Randall 2018: 205–10). Hume subsituted for these the passionate relations between men and women – not, as in the Platonising Bembo of Baldassare Castiglione's (1478–1529) *The Book of the Courtier* (1528), as a ground on which to ascend towards Platonic love (Castiglione 1976: 255, 260–4, 266 [Bk 3], 291–2, 296, 307–8, 324–42 [Bk 4]; D. Randall 2018: 134–6), but as an irreducible passion on which to construct sociability and all its derivatives. God's role, if any, had been to create a natural order that contained men and women united by complementary passion and interest; remove God, as one easily could, and the predicate of Hume's philosophy was simply the mutual affections of men and women who, although alike in these shared passions, were themselves essentially and necessarily dissimilar.

Yet while Hume grounded the motive force of sociability on the complementary dissimilarity of men and women, that dissimilarity did not extend to any of the derivatives of sociability. Sociability, after all, was the basis of virtues – but of *artificial virtues*, such as justice, intended to constrain the passions. These virtues' artificiality separated them sharply from the realm of nature.[10] Hume wrote in the *Treatise* that 'The remedy, then, is not derived from nature, but from *artifice*; or, more properly speaking, nature provides a remedy, in the judgment and understanding, for what is irregular and incommodious in the affections' (Hume 1996: II, 254–5 [*Treatise* 3.2.2]). Most significantly, Hume's conception of the virtues derived from sociability as artificial separated him from those theorists, generally patriarchalists, who took the nature of man and woman to imply some corollary structuring of human society and politics (Schochet 1988: 18–36; and see Foster 1994; Pfeffer 2001; Schochet 1988: 225–67; Shanks 2015: 70–2; Ward 2010: 134–70). Hume's rejection of patriarchy did resemble John Locke's (1632–1704) – but while Hume's shift to artificial virtue discarded restraints derived from male and female duality, Locke's shift to social atoms recast in liberal garb the usual implicit masculinities of universalising theory (Baier 1988: 770–2; Forbes 1975: 68–80). Hume was not unique either in his conception of sexual passion yoked to familial interest or in the freedom he allowed to the world of human society and politics – but he was sharply distinctive in linking these two conceptions together as natural complements.

Although Hume took the world formed by sociability as one of artificial virtues, he and his peers still took the presence of women as informing the different aspects of this world formed by artifice. Manners, politeness, were inconceivable without women, for the exercise of politeness was significantly gendered, both in its conception of male gallantry and in its conception of female modesty and tact (J. Davidson 2004: 46–107). So Hume, building upon the arguments of seventeenth-century French thinkers (e.g., C. 1673: 118), emphasised the complementary interrelation of men and women in the realm of manners by means of an exploration of the concept of *galanterie* in 'Of the Rise and Progress of the Arts and Sciences' (Hume 1996: III, 141, 145). Hume (for all his emphasis on mutuality and complement between the sexes) considered gallantry a condescension by man to woman, his inferior in 'mind and body'; and it was not least a way to give the ineradicable, mutual 'bodily appetite' of the sexes a 'garniture of reason, discourse, sympathy, friendship, and gaiety' that would make it acceptable 'in the judgment of the truly elegant and luxurious' (Hume 1996: III, 142–5). Yet despite this significant tinge of inequality and erotic physicality, the consequence was still to make the complementary manners of men and women the measure and the summit of politeness.

Politeness and manners were also themselves associated with femininity by way of their alliance with commerce and luxury. With a more hostile polemical spin, the same gendering of politeness associated it with effeminacy: the advocates of politeness had persistently to counter the argument that feminine manners contrasted with masculine virtue, that the supple were as supine as the mannerless were martial (Harrington 2001: 36). But both by praise and by blame, politeness was inextricably linked with the female qualities.

So too was conversation, that happy result of politeness. The role of women in conversation had already been quite prominent in seventeenth-century France (D. Randall 2018: 77–8). Hume maintained this estimate, or even increased it, for he conceived of women as the regulators of manners, who allowed conversation to persist (Hume 1998: 3 ['Of Essay Writing']; Dickins 2008: 32–3). But perhaps more important than making women the empresses and arbiters of conversation was to make the mutual discourse of men and women constitutive of proper conversation. This preference for mixed conversation also had seventeenth-century French precedent, as noted in *Concept of Conversation*, but it received yet further emphasis in eighteenth-century England. A few years before the beginning of the century, Judith Drake [?] in *An Essay in defense of the Female Sex* (1696) centred polite conversation on both the presence of women and the female condition. So far as men were concerned, 'there are other Quallifications, which are as indispensably necessary to a Gentleman, or any Man that wou'd appear to Advantage in the World, which are attainable only by Company, and Conversation, and chiefly by ours' (Drake [?] 1696: 26; L. Klein 1993: 107). Women were more polite than men perforce: they were not educated to contentious and unsociable pedantry, deadly to conversation (Drake [?] 1696: 36–8, 57–8, 136–43). Hannah More provided a late and lucid exposition of the argument in *Strictures on the Modern System of Female Education* (1799):

> The sexes will naturally desire to appear to each other, such as each believes the other will best like; their conversation will act reciprocally; and each sex will appear more or less rational as they perceive it will more or less recommend them to the other. (H. More 1799: 43–96 [Ch. 14: Conversation])

The motivation for the reason and virtue of conversation depended much, if not solely, upon that discourse being mixed.

We should note here that More's phrase that men and women's 'taste and principles thus mutually operate' (H. More 1799: 44 [Ch. 14: Conversation]) implied a wider application than the world of conversation alone. Men were not merely to exercise their taste upon women, as conoisseurs upon aesthetic objects (Bermingham 1995); men and women were to exercise taste, judgement, upon one another, and mutually improve themselves by mutually subjecting themselves to one another's judgement. The entire relation of men and women, by implication, was now one of the mutual operation of taste. While this generalisation has contemporary application that we will pursue later, in late-eighteenth-century Scotland it helped to constitute that separate-spheres ideal which would exert such very great influence on nineteenth-century thought. So David Fordyce (1711–51) in *Dialogues Concerning Education* (1745–8) and *The Elements of Moral Philosophy* (1748) integrated the complementary role of male and female conversation into a broader conception of the complementary moral interrelation between men and women, especially in marriage. Marriage, among other things, was now the paradigmatic relationship of sensibility and sympathy; the core of the sympathetic relationship that embraced the entire family, even (to some extent) the servants (D. Fordyce 1757: 111 [Dialogue XIV]; 1758: 13; Harrington 2001, esp. 41; and see also Dwyer 1987: 109–10, 112).

James Fordyce (1720–96), David's brother, likewise argued in *Sermons to Young Women* (1766) that,

> The influence of the sexes is, no doubt, reciprocal; but I must ever be of opinion, that your's [women's] is the greatest. . . . To form the manners of men, various causes contribute; but nothing, I apprehend, of [*sic*] much as the turn of the women with whom they converse. (J. Fordyce 1809: 16–17 [Sermon I]; Harrington 2001: 41; Mee 2011: 64)

Conversation with women trained men to sympathy, sociability, sensibility, the moderation of passion, and the habitual, everyday (private) virtue more necessary to ordinary men in ordinary times than its heroic (public) counterpart, rare in value but rarely needed. A corollary of this thematic complementarity of men and women was their separation into the complementary, but separate, spheres of the public and private world. Women's seclusion in the private world, the world of *domus* and family, was meant to foster those sympathies and sentiments to which they naturally inclined, which in turn would help them both to render the family into pleasing harmony and to educate their brothers, sons and husbands for their exertions in the world beyond the family (Dwyer 1987: Ch. 4 [on family, 95–116] and Ch. 5 [on women, 117–40]; and see also Harrington 2001: 42). The very importance of women now served to underwrite their circumscription within the private sphere.

Moreover, we may add the role of women in the conception of the historical progress of society to women's thematic role in sociability, manners, conversation and virtue. As sociability and its derivatives were meant to operate in history, and the status of women was now firmly allied to them, so the increasing status of women itself became thematic in the Enlightenment's (conjectural) histories. Hume contrasted the ancient world with the modern by noting that, '[a]mong the ancients, the character of the fair-sex was considered as altogether domestic; nor were they regarded as part of the polite world or of good company' (Hume 1996: III, 145 ['Of the Rise and Progress of the Arts and Sciences']). John Millar (1735–1801) wrote in *The Origin of the Distinction of Ranks* (1771) that,

> Women of condition come to be more universally admired and courted upon account of the agreeable qualities which they possess, and upon account of the amusement which their conversation affords. They are encouraged to quit that retirement which was formerly esteemed so suitable to their character, to enlarge the sphere of their acquaintance, and to appear in mixed company, and in public meetings of pleasure.

> (J. Millar 1960: 224; cf. Hume 1996: III, 141 ['Of the Rise and Progress of the Arts and Sciences']; Dwyer 1998: 81–96)

As Pocock generally notes,

> [t]he refinement of the passions and the growth of politeness were central to the [historical] process; it is not by accident that Kames, Millar and (with modifications) Smith and William Robertson (1721–93) preface their accounts of social development with a chapter on the condition of women. (Pocock 1983: 242; and see also Kames 2007: 259–312; J. Millar 1960: 183–228; M. Moran 2000)

Where women had once been silent and ignored, now their status and their speech were the touchstones by which to judge mankind's historical progress. The revolution in women's status between the time of Petrarch (Francesco Petrarca, 1304–74) and the time of Millar had been extraordinary.

And yet . . . as noted above, the limitations inherent in the nascent separate-spheres ideal ought not to be minimised either, and they reflected a general tendency to ascribe distinct limits to women's role, to admire women only so long as they remained within those constraints. In the realm of conversation, Addison and Steele disliked women's tendency to talk of politics, and wished they would eschew 'that Party Rage which of late Years is very much crept into their [women's] Conversation' (Bond 1965: I, 242 [No. 57, 5 May 1711]; Mee 2011: 54). Hume was ambivalent. On the one hand, he noted with reasonable approbation that

> [i]n a neighbouring Nation [France], equally famous for good Taste, and for Gallantry, the Ladies are, in a Manner, the Sovereigns of the *learned* World, as well as of the *conversible;* and no polite Writer pretends to venture upon the Public, without the Approbation of some celebrated Judges of that Sex.

On the other hand, he distinguished the 'Empire of conversation' from the Republic of Letters, and noted that his 'Countrymen, the Learned' stubbornly objected to letting women have 'the sovereign Authority over the Republic of Letters'. He also articulated some pointed reservations about women's lack of erudition, and sentimental weakness for 'Books of Gallantry and Devotion' (Hume 1998: 3–4 ['Of Essay Writing']; Dickins 2008: 32–3). Hume's compliments to women included some that were distinctly backhanded.

Furthermore, the flip side of *social* conversation and commerce was taken to be *sexual* conversation and commerce; women's conversation threatened women's corruption. So Edward Gibbon in his *Decline and Fall* (1776):

> Although the progress of civilisation has undoubtedly contributed to asswage the fiercer passions of human nature, it seems to have been less favourable to the virtue of chastity, whose most dangerous enemy is the softness of the mind. The refinements of life corrupt while they polish the intercourse of the sexes. (Gibbon 1776: 232 [Ch. 9]; Pocock 1985: 118)

Millar likewise associated female freedom with luxury and corruption (J. Millar 1960: 225; and see also Dwyer 1998: 92–6). The sexual implications of female conversation continued to inhibit its wholehearted acceptance.

Finally, as Pocock notes, the civilising function of women in society paralleled the civilising function of property not least because women were still regarded 'as a species of property, or as a medium of exchange'; women's emergence from the household was an analogue to the shift of economic production from the household to the market, and so implied that women, as any other element of the *oikos*, remained objects for the use of men (Pocock 1985: 117–18). Women's roles as the maintainers of conversation required a distinct abnegation: Hume's sovereign ladies were also, perforce, handmaidens (Dickins 2008: 33). The separate-spheres ideal noted above was in some ways merely a restatement of the old restriction of women to the *oikos*, which derived naturally from a conception of women that had never fully disentangled them from domestic subordination. At the end of the day, women in many ways remained no more than golden harps, whose voices served their mastering men.

Both the revolutionary increase in and the enduring limitations on women's status were part of the narrative of eighteenth-century British conversational thought. But however limited the status of women might remain in that tradition, at least it granted women such a status, as women – and made the whole range of its philosophy, from sociability to historical progress, depend upon the existence of women as women. The rival traditions of the Enlightenment, the universalisms of Locke and Immanuel Kant (1724–1804), offered them only the possibility of inclusion in a putatively featureless but implicitly male humanity.

Education

Making conversation a universal model of discourse also led to the application of the conversational model to pedagogy. Some qualifications and elucidations are at once necessary. First, much of this narrative involves 'education' in the broadest sense: the conversational impulse overlapped variously with the education of one's own mind, the prince's mind, the people's minds. The application of conversation to pedagogy therefore is in one sense only a formalisation of this educative ambition, and a narrowing of its scope to youth. On the other hand, the application of conversation to pedagogy also registered the spread of conversational education, from that of a narrow elite to that of the people as a whole. The rise of explicitly conversational pedagogy in the Enlightenment also registered the spread of conversation-as-education from its Renaissance use primarily to educate women to the education of both sexes. Such conversational education now effectively applied to all mankind.

The conversationalisation of education, as of so much else in European culture, operated upon a discipline already set into a rhetorical frame. Aside from the obviously rhetorical subject matter of much Renaissance and early modern education, the humanist pedagogy of the Renaissance was conceived of in rhetorical terms. This Renaissance pedagogy first bore an oratorical, agonistic stamp: there was a strong (albeit contested) tradition that the pedagogue should be a sort of educational prince who ruled by a harsh discipline that elicited fear and obedience from his students (Bushnell 1996, esp. 23–116; and see Grafton and Jardine 1986). In seventeenth-century France, the structure of Jesuit education preserved the oratorical note, for it strongly emphasised agonistic competition: the Jesuit

> intellectual climate . . . encouraged combat at every turn. During their weekly and monthy debates students sparred verbally in teams named for the Romans, Spartans, and Trojans and led by decurions. The *Ratio studiorum* regulating all the Jesuit colleges laid out guidelines for these 'jousts', 'contests', or *concertationes*. (Van Orden 2005: 226)

The infiltration of conversation into pedagogy would proceed against the background and alternative of an oratorical pedagogy (and see J. Gibson 2008: 402–3).

The first steps of this infiltration occured no later than the sixteenth century, at which point conversation was already taken to be a means of female education. Women could not attend male institutions of education, women were less likely to be able to read the (Latin) books that formed the male curriculum, and women were not supposed to engage in agonistic competition. So, while male education retained agonistic disputation as its primary mode, conversation emerged *faute de mieux* as a means for women to educate themselves. In the discussion of female education in Agnolo Firenzuola's (1493–1543) *Ragionamenti* (1525), he prized conversation over reading by oneself (Firenzuola 1802: 54, translated in Smarr 2005: 15; 2005: 15–16). Tellingly, Lodovico Dolce's (1508–68) Italian adaptation of Juan Luis Vives' (1493–1540) *De institutione feminae Christianae* (1524), *Dialogo della instituzion delle donne* (1545), became a conversation opened by Dorothea, who suggested that Flaminio tell her something of the Latin book he had been reading (Dolce 2015: 83; Smarr 2005: 16–17). In Desiderius Erasmus' (1466–1536) 'The Girl with No Interest in Marriage' (1523), such pedagogical conversations among women were taken for granted: 'And if you see some lady or unmarried woman of outstanding moral excellence, you can improve yourself by her conversation' (Erasmus 1965: 110; Smarr 2005: 103). Sixteenth-century education made common use of conversation, but mostly for women.

In seventeenth-century France, while conversation and letter writing remained the especial subjects of female education, conversational education began to broaden to include high-born boys. French aristocratic education now included academies for young noblemen, whose Castiglionean curricula aimed to produce a courteous *uomo universale*, and which taught, jointly, conversational skills, a polishing of *je ne sais quoi*, and aristocratic accomplishments such as riding, dancing and fencing. At the same time, Claude Fleury's (1640–1723) *Traité du choix et de la method des études* (1686) emphasised the importance of teaching conversation as a component of rhetoric (Fleury 1686: 239–40; Maland 1970: 47, 49; Motley 1990: 72–3, 84, 86–90, 95, 116, 127, 140, 142–50). Both the practice and the theory of French education were shifting in a conversational direction.

If Castiglione inspired the curriculum of the academies, the early modern shift towards *delectare* (delight) likewise inspired (by way of a series of pedagogical thinkers including Quintilian (c. 35–c. 100), Erasmus, John Amos Comenius (1592–1670), Michel de Montaigne (1533–92) and Locke) the emphasis by Fleury, Jean-Pierre de Crousaz (1663–1750) and Charles Rollin (1661–1741) on making education pleasurable. Crousaz put it in *Traité de l'éducation des enfans* (1722) that 'Il faut semer de Roses le chemin par lequel on conduit un Enfant aux Sciences, il en faut arracher toutes les épines';

and Rollin wrote in *De la Manière d'Enseigner et d'Etudier les Belles Lettres, par rapport à l'esprit et au coeur* (1726–8) of education that

> Its government is gentle and engaging, an enemy to violence and constraint, which delights to act only by motives of persuasion, which endeavours to make its instructions relished, by speaking always with reason and truth, and tends only to make virtue more easy, by making it more amiable. Its lectures, which begin almost as soon as a child is born, grow up and gather strength with it, in time take deep root, soon pass from the memory and understanding to the heart, are daily imprinted in his manners by practice and habit, become a second nature in him. (Fleury 1686: 103, 107, 146, 174; Crousaz 1722: I, 204, 221; Rollin 1737: IV, 249; N. Gill 2010: 80–2, 90–1; and see also Boyer 1702: 164; N. Gill 2010: 23–62, 67–8)

The application of *delectare* to pedagogy was partly the result of a recognition of the rational capabilities of children. Partly, however, it also transferred the attitude of the courtier towards the prince to the attitude of the pedagogue towards his students: they had minds capable of reason, but their will had to be wooed towards reason's practice. Such pedagogy harked back to Castiglione, looked forward to Smith's conception of an education towards conscience, and was pervaded by the spirit of conversation.

Eighteenth-century British pedagogy partook of both the Italian and the French inheritances (see also Dwyer 1987: 73; N. Gill 2010: 181–226; Hanley 2011). As in sixteenth-century Italy, education by means of conversation was common, especially among women and children of both sexes (Bygrave 2009: 28; Cohen 2008; and see Bygrave 2009: 94–122; Gleadle 2003: 68–70). As had the educators of seventeenth-century French noblewomen, girls' boarding schools in eighteenth-century England aimed to inculcate conversational facility in their students – and now were ridiculed for teaching nothing more (Valenza 2009: 46). Locke in his widely influential *Some Thoughts Concerning Education* (1693) described a proper pedagogue as a most perfect classroom courtier: 'He should be a Person of eminent Vertue and Prudence, and with good Sense, have good Humour, and the skill to carry himself with gravity, ease, and kindness, in a constant Conversation with his Pupils' (Locke 1693: 212). In all these affiliations, British pedagogy drew upon enduring conversational conceptions.

Far more important than these inheritances, however, was the innovative and explicit remodelling of pedagogy upon conversation. The Dissenting Academies, above all the Warrington Academy, began to popularise conversation as a pedagogical technique: John Jennings (c. 1687–1723), Philip Doddridge (1702–51) and John Aiken (1713–80) successively expanded and popularised the use of the conversational mode – free inquiry, dialogue between student and teacher, and the student's freedom to judge (Mee 2011: 68; White 2006: 25–6). The Nonconformist Isaac Watts' *The Improvement of the Mind: or, a Supplement to the Art of Logick* (1741) likewise inserted conversation into pedagogical theory:

> In free and friendly *Conversation* our *intellectual Powers are more animated and our Spirits act with a superior Vigour in the quest and pursuit of unknown Truths*. There is a Sharpness and Sagacity of Thought that attends *Conversation* beyond what we find whilst we are shut up reading and musing in our Retirements. (Watts 1743: 42–3; Mee 2011: 69–70)

Conversation linked with sociable reading would prompt students 'to consider whether their Opinions are right or no, and to improve your own solid Knowledge'. Yet if '*free Conversation* . . . is designed for mutual Improvement in the Search of Truth', the goal of 'all our Studies and Pursuits of Knowledge' remained 'the Conformation of our Hearts and Lives to the Duties of true Religion and Morality'. The truth for Dissenters was still very much that of religion; and conversation a means to that truth (Watts 1743: 63, 73, 138; Mee 2011: 72–3). The conversationalisation of pedagogy was real among eighteenth-century Dissenters, but still had equally important limits.

Eighteenth-century Germany, meanwhile, saw the first steps of the parallel conversationalisation of pedagogy at the university level. Here, notably first at the Universities of Halle and Göttingen, the seminar model of dialogue as a mode of inquiry began to penetrate German education – first in philology, and from there colonising discipline after discipline. We may note that the introduction of the philological seminar was associated, significantly, with the training of taste and judgement; it was also associated (especially at Göttingen) with an aristocratic student body, for whom the seminar would presumably have invoked the by-now-pervasive resonances of conversation in European aristocratic culture. Not coincidentally, Göttingen provided not only seminars but also classes in courtly subjects – '[d]ancing, drawing, fencing, riding, music, and conversation in modern languages'. By the beginning of the nineteenth century, the extension of the seminar model would dovetail with the forwarding of the ideal of neo-humanism in the German universities. The spontaneous conversation of the seminar, led by a professor of quasi-aristocratic character, aimed (in semi-Shaftesburian fashion) at *Bildung*, the improvement and individuation of the character of the characteristically aristocratic or patrician students so as (in good measure) to develop that inquiring habit of mind prerequisite for conversation. The German articulation of the ideal of academic freedom would derive not least from a desire to establish the preconditions for proper academic conversation (Humboldt 1854, esp. Ch. 2; Bruford 2010; McClelland 1980: 38–9, 45, 60, 111–12, 124–5, 128–9; Watson 2010: 52–3).

If England saw conversation made into pedagogical practice in Dissenting Academies, and Germany likewise saw it institutionalised in its universities, eighteenth-century Scotland saw a particularly radical variant in this constellation of pedagogical innovation: education that did not merely use the means of conversation, or aim only to produce a conversationalist as the capstone to an education, but was fundamentally oriented throughout towards producing a conversational character. Scots such as Hugh Blair (1718–1800), David Fordyce, James Fordyce, Lord Kames (1696–1782), Henry Mackenzie (1745–1831) and George Turnbull (1698–1748), carrying forward the French emphasis on education to sociability, now argued the corollary that this required an extended period of education, of character formation, throughout the youth – the adolescence – of the scholar. Some part of the necessity for an extended education arose from the changing circumstances of the world: the new commercial society brought with it luxuries that could all too easily corrupt heedless youth unless it was steadied by a prolonged education (J. Fordyce 1777: 20–1 [Address I]; see also Mackenzie 1773: 53–75; Dwyer 1987: 72–94; 1990; Hanley 2011). A different way to put it was that a luxurious society stimulated the passions, and thus youth required more than ever an education that would transmute and rationalise their passions into sentiments. A prolonged schooling could preserve youth from temptation, and allow for the proper education of their sentiments, sympathy and sociability. This education was partly to be familial – an instruction, above all, from the women of the family. Women, after all, were naturally sociable, sympathetic, sentimental, polite and apt to the art of pleasing. Hence, by being themselves (lightly polished, and if they were gentlewomen) in their proper, domestic sphere, they could model those qualities for (presumably male) youth, and educate them with yet another variation on *sprezzatura*, an invisibly artful artlessness. The lengthened tutelage of youth, and a further justification for women's segregation within the domestic sphere, both followed from the imperatives of a sentimental and sociable education.

In England, Germany and Scotland, conversation was now an essential ingredient in the theory, the practice and the ends of Enlightenment education. All these changes, however, were limited innovations within a system of education that remained largely traditional. Moreover, these shifts towards a conversational mode of education were made with an awareness that they contrasted with the old oratorical mode of education. The oratorical mode educated towards action – agonistic effort – while the conversational mode, even its adherents acknowledged, tended to educate towards refined sensibility shorn of consequent action (Dwyer 1990: 177). Some major portion of the debates concerning pedagogy coming forward from the Enlightenment would, in effect, concern themselves with the proper balance between education in the oratorical mode, oriented towards virtue and action, and education in the conversational mode, oriented towards sensibility and the search for truth. Adam Smith's examination of the educative effects of labour may be taken to encapsulate the debate: labour educated to the active virtue of prudence, but labour (at least in its more mechanical forms) also tended to stultify the mind, to render it, in effect, incapable of conversation (A. Smith 2003: 987–9, 993–4 [5.1]; Hanley 2011: 598; D. Randall 2016b: 340–1). The old divide between the few and the many suggested one solution: the few were to be educated to converse properly, while the many were to be educated to industrious labour. Yet the universalising dynamic of conversation suggested as a corollary long-term goal that all children could and should be educated to acquire a conversational character. This inexorable aspiration lay behind all the other aspects of the Enlightenment's conversationalised pedagogy.

Conclusion

The *salon*, expanding from its Paris heartland to the far corners of Europe, provided an influential model for the larger culture of conversation – but not by itself a sufficient one. The range of the Enlightenment's culture of conversation was expanded by the democratising project of politeness, the full thematisation of women in theories of conversation, and the extension of conversation to pedagogy. These developments give some sense of how conversation, and the impulse to spread conversation, became an omnipresent background to the century's varied intellectual endeavours. The particular innovations of conversation in eighteenth-century genres, media and disciplines all took place against this pervasive conversationalising background.

We will now turn to the conversationalisation of the arts – the *belles lettres* and the *beaux arts*. Here an enormous portion of the European intellectual map, while retaining its broadly rhetorical framework, was transmuted from an oratorical mode to a conversational one. The next chapters' detailed study of the oratorical and conversational arts will flesh out this chapter's sketch of the society and culture of conversation and examine how the conversational impulse worked itself out in all the sister arts.

Notes

1. These *salons* in their own day were given names such as *ruelles* and *académies*. Nineteenth-century Frenchmen applied the word *salon* retrospectively to these pre-Revolutionary social gatherings; the term is anachronistic, if too well established to abandon now. Lilti 2015: 25–9; Pekacz 1999a: 1.
2. Before 1641, several *salons* appeared in England, associated with the countesses of Bedford and Carlisle – but *salons* disappeared in the upheavals of the British Civil Wars, not to reappear until the eighteenth century. Melton 2001: 211.
3. Scientific discourse operated within several overlapping social venues in early modern Europe (Biagioli 1996), including the courtly (Biagioli 1993; B. Moran 2006), the genteel (Shapin 1994) and the learned (McClellan 1985; Wood 1994). It also intersected with the world of the *salons*, notably in conversational works such as Fontenelle's *Conversations on the Plurality of Worlds* (1686) (Delon 1981; Fontenelle 1990; Russo 2007: 65–6; G. Sutton 1995; Terrall 1995; 1996). For intersections of the polite and conversational worlds with the history of scientific culture, see Bertucci 2008; Secord 1985; G. Sutton 1995; Walters 1997. For more general considerations of the role of science in the society and culture of the Enlightenment, see Broman 1998; Golinski 1986; 2011; Lynn 2006.
4. The *philosophe* critique of *salon* conversation also revived the tradition of compelling eloquence, the Renaissance emperor of men's minds reborn as the republican orator. Mercier 1773: 233–4 [22]; D. Randall 2011c: 209–13; 2016a: 130–2; 2018: 62–4; Rebhorn 1995: 23–54, 83–6, 93; Russo 2007: 12, 17–18, 32–3, 203–4, 215, 217–18; A. Thomas 1819: 172–3 [28], 253–4 [38].
5. Bembo 1954: 13–14; Bending 2006; Fonte 1997: 46–57; Langer 1994: 67–8; Lipsius 1594: 59–67 [2.1–3]; Logan 1983: 37; Marsh 1980: 36, 104, 106–8; T. More 2003: 53; Smarr 2005: 5, 10; Tinkler 1988: 211; K. Wilson 1985: 144 (note 7); Johnson Wright 1997: 72, 191–2.
6. Bruni 1987: 75 [Bk II]; Erasmus 1965: 48 [*The Godly Feast*]; Langer 1994: 67–8; Lipsius 1594: 66 [II.3]; Marsh 1980: 9, 14–15, 36–7, 53–4; Tinkler 1988: 211–12; Johnson Wright 1997: 72, 191–2.

7. For the sociability of the walk, that strenuous sibling of the promenade, see De Jong 2007. For an introduction to the history of the pleasure garden in seventeenth- and eighteenth-century England – garden leisure in a less improving and philosophical mode – see Borsay 2013; Crane 2009: 12; Greig 2012.
8. For the garden as a site of private and solitary meditation, see Crane 2009: 15–16.
9. The expansion of royal gardens paralleled the royal attempt to appropriate the realms of conversation and inquiry into truth. Baridon 2008; Conan 2007: 43–4; Crane 2009; F. Millar 1977: 27. Where an aristocratic republic endured, the gardens likewise remained aristocratic. Puppi 1972.
10. For the above paragraphs on Hume and Smith, see Hume 1996: II, 248 [*Treatise* 3.2.1]; A. Smith 2002: 17, 135 [1.1.2.1, 3.2.6]; Baier 1988, esp. 769–74; Clark 1993; J. Dunn 1983: 120–2, 128–34; and also see Forbes 1982; Moore 1976; Stein 1980: 12–14.

Chapter 2

The Oratorical Arts

Introduction

During the Renaissance, both theoreticians and practitioners began to apply the strictures of rhetoric to the several fine arts – to art, architecture, music, dance and poetics, among other fields. These rhetorical strictures were at first those of oratory, and the fine arts of the Renaissance thus emphasised moving the passions, seizing the will, and all such features of a fine oration. The shift in the default conception of rhetoric from oratory to conversation during the seventeenth and eighteenth centuries therefore caused, as a corollary, a shift in these various arts towards the model of conversation. The emergence of a conversational aesthetics transformed both the fine arts and poetics, and gave birth to those tight-yoked siblings, the *beaux arts* and the *belles lettres*. The same centuries also saw the culmination of rhetoric's metaphorisation, such that the principles of rhetoric were applied not only to the genres of the word but also to the several nonverbal genres. Music, art and dance were now taken to persuade in and of themselves, by wordless conversations composed of sound, sight and gesture.

The next two chapters address these rhetorical and conversational arts as a discrete unit, from ancient times to the Enlightenment, and address a remarkable thinness in Habermas' discussion of culture. I believe that this results partly from his personal predilection towards the culture of the word, which limits his interest in the realms of nonverbal arts. Unlike Adorno, for example, who wrote significantly on music (Adorno 2002), Habermas has not accompanied his limited engagement with aesthetics (Duvenage 2003) with a major and direct discussion of a particular genre of the fine arts. This is also a result of his theory of communication, which focuses strongly on media of communication amenable to rational, *verbal* exposition and justification – a focus which tends inherently to exclude the nonverbal arts. Habermas' public sphere theory is therefore hampered precisely because it cannot speak adequately of the nonvisual culture of the Enlightenment. Habermas' theory can analyse the novel and art criticism, but it is much less useful for an analysis of the nonverbal artistry of Watteau, Mozart or Noverre. It is precisely the strength of a rhetorical mode of analysis that rhetoric can speak of, to and through the arts, as communicative rationality cannot. The richness of the history, and historiography, of rhetoric and the fine arts is meant both to present the enormous amount of cultural history that must be ignored in a Habermasian mode of analysis, and to challenge that Habermasian mode by showing precisely how much broader a history can be provided by use of the rhetorical mode.

I note finally that my discussion of poetics in these two chapters[1] combines a narrative of rhetorical poetics in general with an analysis of the specific transformations associated with *ethos* (character) and the prologue. I follow this procedure in part because the effects of the conversationalisation of poetics were most marked in their effects on *ethos* and the prologue. More importantly, I follow this procedure because the conversationalisation of *ethos* and the prologue shifted the persuasive authority of character from the author's address to the audience in the prologue to the character's address to the audience in the narrative. This shift redescribes precisely what Habermas refers to as the literary public sphere, whose favoured genres – letters and novels that revealed the interiority of the self – emphasised 'subjectivity, as the innermost core of the private, [which] was always already oriented to an audience (*Publikum*)' (Habermas 1991: 29, 36, 49; and see also Habermas 1984–7: I, 85–6, 90–4). The somewhat more complicated treatment of poetics thus allows for a direct and extended critique of Habermas, to complement the more implicit critique provided by this entire section.

Ancient Arts

The Renaissance did not invent the association of rhetoric with the fine arts. Quintilian, for one, had associated oratory strongly with music (Quintilian 1920–2: I, 165, 171 [1.10.11, 24–5], and more largely 159–75 [1.10.1–33]; Kim 2008: 75–6). Plato (c. 428–c. 348 BC) and Saint Augustine (354–430) – to bookend the ancient world – also suggested similarities between music and rhetoric, if only as modes of communication whose allure they both, in their different ways, simultaneously feared and wished to employ (Winn 1981: 23–6, 43–55). The practice of art and architecture in ancient Rome were likewise significantly influenced by rhetoric (Vitruvius 1960: 13–14 [1.2.2–3, 1.2.5]; Elsner and Meyer 2014; Lamp 2013). Quintilian also made the relevant comparison between rhetoric and painting: 'pictures, which are silent and motionless, penetrate into our innermost feelings with such power that at times they seem more eloquent than language itself' (Quintilian 1920–2: IV, 281 [11.3.67]). In the Greek world, Plutarch (45–120) had ascribed to Simonides a notable parallel: 'Simonides, however, calls painting inarticulate poetry and poetry articulate painting' (Plutarch 1972: 501 [346F]; Vickers 1988: 340). We need not exaggerate the importance of rhetoric in ancient aesthetics and practice, but there was already a significant conceptual association (and see E. Thomas 2014).

More broadly, the ancient conception of the underlying unity of the different arts and sciences underwrote a rhetorical conception of other fields of endeavour. Cicero (106–43 BC) wrote in *De oratore* (55 BC) that

> the whole of the content of the liberal and humane sciences is comprised within a single bond of union; since, when we grasp the meaning of the theory that explains the causes and issues of things, we discover that a marvellous agreement and harmony underlies all branches of knowledge. (Cicero 1967: II, 19 [3.6.21]; and see 1979: 9 [1.2])

Vitruvius (d. c. 15 BC) likewise stated in *The Ten Books on Architecture* that 'all studies have a common bond of union and intercourse with one another' (Vitruvius 1960: 10–11 [1.1.12]). 'A single bond of union' did not in itself argue that all fields of endeavour should be thought of as forms of rhetoric – but rhetoric's pedagogical primacy in both the ancient world and Renaissance and early modern Europe inclined theoreticians of the different arts to take the argument of unity as an argument for rhetoricity. There were, to be sure, some intrinsic difficulties in taking the verbal art of rhetoric as a model for nonverbal modes of expression. But rhetoric also included the nonverbal – above all, the tones, aspects and gestures of delivery (*pronuntiatio*) (Cicero 1967: II, 169–83 [3.56.213–3.61.227]; Quintilian 1920–2: IV, 243–349 [11.3]). The orator's reliance on such means gave both impetus and warrant to further expansions by rhetoric into the several wordless realms of sight, sound and motion (Lichtenstein 1993: 6).

We may also note that in Rome the shift in applying rhetoric towards the 'productive arts' – what would later be called the 'fine arts' – was a development of the Principate (Lamp 2013: 27–9).

In other words, the shift from Republic to Empire, and the attenuation of the sphere of political debate, saw a displacement of rhetoric from oratory to the arts, parallel to the displacement of rhetoric from the deliberative mode to the epideictic. It is interesting to note that the development of politics and of rhetoric in early modern Europe, above all in early modern France, would recapitulate these linked attenuations and displacements. Thus the recuperation of Quintilian was also a recuperation of rhetoric in an Imperial key: the assimilation of Quintilian from the fifteenth century onwards, and the consequent shift in rhetoric towards the fine arts, did not merely suit the shift to a political climate of latter-day *principes*, but may positively have reinforced it.

Ancient Poetics

The association between rhetoric and poetics was naturally stronger than that of rhetoric with music or art, for both rhetoric and poetics concerned themselves with the word itself, and not with the word turned into a metaphor. Oral rhetoric became the model for much of ancient literature. In general, antiquity saw a progression whereby epideictic rhetoric – the rhetoric of praise and blame, intended for display and aiming to persuade an audience to provide aesthetic approbation – expanded to incorporate all the literary and poetic genres (G. Kennedy 1963: 10; McKeon 1982: 16–17). Where literature's subject matter was public affairs, or any interplay of persuasive discourse, rhetoric structured its content (Dominik 1997: 131–245 [Part III]; J. Walker 2000; Xanthakis-Karamanos 1979). More profoundly, the various literary genres were to a great extent conceived of as exercises in persuasion (and see G. Kennedy 1963: 37; J. Walker 1996). In the *Republic* (c. 380 BC), Plato described the poet as holding implicitly rhetorical sway over an audience (Plato 1945: 337–8 [X.605]). That Aristotle (384–322 BC) delivered his *Poetics* (c. 335 BC) separately from his *Rhetoric* shows that he distinguished poetry from rhetoric; not least among the differences was that in the *Poetics* he conceived of the audience of poetry as unspecified and universal, hence rendering rhetoric's assumption of a specific audience as apparently irrelevant (Aristotle 1996, *passim*; Weinberg 1961: I, 351). Indeed, for Aristotle poetics and rhetoric possessed fundamentally different modes, analytic vocabularies and aims (Prill 1987: 130). Yet Aristotle also stated that because of 'the weakness of audiences; the poets follow the audiences' lead and compose whatever is to their taste'; this implied a grudging acknowledgement of the practice of rhetorical specificity on the part of the poet, if not its desirability (Aristotle 1996: 22 [14]). Furthermore, Christopher Gill notes that in the somewhat obscurely worded seventeenth chapter of the *Poetics* Aristotle's advice to the dramatist 'seems to imagine the playwright himself, like an orator, standing before the audience himself, and playing on their emotions (being "persuasive" or "realistic") through his own capacity for emotional self-involvement' (Aristotle 1996: 27–8 [17]; C. Gill 1984: 152; and see also Aristotle 1996: 31 [19]; C. Gill 1984: 154). We should not over-interpret these moments, yet it would appear that with both Plato and Aristotle the oral assumptions of literature, and the corollary assumption of a visible audience amenable to persuasion, had begun to cast poetic thought in a rhetorical frame.

This frame strengthened in the Roman world – a matter of great importance for the future, since Aristotle's *Poetics* had limited influence on Western European theory or practice until after the publication of Giorgio Valla's (1447–1500) Latin translation in 1498 (Weinberg 1961: I, 71, 351, 361). In practice, Roman poetry became significantly rhetoricised from the Augustan age, as rhetoric became the standard education for would-be poets and as the shift to Empire left would-be rhetors little outlet for their skills but in verse (D'Alton 1962: 438–524; Prill 1987: 131–2). Ovid (43 BC – AD 17/18) and Virgil (70–19 BC) both incorporated rhetorical elements into their poetry, and the *Georgics* (c. 29 BC) were, *inter alia*, exercises in persuasion (G. Kennedy 2008: 387–97, 405–19; Prill 1987: 132). In theory, Cicero reaffirmed the importance of an orator's *ethos*: in *De oratore* he stated both that 'no man can be an orator complete in all points of merit, who has not attained a knowledge of all important subjects and arts', and that 'the poet is a very near kinsman of the orator' (Cicero 1967: I, 17 [1.6.20], 51 [1.16.70]). In the *Orator* (46 BC), Cicero also affirmed that the relationship of rhetor to audience found a parallel in poetry:

> The universal rule, in oratory as in life, is to consider propriety. This depends on the subject matter under discussion, and on the character of both the speaker and the audience . . . the literary critics consider it in connexion with poetry; orators in dealing with every kind of speech. (Cicero 1971: 359 [xxi.71–2])

Horace's (65–8 BC) *Ars poetica* (c. 19 BC), which emerged as the most important authority for medieval and early Renaissance poetics, was at best ambiguously rhetorical (Horace 1977: 85–95; Grant and Fiske 1924; G. Kennedy 2008: 398; Prill 1987: 131; Vickers 1988: 50–51;

Weinberg 1961: I, 71–2), but later Roman theorists clearly emphasised the affinity or identity of poetics and rhetoric (Prill 1987: 132–4). Quintilian noted the resemblance of poetry to epideictic rhetoric (Quintilian 1920–2: IV, 19 [10.1.28]; Prill 1987: 133), while Tiberius Claudius Donatus (*fl.* c. 430s) and Macrobius (*fl.* early fifth century) both conceived of poets as orators (Donatus 1905–6: I, 4; Macrobius 2011: 215 [5.1]; Prill 1987: 133). The direction of Roman thought was towards an amalgamation of rhetoric and poetics.

The poet's persuasive *ethos* resided particularly in the prologue. The parallel with rhetoric seems to have fostered this habit: as the orator sought to gain the goodwill of his audience by presenting his *ethos* in the introduction (*proemios*, *exordium*) to his speech, so the poet presented his own authority in the prologue (G. Kennedy 1963: 91–3). Thus Aristophanes (c. 446–386 BC) used Xanthias' speech near the beginning of *The Wasps* (422 BC) 'by way of preface' to address the audience and seek its goodwill; Aristotle compared the forensic exordium to the dramatic prologue; and Terence's (c. 195/185–c. 159 BC) prologues in *The Lady of Andros* (166 BC), *The Self-Tormentor* (163 BC) and *The Eunuch* (161 BC) illustrate the use of the prologue to gain the audience's favour (Aristophanes 1978: 413–15 [ll. 54–66]; Aristotle 2004: 145 [3.14.1415a]; Terence 2001: 51–3, 181–5, 317–19; and see T. Hunt 1970: 1). Indeed, the Prologue in *The Self-Tormentor* expresses persuasion in the particular legal idiom of Roman rhetoric: 'The playwright wanted me as an advocate [*oratorem*], not as a prologue speaker [*prologum*]. He has turned this into a court [*iudicium*], with me to act [*actorem*] on his behalf' (Terence 2001: 181; K. Dunn 1994: 3). This association of prologue and *ethos* would have a continuing influence on later poetics.

Medieval Art and Architecture

The evidence for the influence of rhetoric on the medieval arts is scattered – not absent, but slender and ambiguous. In the Latin West, the vocabulary of rhetoric appears to have influenced art and architecture – notably in concepts such as *ductus*, *auctor* and *memoria*. Evidence for a rhetorical conception of art and architecture, while still more inferential than direct, becomes stronger in the High Middle Ages, although it is not clear whether this registers a shift in thought or increasingly plentiful source material (Carruthers 2010, esp. 14–51, 96–123, 190–213, 214–49). In Byzantine art – whose influence on the arts of the medieval and Renaissance West need not be underscored – rhetoric appears to have had a general influence.

This influence was especially strong in the twelfth century, linked particularly via the rhetorical concept of *ekphrasis* (verbal description of a work of art) (Belting 1994: 261–96; Brubaker 2003; Cormack 2003; Maguire 1994).

Yet although rhetoric was the general system of education in Byzantium for the gently born, and although art may have been appreciated in rhetorical terms, we do not know to what extent Byzantine artists – still only artisans, not gentlemen – received any specific rhetorical education (Brubaker 2003: 264–5; Cormack 2003: 245–6). This point should be generalised, not only to the medieval West but also to the entire narrative of the rhetoricisation of arts. The application of rhetoric to the fine arts correlated with the rise of education of artists, and with the rising social status of artists. Where rhetoric was effectively the preserve of the gentleman, to apply rhetoric to the fine arts was a claim to gentle status, both personally and for one's profession (cf. Crow 1985: 72). The steady rhetoricisation of the arts over the centuries registered a social claim by artists, and its slow acceptance by gentlemen.

Medieval Music

Early medieval music may have been thought of rhetorically, but here also the paucity of written evidence vitiates either precision or certainty. Isidore of Seville (c. 560–636) wrote in his *Etymologies* (c. 600–25) that, 'Music rouses emotions, and it calls the sense to a different state' – but this, although apparently rhetorical in its conception of music, is only broadly descriptive. It is also a slight piece of evidence by which to characterise an epoch (Isidore 2006: 95 [3.16.1]; Neubauer 1986: 32). From the ninth to the eleventh centuries, music began to be considered in terms of the constituent parts of language – colon, comma, period – with sound and phrase analysed as the elements of a song, as phonemes and phrases had been analysed as the elements of prose or poetry. This began a written tradition wherein music could be analogised to poetry, grammar or rhetoric, and generally rendered subject to detailed rational analysis – not to mention subject to the practical division of musical notation – as the long tradition of rational analysis of language could now be extended to music (Jonsson and Treitler 1983: 7–8).

In the following centuries, different aspects of rhetoric appear to have been applied to the theory and practice of music. The clearest evidence comes from the application to music of rhetorical terms such as *clausula*, *colores*, *copula*, *diminutio*, *elocutio*, *figurae*, *trope* and *variatio* (Buelow, Hoyt and Wilson 2001, esp. 260–1; Van Deusen 1985). Rhetorical techniques for memorisation and delivery were also applied to medieval music, although it remains uncertain to what extent these words and techniques were used as loose analogy and to what extent as tight model (Berger 1981; Enders 1992). As with Byzantine artists, a great unknown is the extent to which medieval composers and performers – frequently monks and clergy – were educated in rhetoric. An education in music and an education in rhetoric may have been alternatives or complements, depending on the time and place (Berger 1981: 119; Perkins 1984: 386–7; and see Witt 2011: 17–70, esp. 31–7).

Yet with all uncertainty acknowledged, there does appear to have been some rhetorical element in medieval music, for which the evidence thickens in the late medieval centuries. By the early fourteenth century, Marchetto of Padua (*fl.* 1305–19) made a parallel in his *Pomerium* (1318?) between rhetoric's *colores rhetorici ad pulchritudinem sententiarum* and music's *colores ad pulchritudinem consonantiarum* (Marchetto 1961: 71 [4.3]). Towards that century's end Heinrich Eger von Kalkar (1328–1408) wrote in *Das Cantuagium* (1380) that *Ornatus etiam habet musica proprios sicut rhetorica* (Eger 1952: 57). The rhetorical mode of Renaissance music built upon, and transformed, a prior rhetorical mode of medieval music, rather than creating the conception *de novo* (Bent 2010; MacClintock 1959; Perkins 1984; C. Reynolds 1995: 280–97; John Stevens 1992).

To some extent, the association of rhetoric with music appears to have preserved the traditional primacy of the sung word within medieval music. Yet medieval writers on music, although far from ready to grant music an autonomous status independent of the word, increasingly recognised (if usually hesitantly and hazily) the distinctness of word and tone (Jonsson and Treitler 1983: 8–11; Harrán 1986: 39–75). Stevens argues persuasively that this development registers the particular influence of rhetorical thought, as the rhetorical conceptualisation of music began to be applied not just to words, but also to tone (John Stevens 1992: 904–7). The medieval centuries saw rhetoric begin to be used as a mode for music in and of itself.

Medieval Poetics

Early medieval Europe also preserved a connection between rhetoric and poetics by applying epideictic, panegyric oratory to eulogistic poetry; this tradition continued from late antiquity through the Carolingian age and beyond (Curtius 1963: 154–66, 174–6; Prill

1987: 134; and see Hermogenes 1987: 114 [389]). Furthermore, a rhetoricised interpretation of Horace's *Ars poetica* began to influence medieval poetics. Manuscripts of the *Ars poetica* were disseminated along with late antique commentaries by Helenius Acron (*fl.* third century AD?) and Porphyrion (*fl.* second century AD?) – the bundling of Horace with these commentators is extant in manuscripts from the ninth century on – and these commentaries recast Horace's ambiguously rhetorical prescriptions as emphatically rhetorical doctrine. So Acron expanded on Horace's *omne tulit punctum* with the comment, 'He alone obtains the votes and [favourable] judgment of the people who writes a poem in a useful and pleasant fashion and who can both profit and delight' (Horace 1977: 92 [l. 343]; Hauthal 1866: 661, translated in Weinberg 1961: I, 76; 1961: I, 72–9). Rhetorical poetics claimed Horace as its avatar, and medieval poetics, insofar as they were Horatian, became heavily rhetorical.

Horace became a widespread influence in post-Carolingian Europe: more than thirty copies of the *Ars poetica* are listed in medieval library catalogues between the ninth and thirteenth centuries (Schultz 1984: 2). The early-thirteenth-century poetics of Geoffrey of Vinsauf (*fl.* 1200) and John of Garland (c. 1190–c. 1270) betray a pronounced Horatian influence – not least in their titles, *Poetria nova* (c. 1210) and *Parisiana poetria* (c. 1240), which allude directly to Horace's *Poetria* (as the *Ars poetica* was frequently called in the medieval centuries) (Curtius 1963: 153; Schultz 1984: 4–5). In his letter to Cangrande della Scala (1291–1329), Dante Alighieri (c. 1265–1321), making reference to the *Paradiso*, affirmed the rhetorical form of literature; in *De vulgari eloquentia* (c. 1302–5), he defined poetry as 'a rhetorical composition set to music [*fictio rethorica musicaque poita*]' (Alighieri 1966: 202–4 [10.17–19]; 1969: 77 [2.4]).

At this point, a form of *ethos* assumed increasing importance in medieval poetics: *auctoritas*. The tradition of *auctoritas*, a rhetorical concept, originates in Cicero's *Topics* (44 BC) as (in Ascoli's summary) 'that quality in a (juridical) witness, the *auctor*, that inspires faith in his testimony'. Cicero himself extended *auctoritas* to the written word, to the judgement of 'orators, philosophers, poets, and historians. Their sayings and writings are often used as authority [*auctoritas*] to win conviction' (Cicero 1960: 439–43 [19.73 – 20.78]; Ascoli 1989: 27). *Auctoritas* acquired a more transcendental and essential character in late antiquity, when Saint Jerome (347–420) reconceived scripture as the *auctor*, the witness, to God's actions in history; medieval commentary followed up on this reconceptualisation to make *auctoritas* a divine attribute and

God the ultimate *auctor* – creator as much as witness (Ascoli 1989: 27; Curtius 1963: 464; Minnis 1984: 81–2, 114). So Albertus Magnus (c. 1200–80) wrote in his *Commentarii in Baruch*,

> Psalm cxvii. 26, 'Blessed is he who comes in the name of the Lord'. In this statement the author and the cause of the following work is demonstrated, and the authority of this Scripture. The author, because the 'blessed' man may be interpreted as Baruch . . . The authority of the Scripture is noted in that it is said 'in the name of the Lord'. For a name is applied from knowledge, and knowledge of God, who is truth alone, supplies the authority of the words. For the authority [of the Book of Baruch] is a revelation, and revelation is the most firm foundation which is to be had. (Albertus 1893: 355, translated in Minnis 1984: 82)

As a corollary of this development, the *auctores* of antiquity also acquired transcendental and essential status, as revealers of truth rather than as writers of persuasive texts (Balbi 1506: *s.v. auctoritas*; Ascoli 1989: 28; Curtius 1963: 51–2; Losse 1994: 20; Minnis 1984: 10–11). Modern writers, dwarves on giants' shoulders, could scarcely be proper *auctores*. Walter Map (1140–c. 1210) registered this belief in his somewhat embittered prediction in *De nugis curialium* (1181–3) about the future attribution of his *Dissuasio Valerii ad Rufinum philosophum ne uxorem ducat* (c. 1170s):

> I know what will happen when I am gone. When I have begun to rot, the book will begin to gain savour, my decease will cover all its defects, and in the remotest generations my ancientness will gain me dignity; for then, as now, old copper will be of more account than new gold. (Map 1983: 313 [Dist. v, cc. 5]; Minnis 1984: 11–12).

Yet after a while these modern poets acquired a certain status once more. From the twelfth century on, the assimilation of Aristotelian logic into textual analysis gave the human *auctor* a role as 'efficient cause', under God, of his text; hence *auctores* were susceptible to analysis as human beings with individual purposes in writing (Minnis 1984: 13–159). Richard Fishacre (c. 1200–48) wrote in his prologue to his *Commentary on the Sentences* (c. 1241–8) that

> Although therefore some part of sacred Scripture seems to have been written by Moses, and similarly some part by the prophets, some by the Evangelists, and some by the Apostles, yet not they themselves but God both wrote and spoke by them, as the principal efficent cause by the instrument. (Long 1972: 88, translated in Minnis 1984: 78)

Nicholas of Lyre (c. 1270–1349) likewise wrote in the *Praefatio autoris* of his *Psalterium* of God's inspiration working in conjuction with the mental processes of his instrument David (Nicholas 1545: 83v; Minnis 1984: 91). In short, as the *auctor* shed his transcendence and reassumed his humanity, he could once again be regarded as a *rhetor* (and see Ascoli 1989: 29).

While this analysis first transformed the study of classical *auctores* and scripture, it also gave modern poets a way to put themselves on a level with the *auctores* of old: a modern poet could aspire to rhetorical authority more easily than to transcendental authority. Poets, therefore, increasingly claimed *auctoritas* for themselves – *auctoritas* now characterised as the capacity to provide creative renditions of source material. Significantly, both scripture and the *auctores* of antiquity themselves were coming to be regarded (*sotto voce*) more as 'source material' than as transcendental authorities, subjects as fit for poetic reworking as any other story (Weimann 1996: 149). Losse notes that

> in his preface to *Erec et Enide* [(c. 1170)], Chrétien [de Troyes, *fl.* c. 1160–1190] points out the weakness of his source, a *conte d'aventure* without merit, and praises his own efforts to create a work which will last as long as Christianity. (Troyes 1987: 1 [*Erec and Enide*, ll. 1–26]; Losse 1994: 21)

In the prologue of *Tristan* (c. 1200) Gottfried von Strassburg (d. c. 1210) based a part of his *auctoritas* on the claim to have found 'the true and authentic version of Tristan', but Gottfried gave 'true and authentic' a connotation more archival than transcendental: 'I made many researches till I had read in a book all that he [Thomas of Britain] says happened in this story' (Strassburg 1960: 43). The source established, Gottfried's creative *auctoritas* could now take wing. The claim by modern poets that they, too, were *auctores* became more and more influential: by the fourteenth century Guido da Pisa (*fl.* 1320s) (among others) could write a commentary on that modern *auctor*, Dante (Guido 1974; Minnis 1984: 165).

Merely human *auctoritas* was essentially more problematic than its transcendental predecessor. Dante wrote in his *Convivio* (c. 1304–7) that his exile from Florence had compromised his poetic authority:

> I have seemed cheap in the eyes of many who perchance had conceived of me in other guise by some certain fame; in the sight of whom not only has my person been cheapened, but every work of mine, already accomplished or yet to do, has become of lower price. (Alighieri 1912: 15–16 [I.iii]; and see Ascoli 1989: 32)

His self-presentation of his character, his persuasive authority, was a reaction to his fallen estate: the deliberate evocation of human *auctoritas* could recoup his authority, but human *auctoritas* had compromised his authority in the first place (Ascoli 1989: 33). *Auctoritas* was essentially unstable once made human and rhetorical.

The effects of medium should also be noted. In distinction from antiquity, medieval literature began to be conceived of as a fundamentally written activity, rather than as an oral one: the claim of Chrétien de Troyes and his peers to *auctoritas* depended in good part on the fact that they were writing down their work (Ollier 1974: 27–9). As a consequence, the narrator of the written work began to disjoin from the author of the oral work: *auctoritas*, the modern conception of the author itself, was in part a necessary suture narrowing this widening gap (Scholes and Kellogg 1966: 52–3; Weimann 1996: 124). The use of the prologue as a frame, to set the written text as a tale told out loud, was another attempt to suture the gap between the spoken and the written word (Ong 1975: 16; Scholes and Kellogg 1966: 55). Rhetorical, oral assumptions, of an author essentially identical with a narrator and therefore capable of presenting *ethos* to an audience, still governed literature as it came to be considered a thing of writing – but with more and more strain.

Finally, as *ethos* had been associated with the prologue in antiquity, so the general influence of rhetoric on medieval poetics, and the specific influence of Horatian rhetorical poetics, meant that *auctores* now sought the goodwill of their audiences by means of exordial prologues. Dante identified the prologue as the place where the author sought the goodwill, attention and interest of his audience (Alighieri 1966: 203–4 [X.18–19]; and see Losse 1994: 12–13, 15). Arthurian prologues (especially those of Chrétien), and the prologues of Jean de Meun (c. 1240–c. 1305), Giovanni Boccaccio (1313–75) and Geoffrey Chaucer (1343–1400), among others, were strongly exordial in structure and function; within them, the poet presented himself to his listeners (and they were still conceived of as listeners) and so sought to gain their goodwill in several ways, not least by the presentation of his *ethos* (T. Hunt 1970; 1972; Losse 1994: 19; Nolan 1986: 154). So Chrétien inserted some *ethos* into his prologue to *The Knight of the Cart* (c. 1177):

> I am not one, I swear, who would wish to flatter his lady . . . [the book's] subject-matter and treatment are supplied and given to him by the countess [Marie of Champagne], and he puts his mind to it without contributing anything beyond his effort and application. (Troyes 1987: 185 [*The Knight of the Cart*, ll. 1–30])

By Chrétien's time the persuasive claims of *auctoritas* had become firmly associated with the prologue.

Renaissance Art

In the visual arts – painting above all – rhetoric assumed a swift ascendancy (Plett 2004: 297–364; Vickers 1988: 340-60; and see Jensen 1976: 47–88). Here, although the humanists had commented on art from Petrarch onwards, the crucial event was the appearance of Leon Battista Alberti's (1401–72) *De pictura* (1435; Italianised as *Della pittura*, 1436), which played a decisive role in the transformation of art from a craft to a liberal art (Baxandall 1971: 51–139; Plett 2004: 309–11; Van Eck 2007: 17–30; Vickers 1988: 342–53). For his initial audience – Baxandall takes *De pictura* to have been written for someone with humanist education, solid geometry, and some practice in drawing or painting – Alberti applied rhetorical concepts such as *compositio*, *copia*, *varietas* and *dissolutus* to painting (Alberti 1966: 72–6; Baxandall 1971: 126–7, 129–31, 136–7). It is worth noting, incidentally, that Quintilian's influence on Alberti – the *Institutes* had been rediscovered only a generation earlier – extended not only to his willingness to apply rhetoric to art but also to the very structure of *De pictura*, which was modelled on the *Institutes* (c. 95 AD) (Vickers 1988: 342–3). The Renaissance analysis of art, as well as its production, was to be deeply embedded in (Quintilianic) rhetoric.

Painters from the *quattrocento* to the seventeenth century became increasingly rhetorical in practice, as they applied Alberti's conceptions to their craft. They did so not least with an eye to the eminently rhetorical goal – the eminently oratorical goal – of moving the passions of the spectator (Van Eck 2007: 55–88). The theoretical understanding of art, and proto-aesthetics, followed practice only after a lag, and did not become pervasively and explicitly rhetorical until the *cinquecento*. Even then, and thereafter, neo-Platonic philosophy also influenced the theoretical understanding of art in complement and challenge to the rhetorical framework. The rhetorical framework, nonetheless, was at least equal in strength as a means to understand the nature and purpose of art. Plett cites a lengthy list of exemplars of this rhetorical approach to understanding art, including Francesco Lancilotto's *Trattato di pittura* (1509), Paolo Pino's (1534–65) *Dialogo di pittura* (1548), Raffaello Borghini's (1537–88) *Il Riposo* (1584), Ludovico Dolce's *Dialogo della Pittura, intitolato l'Aretino* (1557),

Giovanni Paolo Lomazzo's (1538–92) *Trattato dell'arte della pittura* (1584), Gianbattista Armenini's (1530–1609) *De veri precetti della pittura* (1587), Franciscus Junius' (1591–1677) *De Pictura Veterum* (1637), Roland Fréart, Sieur de Cambray's (1606–76) *Idée de la perfection de la peinture* (1662), and John Dryden's (1631–1700) 1695 preface to his English translation of Charles Alphonse du Fresnoy's (1611–68) *De arte graphica* (1668). These theorists collectively rehearsed rhetorical terms including color (the *colores rhetorici* translated into *colores pictoris*), composition, decorum, design, disposition, *evidentia*, *enargeia*, imitation, invention and style (Plett 2004: 315–29; Van Eck 2007: 139–66; and see Lichtenstein 1993; Vickers 1988: 353). Franciscus Junius in *De Pictura Veterum* (1637) provided a particularly striking passage illustrating the rhetorical approach to art:

> Both [poet and painter] doe hold the raines of our hearts, leading and guiding our Passions by that beguiling power they have, whithersoever they list. . . . both then have a hidden force to move and compell our minds to severall Passions, but Picture for all that seemeth to doe it more effectually; seeing *things that sinke into our hearts by means of our eares*, sayth *Nazarius* [*In Panegyrico*], *doe more faintly stirre our minde, then such things as are drunke in by the eyes. Polybius* [*Lib.XII.*] doth likewise affirme, that *our eyes are more accurate witnesses then our eares.* (Junius 1638: 55–6; Plett 2004: 329)

This approach found a parallel in the words of a notable seventeenth-century practitioner of painting, for Nicolas Poussin (1594–1665) evidently also conceived of art on a rhetorical model (Poussin 1964: 170, translated in J. R. Martin 1977: 86; L. Brown 1980: 103 (note 10)). The rhetorical approach to art – the oratorical approach to art – was prevalent by the mid-seventeenth century.

Renaissance Architecture

Smith argues that Byzantine émigré Manuel Chrysoloras (1355–1415) provided the first impulse in *quattrocento* Italy to apply a rhetorical framework to architectural thought, by way of the genres of architectural description and the *laus Urbis*' melange of architectural description, panegyric and history (C. Smith 1992: 133–97). Yet it was Alberti (as he did in art) who crystallised the rhetorical approach to architecture, both in his *Profugiorum ab aerumna* (1441–2), which applied rhetorical conceptions of harmony and style to architectural description (C. Smith 1992: 80–97), and in his eminently rhetoricising treatise *De re aedificatoria* (1443–52). Van Eck notes that the structure of *De re aedificatoria* more closely resembled a treatise of rhetoric than that of its classical forebear, Vitruvius' *De architectura* (Van Eck 1998). Furthermore, Alberti imported into his discussion of architecture various key terms originating in rhetoric, most notably *concinnitas* and *varietas* (Alberti 1988: 20 [1.8], 35 [2.1], 313–14 [9.9], 421–22, 426). The very function of architecture was now to move the passions of the spectator by means of a visual analogue of an epideictic speech, praise by means of splendid brick and stone of the virtues of a building's honoree or owner (Alberti 1988: 194 [7.3]; Van Eck 2000).

The rhetorical conception of archictecture spread out from Alberti, and, as had the rhetorical conception of art, became increasingly common in Europe (Van Eck 2007: 31–52, 89–110, 167–202). Among the details of this transformation, recent scholarship has noted the transfer of *imitatio* from rhetoric to architecture, not least by way of the Italian academies (Brothers 2000; Payne 2000), the influence of *varietas* and *decorum* in the *quattrocento* city plan for Pienza (C. Smith 1992: 98–129), the debt of Michele Sanmicheli's (1484–1559) *all'antica* style in the *cinquento* to contemporary rhetorical conceptions of imitation, ornamentation, style and ordering (Davies and Hemsoll 2000), and the influence of the rhetorical conception of architecture during the Renaissance in such transalpine locales as France (Pauwels 2000), England (Anderson 2000) and Scotland (Howard 2000). Daniele Barbaro (1514–70) summarised a thorough rendition of the Renaissance's rhetorical conception of architecture in his commentaries on *I Dieci Libri dell'architectura* (1567): 'si come la oratione ha forme, & idee diverse per satisfare alle orecchie, cosi habbia l' Architettura gli aspetti, & forme sue per satisfar a gli occhi' (Barbaro 1567: 36, 115, 124; Cellauro 2004: 321).

The rhetorical conception of architecture would persist into the seventeenth century, to inform the architecture of Italy and Austria (Polleross 1998). Gian Lorenzo Bernini (1598–1670) (said his biographer Filippo Baldinucci (1624–97)) counselled his students

> Firstly to consider the invention and then the arrangement of its parts and lastly to endow the work with its perfecting grace and elegance. In so doing he was following the example of an orator who first invents, then arranges, garnishes and embellishes. (Baldinucci 1682: 71, translated in Polleross 1998: 126)

Baroque architecture, as much as its Renaissance forebear, was rhetorical.

Renaissance Music I: The Sixteenth Century

Not least, perhaps, because medieval music already possessed so strong a rhetorical stamp, the humanist intertwining of rhetoric and music appears to have been a somewhat slower process than that of rhetoric with either art or architecture (Kim 2008: 16–17 (note 74), 17–18 (note 76); Kristeller 1965: 142–62; Plett 2004: 365–412; Vickers 1988: 360–74; Winn 1981: 122–93). To begin with, the education of musicians and composers remained traditionally liturgical throughout the *quattrocento*, and seems not to have been subsumed within the *studia humanitatis* until the triumph of the Erasmian educational model during the *cinquecento* (Meconi 1994: 170–2). In consequence, the Renaissance reconception of how rhetoric should relate to music seems to begin late in the *quattrocento*, to gather strength throughout the *cinquecento*. The timing roughly aligns with the recuperation and integration of Quintilian's thought following the rediscovery of his *Institutes* in 1416: a large part of musical thought in the next centuries may be summarised as meditations and innovations upon Quintilian's relatively brief treatment of music as allied to oratory (Palisca 1972: 39; and see H. Brown 1982; Burkholder 1985; Meconi 1994; Perkins 1984). As in the medieval centuries, the extent of the influence of rhetoric on musical composition in the *cinquecento* remains controversial; but case studies have highlighted the influence of rhetoric on the work of composers such as Orlandus Lassus (1532–94) (Palisca 1972), Adrian Willaert (c. 1490–1562) (H. Brown 1980) and John Dowland (1563–1626) (Toft 1984).

The explicit parallel between music and oratory simultaneously grew stronger throughout the *cinquecento*, as musical humanists incorporated the rhetorical thought of (above all) Cicero and Quintilian (B. Wilson 1995). The affinities perceived by sixteenth-century humanists between rhetoric and poetry on the one hand, and between poetry and music on the other, further aligned rhetoric and music (Kim 2008: 144–5; and see Harrán 1988: 434–8). So, slightly in advance of the sixteenth century, Franchinus Gaffurius (1451–1522) described the first kind of musicians in his *Practica musicae* (1496) as 'those who are versed in prose, as orators and lectors, and who express their thoughts in words rather than in melody' (Gaffurius 1968: 22; Kim 2008: 146). Some decades later Nicola Vicentino (1511–75/6) wrote in *Ancient Music Adapted to Modern Practice* (1555) that

> The experience of the orator can be instructive, if you observe the technique he follows in his oration. For he speaks now loud and now soft, now slow and now fast, thus greatly moving his listeners. This technique

> of changing the measure has a powerful effect on the soul. For this reason music is sung from memory, so as to imitate the accents and effects of the parts of an oration. (Vicentino 1996: 301 [4.42]; Palisca 1972: 39; Kim 2008: 143–4)

By the later decades of the century, the English liturgicist John Merbecke (c. 1510–c. 1585) would refer to himself as an 'Orator' in his prefaces to *The Lyues of Holy Sainctes* (1574) and *Examples Drawen Out of Holy Scripture* (1582) (Merbecke 1574: sig. Aiii^{v}; 1582: sig. Aii^{r}; Kim 2008: 62, 62 (note 209); and see Heyden 1972: 19; Kim 2008: 144; Vickers 1984: 14).

Reformation theology, dovetailing with the sixteenth century's musical humanism, also emphasised the rhetorical aspect of sacred music. Martin Luther (1483–1546) wrote in 1538, in his preface to a collection of part-songs, that music is 'beyond the reach of the greatest eloquence of the greatest orators' (Luther 1873: 552, translated in Buszin 1946: 81; Kim 2008: 74). John Calvin (1509–64), meanwhile, wrote in his Preface to the Geneva Psalter (*La forme des prières*, 1542) that, 'in truth we know from experience that song has great force and vigor to arouse and inflame people's hearts to invoke and praise God with a more vehement and ardent zeal' (Calvin 1542: sig. a5^{r}, translated in Calvin 2001: 94; Kim 2008: 72). Music served the Word of God, its function to convey that Word to the auditor. Vocal music, which appealed to the intellect, in consequence was superior to purely instrumental music, which appealed only to the senses (Kim 2008: 69, 72, 79–80, 91, 93–4, 142; and see Vickers 1984: 10).

Yet if a rhetorical conception of music emphasised the word, especially in the Protestant tradition, the sixteenth century also saw a shift of the relationship of rhetoric to music that began to apply rhetoricity to the character of music itself. Where the persuasive character of rhetoric had been taken to reside in the words, the sixteenth century saw an increasing shift towards regarding the persuasive character as inherent in the sounds themselves. Mace argues plausibly that Pietro Bembo's reconception in *Prose nelle quali si ragiona della volgar lingua* (1525) of the persuasive and expressive power of poetry as deriving from the very sound of language lay behind the *cinquecento* shift towards regarding the persuasive and expressive power of music as inhering in the music itself, rather than in the words sung and accompanied. The development of the madrigal, and then the opera, echoed in a musical mode Bembo's conception of persuasive and expressive sound. Mace further notes that Filippo Massini (1559–1618), for one, echoed Bembo's language extraordinarily closely when he wrote of the madrigal in *Del madrigale* (1581) that,

> I should wish then above all else that the madrigal should contain some rare and ingenious thought, and that its elocution should be very pure and artful, and that both thought and elocution in the graver madrigals should be such that they would produce honesty, dignity, majesty, magnificence, and greatness, and in the more amusing ones, grace, suavity, loveliness, sweetness, jokes, and playful expressions. (Bembo 1525: XXVIII^r, XXXII^r; Massini 1588: 181, translated in Weinberg 1961: I, 208)

The *cinquecento* reconception of rhetoric as applying to pure sound made possible the conception of music itself as a form of rhetoric (D. Mace 1969; and see Harrán 1986).

Renaissance Music II: The Baroque

The relatively casual equation of rhetoric and music became common in the seventeenth century: so René Descartes (1596–1650) wrote in *Compendium musicae* (1618) that there was 'a type of figure of speech in music, just as there are figures of speech in rhetoric' (Descartes 1961: 51; L. Brown 1980: 105), while Henry Peacham the Younger (1578–c. 1644) likewise remarked in *The Compleat Gentleman* (1622) that, 'in my opinion, no Rhetoricke more perswadeth, or hath greater power ouer the mind [than does music]: nay, hath not Musicke her figures, the same which Rhetorique?' (Peacham 1622: 103). Beyond such brief analogies, the link between rhetoric and music finally achieved full theoretical articulation about 1600. Joachim Burmeister's (1564–1629) *Hypomnematum musicae poeticae* (1599) dealt extensively with the link between music and oratory, but his *Musica poetica* (1606) provided the first consciously rhetorical treatise of musical composition, emphasising (among other rhetorical concepts) the movement of the affections (Burmeister 1993, esp. 57, 155–97, 203–5, 207–11). So Burmeister applied the rhetorical definition of an *exordium* to music, explicitly and precisely: 'The exordium is the first period or affection of the piece. It is often adorned by fugue, so that the ears and mind of the listener are rendered attentive to the song, and his good will is won over' (Burmeister 1993: 203). The full flowering of rhetorical music, albeit building upon substantial sixteenth-century precedent, is therefore a seventeenth-century development, baroque rather than High Renaissance (Kim 2008: 16–17; W. Kirkendale 1979: 30; Meconi 1994: 156–7; and see also Vickers 1984: 19–20; 1988: 360–72).

Burmeister and later theorists (frequently but not exclusively German) proceeded to import the full panoply of rhetorical aims and terminology into music, including not only the movement of the affections (*actio*), greatly emphasised throughout the seventeenth and eighteenth centuries, but also *collatio*, *dispositio*, *copulatio*, *elocutio* (in music, decoration), *inventio*, *mimesis* and *pronuntiatio* (Barros 2010; 35–8; Bose 1996: 4; L. Brown 1980; Butler 1977: 51–2; Farnsworth 1990; Plett 2004: 371–81). Marin Mersenne (1588–1648) wrote in his *Traité de l'harmonie universelle* (1627) that,

> First of all, it is necessary that he [the musician] imagine that he is an Orator who forgets nothing in his oration of everything that he believes can serve him in pleasing his listeners and can move them to that which he wishes. (Mersenne 1627: 181 [1.22], translated in L. Brown 1980: 102)

Athanasius Kircher (1602–80) likewise wrote in his *Musurgia universalis* (1650) that,

> Our musical figures are and function like the embellishments, tropes, and the varied manners of speech in rhetoric. For just as the orator moves the listener through an artful arrangement of tropes . . . so too music [moves the listener] through an artful combination of the musical phrases and passages. (Kircher 1650: I, 366 [5.19], translated in Bartel 1997: 107)

Jean-Philippe Rameau (1683–1764) in his *Traité de l'harmonie* (1722) wrote of the recitative that

> a good musician . . . should always strive to set the long syllables of the discourse by means of notes having an equivalent duration, and those which are short, by the notes of shorter duration; all this is done so that the audience can understand all the syllables as easily as if they were being declaimed by an orator. (Rameau 1722: 162, translated in Farnsworth 1990: 218)

Johann Mattheson (1681–1764) in *Der vollkommene Capellmeister* (1739) spoke of *Klangrede*, musical eloquence, and carried the rhetorical conception of music to an extraordinary level of detail (Mattheson 1981: 63; Plett 2004: 380–1; Buelow 1983).

As with discussions of previous centuries, there is a continuing debate among scholars both as to whether rhetoric did actually provide a tight guide rather than a loose analogy to musical composition in this era, and as to whether rhetoric, inherently verbal, could in fact provide any real guidance to a nonverbal art such as music (Maniates 1983; Vickers 1984: 38–44). Yet the aspiration to apply rhetoric to music certainly existed, whether as tight guide or loose analogy (Dreyfus 1996, esp. 1–10; U. Kirkendale 1980; W. Kirkendale 1979; 1997; Schulenberg 1992; Street 1987; P. Walker 1995; Williams 1983). Musical rhetoric both pervaded works of the period and achieved twin summits in the work of Johann Sebastian Bach (1685–1750) and Jean-Philippe Rameau.[2]

Parallel developments strengthened these trends. The application to composition of Descartes' peculiarly mechanical theory of the passions in *Les Passions de l'âme* (1649), for example, strengthened the idea that a particular type of music could produce with some reliability a particular passion. Thus Rameau wrote in his *Traité de l'harmonie* (1722) that

> the major mode in C, D, or A, is appropriate for songs of rejoicing and happiness; in F or B flat, it is appropriate for storms, furies & other similar subjects. In G or E, it is also appropriate for tender & gay songs; the grand & the magnificent occur in D, A or E. (Rameau 1722: 157, translated in D. Thomas 1995: 30; and see L. Brown 1980: 105)

This conception aligned well with the musical rhetorical ambition to detail the means by which music could move the passions (L. Brown 1980: 104–5; Neubauer 1986: 49). So, returning to Johann Mattheson, his theory of music notably blended Descartes' philosophy of the passions with his rhetorical framework (Mattheson 1981: 103–11; Buelow 1983: 399–401). Musical rhetoric was by no means exclusive of other approaches to music, and could work in nice complement with them.

One strand of this rhetoricisation of music furthered the conception of music as rhetorical in and of itself, independent of the word: thus Kircher in his *Musurgia universalis* (1650) wrote, 'There is a great power yet still latent within music – a greater energy and capacity to influence effectively the human mind, than that possessed by rhetoric' (Kircher 1650: II, 141 [8.8], translated in Farnsworth 1990: 212). In France, Ranum characterises French baroque instrumental music as having been structured as small-scale orations (Ranum 2001: 25). Music's irreducibly nonverbal character meant that this application of rhetoric to nonverbal music necessarily remained in some ways more a programmatic ambition than a realizable practice – but the ambition still characterised the age's approach to music (Bose 1996, esp. 10–11, 18, 21; Vickers 1984: 38–44).

But the emphasis on the word also continued: the rise of opera, that quintessentially baroque genre which combined a high value on the word and an emphasis on moving the affections, was an eminently rhetorical moment. Claudio Monteverdi's (1567–1643) relevant maxim was that 'l'oratione sia padrona del armonia e non serva' (Monteverdi 1973: 396; Plett 2004: 369); while in the Prologue of his *Orfeo* (1607), Musica proclaimed that 'Io la Musica son, ch'à i dolci accenti So far tranquillo ogni turbati core, Et hor di nobil ira et hor d'amore Poss' infiammar le più gelate menti' (Monteverdi 1992: 35; Vickers 1984: 14). The related baroque forms of recitative (itself subsumed into the opera), cantata and oratorio also registered the continued importance of the word to baroque music (Farnsworth 1990: 218). Both the rhetoric of the word united with music and the rhetoric of pure music were aspects of the oratorical, passionate, baroque *musica rhetorica* (Farnsworth 1990: 212).

Renaissance Dance

The ancient theorists do not appear to have applied rhetoric to dance, and the medieval tradition of dance does not appear to have been especially rhetorical either. Nevertheless, dance, at least from the *quattrocento* onwards, appears to have been influenced by conceptions of rhetoric. This shift came as part and parcel of a claim by Italian *quattrocento* theorists of dance – notably Domenico da Piacenza (c. 1400–c. 1470) (*De arte saltandi et choreas ducendi*, 1416), Antonio Cornazano (c. 1430–84) (*Libro dell'arte del danzare*, 1455) and Guglielmo Ebreo da Pesaro (c. 1420–c. 1484) (*De pratica seu arte tripudii*, c. 1463). These theorists claimed that dance, via its association with music, was an intellectually delightful liberal art, a component of the *studia humanitatis*, and a discipline for the gently born and properly educated that involved both mind and body (A. W. Smith 1995: 126 [Guglielmo, *De pratica seu arte tripudii*]). That the gentle and the noble danced was not new in the *quattrocento*, of course; but the urge to write theoretical justifications of dance as a humane and liberal study was, as was the elaboration of a precise technical vocabulary with which to analyse its movements.

This humanist justification of dance was not entirely a matter of rhetoric. Neither the basic linkage between the excellent virtues of the body and the mind nor the ritual use of dance to express both communal identity and social status within that community required a specifically rhetorical commitment (Nevile 2004: 12–57). Dance's link to music also connected it to the *quattrocento*'s spiritualising esteem for Pythagorean geometries – hence, in good measure, the taste for geometric dances (Nevile 2004: 104–30). But dance, fundamentally, expressed and revealed – communicated – the dancer's character. Dance was now also taken to express *ingegno* (wit, genius) and grace, and to require memory and decorum – this last displayed physically in dance by self-control, moderation and propriety (Nevile 2004: 86–103). To reveal these qualities of the dancer's body likewise revealed the qualities of the dancer's mind: Guglielmo wrote that

> The virtue of dancing is an external demonstration of spiritual *movimenti* which corresponds with the orderly arranged and perfect consonances of the harmony. This descends with delight through our hearing to the brain and the warm senses, where certain sweet sympathetic *movimenti* are generated. As if trapped against nature, they try to exit as much as possible and are manifested by action. (A. W. Smith 1995: 126 [Guglielmo, *De pratica seu arte tripudii*])

Dance was character in motion.

Dance not only expressed but also exercised and improved the dancer's character. Domenico da Piacenza explicitly associated the virtue of prudence with the cultivation of memory, moderation and temperance, those virtues prerequisite for proper dance:

> Don't we know that the *misura* is part of prudence and of the liberal arts? Don't we know that the *memoria* is the mother of prudence which is acquired after long experience? Don't we know that this virtue is part of harmony and of music? (A. W. Smith 1995: 15 [Domenico, *De arte saltandi et choreas ducendi*]; Nevile 2004: 96)

Guglielmo wrote that

> when it is exercised by gentle, virtuous, and honest persons, I say this science and art is good, virtuous, worthy of commendation and praise, and more. It makes not only the virtuous and honest persons become gentle and wise, but also those who are badly mannered and born of vile conditions. It makes them become gentle, and gives very much which allows the quality of all to be openly recognized. (A. W. Smith 1995: 144 [Guglielmo, *De pratica seu arte tripudii*]; Nevile 2004: 63–74)

Thomas Elyot (c. 1490–1546) likewise wrote in *The Boke Named the Governour* (1531) that dancing instructed men in prudence: 'A double in dancing is compact of the number of three, whereby may be noted these three branches of prudence: election, experience, and modesty' (Elyot 1962: 78–88, esp. 85). Knowing what steps to take on the dance floor was no small education in knowing what steps to take in the governance of realms (Nevile 2004: 96–7). The orator had been, and hence the courtier now was, supposed to be master of the motions of his body; excellence in dance both practised and provided witness of such bodily self-mastery. Moreover, the proper dancer – the virtuous dancer – taught his virtues to his audience, which by observing him could imitate him, physically and morally (Nevile 2004: 92–3, 96).

As the rest of the rhetorical arts, dance was taken to rely upon both natural ability and practical cultivation – nature and art – to reach its highest form. Guglielmo wrote that 'The science of dancing is both natural and artificial. Therefore it is perfect and meritoriously commended' (A. W. Smith 1995: 144 [Guglielmo, *De pratica seu arte tripudii*]; Nevile 2004: 102–3; and see A. W. Smith 1995: 133–4 [Guglielmo, *De pratica seu arte tripudii*]). Dance's division between the natural and the learnt expressed its rhetoricity.

The form of dance, as well as the qualities of individual dancers, also expressed rhetorical elements. Dances frequently were geometric – but the choreography not infrequently integrated dance into dramatic spectacle, implicitly if not yet explicitly persuasive in its aesthetics (Nevile 2004: 28–9, 36–43, 46–7, 49–52). Dance's emphasis on heterosocial interaction (Nevile 2004: 52–7) also aligned it with the conversation of men and women. The vocabulary of dance appropriated concepts from rhetoric, such as variety (*diversità di cose*) and elegance – the happy median between violent motion and rigidity (A. W. Smith 1995: 13 [Domenico, *De arte saltandi et choreas ducendi*]), 85–6 [Cornazano, *Libro dell'arte del danzare*]; Nevile 2004: 77–82). The flexible *maniera* of the dancer (if we may push the parallel a little) recapitulated the flexible demeanour of the courtier (A. W. Smith 1995: 90 [Cornazano, *Libro dell'arte del danzare*]; Nevile 2004: 82–6). As evidence of the affinities between rhetoric and humanist dance, we may finally note that some pages of the second half of Guglielmo Ebreo da Pesaro's *De pratica seu arte tripudii* were written as a dialogue (A. W. Smith 1995: 142–8 [Guglielmo, *De pratica seu arte tripudii*]; Nevile 2004: 62).

As the Renaissance progressed, certain genres of dance continued their long approach towards the arts of language. In geometric dances, the dancers' bodies now formed written characters, a living alphabet, and the motion of their dance thus created words, language, a text. In *Le Ballet de Monseigneur le duc de Vandosme* (1610), 'se trouuoient toutes en rond, d'où elles commençoient leur ballet, changeant d'air, de pas, & de cadence, & formoient ceste premiere figure, A' (*Ballet* 1610: 24; Franko 1993: 15–19). At the same time, the spectacle of courtly *ballet de cour* emerged as a hybrid of dance, drama and music. This, in the first instance – just as the *quattrocento* dances it succeeded, and as the masque, which it paralleled and perhaps influenced – expressed the cosmological harmonies under God and King. The *logos* (rational argument) it represented was a divine and royal soliloquy, a statement fundamentally of identity, even where king and nobles did not themselves dance (Christout 1987; Franko 1993: 32; Rygg 2000: xvi–xxii).

Quattrocento dance treatises had used rhetorical vocabulary, and the alphabetical dances and masques of the Renaissance were communicative in a quasi-rhetorical fashion – but dance came to model itself explicitly on rhetoric as the Renaissance progressed. Thoinot Arbeau (Jehan Tabourot, 1519–95) put it in his *Orchésographie* (1588) that

> most of the authorities hold that dancing is a kind of mute rhetoric by which the orator, without uttering a word, can make himself understood by his movements and persuade the spectators that he is gallant and worthy to be acclaimed, admired, and loved. . . . And, when miming is added, she has the power to stir his emotions, now to anger, now to pity and commiseration, now to hate, now to love. (Arbeau 1967: 16–17; Brainard 2016: 16)

Michel de Pure (1620–80) wrote in *Idée des Spectacles Anciens et Nouveaux* (1668) that 'Il est de la division du Balet, comme de celle de l'Oraison. Si elle n'est pas necessaire au discours de l'Orateur, elle l'est à l'intelligence des Auditeurs' (De Pure 1668: 230; Barros 2010: 44). John Weaver (1673–1760) conceived of the best dramatic dance in similarly rhetorical terms in *Anatomical and Mechanical Lectures upon Dancing* (1721):

> *Rhetorick* . . . is only requir'd of a Master of *Dramatick Dances*; and then only, as far as such *Dances* have relation to the *Manners*, *Passions*, &c. . . . What *Rhetorick* is to the *Orator* in Speaking, [also] is to the *Dancer* in Action; and an Elegance of Action consists, in adapting the Gesture to the Passions and Affections; and the *Dancer*, as well as the *Orator*, allures the Eye, and invades the Mind of the Spectator; for

> there is a Force, and Energy in Action, which strangely affects; and when Words will scarce move, Action will excite, and put all the Powers of the Soul in a ferment. (Weaver 1721: 144; Brainard 2016: 20)

The very stances and gestures of dancers by the seventeenth century (if not earlier) echoed those of orators: dance was in some sense a purified aesthetic focus upon the gestural component of oratory (Brainard 2016: 27–36; Ranum 2001: 26; and see Rebhorn 1993).

The conceptual framework of rhetoric also began to be applied to dance in detail. Early in the seventeenth century, Mersenne in his *Harmonie universelle* (1636) analysed dance as a mode of communication – the posture, gestures and steps the components of its language – implicitly subject to such rhetorical arts as collocation and disposition (Mersenne 1636: third pagination, 159–61; Duncan 1989: 161). Mersenne's relatively brief discussion of dance was elaborated as the century progressed, and baroque dance became progressively more subject to rhetorical strictures. In 1680, for example, Rault's 'De L'Origine de La Danse' (*Mercure galant*, April 1680) described dance as

> nothing other than a certain faculty and Disposition of the body, which by proportional movements and postures attuned to the sound of instruments or the voice, is animated and moves rhythmically, and which, according to the Numbers, *modes*, and meters of the Art, imitates and expresses the passions of the soul by the actions of the body. (Rault 1680: 189, translated in Ranum 2001: 26; 2001: 25–6)

Barros supplements these theories of dance with a close analysis of the choreography of baroque dances in France; they too are orations *dansées* (Barros 2010). The baroque mode of dance still represented authority, but as it was now an authority founded in persuasion, the art of persuasion came to govern the movements of this dance, of this *ballet* (and see Cowart 2008).

Renaissance Poetics

The rhetorical conception of poetics strengthened further in the Renaissance as literature was increasingly seen not merely as analogous to rhetoric but as itself a form of rhetoric, with rhetorical prudence as the wellspring of an ideal of artistic decorum (Kahn 1985: 37, 39; and see Plett 2004: 85–293). Humanists began to read Aristotle's *Nichomachean Ethics* to support a conception of literature as persuasive activity, thus superseding the Platonic conception of literature as an activity dedicated to expressing transcendental ideas (Kahn 1985: 32–3). Cristoforo Landino's (1424–98) 1482 commentary on the *Ars Poetica* conceived of Horatian poetics as close to, and elaborately parallel to, the strictures of rhetoric: 'Because in the writing of a poem the first thing to be investigated is invention, disposition, and elocution, at the very beginning he explains immediately those things which relate to invention and disposition' (Horace 1482: CLVII^{r}, translated in Weinberg 1961: I, 80; 1961: I, 79–81). So too did Iodicus Badius Ascensius' (1462–1535) 1500 commentary, which also used the rhetorical ideas of Quintilian and Cicero to interpret Horace's poetics (Horace 1536, *passim*; Weinberg 1961: I, 81–5).

The sixteenth-century reintroduction of Aristotle's *Poetics* was also at first assimilated to Horatian, rhetorical poetics. Francesco Robortello's (1516–67) *Utinensis in librum Aristotelis de arte poeticae explicationes* (1548) interpreted Aristotle's work in a rhetorical light, paying attention to *ethos* and specific audience. Robortello wrote that 'the exordium and the epilogue' were nothing else but 'certain episodes of some forensic oration' (Robortello 1548: 205, translated in Weinberg 1952: 345); in poetic works more generally, 'Those speeches persuade and move most of all which are not invented by art but which are true and come from nature itself' (Robortello 1548: 198, translated in Weinberg 1952: 337; W. Kennedy 1978: 12; Weinberg 1952). Antonio Sebastiano Minturno (1500–74) in his *De poeta* (1559) applied Cicero's description in *Orator* of the eloquent man ('ut probet, ut delectet, ut flectat') to the poet: 'erit Poetae sic dicere versibus, ut doceat, ut delectet, ut moveat' (Cicero 1971: 357 [21.69]; Minturno 1559: 102; Herrick 1946: 41; Weinberg 1961: II, 743).

Renaissance rhetoric itself preserved the Aristotelian and Ciceronian emphases on gaining the goodwill of an audience and the persuasive authority of a rhetor's *ethos*. Leonard Cox's (c. 1495–c. 1549) *The art or crafte of rhetoryke* (1532) put it succinctly that 'Benevolence is the place whereby the herer is made willyng to here us / and it is conteyned in the thynge that we speke of / to them whom we speke to / + in our owne persone' (Cox 1532: sig. Bii^{v}; and see also Cox 1532: Bii^{v}–Bvii^{v}; T. Wilson 1553: 55^{r}–57^{r}). Furthermore, in *De laboribus Herculis* (1383–1406), Coluccio Salutati (1331–1406) transferred Cicero's definition of the *vir bonus* from the orator to the poet and made his personal virtues prerequisite for his poetic ones: 'Thus the poet is a good man skilled in the art of praise and blame, who by means of a material and figurative speech, hides truths under the mysterious narration of some event' (Salutati 1951: I, 63, translated in Greenfield 1981: 140–1). Persuasive *ethos* was now more explicitly than ever transferred from the orator to the poet – and, in consequence, retained a strong association with the prologue (and see K. Dunn 1994: 11).

The flourishing of the dedicatory epistle was one expression of this link: the dedication, a form of prologue, not only associated the author with the authority of his (would-be) patron's social rank but also, as a corollary, recapitulated in print the author's own social *ethos* (K. Dunn 1994: 7; P. Schaeffer 1986: 215–19; see also Bergeron 2006). The prefaces of French *nouvelles* expressed the link in another manner: where unjustified prolixity was a sign of dubious character, the *conteurs*' expositions of the circumstance that occasioned and justified their decision to write in the first place – illness, flood, a plentiful grape harvest and the like – presented their *ethos* so as to gain the goodwill of their readers (Losse 1994: 62–7). So Bonaventure des Périers (c. 1500–44) 'by way of preamble' in his *Novel Pastimes and Merry Tales* (printed 1558) proferred war as a rationale for publishing his stories:

> when I saw that the broom of peace was missing its handle and that people didn't know how to hold on to it, I decided to go ahead and give you a way to outfox time, sprinkling merriment upon your anxieties, until such time as peace might be made by the will of God. (Des Périers 1972: 35)

As Dante's had done, the *conteurs*' presentation of their *ethos* sought to counter the essential unreliability of human *auctoritas*.

Yet *ethos*' persuasive authority came under strain during the Renaissance, buckling under the pressure applied by the printing press and the widening, revolutionary ramifications of print culture (for which see Beal 1998; Eisenstein 1983; Fox 2000; Johns 1998; Love 1993). The attractions of print, both for remuneration and for fame, increasingly meant that authors wrote for sale to the press, and its unknown readership, rather than for gift-exchange to a select audience connected by the spoken word or the copied manuscript (Weimann 1996: 148). In the French *conteur* tradition, rooted in oral tale-telling and an audience of listeners, prefatory titles had begun to address themselves to an audience of readers – *au lecteur, aux lecteurs, aux lisantes, aux liseurs* – by the mid-sixteenth century (Losse 1994: 17–18). Nicolas de Cholières (1509–92) in *Les Après disnées* (1587) addressed himself generally 'aux liseurs' and specifically to 'debonnaires liseurs' (Cholières 1587: 3). The increased literacy that came with the print revolution, and the increased numbers of copies of printed material, slowly promoted private, silent reading, as opposed to public, vocal reading (Coleman 1996; Cressy 1980). The default assumptions of writing, already under strain from at least the time of Chrétien de Troyes, shifted as the print revolution progressed, from an oral medium and a visible audience to a print medium and a readership of individuals (Glidden 1981: 28; Weimann 1996: 148; but see Ong 1968: 40, 49–50). Sixteenth-century texts, such as John Lyly's (1553–1606) *Euphues* (1578) and *Euphues and his England* (1580) exaggerated their oral and rhetorical nature, in an anxious, desperate attempt to retain orality's prestige and pin down the vanishing spoken word within the world of print (Lyly 1578; 1580; Cave 1979: 155–6; Ong 1975: 16).

But the most drastic effect of print on rhetoric was that it made literature *anonymous*, 'a relation among strangers' (Warner 2002: 74). Print multiplied the copies of a text and therefore the number of possible readers; however vast a readership had been over time before, it now expanded towards unknowability at the very moment of printing. The author became unknown. *Unknown* had multiple meanings. In one sense, there was the author known only by means of the bought and printed work, whose identity came through the text alone, without extratextual support or reliability. This form of anonymity, ultimately implicit in all resorts to writing and print, became more pronounced during the early modern centuries as the multiplicity of authors unknown outside the text pressed the bounds of credibility – one reason, of course, for the insistent growth of extratextual claims of authorial identity in early modern Europe, a growth which should be taken to complement the process described here (Barthes 1977; Foucault 1979; Pask 1996). In another sense, there was the literally unknown author – not just the modest, courtly and discreetly anonymous aristocrat, who feared the stigma of print and winked to his coterie through a veneer of anonymity, but rather the truly anonymous author, unknown to all readers save (perhaps) the printer (North 2003: 159–210; and see S. May 1980; Saunders 1951). Statistically speaking, Joad Raymond notes that in England between 1588 and 1688,

> anonymity (no name or initials, or the use of a pseudonym) became increasingly frequent. Only a handful of publications in 1588 were anonymous, conspicuously the Marprelate tracts. In 1614 about 8 per cent

> of all publications were anonymous: mainly consisting of news items and literary works, suggesting two of the main causes of anonymity at this point. By 1644, this had risen to around 60 per cent; it was around 57 per cent in 1688. (Raymond 2003: 168–9)

Rhetoric's traditional conception of an author addressing a specific audience, each of them known to the other, could not encompass all these anonymities. In particular, print culture attacked the underpinnings of *ethos*: as the socially disembedding transformations of print and commerce disrupted the link between author and audience, made it a relationship of mutually unknowns, *ethos* lost its persuasive power (J. Agnew 1986: 17–56; Glidden 1981: 28).

The Martin Marprelate tracts of 1588–9, the *locus classicus* of the pamphleteering tradition in England, highlight some of the difficulties that the anonymity of print culture imposed on *ethos*' ability to persuade. These pioneeringly anonymous Presbyterian assaults on the ecclesiastical policy of the Church of England were written under the nom de plume of Martin Marprelate, represented variously in the pamphlets as their author, their narrator and a character in them (Raymond 2003: 41–3, 63–5). Anonymity gave the Marprelate tracts much of their power: Martin as character could assume the persona of a fool and so, according to the rules of *decorum personae*, use a fool's railing and jests to mock the bishops themselves as fools (Anselment 1970; Raymond 2003: 42), while Martin as unknown author, unable to gain authority from an epistle dedicatory, was free to 'dedicate' an abusive epistle to the bishops and thereby gain another avenue of satire ([Marprelate 1588]: title page). But anonymity also had its drawbacks. Martin defied the bishops by claiming that

> you will go about I know, to proue my booke to be a libell, but I haue preuented you of þt aduantage in lawe, both in bringing in nothing but matters of fact, whiche may easily be prooued, if you dare denie them: and also in setting my name to my booke

– but of course his name was a fake ([Marprelate 1588]: 40; and see Stamp 2002: 47–74). Martin's claim to witness his claims by the *auctoritas* of his name harked back to the Ciceronian origins of the term, juridical *ethos*, and so underlined how anonymity crippled his ability to call on *ethos* to persuade (cf. North 1999: 8).

Significantly, the negative responses to the Marprelate tracts (albeit overdetermined responses, since they were commissioned by the aggravated Elizabethan state) focused on Martin's anonymity. Thomas Nashe (1567–c. 1601) characterised his anonymity as a cover for a bestial, heretical Machiavel (Nashe 1589a: sig. A3v; 1589b: sig. G2r), while Lyly saw vulgarity, bastardy, bestiality and essential knavery behind his disguise: '*Martin*, of what calling so euer he be, can play nothing but the knaues part, *qui tantum constans in knauitate sua est*' (Lyly [1589]: sigs. B3v, D3r; see also [1589]: sig. *A4v*). The attacks on Martin as vulgar, a bastard, a devil and a knave – the attacks on his *ethos* – registered the perception of Elizabethan contemporaries that while *ethos* continued to provide authority, it could not easily persuade across the barrier of printed, commercial anonymity.

Similarly, the prologue decayed as a site of authority. Francis Bacon (1561–1626) was ambivalent about prologues and prefaces in spoken speech; although 'pre-occupation of mind ever requireth preface of speech', he rather thought that 'prefaces and passages, and excusations and other speeches of reference to the person, are great wastes of time; and although they seem to proceed of modesty, they are bravery' (Bacon 1909: 67 [XXV, 'Of Dispatch']). In the *conteur* tradition, prefaces had grown enormous during the sixteenth century, anxiously asserting authorial *ethos*, but they shrank as the century passed: the *préface* of the seventeenth century was a vestigial appendix largely shorn of persuasive power (Losse 1994: 77–8, 103). The tradition of mocking the preface – used during the Renaissance by Erasmus, Thomas More, François Rabelais (1494–1553), Nashe and others – had become common in England by the eighteenth century; Swift swelled his parodic prefatory material in *A Tale of a Tub* (1704) to gargantuan proportions (Swift 1704: sig. A3r–[A6v], 1–53; K. Dunn 1994: 149–50). The decline of the prologue's persuasive powers further weakened the ability of *ethos* to express itself as *auctoritas*.

Finally, scepticism re-emerged as a philosophy of growing strength during the sixteenth century – an articulate recognition of and meditation on unknowability that was very much a response to and counterpart of the anonymity of print culture. Scepticism, in its Academic variant, had been allied with rhetorical thought during the fifteenth century; the attitude had been that 'since man, according to the sceptic, can know nothing absolutely, he is always concerned with the realm of the contingent and the probable, that is, the realm of rhetoric' (Kahn 1985: 35–6). But in the sixteenth century, and particularly from the translation of Sextus Empiricus' (c. 160–c. 210) *Outlines of Pyrrhonism* into Latin in 1562, and the publication of Gentian Hervet's (1499–1584) *Against the Mathematicians* in 1569, a more intense, Pyrrhonist scepticism undermined the assumptions of rhetorical thought (Kahn 1985: 47; and see Popkin 1979: 1–86). In the *Essays* (1570–92) of Montaigne, (Pyrrhonist) scepticism's most eloquent advocate and, as an extraordinarily influential exemplar, a crucial figure in the transformations of the Renaissance's rhetorical poetics, sceptical thought eroded the means of persuasion that made rhetoric possible. He did not believe in the effectiveness of reason: 'Our mind is an erratic, dangerous, and heedless tool' (Montaigne 2003: 509 ['Apology for Raymond Sebond']). *Ethos* was no more reliable, since the *rhetor*'s character was itself fundamentally unreliable: 'I cannot keep my subject still. It goes along befuddled and staggering, with a natural drunkenness . . . I may presently change, not only by chance, but also by intention' (Montaigne 2003: 740 ['Of repentance']). Nor did Montaigne believe that one could accurately perceive the nature of other people: 'We cannot distinguish the faculties of men; they have divisions and boundaries that are delicate and hard to determine' (Montaigne 2003: 923 ['Of vanity']). Significantly, Montaigne connected this inability to distinguish audience with the novel conditions of print culture, in which an author addressed an unknown and dispersed public: 'I would have been more attentive and confident, with a strong friend to address [in a letter], than I am now, when I consider the various tastes of a whole public' (Montaigne 2003: 225 ['A consideration upon Cicero']). But if men's faculties could not be determined, the use of rhetoric to evoke *pathos* (passion) in an audience became untenable. With reason useless, and both self and audience unknowable, rhetorical poetics as traditionally conceived could not survive.

Notes

1. An earlier version of my discussion of poetics appears in D. Randall 2008.
2. Allanbrook 1983, esp. 1–9; Barth 1992; Beghin 1997; Beghin and Goldberg 2007; Bonds 1991: 53–131; Buelow 1966; Butler 1977; Duncan 1989; Farnsworth 1990: 212–16; Ranum 2001; Sisman 1993; Sloan 1990; Vial 2008: 13–43; Vickers 1984: 15–16, 18, 35.

Chapter 3

The Conversational Arts

Conversational Aesthetics: *Belles Lettres* and *Beaux Arts*

Two linked shifts transformed arts and poetics during the early modern inflexion between the Renaissance and the Enlightenment. In the first place, the early modern shift away from oratory caught up the different fields of arts and poetics, and set them all in a conversational mode. More fundamental, however, was the effect of the interiorisation and universalisation of rhetorical poetics, in combination with the subsumption of the various arts and letters within rhetoric. The first change transformed rhetoric from a skill towards an inward faculty; the second detached the rhetorical relation from a tight link to the written word. These two transformations together abstracted the relationships and attitudes that constituted rhetoric from the genre itself; the *belles lettres*, *beaux arts* and aesthetics emerged to supplant rhetoric as the defining models of the arts and letters, and indeed to reduce rhetoric (oratory) to one genre only of the *belles lettres*. We shall now examine the emergence of these new abstractions, constituted and defined by the conversational mode.

We should note first that the neoclassical, conversationalising aesthetic propounded in France constituted itself in explicit opposition to the baroque. This is not merely a retrospective judgement of modern scholars. *Baroque* – from the Portuguese *barroco*, an irregular or bulbous pearl – had from the beginning of its aesthetic application in the early eighteenth century the significations of singular, unusual, rough, incongruous, bizarre, uneven, irregular – and thus violated the nature-imitating, simplifying *honnête* norms (Palisca 1989: 7–10). The anonymous *Lettre de M. *** à Mlle *** sur l'Origine de la Musique* in *Mercure de France* (May 1734), for example, spoke thus of Rameau's *Hippolyte et Aricie* (1733):

> No genius animated it; it shied from nature and sentiment. Art should have served only to seek out the one and the other and to decorate them and to reveal them in the best light. . . . The music had no relationship

> to the dance except for its more or less lively movement. There was consequently no thought, no expression at all. . . . The uncommon had the character of the baroque, the fury of din. Instead of cheer, restlessness, and never any graciousness, nor anything that could reach the heart. (*Lettre* 1734: 868–9, translated in Palisca 1989: 7–8)

Nor, it is worth emphasising, was this merely hostile polemic: the self-understanding of those who would later be called baroque theoreticians indeed endorsed the aesthetic condemned as baroque. Montgomery's survey of seventeenth-century baroque literary theory – especially the works of the Italians Sforza Pallavicino (1607–67) (*Del bene*, 1644; *Considerazioni spora l'arte dello stile e del dialogo*, 1646), Matteo Peregrini (1595–1652) (*Delle acutezze*, 1639) and Emmanuele Tesauro (1592–1675) (*Connoccchiale aristotelico*, 1654) – notes that their innovation upon High Renaissance rhetorical poetics (as the innovations of the *honnête*) shifted towards an emphasis on audience reaction, and (also as the innovations of the *honnête*) towards the autonomous realm of beauty, detached from the framework of virtue. So Pallavicino: 'poetry is not the inventor of events that might be true and useful to know, but feigns those things which happen to be false and enjoyable to imagine' (Pallavicino 1831: II, 47, translated in Montgomery 1992: 41). These theoreticians therefore prescribed a style to entertain the audience so as to attract its attention – but to do so used, and prized, novelties of wit (*acutezza, argutezza*), vivacity, perspicacity, grace, versatility, artifice and metaphor. Tesauro put it that

> there is nothing man loathes more than learning, so that he listens to elevated and useful doctrines with yawning and daydreaming. Unless keenness and novelty of style pierce his wit, he cannot stay awake. . . . Thus all that, which to relieve the boredom of the listener, differentiates words, aphorisms, and enthymemes from the plain, unadorned, daily style, is called rhetorical schemes and figures. Whence comes delight and the listener's applause for words that are new and perspicacious, not to mention whatever sets before the eyes a strange and foreign experience. (Tesauro 1670: 122–3, translated in Montgomery 1992: 23)

These theoreticians advocated deliberately breaking the laws of nature rather than imitating them, precisely because such devices addressed and allured the intelligence, which became jaded and bored far more quickly than the emotions. So Peregrini:

> When the means of joining and the things joined remain in their natural condition, they cannot form anything rare, and lacking any other artifice of value they can only give off a good and clear syllogistic connection, and so they are quite satisfying to the intellect but not to the wit . . . the

> wonderful is so much more the wonderful as it has more of appearance and less of substance. (Peregrini 1639: 42–3, 46, translated in Montgomery 1992: 30–1; 1992: 11–47)

In all this we may note that these theoreticians of the baroque differed from their *honnête* peers in continuing to prize the intellect so highly – but their similarities in other theoretical aspects are at least as striking as their differences. Fundamentally, the two schools had similar aims, and both understood the purpose of the baroque aesthetic; but those who liked baroque enjoyed its artificiality and conceits, while the *honnête* found these qualities abrasive. Peregrini was confident that 'our nature is friendly to novelty' (Peregrini 1639: 57, translated in Montgomery 1992: 33); but the baroque nature did not extend to Paris (but note Russo 2007: 141–3, 146).

So the baroque; let us now look at the contrasting development in France of neoclassicism. Neoclassicism was in good measure a reaction against the Renaissance emphasis on *copia*, verbal abundance, and brought with it both praise of the fidelities of *vraisemblance* and a greater chasteness of plot and style. Jean-Louis Guez de Balzac (1597–1654), Jean Chapelain (1595–1674) and Pierre Corneille (1606–84) all prepared the way for this transformation, and among the notable works propounding this stylistic shift were Dominique Bouhours' (1628–1702) *Les Entretiens d'Ariste et d'Eugène* (1671) and *La Manière de bien Penser dans les Ouvrages d'Esprit* (1687), and Nicolas Boileau-Despréaux's (1636–1711) *Art poétique* (1674), translation of Longinus (1674) and *Réflexions critiques* (1674–1711) (Montgomery 1992: 49–67, esp. 50–2). Bouhours encapsulated neoclassicism's aesthetics nicely in *La Manière de bien Penser dans les Ouvrages d'Esprit*:

> Les pensées . . . sont les images des choses, comme les paroles sont les images des pensées; & penser, à parler en général, c'est former en soi la peinture d'un objet ou spirtuel ou sensible. Or les images & les peintures ne sont véritables qu'autant qu'elles sont ressemblantes: ainsi une pensée est vraye lorsqu'elle represente les choses fidellement; & elle est fausse quand elle les fait voir autrement qu'elles ne sont en elles-mêmes. (Bouhours 1743: 11; Montgomery 1992: 53)

Now, while neoclassicism overlapped significantly with the conversationalising transformation, it was not identical to it. The conversational topics I will describe below should be taken as components of neoclassicism, but not its entirety.

The first component of the conversationalisation of aesthetics derived from the Montaignean redefinition of friendship. Circa

1600, particularly in the thought of Montaigne and Antoine Hotman (c. 1525–96), friendship had shifted decisively from shared reason or virtue towards the familiar friendship of voluntarily revealed interior selves, whose friendship was based on nothing more than a mutual movement of the passions (Hotman 1616: 114, 128–9; Montaigne 2003: 165, 169 ['Of friendship']; James and Kent 2009: 149–54; Langer 1990: 182–90; 1994: 69–87, 157–76; D. Randall 2018: 90–1; but see Bond 1965: I, 397 [No. 93, 16 June 1711]; Mee 2011: 41–2). The development of this new form of friendship was part and parcel of the triumph of conversation. Guez de Balzac, in his description of the quintessential conversationality of the Romans in 'A Discourse of the Conversation of the Romans' (1634), also described them as partakers of intimate and private friendships: 'These sentiments which parted from the heart, were hidden in great Assemblies, and were discovered but between two or three friends, and as many faithful domesticks, and with whom hee communicated this secret felicity' (Guez de Balzac 1652: 72–3). Conversation was the communication of this intimate friendship.

And taste would be a transposition of such friendship into the realm of beauty. Bouhours, in his *Les Entretiens d'Ariste et d'Eugène* (1671), derived his conception of *je ne sais quoi* from his conception of friendship. Recapitulating Montaigne's 'Because it was he, because it was I', Bouhours took friendship to be purely a matter of the heart, independent of reason and the will. It was this instinctive, unexplainable relationship of friendship, the relationship of heart to heart, that Bouhours referred to as *je ne sais quoi*: 'c'est le penchant & l'instinct du cour; que c'est un tres exquis sentiment de l'ame pour un objet qui la touche'. Bouhours then applied *je ne sais quoi* to the realm of beauty: the relationship of the percipient to the perceived object, in other words, was a relationship of friendship applied to the realm of aesthetics. It was, furthermore, a relationship accessible to all: the faculty of friendship was universal, and so, potentially, was the aesthetic sense of *je ne sais quoi*, of *goût*: 'Tous les hommes ont un je ne sçay quoy particulier.' Genius was a rarer talent – a gift, like divine grace – but it operated upon this universal faculty, for what it did was to allow an artist to create a work that could produce the relation of *je ne sais quoi* in a percipient (Bouhours 1682: 246–7, 257; Delehanty 2013: 57–63). In his *La Manière de bien Penser dans les Ouvrages d'Esprit* (1687), significantly, Bouhours used the genre of the dialogue, and stated explicitly that the genre, which allowed liberty of judgement, was meant to model the very *ouvrages d'esprit* that he discussed. The friendly spirit of *je ne sais quoi*, the liberty granted to differing tastes, the loose pedagogy of the example rather than the tight pedagogy of the rule – the several components of the conversational stance of this new aesthetic – still found their genre correlate in the dialogue (Bouhours 1743: iv–vii; Delehanty 2013: 65–7, 69).

The intimately friendly, universal faculty of taste – *je ne sais quoi*, *goût* – thus became central to aesthetics. The abstraction of rhetoric aligned with this development: so, for example, René Rapin's (1621–87) influential works weakened the primacy of public oratory as they redefined rhetoric towards a more general focus on the relation between writer and reader: 'This Work, which may serve for some sort of Rule in Speaking and Writing, is a Collection of eight Pieces upon all the principal Subjects of fine Letters, compos'd one after another, without any particular relation between them' (Rapin 1706: I, sig. b^{r}; H. Davidson 1965: 27–8). Largely via the intellectual transformations in seventeenth-century France, the concepts of *decorum* and *sprezzatura* also sublimated into the concepts of *bienséance*, taste (*goût*) and aesthetics (Fader 2003: 8–20; Monk 1944; D. Randall 2018: 18, 23, 31–2, 71, 78, 88, 126–7, 131–3, 139–40, 149, 152, 158, 164, 170, 189–90, 194, 197, 212, 214; and see Buchenau 2013; Minor 2006: 4–60): these thus combined the intimately friendly, the appropriate and the artfully artless into a faculty both universal and detached from the formal practice of rhetoric.

This concept of taste lay behind the concept of *belles lettres*, pioneered in works such as René Rapin's *Réflexions sur l'éloquence, la poétique, l'histoire et la philosophie, avec le jugement qu'on doit faire des auteurs qui se sont signalés dans ces quatre parties des belles lettres* (1684), Dominique Bouhours' *La Manière de bien Penser dans les Ouvrages d'Esprit* (1687) and Charles Rollin's (1661–1741) *De la Manière d'Enseigner et d'Etudier les Belles Lettres, par rapport à l'esprit et au coeur* (1726–8). Bouhours in his *Manière de bien Penser* took the genres of *ouvrages d'esprit*, those subjects of the exercise of *je ne sais quoi*, to include history, poetry and rhetoric (Bouhours 1743: iv). Rhetoric, we should emphasise, was now only one genre among many, rather than a model; these works generally made rhetoric only one of several of what now came to be called the *belles lettres*. The *belles lettres* were defined by the exercise of taste rather than modelled on the practice of rhetoric (Delehanty 2013: 64–5; Howell 1971: 524, 530).

The taste that underpinned the *belles lettres* was rhetorical in structure – but more particularly, its practice and genre correlates both overlapped considerably with *sermo*, sociability and the varied attributes of the age's parfit conversationalist, the *honnête homme*. Rapin perceived the unity of the *belles lettres* as lying in the taste of the gentlemen who studied them:

> 'Tis certain, a Man cannot arrive at any tolerable degree of Politeness, or of that Genteelness which gives such an Air to Human Converse, but by some tincture of these Faculties, and some knowledge of those who have excell'd in them. (Rapin 1706: I, sigs. b[r], b2[r] ['The Design of the Work in General, and in Particular']).

For Rapin, oratory and history – and also philosophy, the subject of conversation – were species of reciprocal rhetorical activity whereby the rhetor spoke to an audience presumed to consist of a homogeneous elite of *honnêtes gens*, whose judgement and taste were equal to the rhetor's skills (Rapin 1706: II, 347). Furthermore, although rhetoric had to adapt itself to the diversity of speakers, auditors and circumstances (Rapin 1706: II, 16–17), it was ultimately directed at that same *honnête* audience (Rapin 1706: II, 30).

Rapin's emphasis on delight rather than persuasion followed from this high estimation of the audience's ability: an audience expert in rhetoric was not to be moved by the crudities of persuasion, but rather to be allured by the subtleties of delight (Rapin 1706: II, 25; H. Davidson 1965: 44–53). Bouhours, meanwhile, aimed to educate his reader to exercise proper taste upon both eloquence and the *belles lettres*; he also gave to the latter literary qualities associated with Attic style, and hence with *sermo*. So he wrote that

> it is not enough that every thought in the Works of the Learned shou'd be proportionable to the Subject they treat of, nor that the style must be embellish'd, agreeable without affectation, nice without refining; but it must be clear, and intelligible. (Bouhours 1705: 79 ['Dialogue IV']; Howell 1971: 526–7)

Rollin – whose work, in English translation, appears to have naturalised the term 'belles lettres' in English in the mid-1730s (but see Bond 1987: III, 191 [No. 230, 28 September 1710]) – likewise praised an Attic, *honnête* taste (Rollin 1734: I, 50, 54, 58; Howell 1971: 528–9, 532–3; and see also Warnick 1985: 55–6). Rollin's description of the natural habitat of this good taste explicitly associated it with conversation and its correlates of epistles and manners: 'Even those, who live in the politer ages without any application to learning or study, do not fail to gain some tincture of the prevailing good taste, which intermixes without their perceiving it themselves in their conversation, letters, and behaviour' (Rollin 1734: I, 53).

Rollin's work, the last and fullest of this sequence, explored at some length both the characteristics of this taste and its precise relationship to the study of the *belles lettres*. First, he elaborated the universalising implication of taste as faculty of the mind:

> all men bring the first principles of taste with them into the world, as well as those of rhetorick and logick. As a proof of this we may urge, that every good orator is almost always infallibly approved of by the people, and that there is not difference of taste and sentiment upon this point, as Tully observes, between the ignorant and the learned. (Rollin 1734: I, 51)

This was a very important shift in emphasis: where a successful conversationalist was able to address all audiences, all audiences were able to appreciate a work in good taste. Understanding, not discourse, was now the crux. This understanding – this cultivation of the mind – was the product of a form of conversation:

> In reality the mind is nourished and strengthened by the sublime truths, which are supplied by study. It encreases and grows up as I may say with the great men, whose performances are the objects of its attention, in the same manner as we usually fall into the practices and opinions of those, with whom we converse. (Rollin 1734: I, 5)

The precise purpose of the *belles lettres*, therefore, was to apply the now-traditional conception of a conversation with ancients towards the education of taste (Rollin 1734: I, 25, 6). The sovereignty of the *auctores* was not so much at issue, however, as was their status as 'finished patterns': they were meant to inspire imitation. This education in the *belles lettres* was not intended to induce the student to abdicate his judgement of taste, but rather – as conversation had always been meant to inspire further inquiry – to encourage the student himself to exercise his judgement, his taste (Rollin 1734: I, 49–50). By learning to exercise his taste, the student could in turn take part in modern conversation and society (Rollin 1734: I, 10–11).

It is worth noting here another shift in emphasis: Rollin still prescribed the imitation of the virtues of the ancients, but he took them as no longer such fit models for action as they were for taste:

> The customs, manners, and laws of the antients have changed; they are often opposite to our way of life and the usages that prevail among us; and the knowledge of them may be therefore less necessary for us. . . . But good taste, which is grounded upon immutable principles, is always the same in every age; and it is the principal advantage, that young

> persons should be taught to obtain from reading of antient authors, who have ever been looked upon with reason as the masters, trustees, and guardians of sound eloquence and good taste. (Rollin 1734: I, 60; and see Hampton 1991)

Rollin's culminating rendition of bellelettrism thus shifted the predicates of discourse away from persuasion towards the exercise of a faculty of taste conceived of as educated by conversation with and imitation of the ancients, to be used in conversation with one's peers, and whose prescription of a lucid, natural, artless Attic style overlapped with the prescribed style of conversation. The shift to *belles lettres* was partly an abstraction of rhetoric, but partly it also effectively substituted *sermo*'s mode and genre characteristics for those of oratory as the constitutive character of literary discourse (and see Astell 1697: Part II, 191–2; Sterne 1980: 77 [II.11]; L. Klein 1984–5: 208).

We may note here the importance of that key concept of *vraisemblance* – the probable, the plausible, verisimilitude made French. *Vraisemblance*, crucially, was a quality deriving from the audience rather than the author – for though the achievement of *vraisemblance* was incumbent upon the author, the judgement of *vraisemblance* fundamentally belonged to the audience. As Rapin put it in *Réflexions sur la poétique de ce temps* (1675), 'Le vray-semblable est tout ce qui est conforme à l'opinion du public' (Rapin 1675: 34). (*Public opinion*; we shall return to this later.) As much as any of the age's definitions of the audience, the people, etc., this audience could be restricted to a properly self-constituted *gens raisonnables, bien sûr honnéte* – but the adoption of the ideal of *vraisemblance* encapsulated the shift in aesthetic emphasis to the judgement of the audience – a judgement that was eminently rhetorical in its emphasis on the probable (Moyes 2011, esp. 328–31; and see Doran 1963: 53–84).

The French bellelettristic movement was generally influential in Britain. Bernard Lamy (1640–1715), François Fénelon (1651–1715), Rapin, Bouhours and Rollin were all translated into English, and Warnick has described in detail their influence on figures such as Hugh Blair, George Campbell (1719–96) and Adam Smith (Howell 1971: 524–5, 527–9; Warnick 1993). Smith's statement concerning judicial eloquence, that '[t]he eloquence which is now in greatest esteem is a plain, distinct, and perspicuous Stile, without any of the Floridity or other ornamentall parts of the Old Eloquence', may stand (*mutatis mutandis*) for the general influence of bellelettristic Atticism on eighteenth-century British conceptions of rhetoric (A. Smith 1985: 196 [ii.245]). Smith also indicated the sentimental variation that eighteenth-century British rhetoricians applied to French bellelettrism:

> the perfection of stile consists in Express<ing> in the most concise, proper and precise manner the thought of the author, and that in the manner which best conveys the sentiment, passion or affection with which it affects or he pretends it does affect him and which he designs to communicate to his reader. (A. Smith 1985: 55 [i.133])

The appearance of the concept of *belles lettres* was paralleled by the appearance of the cognate concepts of the *arti di disegno*, *le buone arti*, *beaux arts*, the polite arts and the fine arts, all of which united the various rhetoricised arts – along with conversation and 'prudent Behaviour' – without explicit reference to their rhetorical status (Kristeller 1965: 163–227; L. Klein 1984–5: 201, 201 (note 39)). The term *beaux arts* became famous and influential by means of Charles Batteux's (1713–80) *Les beaux arts réduits à un même principle* (1746), which, eponymously, redefined the nature of the unity of these endeavours, and gave that new unity both system and theoretical heft (Maniates 1969: 122). In discussing Batteux's scheme, it is worth noting how it preserved various aspects of *honnête* aesthetics. For example, Batteux prescribed the usual *honnête* style:

> Clarity is of prime importance . . . Each mood must be exactly right. . . . The expression must be lively, and frequently fine and delicate. . . . The expression must be straightfoward and simple; everything that smacks of effort is painful and tiring. . . . In conclusion, the expression must be fresh, especially in music. (Batteux 1981: 51–2)

More generally Batteux saw taste (*goût*) as applicable to all of the arts, as well as the (sentimental) combination of taste, reason and genius (Batteux 1981: 41–2). The *beaux arts* – music, poetry, painting, sculpture, dance – shared the imitation of nature, the *vraisemblable*, and the purpose of delight; albeit eloquence and architecture aimed at use as well as at delight (Batteux 1981: 44–6). The qualities they shared, however, were broad enough to allow for the individual exercise of taste:

> Nevertheless, men and nations of reputed enlightenment and urbanity do differ in their tastes. . . . This can be explained on the one hand by the richness of nature herself; and on the other hand by the limitations of the human heart and mind. [Paragraph] The riches of nature are manifold, and each may be considered from an infinite number of viewpoints. . . .

> A single object can be represented in an infinite number of ways, all however entirely regular and wholly conformable to nature and good taste. (Batteux 1981: 47)

Rollin's discussion of the *belles lettres* had posited a cognate conception of taste:

> Taste, simple and uniform in its principle, is varied and multiplied an infinite number of ways, yet so as under a thousand different forms, . . . 'tis always the same, and carries with it a certain character of being true and natural, which is quickly perceived by all persons of judgment. (Rollin 1734: I, 50)

Here as elsewhere, Batteux's articulation of the *beaux arts* largely recapitulated the articulation by Rollin and his predecessors of the principles of the *belles lettres*, applying the universality and abstraction of taste not only to the various genres of the word but also to the various genres of nonverbal art – visual, aural, gestural. A common conversational aesthetics united the *belles lettres* and the *beaux arts*.

Conversational Art

After c. 1600, art's persistingly rhetorical orientation shifted towards a conversational mode. So the Dutch painters of the seventeenth century introduced the genre of the 'conversation piece', whose subject matter recapitulated the correlates of conversation. Conversation pieces such as Gabriel Metsu's (1629–67) *Family of the Merchant Geelvinck* (1650s–60s) portrayed domestic life (familial, intimate), sociable groups and, above all, conversations – in and out of doors, in gardens, engaged in sporting and musical conversations. In eighteenth-century England, the conversation piece found an early exemplar in James Thornhill's (1675/6–1734) group portrait *Andrew Quicke in Conversation with the 1st Earl of Godolphin, Joseph Addison, Sir Richard Steele, and the Artists* (c. 1711–12), emerged in the 1720s and 1730s as a major genre in the visual arts, and flourished throughout the mid-century in the hands of artists such as William Hogarth (1697–1764) and Johann Zoffany (1733–1810). By the mid-eighteenth century the subgenre of English family portraiture had become eminently conversational – informal, natural and domestic. It also focused upon both the communication of sentiments and a portrayal of the interior and private character for a public, unknown audience (Mee 2011: 5–6, 48; Paulson 1975: 121–36; Praz 1971, esp. 68; Retford 2006, esp. 3–17; Solkin 1993: 48–77; and see E. Goodman 1982, esp. 251).

In France, Antoine Watteau (1684–1721) both adapted into painting the polite, sociable and conversational mode of *honnête* and *salonnier* France, and included conversation as a subject matter throughout his oeuvre (Vidal 1992: 13–98; and see Barker 2007; Crow 1985: 55–74). Moreover, Watteau innovated in ways of presenting conversation pictorially. In addition to exploring ways of using both head movements and scenes of leisurely movement (e.g., promenades) to convey conversation, Watteau, Vidal writes, '[b]y depicting very reserved gestures, or no gestures at all, . . . constructs a more convincing image not of speeches, but of refined, generalized conversation' (Vidal 1992: 19–20). Watteau also appears to have been an early innovator in presenting the relation of viewer and subject as a form of conversation (Vidal 2006: 83; and see also 1992: 63, 65, 99–142). Not only the artist but also the figures in his paintings engaged in familiar, conversational address to the viewer (Vidal 1992: 134). The very structure of the painting became conversational: 'multiple or shifting points of view perfectly corresponded to the open-endedness of Watteau's subjects, which do not claim a didactic authority over the viewer'. Their proportions were equally conversational: 'the size of Watteau's paintings – small, accessible, with diminutive figures – never overpowers, but beckons us to approach the painting to stand as close as we would to a conversational partner' (Vidal 1992: 136). Finally, such painting was also meant to act as a conversation, to stimulate further thought and judgement by the viewer (Vidal 1992: 134).

Roger de Piles' (1635–1709) discussions of art provided a theoretical counterpart to Watteau's practice. Piles began by comparing the painter to the orator in his *Conversations sur la connoissance de la peinture* (1677): 'Le Peintre est comme l'Orateur . . . Le peintre doit persuader les yeux comme un homme Eloquent doit toucher le coeur' (Piles 1677: 102–3; Plett 2012: 162). But Piles also described painting in *Conversations* as a discourse more akin to conversation in its quiet intimacy: 'un discours muet a la verite, & qui n'est que pour le coeur; mais tout muet qu'il est, il se fait tres bien entendre' (Piles 1677: 16; Vidal 1992: 136). By the time Piles wrote *Cours de peinture par principes* (1708), his image of painting had become explicitly conversational: 'le Spectateur surpris doit aller a elle comme pour entrer en conversation avec les figures qu'elle represente' (Piles 1708: 6; Vidal 1992: 136). Connoisseur and painter were supposed to be in conversation: 'la conversation des habiles connoisseurs & des savans Peintres' (Piles 1708: 26). The painter was no longer to aim at oratorical power over his viewers, but to engage them in a visual conversation (Vidal 1992: 136; cf. Bond 1965: III, 538 [No. 411, 21 June 1712]).

In addition to being conversational, *après* Watteau and Piles, French paintings were also meant to be natural. The art critic André Félibien (1619–95) wrote in *Entretiens sur les vies et sur les ouvrages des plus excellens peintres anciens et modernes* (1685) that

> diversity [in the composition of paintings] must be natural, without anything affected or constrained. The figures must seem to be arranged and posed on their own, without too much care or study, and it is that which brings grace to the arrangement. (Félibien 1705: II, 295, translated in J. Gibson 2008: 423)

Denis Diderot's (1713–84) praise of Jean-Baptiste-Siméon Chardin (1699–1779) at the Salon of 1763 was notably for providing the appearance of 'la nature même' (Diderot 1975: 222); and at the Salon of 1769 he praised Maurice Quentin de la Tour (1704–88) on similar grounds: 'I have never seen such examples of simplicity and truth; not a shadow of mannerism, just pure, artless nature, no pretention in the touch, no assignment of contrast in the colors, no discomfort in the position' (Diderot 1995: 50, translated in Milano 2015: 27–8). The development of *plein air* painting in eighteenth-century France combined the subject matter of the natural landscape with quick and direct execution of the painting, both to capture the evanescent aspects of nature and to make unstudied, direct apprehension of nature part of the artistic process (A. Miller 2013: 6–8). The imitation of nature would be as strong in painting as in any other genre of the conversational arts.

In late-seventeenth- and early-eighteenth-century England, meanwhile, Mee analyses Godfrey Kneller's (1646–1723) paintings as 'much more aware of the involvement of their subjects in circuits of exchange, which include the viewers of the picture. This "audience-oriented subjectivity", to use Habermas's term, looks to bind its viewers into its construction of a conversable community' (Mee 2011: 48). Paulson takes Hogarth's conversation pieces as translating into conversational idiom the principles of history painting, articulated from Alberti onwards, which also prescribed one person's actions moving the passions of an audience. Hogarth's works showed a 'situation in which one person is reacted to as a person or as a thing by a number of other people, all of whom – essentially audience – are interacting only with this person, not with each other' (Paulson 1975: 128–9).

Hogarth's conversation pieces, moreover, provided the viewer with greater interpretative freedom than did traditional history paintings, because they were of unknown subjects, where the diverse affections and responses told the story without the key of a known historical subject matter (Paulson 1975: 129–30; and see Solkin 1993: 78–105). In France also Louis-François Dubois de St Gelais (1669–1737) in his *Description des tableaux du Palais Royal* (1727) made such interpretative freedom explicit when he stated that he 'abstained from any critical judgement . . . in order to leave each viewer the liberty to make judgements according to the impression made on him by each picture' (Dubois de St Gelais 1728: viii–ix, translated in Crow 1985: 41).

At the level of theory, Jonathan Richardson's (1667–1745) *An Essay on the Theory of Painting* (1725) articulated a conversational theory of portraiture. Like a letter, a portrait was a communication between absent friends:

> To come to Portraits; the Picture of an absent Relation, or Friend, helps to keep up those Sentiments which frequently languish by Absence and may be instrumental to maintain, and sometimes to augment Friendship, and Paternal, Filial, and Conjugal Love, and Duty. (J. Richardson 1725: 13; De Bolla 2008: 172)

A portrait painter needed to understand men's inner characters:

> A Portrait-Painter must understand Mankind, and enter into their Characters, and express their Minds as well as their Faces: And as his Business is chiefly with People of Condition, he must Think as a Gentleman, and a Man of Sense, or 'twill be impossible to give Such their True, and Proper Resemblances. (J. Richardson 1725: 22; De Bolla 2008: 174)

Finally, portraits, and the act of sitting for a portrait, were meant themselves to communicate one's character and so make it a subject to inspire further conversation: 'Upon the sight of a Portrait, the Character and Master-strokes of the History of the Person it represents are apt to flow in upon the Mind, and to be the Subject of Conversation' (J. Richardson 1725: 13–14; De Bolla 2008: 175).

Conversational Architecture

Much of French architecture shifted towards the neoclassical – that chaste and Attic style whose rhetoric overlapped with, although it was by no means identical with, the conversational mode (and see Gerbino 2010). Within that broader shift, we may note certain aspects that emphasised the growing importance of conversation. The Hôtel de Rambouillet, site of the earliest *salon* in the continuous tradition, was redesigned to foster conversation: Maland writes that

> [f]ollowing a pattern already established in a few *hôtels*, the staircase was removed from the centre and put to one side of the *corps de logis*, leaving a suite of communicating rooms in which small groups could hold intimate conversation and yet be free to move easily to others. (Maland 1970: 47)

More broadly, the architecture of the French *hôtels* shifted from baroque to rococo to neoclassical over the course of the seventeenth and eighteenth centuries, the shift incorporating the ever-greater valuations of intimacy, privacy, individuality and freedom so enduringly characteristic of the conversational mode (Dennis 1986: 52–171).

From the late seventeenth century onward, French architectural theory also shifted in a conversational direction. Buildings persuaded as much as did their Renaissance forebears, but ever more by means of their individual character. Prerequisite for this development was the idea that architecture could and should vary. François Blondel (1618–86) still argued in the last decades before 1700 that the character of persuasive architecture was universal and the natural, but Claude Perrault (1613–88) now began to conceive of architecture as also governed by the purely customary conventions of 'arbitrary beauty' (Perrault 1684: 12 (note 13); Kruft 1994: 134: Pelletier 2006: 12–13). This shift towards 'arbitrary beauty' in turn led to a new emphasis on the equally arbitrary discrimination of individual taste. Germain Boffrand (1667–1754) would write in *Livre d'architecture* (1745) that 'What is excellent for one is not always excellent for another. . . . Enthusiasm is as dangerous as dullness. Excellence of taste resides in a judicious fitness' (Boffrand 2002: 6). Arbitrary beauty and individual taste between them opened up the possibility of an architecture built upon the individual expressivity characteristic of conversation.

This theory of individually expressive architecture emerged in the course of the eighteenth century, in the concept of *caractère* articulated in the works of Germain Boffrand (*Livre d'architecture*, 1745) and Jacques-François Blondel (1705–74) (*De la Distribution des maisons de plaisance*, 1737–8; *Cours d'architecture*, 1771–7). In the theory of *caractère*, the unifying stamp of architecture lay in the individual nature of the building rather than in abstract conceptions of decorum. Boffrand wrote '*Let the work maintain the same character from beginning to end, so that every part may relate to the whole*' (Boffrand 2002: 11). Blondel, who conceived of architecture as analogous to facial physiognomy in the way it expressed character, in turn wrote that an architect needed to 'assigner à chaque bâtiment le caractere qui lui est propre' (Blondel 1771: 374; Archer 1979: 341–2; Pelletier 2006: 19). Boffrand put the theory of unifying *caractère* into practice in his own work, notably in his 1735–6 execution of the Princesse de Soubise's apartments in the Hôtel de Soubise (Gallet and Garms 1986: 46–7, 108–9, 221–35; Van Eck 1995: 93.

Caractère acquired communicative aspects as the century wore on. Boffrand, for one, drew on Horace's *Ars poetica* to explain his architectural theory, and thus allied the architecture of *caractère* with the long tradition of rhetoricised poetics that aimed at affecting the passions of an auditor – or in the case of architecture, a spectator. Horace's recommendation that poets 'Correctly represent the marks of every phase of life, / and give your characters what suits their varying years' now became Boffrand's recommendation to architects (Horace 1977: 88 [lines 156–7]; Boffrand 2002: 8–12; Archer 1979: 342; Van Eck 1995: 93). Boffrand made explicit the analogy of architecture with words: 'The profiles of mouldings, and the other members that compose a building, are in architecture what words are in a discourse' (Boffrand 2002: 9). He likewise made explicit the communicativity of architecture's *caractère*:

> *It is not enough for a building to be handsome; it must be pleasing, and the beholder must feel the character that it is meant to convey; so that it must appear cheerful where it is intended to communicate joy, and serious and melancholy where is is meant to instil respect or sadness.* (Boffrand 2002: 10–11; Pelletier 2006: 19; Van Eck 1995: 95)

By the time of Blondel's *Cours d'architecture* (1771), the *caractère* of a building was meant explicitly to move the passions of the spectator (Blondel 1771: 259–60; Archer 1979: 345). Nicolas Le Camus de Mézières (1721–89) added in *The Genius of Architecture* (1780) that

> A structure catches the eye by virtue of its mass; its general outline attracts or repels us. When we look at some great fabric, our sensations are of contradictory kinds: gaiety in one place, despondency in another. One sensation induces quiet reflection; another inspires awe, or maintains respect, and so on . . . The arrangement of forms, their character, and their combination are thus an inexhaustible source of illusion. We must

> start from this principle whenever we intend to arouse emotion through Architecture, when we set out to address the mind and to stimulate the soul. (Le Camus 1992: 70–2, 160; Archer 1979: 346; Pelletier 2006: 22; and see Boullée 1968: 73; Grignon and Maxim 1995: 36)

For all these theorists of the French Enlightenment, the character of architecture communicated itself to the viewer and moved his passions.

A parallel intensification of the conception of *style* in architecture accompanied the rise of *caractère*. Architectural theory had included scattered mention of style back to the *quattrocento*: Filarete (Antonio di Pietro Averlino, c. 1400–c. 1469) had written in his *Treatise on Architecture* (c. 1464) that 'The painter is known by the manner of his figures, and in every discipline one is known by his style' (Filarete 1965: I, 12 [Bk I, fol. 5v]; Van Eck 1995: 91). *Style* had generally come into more common usage in all the arts from the Renaisance onwards, and become increasingly common in the architectural world (Wren 1750: 302; Germann 1972: 11–27; Van Eck 1995: 91). By the eighteenth century, it had come to be a commonplace. The *Dictionnaire universel* (the *Dictionnaire de Trévoux*) stated simply that

> Le *style*, tel qu'on le définit ici, est en quelque sorte l'ame du discours, l'attrait & le charme qui soutient l'attention de l'esprit par la suite des matières qu'il enchaine ensemble . . . non seulement dans la Musique, mais en tout genre de composition. (*Dictionnaire Universel* 1771: 861; Van Eck 1995: 92, 94)

The same architects brought both *caractère* and style into common use, as complements. Boffrand linked the two concepts:

> Architecture, although its object may seem to be no more than the use of material, is capable of a number of genres that bring its component parts to life, so to speak, through the different characters that it conveys to us. . . . The same is true of poetry: this, too, has its different genres; and the style of one does not suit another. (Boffrand 2002: 8; Van Eck 1995: 92).

Blondel added that 'style can express in particular the character: regular or irregular, simple or composed, symmetrical or varied' (Blondel 1771: 401, translated in Van Eck 1995: 94). Style unified architecture as did *caractère*, and a building communicated by means of its style (Blondel 1771: 373–4; Van Eck 1995: 94–6). Yet above all, style communicated character. Antoine-Chrysostome Quatremère de Quincy (1755–1849) wrote in his article 'Style' in the *Encyclopédie méthodique* (1825):

> the word 'style' signifies in a much more generally accepted sense, that typical and characteristic form, which very general[ly] causes impress on products of the mind . . . Style, as we say, becomes synonymous with *character*, or with the individual manner (*la manière propre*) of the distinctive physiognomy which belongs to each work of art, to each author, each genre, each school, each country, each period. (Quatremère 1825: III, 411, translated in Van Eck 1995: 98)

Caractère was not fully individuated. As a building's *convenance* had in the seventeenth century – or indeed as Vitruvius himself had suggested – so a building's *caractère* in the eighteenth century was largely meant to echo the social status of its owner, or to ascertain the building's genre (Vitruvius 1960: 181–3 [6.5]; Blondel 1771: 389–90; Grignon and Maxim 1995; Szambien 1986: 167–99). Boffrand wrote that 'A prince's house is not to be built like that of a private person; nor that of a private person like the house of a man with a public position to maintain' (Boffrand 2002: 6; and see Le Camus 1992: 72). Style also tended to the typological, to characterise a nation more than an individual artist (Vidler 1987: 147–64). *Caractère* and style, inasmuch as they were not fully individualised, were not fully conversational. Yet Boffrand and Le Camus associated *caractère* with good taste (Boffrand 2002: 4–7), simplicity (2002: 10), common sense (2002: 11), artless art (Le Camus 1992: 89), and sincere friendship (Boffrand 2002: 12) – all the conversational aesthetics of the age (Kruft 1994: 142–3). If *caractère* was not fully conversational, it aligned significantly with conversational aesthetics.

The rise of *caractère* registered one aspect of the shift towards conversational aesthetics in French architecture; so too did the combination of the increasing interest in interior décor – the aesthetics of the furnishings rather than of the architectural bones – and the shift away from using such décor merely to impress. This shift – which would also affect England profoundly – registered the greater value of personal convenience, *commodité*, as against the public display of status, *magnificence*. In effect, architectural decorum, the consideration of the *vraisemblable* and the appropriate, shared in the shift from public to private, from the oratorical to the conversational, from the Latin *decorum* to the French *décor*. Décor's association with female interests and tastes also registered the feminisation of the world of architecture. So far as timing was concerned, the shift from a heroic decorative mode to a *mondain* one correlated with the shift from Louis XIV to the Regent Philippe d'Orléans (Boffrand 2002: 16–17; Gallet and Garms 1986: 108–9, 221–35; M. Martin 2010; K. Scott 1995: 97, 103–17, 177–239).

In this new dispensation, *honnête* and *mondain* taste in interior décor would be registered by a taste for the *burlesque* – a playful and deliberate breach of decorum – and the *grotesque* – which likewise breached the rules of classicising taste by appealing directly to the senses of the beholding amateur. Claude-Henri Watelet's (1718–86) definition of 'grotesque' in Diderot's *Encyclopédie* happily put it that

> since good sense does not preclude a place for a kind of amiable unreason, which when carefully managed may serve as its ornament, [so] the Arts, sober and reserved by nature, have no less the right occasionally to derogate from the austerity of their grand principles. (Diderot 1782: 707, translated in K. Scott 1995: 124; Bédard 2011: 26–7; K. Scott 1995: 123–36)

Burlesque and *grotesque* together helped form the emerging mode of rococo décor, whose extravagance continued to register *honnête* subversion of decorum. That subversiveness, however, would be lost as rococo décor became commodified, the rococo objects detached from noble *hôtels* and sold to all with the francs to buy. The vulgarity of rococo, soon condemned at the time, derived not least from losing its subversive *raison d'être* when removed from its rhetorical frame (Bédard 2011: 26–7; 29; K. Scott 1995: 241–65; and see Bédard 2003; 2011; Russo 2007).

Yet interior décor was not supposed to be commodified and autonomous, but rather an integral part of a building's architecture – for a building was now supposed to be the same inside and out, in architectural counterpart to the ideal of sincerity (Le Camus 1992: 102). Quatremère added in his 1788 article on 'Caractère' in the *Encyclopédie méthodique* a generalisable note on the architecture of theatres:

> Cette forme intèrieure devint aussi celle de l'extérieur de l'édifice . . . Quelle étrange bisarrerie a voulu établir entre leur conformation interne & leur configuration extérieure une contradiction telle, que sans le secours d'une inscription, il seroit impossible de savoir devant quel monument on se trouve? (Quatremère 1788: 511–12; Vidler 1987: 160).

Naturally, décor could communicate as much as any other component of architecture: 'La décoration, considérée dans ses ressources partielles ou dans ses détails, est un language dont des signes, les expressions doivent ètre douès d'une signification prècise & capable de rendre des idées' (Quatremère 1788: 515; Vidler 1987: 160). The quintessence of French conversational architecture was a building whose character spoke as much from its porcelain as from its pediment.

Across the Channel, a similar transformation occurred. As conversation and sociability flourished in late-seventeenth- and early-eighteenth-century England, as the country increasingly prized casual negligence of rank and formulated innumerable informal rules to maintain conversation by regulating speech and maintaining concord, as England became a nation of societies and clubs, of academies and coffeehouses – so much of English architecture shifted to a conversational mode, both reflecting the spirit of the age and seeking to foster these practices. Accordingly, much urban architecture was built in eighteenth-century England to promote the practice of polite conversation (Borsay 1989: 136–9, 145–6, 150–62, 273–6; cf. Le Camus 1992: 139; but see Van Eck 2007: 111–36). The design of these new public spaces also became conversational: the axial vista focused on the palace of the king (or whatever locus of authority) shifted to a design centred on 'a series of focal points – the different baths, the assembly rooms, the pump room and the abbey – surrounded or linked by terraces and crescents'. In this uncentred public place, '[p]eople strolled from one to the other, meeting friends on the way and talking to them' (Girouard 1978: 183).

For those who could afford it, architecture became polite in eighteenth-century England – hence Palladian, since classical style then connoted politeness. But Palladian style was also polite both because it embodied the conversational virtues of naturalness and simplicity and because the appreciation of that style presupposed the exercise by the well bred of that conversational mode of judgement, good taste. Isaac Ware (1704–66) wrote in *A Complete Body of Architecture* (1767) that

> there is a nobleness in simplicity which is always broke in upon by ornament . . . the simple and the natural is the proper path to beauty . . . Whatever the false taste of any particular time may adapt, the builder . . . must never suppose that caprice, or fashion, can change the nature of right and wrong. He must remember that there is such a thing as truth. (Ware 1768: 136–7, 295)

Robert Morris (1701–54) concurred in *Rural Architecture* (1750):

> *I think a Building, well proportioned, without* Dress, *will ever please; as a plain Coat may fit as graceful, and easy, on a* well-proportioned

> *Man; . . . But if you will be lavish in Ornament, your* Structure *will look rather like a* Fop, *with a Superfluity of* gaudy Tinsel, *than a real* Decoration. (Morris 1757: Preface, first page; L. Klein 2002: 886; Borsay 1989: 235, 305–7)

The interior decoration of the polite house came to promote informality and comfort over grandeur, polite conversation over ceremonial display, sociability between equals over grand hospitality for social inferiors. The interior design likewise promoted sociability: as Klein summarises, 'Formal axes within the house gave way to circuits of large rooms, suited for balls, assemblies, and other receptions.' Norfolk House (designed c. 1750) in St James' Square in London set its stamp on this mode; the fashion quickly spread throughout London, and then on to the country houses of England (L. Klein 2002: 886–7; Girouard 1978: 181–212, esp. 194–5, 199; and see Sloboda 2010: 137–8). The internal variation of the rooms – Norfolk House had varying colour schemes in its circuit's several rooms – reflected the varying character of society (Girouard 1978: 195). The age's emphasis on the cohesion and uniformity of the design of external architecture, however, was meant to echo not the individuality but the commonality of mankind, that great prerequisite for sociability (Borsay 1989: 270–1).

Even beyond the aristocratic elite, the accent of prosperous urban culture shifted architecture and décor towards the politely conversational: both the renovation of interiors to facilitate comfortable and attractive domesticity and the participation in the shared urban architecture of polite sociability – e.g., assemblies – made conversational architecture a possession or an aspiration among a remarkably wide, and widening, portion of eighteenth-century Englishmen (L. Klein 2002: 887–8). For all, architecture was meant to civilise, the incubator as well as the consequence of politeness. As Richard Neve put it in the *Builder's Dictionary* (1726), 'where there is no *Architecture* in a Nation, there can, by Consequence, be no Princely Government . . . where such a Power is wanting, People are so *Savage* and *Barbarous*, that they live more like Brutes than Rational Men' (Neve 1726: viii; Borsay 1989: 260–1, 265).

Out of doors, a great many walks and gardens were built to foster still more the practices of conversation and sociability. These became more prevalent in the seventeenth and (especially) the eighteenth centuries, and spread from exemplary sites in London such as St James' Park and the walks at Moorfields to the provinces. The focus at first was more on providing a location for public promenade, but the midddle and later eighteenth century saw the appearance of specialised commercial pleasure gardens (Borsay 1989: 162–72). The design of these walks, gardens and parks echoed that of the rooms within a house, and of the urban architecture of sociability: circular planning (such as at Stowe or Stourhead) progressively replaced axial planning over the eighteenth century, and the garden walk became a circuit where varied sites – 'temples, obelisks, seats, pagodas, rotundas' – echoed the varied décor indoors (Girouard 1978: 210). Gardens and houses were both now intended to be seen from a variety of shifting perspectives, rather than from one commanding one, and the decentring of perspective now encouraged planned asymmetry (Girouard 1978: 211–12; and for later developments, see Girouard 1978: 213–44).[1]

English landscape theory also saw a transposition of the idea of 'character' into landscape itself. Where the French had applied *caractère* to the social class of a building's owner, or to that building's social function, Thomas Whately's (1726–72) *Observations on Modern Gardening* (1770) – following precedents in such works as Timothy Nourse's (d. 1699) *Campania Foelix* (1700), Roger de Piles' *Cours de peinture par principes* (1708), Robert Morris' *Lectures on Architecture* (1734) and Lord Kames' *Elements of Criticism* (1762) (Nourse 1700: 341; Piles 1708: 200, 219; Morris 1734: 73; Kames 1967: III, 299; Archer 1979: 354–63) – applied 'character' rather to the quality of the land itself.

> The *style* also of every part must be accommodated to the character of the whole; for every piece of ground is distinguished by certain properties: it is either tame or bold; gentle or rude; continued or broken; and if any variety, inconsistent with those properties, be obtruded, it has no other effect than to weaken one idea, without raising another. (Whately 1770: 13–15; Archer 1979: 350; and see Whately 1770: 46–7, 99, 256–7)

The character of the landscape was also communicative, for it moved the emotions. Torrents of water, for example, 'alarm the senses; the roar and the rage of a torrent, its force, its violence, its impetuosity, tend to inspire terror; that terror, which, whether as cause or effect, is so nearly allied to sublimity' (Whately 1770: 61–2; Archer 1979: 350–1; and see 61–2, 153, 156).

Character did not pertain simply to nature unimproved, but rather to nature improved by art: 'the art of gardening aspires to more than imitation: it can create original characters, and give expressions to the several scenes superior to any they can receive from allusions' (Whately 1770: 153–4; and see 106). Yet such improvement was supposed to give the impression of nature – artless art, in landscape design. So the English recoil from symmetry: 'regularity always suggests a suspicion of artifice; and artifice detected, no longer deceives' (Whately 1770: 19; and see 144–5). This note of *sprezzatura* in landscape design was eminently conversational. The character of landscape was also conversational in that it was meant to spark new chains of thought:

> The power of such characters is not confined to the ideas which the objects immediately suggest; for these are connected with others, which insensibly lead to subjects, far distant perhaps from the original thought, and related to it only by a similitude in the sensations they excite. (Whately 1770: 154–6; Archer 1979: 351; and see Whately 1770: 131–2)

Whately largely confined his discussion to landscape design, but also began to apply 'character' to building itself – the main subject of architecture – in his discussions of buildings within gardens (Whately 1770: 116–35). Such buildings were 'intitled to be considered as *characters* . . . The same structure which adorns as an object, may also be expressive as a character' (Whately 1770: 118, 123–4; Archer 1979: 350–1; and see Whately 1770: 224–5, 243). These buildings also moved the passions of the spectator: 'the peculiar excellence of buildings is, that their effects are instantaneous, and therefore the impressions they make are forcible' (Whately 1770: 126). In Whately's landscape theory, the quasi-conversational theory of character abandoned its role as a proxy for social status and integrated itself into the pure language of the fashioning of buildings and nature.

Whately's influence soon became pervasive within the field of English architecture. Archibald Alison (1757–1839) wrote in *Essays on the Nature and Principles of Taste* (1790) that

> the different Forms of rooms, their difference of magnitude, and various other causes, give them distinct characters, as those of Gaiety, Simplicity, Solemnity, Grandeur, Magnificence, &c. No room is ever beautiful, which has not some such pleasing character; the terms by which we express this Beauty are significant of these characters. (Alison 1790: 2, 385)

Humphry Repton (1752–1818) wrote in *Observations on the Theory and Practice of Landscape Gardening* (1805) of '*Characteristic Architecture*', marked by

> the adaptation of buildings not only to the situation, character, and circumstances of the scenery, but also to the purposes for which they are intended . . . it is obvious that every building ought 'to tell its own tale', and not to look like any thing else. (Repton 1805: 206; Archer 1979: 364–5)

By such individualised tale-telling, affectively expressive of individuality, conversation became English architecture's keystone.

Conversational Music

A first wave of conversationalising influence in early modern music apparently derived from the late-*cinquecento* attempt by the circle around Vincenzo Galilei (c. 1520–91) to imitate the (lost and idealised) expressiveness of ancient Greek music. This school's influence emphasised the importance of using music to express a person's particular character, and the preferability of clarity and the imitation of nature to clever artificiality. Galilei himself put it in his *Dialogue on Ancient and Modern Music* (1581) that

> Before singing a poem, an ancient musician first examined diligently the quality of the person speaking, the age, sex, with whom, and the object of the speech. After the poet clothed these ideas in words suited to their needs, the musician expressed them in that tonos, with those accents, gestures, quantities and qualities of sound, and with a rhythm that suited the action of the personage. (Galilei 2003: 90)

The Galilean school had significant influence on attempts to make the madrigal more expressive, and thus upon the nascent opera (Neubauer 1986: 25–7).

Yet though Italy thus played a role in the conversationalisation of music, most of this transformation occurred in France. Now, we may recollect that French music of the seventeenth century still largely worked within a rhetorical framework. Claude-François Ménestrier (1631–1705) wrote in *Des Représentations en musique anciennes et modernes* (1681) that

> there are no emotions that our poetry and our music, as well as our eloquence, cannot express and excite whenever they wish . . . this, skillful masters do without much difficulty when they understand equally the nature of languages and the perfection of music. (Ménestrier 1681: 146, translated in J. Gibson 2008: 395 (note 2))

Jean-Laurent Le Cerf de la Viéville (1674–1707) likewise wrote in *Comparaison de la musique italienne et de la musique française* (1704–6) that 'I have taken the method of clarifying and proving my thoughts on music by inference, from rhetoric, from poetry, and from the other fine arts that music resembles, and since that resemblance is certain, my method cannot be wrong' (Le Cerf de la Viéville 1972: 3:51, translated in J. Gibson 2008: 395 (note 2)). Yet French rhetoric had already begun to deprecate the figures of rhetoric as excessively formal and artificial, and to prize instead of rote rules of rhetoric an eloquence rooted in the natural expression of the passions, flexible good taste and decorum. French writings on music in the late seventeenth century, therefore, likewise rooted their *musica rhetorica* in nature, good taste and decorum. Unlike their German musical contemporaries, but as the French rhetoricians of the age, they deliberately eschewed specific mention of rhetorical figures or parts of rhetoric, and emphasised delivery (*pronuntiatio*) rather than *elocutio* (associated with rhetorical figures) as best able to convey, without rule or artifice, the natural passions. Bénigne de Bacilly (1621–90), for example, in *L'Art de bien chanter* (1668) contrasted the Italian embrace of dramatic word choice – song in a more oratorical mode – with the French eschewal of such expressions (Bacilly 1968: 42–3; Fader 2003: 31 (note 56); J. Gibson 2008: 396–7, 405–15; and see Ranum 2001: 94–5). This contrast should not be exaggerated: Brown notes that if the German musical tradition codified more than a hundred rhetorical figures, the French musical tradition still made regular use of at least two dozen (L. Brown 1980: 106). Yet the difference between two dozen and a hundred was still substantial: in contrast to the *Klangrede* across the Rhine, the musical rhetoric of France became progressively looser and more informal.

This musical transformation had its roots as far back as the sixteenth century. The composers of the *airs de cour* of the late sixteenth and early seventeenth centuries – among them Adrian Le Roy (c. 1520–98) and François de Chancy (1600–56) – had aimed their works at an aristocratic audience, emphasised their *mondain* simplicity, negligence and grace, and contrasted them with the difficulty and pedantry associated with rival modes of music (Le Roy 1571: [1^{v}] [Dedication]; Chancy 2006: 5 [Au Lecteur]; Brooks 2000: 13–17, 159–67; Fader 2003: 26–7). This *mondain* mode had then receded in importance in France during the rise of court culture during the seventeenth century, marked by professional performances of operas and ballets, but it had survived to be reformulated from the late seventeenth century onwards in terms of *honnêteté*, *politesse* and *bienséance* (Bacilly 1679: 11–13, translated in

Fader 2003: 31; 2003: 30–1). Late-seventeenth-century France therefore saw a mutually reinforcing confluence of the recession of musical rhetoric and the second rise of an *honnête* musical aesthetic, now with decisive effect.

In the succeeding generations, French music's imitation of rhetoric dwindled towards a mere resemblance – and in Michel de Saint-Lambert's (*fl.* 1700) *Principes du clavecin* (1702), oratory was taken to resemble music rather than the reverse: 'it is the piece of rhetoric which resembles the piece of music, since harmony, number, measure, and the other similar things which a skillful orator observes in the composition of his works belong more naturally to music than to rhetoric' (Saint-Lambert 1984: 32; J. Gibson 2008: 401). In Michel Le Faucheur's (1585–1657) *Traité de l'action de l'orateur, ou de la prononciation et du geste* (1657), among others, the emphasis on *pronuntiatio* rather than *elocutio* mentioned above also served to relocate eloquence's beauty and force as originating in music rather than in oratory: ''Tis the same in *speaking* as in *Musick*: *Words* for the *Euphony* of the one, and *notes* for the *Harmony* of the other. If your *Speech* proceeds from a *violent Passion*, it produces a *violent Pronunciation*' (Le Faucheur 1680: 99; J. Gibson 2008: 411–13). Batteux, in turn, made the arts of speech derive significant power from music and dance: 'Music and dance can well shape the accents and gestures of the orator on his rostrum and the way in which the common man recounts a story in the course of conversation' (Batteux 1981: 46).

Music (following the strictures of Fénelon, Lamy and Rapin as to proper eloquence) became eloquent as an unconstrained imitation of nature rather than of oratory – or more precisely, the nonchalant and effortless imitation (*sprezzatura* once more) of unconstrained nature. Fénelon prescribed in his *Dialogues Concerning Eloquence* (1718), 'If you must employ Art, conceal it so well under an exact Imitation, that it may pass for Nature itself'; and this imitation of nature became the key in French musical eloquence as well (Fénelon 1722: 99; and see also 1722: 89, 98, 141; J. Gibson 2008: 421). Phérotée de La Croix (c. 1640–c. 1715) wrote in his *L'art de la Poësie françoise et latine avec une idée de la musique sous une nouvelle méthode* (1694) that 'the art of music is nothing but an imitation of the Natural, otherwise it would not be music; Art must always imitate Nature' (La Croix 1694: 620, translated in J. Gibson 2008: 425). Le Cerf de la Viéville likewise wrote in his *Comparaison de la musique italienne et de la musique française* (1704–6) that, 'I do not at all condemn cultivation in itself, a hidden labor that diminishes faults without damaging the beauty of nature: I condemn labor that adds faults, that conveys false beauty, and that appears' (Le Cerf de la Viéville 1972: 3:161, translated in J. Gibson 2008: 423; and see Crousaz 1715: 295–6; J. Gibson 2008: 423 (note 84)). Contrariwise, Le Cerf de la Viéville took the fault of Italian music as lying in its rulebound laboriousness and its neglect of the imitation of nature (Le Cerf de la Viéville 1972: I, 176–8; J. Gibson 2008: 416–29).

Ranum notes that French music concentrated on dance airs, *airs de mouvement*, precisely because they were taken to possess naturalness, simplicity, order and the commonplace nature of a maxim, all of which could be combined to form a musical oration of Racinean purity. As Étienne de Lacépède (1756–1825) put it in *La poétique de la musique* (1785),

> What then is an air? . . . It is a sort of little musical oration that can be delivered alone and whose effect is, so to speak, independent of its surroundings; that touches more or less forcefully according to the context in which it is performed, but that is always moving, wherever it appears; whose principal charm comes from itself. (Lacépède 1970: II, 106, translated in Ranum 2001: 29–30; Masson 1699: 27; Ranum 2001: 27–37)

French musical rhetoric now concentrated on the expression and movement of the passions by means of the artfully artless imitation of nature.

As the polemic by Le Cerf noted above indicates, the designated opponent of this reformulated mode was Italian music, especially its opera – excessive in its passion and its difficulty, neither natural nor gentle (Fader 2003: 30–1). As early as 1637, the music theorist Marin Mersenne described this musical distinction as a difference in French and Italian national styles (Mersenne 1637: 356, translated in Fader 2003: 30; and see also Van Orden 2005: 102). Even when opera began to naturalise itself in France, Bénigne de Bacilly in *Discours qui sert de Réponse à la Critique de ce Traité* (1679) updated this contrast in the late seventeenth century to contrast *salonnier*, amateur recitative and Italianate, professional opera; his model for *chanson* was Pierre de Nyert (1597–1682), an *honnête homme* of a singer, whose work was the very acme of *politesse du chant* (Bacilly 1679: 9; Fader 2003: 23). Saint-Évremond, very much an advocate that musicians should be *honnête* and music subject to *politesse*, critiqued Italian music in general for its immoderate emotionality and laboured technique (Saint-Évremond 1700: I, 527), and opera in particular because of its non-stop singing irreconcilable with the strictures of verisimilitude (Saint-Évremond 1700: I, 522). Both these faults violated *bienséance*. The French, by contrast, displayed in music their characteristic *je ne sais quoi*, the music that persuaded by artful artlessness (Fader 2003: 23–36).

This line of critique, with its praise of the *honnête* and polite virtues of French music and its polemic against Italianate music, continued long into the eighteenth century, with notable late episodes in the *Querelle des Bouffons* (1752–4) and the Gluck–Piccini *querelle* (1773–9) (with Christoph Willibald Gluck (1714/15–87) counted as an honorary Frenchman in the lists against Niccolò Piccinni (1728–1800)) (Pekacz 1999a: 143–203, esp. 166–88; and see Young 2013). Significantly, several critiques of Italian opera during these later rows also focused upon their unconversational qualities: So Claude-Henri Fusée, abbé de Voisenon (1708–75) [?] wrote during the *Querelle des Bouffons* that 'Un Opéra Italien isolé paroitra bien-tôt aussi insoutenable qu'un bavard impérieux qui usurpe la conversation, qui étonne d'abord, & qui finit par excéder' (Fusée de Voisenon [?] 1753: 7; Pekacz 1999a: 173). When in the mid-eighteenth century a new generation of critics came to argue for Italian opera over French, they did so on the same grounds as the previous polemic for French music over Italian. Now Italian opera was taken to be natural and simple, French to be artificial and studied (Rousseau 1998: 163 ['Letter on French Music']; Fader 2003: 27; but see Batteux 1981: 47; Isherwood 1989). We may note here that the epithet *baroque* from its coinage as an aesthetic term in the eighteenth century was specifically applied to that music, especially Italian, whose laboured qualities contrasted thematically with the natural and effortlessly unartful music of France. Thus Rousseau wrote that 'The Italians claim that our melody is flat and without any tuneful character, and all neutral Nations unanimously confirm their judgment on this point; for our part, we accuse theirs of being bizarre and baroque' (Rousseau 1998: 10 [Letter on French Music']; Palisca 1989: 10, 17; and see 1989: 12–13). As noted above, the dichotomy of *baroque* and *honnête* in general directly derived from contemporaneous contemplation on the oratorical and conversational modes of art – and this is true of music particularly as well.

French music began to acquire a specifically conversational model about the middle of the eighteenth century, building on the long history of musical dialogue in madrigals, motets and other genres, on the rising importance of *caractère* in French music (Jane Stevens 1989), which provided the characters between whom musical dialogue could occur, and on the atmosphere of *salon*, *honnêteté* and conversation that pervaded France at the time. Chamber music in general began to rise in importance as the literal accompaniment to *salon* conversation, and soon French musicians (building upon Italian predecessors) began explicitly to emulate conversation in music – or at least to label their music as conversational for promotional purposes, whatever its actual qualities. As early as 1746, Louis-Gabriel Guillemain (1705–70) published *Six sonates en quatuor ou conversations galantes et amusantes entre une flûte traversière*; in 1764 the publisher Louis-Balthazar de La Chevardière (1730–1812) issued six string quartets by Joseph Haydn (1732–1809) as *Six Symphonies ou quatuors dialogués pour deux violons, alto et basses, composés par M. Haydn, maître de musqiue à Vienne* (Maniates 1969: 184 (notes 11–12)). The *style dialogué* ascribed to music the egalitarian and mutually supporting qualites of proper *honnête* conversations.

In this *style dialogué*, just as subject matter in conversation passed from person to person, among persons sharing equally in the conversation, so melodies and motifs passed from instrument to instrument, each instrument sharing equally in the work. As early as 1703, Sébastien de Brossard (1655–1730) described 'Dialogue' in his *Dictionaire de Musique* as a 'Composition with at least two voices, or two instruments which answer one another and which often come together at the end, making a trio with the B-C [basso continuo]'; musical reference works echoed this definition throughout the following century (Brossard 1703: [DAL' – DIMINUTIONE], translated in Keefe 2001: 26; 2001: 26–7). Antoine Reicha (1770–1836), putting eighteenth-century thought and practice into nineteenth-century words, gave perhaps the fullest description of the way to dialogue a melody in his *Treatise on Melody* (1814):

> Writing a melody in the form of a dialogue involves the distribution of the phrases, members, ideas, and periods among two or more voices or instruments, or even between an instrument and a voice. . . . There are only four ways to write a melody in the form of a dialogue: (1) by alternately performing entire periods, (2) by distributing the phrases, or members of periods, between the different voices which must perform the melody, (3) by creating a dialogue with the figures [*dessins*], that is, through small imitations, (4) by beginning a phrase in one voice, and concluding it in another. (Reicha 2000: 88; Vial 2008: 79)

The genre correlate of the *style dialogué* was the *quatuor concertant* that developed in Paris in the 1770s, the immediate predecessor of the string quartet. In France, at least 200 composers wrote more than 3,500 *quatuors concertants* between 1770 and 1800. Chamber setting, *style dialogué* and the *quatuor concertant* together introduced the conversational model into the heart of French music in the waning years of the *ancien régime*.[2]

Various other aspects of music shifted towards the conversational model. Both in France and in Germany, musical phrasing – punctuation – shifted towards the model of *honnête* speech, and towards conveying conversation properly. This conversational musical punctuation was (at least for Charles-Henri de Blainville (1711–69) in his 1767 *Histoire générale, critique et philologique de la musique*) an essential component of the *style dialogué*: 'En effet, tout chant en musique doit être raisonné, dialogué pour ainsi dire, phrasé, arrondi' (Blainville 1767: 157; Vial 2008: 43–56, 79, 81, 171–6, 195). Solos came to incorporate dialogic internal contrasts (Vial 2008: 81). The very way to hold an instrument was now modelled as natural, negligent, graceful – the artful artlessness of *sprezzatura* once more (Vial 2008: 69–70).

The shift towards the conversationally simple was accompanied by a shift towards making music more like speech itself – expressive of character rather than impersonally persuasive, emulative of speech, of dialogue, in the idiom of music – although, as musical ambitions increased, ever less crudely imitative of the spoken word. Johann Georg Sulzer (1720–79), following up on the earlier French focus on *caractère*, likewise emphasised the importance of character in music in his *General Theory of the Fine Arts* (1771–4): 'Every composition, whether it is vocal or instrumental, should possess a definite character and be able to arouse specific sentiments in the minds of listeners' (Sulzer 1995: 53–4).

This shift towards expression and dialogue was not at first necessarily in a conversational mode. Opera, as noted, only slowly shifted its emulation of expressive dialogue from an oratorical to a conversational mode. The madrigal, opera's immediate predecessor in vocal music, likewise was expressive without necessarily being conversational; consort music, although sometimes described in scholarly literature as conversational (Butler 1977: 63–4; Ledbetter 2002: 76), does not appear to have been conceived so in any tight sense. Contemporary conceptions of the fugue, for example, seem to have been more oratorical. Thomas Mace (1612/13–c. 1706) in *Musick's Monument* (1676) referred to the fugue as '*a subject Matter in Oratory, on which the Orator intends to Discourse*'; while Johann Mattheson in *Critica Musica* (1722) described the fugue as a 'freye Rede' (T. Mace 1676: 116; Mattheson 1964: I, 266; Butler 1977: 63–4).

Mattheson also referred to the fugue as a form of conversation, but his description of conversation was closer to the traditional description of a dispute – agonistic, martial, oratorical (Mattheson 1981: 637; Butler 1977: 64–5). Among eighteenth-century music theorists, Friedrich Wilhelm Marpurg (1718–95) and Luigi Antonio Sabbatini (1732–1809) likewise described the fugue in terms of dispute and combat (Marpurg 1753–4: I, 143; Sabbatini 1802: 1; Butler 1977: 65). Johann Nicolaus Forkel (1749–1818) reported that J. S. Bach arranged the parts of his fugues 'as if they were persons who conversed together like a select company'; but this conversational conception would appear to have played a minor role in the theorisation of the fugue (David, Mendel and Wolff 1998: 455; Butler 1977: 104 (note 60); Keefe 2001: 28–30).

Instrumental music, meanwhile, began its decisive rise in status, and towards autonomy from the word, in accompaniment with the shift in the conception of language towards one of sentiment and passion. This development, it is worth emphasising, was not a necessary consequence of music's conversationalisation: rather, conversational and purely instrumental music shared an affinity based upon the age's shift in emphasis towards the natural and the passionate. Yet this alignment of the two transformations was a feature of the age; music's conversationalisation and instrumentalisation went hand in hand, and their triumph was mutual.

So long as language had been conceived of as fundamentally rational, instrumental music had to remain inferior, as too nebulous to convey meaning more than vaguely – an imitation of language, where language was an imitation of nature, and hence a faint imitation of an imitation. Now, on the one hand, meaning came to be seen to inhere directly in music (and dance). So Batteux:

> Musical sounds and dance steps have meaning, just as words have meaning in poetry; expression in music and the dance then must have natural qualities similar to those of eloquence in speech. Eveything that will be said here therefore will apply equally to music, dance and eloquence. (Batteux 1981: 50)

At the same time, as language came to be conceived of as a passionate discourse – not least, again, in Batteux – where the music of language became its foundation, so instrumental music rose in status as a pure expression of the language of the heart, an unmediated imitation of nature (Batteux 1747: 262–4; translated in Hosler 1981: 63). But Batteux still wanted intelligibility; hence he was not quite a champion of pure instrumental music. Indeed, the French in general – if not universally – continued to shy away from granting full status to instrumental music, as lacking the fuller and more precise communicability of the word. It would fall to Batteux's German successors to develop and champion the idea of fully independent, autonomous instrumental music, whose conversation was entirely disjunct from the discourse of the word (Bonds 1991: 66–7; Hosler 1981, esp. 63–4; Keefe 2001: 13; Maniates 1969).

This last development followed the conversationalisation of music in Germany – and the conversational style of music came late to that nation. The first infiltration was muted and mixed, generally arriving as an import from France, where rhetoric had already begun to shift in a conversational direction. So Johann Mattheson's *Der vollkommene Capellmeister* (1739), although generally oratorical in its conception of rhetoric, included in his prescriptions some distinctly *honnête*, conversational notes. He praised familiarity, facility, clarity, simplicity, the imitation of nature, composition that provided a *je ne sais quoi*, and an artful artlessness, all with an eye to eliciting the audience's enjoyment and approval, for '[w]e cannot have pleasure in a thing in which we do not participate' (Mattheson 1981: 311–15, 324 {48–50, 55, 57, 59, 64, 101}). Carl Philipp Emanuel Bach's (1714–88) trio-sonata *Melancholicus und Sanguineus* (1749), subtitled 'a Conversation between a Cheerful Man and a Melancholy Man', then explicitly and thematically brought dialogue into German instrumental music. The dialogic conception of instrumental music became stronger thereafter in the German lands (Bonds 1991: 65; Finscher 1974: 285–6; Keefe 2001: 14–15). Sulzer's commentary on C. P. E. Bach in his *General Theory of the Fine Arts* (1771–4) turned the composer's practice into theory:

> The possibility of endowing sonatas with character and expression is shown in a number of easy and challenging harpsichord sonatas written by our Hamburg Bach. The majority of these are so eloquent that one almost believes to be hearing not a series of musical tones, but a comprehensible speech that moves and engages our imagination and emotions. . . . The sonatas of C. P. E. Bach for two concerted instruments accompanied by a bass are truly passionate conversations in tone. (Sulzer 1995: 104)

Johann Abraham Peter Schulz (1747–1800) wrote similarly in 'Trio' (1774), part of his contribution to Sulzer's *General Theory*, that 'The proper trio . . . contains three main parts which . . . maintain a dialogue in tones' (Schulz 1774: 1180, translated in Keefe 2001: 29).

This changing conception of music did not only affect Germany. In England, for a notable example, Charles Avison (1709–70) wrote in his 'Advertisement' for his *Six Sonatas for the Harpsichord* (1760) that

> This Kind of Music is not, indeed, calculated so much for public Entertainment, as for private Amusements. It is rather like a Conversation among Friends, where Few are of one Mind, and propose their mutual Sentiments, only to give Variety, and enliven their select Company. (Avison 1760: ['Advertisement'], cited in Finscher 1974: 286)

The culmination of the conversationalisation of music, however, was to take place in the eastern stretches of the German lands.

Austria was a somewhat startling site for such a climax, for it was only in the late eighteenth century that baroque Catholicism, and baroque music, began to recede in Austria, while baroque music had begun to be challenged in France a century before (Melton 2007: 92, 97–8; and see Maland 1970: 197–8). Likewise, *salons* only began to emerge in Vienna in the 1770s and 1780s. Yet if the *salon* and the conversational aesthetic came late to Austria, they had an immediate effect. Among the most notable of these first Viennese *salons* was that of Charlotte von Greiner, in whose *salon* Joseph Haydn (and Wolfgang Amadeus Mozart (1756–91) and Antonio Salieri (1750–1825)) regularly performed. Haydn, exposed to a blossoming conversational Viennese *salon* sociability, was inspired to incorporate into his string quartets the same egalitarian conversational quality characteristic of the *quatuors concertants* (Melton 2007: 103–7). The *salonnier* aspects of his music aroused immediate comment. William Jones (1726–1800) praised the conversationality of Haydn (and Luigi Boccherini (1743–1805)): their music differed 'from some pieces of *Handel*, as the Talk and the Laughter of the Tea-table (where, perhaps, neither Wit nor Invention are wanting) differs from the Oratory of the Bar and the Pulpit' (W. Jones 1784: 50). An anonymous writer for the *Flensburgsches Wochenblat*, on the other hand, was less taken by Haydn's conversationality: 'such things . . . are like an agreeable, entertaining conversation that one hears with relish, but without interest. They are more sleight-of-hand than nourishment for the heart' ('Ueber Musik' 1792, cited and translated in Morrow 1997: 12; Vial 2008: 82–3; Wheelock 1992: 90).

In this generation of Austrian music, symphonies, concertos, trios, sonatas and fantasias all came to be conceived of as disputes, dramatic or passionate conversations, and confrontational dialogues – and Mozart's 'Epistle' Sonatas are thought to have emulated that quasi-conversational genre, the letter. Yet it was above all the string quartet, as perfected in Austria by way of the intermediate *quatuor brillant* upon the model of the *quatuors concertants*, that was conceived of by both composers and auditors as a form of conversation among the instruments. So Giuseppe Carpani's (1751–1825) rendition of an unnamed friend's description of a work by Haydn:

> It seemed to him that he recognized in the first violin a man of spirit and affability, middle aged, well spoken, who was sustaining the major part of the discourse. . . . In the second violin he recognized a friend of the first who was seeking in every way to enhance him, . . . intent on sustaining the conversation more by agreeing with much of what he heard from the other than [by presenting] his own ideas. The bass was a solid man, learned and aphoristic . . . supporting the discourse of the first violin with laconic but secure maxims, and at times . . . [he] predicted what the principal speaker would say, and gave force and regulation to what was said. The viola, then, seemed to him a somewhat loquacious matron who did not really have much of importance to say, but all the same wanted to inject herself into the discussion; at times she seasoned the conversation with grace, and at other times with delightful chatterings that gave the others a chance to take a breath. In the end, she was more the friend of the bass than of the other interlocutors. (Carpani 1823: 101–2, translated in Wheelock 1992: 91–2)

The relationship between the players and the auditors was also supposed to be intimately conversational – and the ideal audience a distinctly *honnête* learned amateur.

This conversational conception indeed applied above all to those perfectors of the string quartet, Haydn and Mozart. Haydn in particular borrowed techniques from *opera buffa* that enhanced the conversational quality of the string quartet, and allowed for a direct address of the audience – and Wheelock suggests that he modelled his string quartets on the actual rhythm and wit of conversation. For the string quartet genre as a whole, the conversations may even be divided into different types: Parker identifies four such – the Lecture, the Polite Conversation, the Debate, and the Conversation.[3]

Mozart's *The Magic Flute* (1791) was likewise conversational in both structure and theme. Kerry writes that in *The Magic Flute* Mozart transmuted the German *Singspiel* into a profoundly conversational work:

> *The Magic Flute* not only featured conversations, it also associated a particular set of eighteenth-century values with speech acts. . . . After a lock is placed on Papageno's mouth [for lying], a homily is sung that extols universal harmony through verbal restraint. . . . The theme of discretion in conversation arises throughout the opera as Tamino is instructed to be discreet. (Kerry 2008: 69)

Keefe adds to this point a study of Mozart's use of musical dialogue in his operas, fused expertly with actual set pieces of dialogue (Keefe 2001: 101–46). The string quartet of Haydn and Mozart, perfectly instrumental and perfectly conversational, registered one triumph of conversational music – and so too did Mozart's reinvention of the opera in a conversational mode. Musical rhetoric's transformation from the mode of oratory to that of conversation may be measured in the distance travelled from Monteverdi's *Orfeo* to Mozart's *Magic Flute*.

Conversational Dance

Since dance had become an art subject to the strictures of rhetoric, it joined in the general shift of the arts towards the conversational mode. So Michel de Pure argued in *Idée des Spectacles Anciens et Nouveaux* (1668) the importance of the ideas of naturalness and nature in the ballet (De Pure 1668: 263, 237, 232, translated in J. Gibson 2008: 424–5; and see De Pure 1668: 250; Barros 2010: 40; Fairfax 2003: 70–8).[4] Claude-François Ménestrier likewise wrote in *Des Ballets anciens et modernes selon les regles du theatre* (1682) that

> Ballet expresses the movements that painting and sculpture can not express, and through such movements it expresses the nature of things and the inclinations of the soul . . . This imitation is made through the movements of the body, which are the interpreters of the passions, and of the inner feelings. (Ménestrier 1682: 41, translated in Barros 2010: 39)

As with music, this shift was reinforced by the reconception – strengthened by the influence classicising mime exerted on early-eighteenth-century ballet – of dance itself as able to convey and express character, of dance as a medium capable of expressing language as purely and as well as the voice (Nye 2011, esp. 38–61, 115–61). Dance capable of expressing character became, logically, dance capable of moving the sentiments, both of other characters and of the audience. Such dance also became capable of expressing dialogue, capable of narrative coherence. It became the material of choreography, the narrative of dance, in which is embedded all its character, dialogue, passion and drama (Nye 2008). As Colley Cibber (1671–1757) recollected in his autobiography,

> To give even dancing therefore some improvement, and to make it something more than motion without meaning, the fable of 'Mars and Venus' [*The Loves of Mars and Venus* (1717)] was formed into a connected

> presentation of dances in character, wherein the passions were so happily expressed, and the whole story so intelligibly told by a mute narration of gesture only. (Cibber 1826: 292–3)

Intensifying transformations to the ballet came in the early eighteenth century from choreographers such as John Weaver, Jean Baptiste De Hesse (1705–79) and Franz Hilverding (1710–68); the culminating innovations of choreographers such as Jean Georges Noverre (1727–1810) and Gasparo Angiolini (1731–1803), in collaboration above all with the composer Christoph Willibald Gluck, produced the mid-eighteenth-century *ballet d'action* – in effect, the modern ballet. In these mid-century works, dance, intimately integrated with music, amalgamated these new aspects into a medium whose character was intensely *honnête*. So Noverre in his *Lettres sur la danse, et sur les ballets* (1760) wrote of the *ballet d'action* in language redolent of the century's conversational aesthetics:

> Action, in the manner of the dance, is the art of transmitting our sentiments and passions to the souls of the spectators by means of the true expression of our movements, gestures, and countenance. Action, therefore, is nothing but pantomime. In the dancer everything must depict, everything must speak; each gesture, each attitude, each port de bras must have a different expression. True pantomime follows nature in all its nuances. If it strays from it for an instant, it becomes wearisome and revolting. (Noverre 1760: 262–3, translated in Giles 1981: 247; 1981: 246–7)

We may note also that the emerging *ballet d'action* gave far wider scope for women to dance, increasingly freed from the conventions of modesty (Fairfax 2003: 219–42); and that from the varied styles of eighteenth-century ballet emerged the idea of individual dancing style, character inhering in the dancer as well as to the character portrayed. The choreographer Gasparo Angiolini wrote in 1773 that

> I not only grant to each [dancer] the freedom to make their own the part that I have composed for him, I always create new dances so that each part is expressly made for those who are to execute them. . . . For the true ballet master, the difficulty consists in fully understanding the level of ability, the style, and the disposition of each dancer in order to be able to make use of and develop over time the merits that remain hidden for some reason. (Lombardi 1998: 84–5 ['Lettere a Monsieur Noverre sopra i balli pantomimi'], translated in Fairfax 2003: 253–4; 2003: 243–55)

The influence of conversational aesthetics on eighteenth-century ballet was deep and wide-ranging (and see Fairfax 2003; Guest 1996).

Conversational Poetics

The scepticism of Montaigne had helped to destroy traditional rhetorical poetics – but Montaigne rather wished to remould rhetoric than to reject it. He criticised rhetoric for its decay into unpersuasive and emptily formal flattery – 'I want my voice not only to reach my listener, but perhaps to strike him and pierce him' (Montaigne 2003: 1016 ['Of experience']) – but his aims remained, *au fond*, persuasive: 'How many times, irritated by some action that civility and reason kept me from reproving openly, have I disgorged it here, not without ideas of instructing the public!' (Montaigne 2003: 613 ['Of giving the lie']). When Montaigne spoke of his distrust of medicine, his significant turn of phrase was that 'I have taken the trouble to plead this cause, which I understand rather poorly, to support a little and strengthen the natural aversion to drugs and to the practice of medicine' (Montaigne 2003: 724–5 ['Of the resemblance of children to fathers']). And for all his interest in a sincere presentation of himself, he was not – obviously! – artless in his self-description. 'Even so one must spruce up, even so one must present oneself in an orderly arrangement, if one would go out in public' (Montaigne 2003: 331 ['Of practice']). Montaigne had abandoned not the goal of persuasion, merely the existing means.

In the transformed poetics of the late Renaissance, rhetoric and *ethos* survived transformed. As noted above, fifteenth- and sixteenth-century thought in fields from politics to aesthetics had slowly shifted in emphasis from the rhetorical values of prudence, decorum and character conceived of as public behaviour to sincerity and character conceived as private essence (L. Agnew 1998: 99; Brinton 1983: 174; Kahn 1985: 35; J. Martin 1997). In his *Ciceronianus* (1528), unprecedentedly, Erasmus transformed the persuasive authority of *ethos* into a function of the truthfully expressed self: 'If you wish to express Cicero exactly, you cannot express yourself. If you do not express yourself, your speech will be a false mirror' (Erasmus 1908: 78; Cave 1979: 42–3; and see Struever 1970: 144–63). So Montaigne (apparently) prized sincerity far above any rhetorical value: 'I have an open way that easily insinuates itself and gains credit on first acquaintance. Pure naturalness and truth, in whatever age, still find their time and their place' (Montaigne 2003: 727–8 ['Of the useful and the honorable']). Indeed, he avowed a low opinion of the effectiveness of rhetoric, partly because of its formulaic misuse:

> There never was so abject and servile a prostitution of complimentary addresses: life, soul, devotion, adoration, serf, slave, all those words have such vulgar currency that when letter writers want to convey a more sincere and respectful feeling, they have no way left to express it. (Montaigne 2003: 225 ['A consideration upon Cicero']; Struever 1989: 245–6)

Rhetoric was generally Montaigne's image of useless ornament: 'Ask a Spartan if he would rather be a good rhetorician than a good soldier' (Montaigne 2003: 723 ['Of the resemblance of children to fathers']).

Yet Montaigne's sincerity was itself a rhetoric, albeit one much transformed. His praise of sincerity is a remarkably rhetorical phrase, in which sincerity is both exordial in function and subject to the strictures of decorum. Traditional rhetoric could no longer persuade – and scepticism limited the ability of any rhetoric to persuade – but the new rhetoric of sincerity was not ineffective in persuasion. Indeed, the rhetoric of sincerity was *ethos* by another name – the presentation of the inner, private character rather than that of the outer, public character, but *ethos* all the same.

Scepticism and sincerity transferred this presentation of *ethos* from the prologue to the narrative of the text. If we return to Montaigne's attempt to persuade against the use of drugs, a fuller quotation provides enlightening detail:

> I have taken the trouble to plead this cause, which I understand rather poorly, to support a little and strengthen the natural aversion to drugs and to the practice of medicine which I have derived from my ancestors, so that it should not be merely a stupid and thoughtless inclination and should have a little more form; and also so that those who see me so firm against the exhortations and menaces that are made to me when my sickness afflicts me may not think that I am acting out of plain stubbornness; or in case there should be anyone so unpleasant as to judge that I am spurred by vainglory. (Montaigne 2003: 724–5 ['Of the resemblance of children to fathers'])

Montaigne argued for his beliefs by presenting his entire character, the entire background of his beliefs, mixed inextricably with his arguments. He did not insist that he possessed unanswerable logic, or unquestionably superior character. He argued only that his character guaranteed that his beliefs were not stupid, thoughtless or vainglorious. He was not even sure that his method would persuade, in a world attuned more to the form of rhetoric than its essence: 'Is it reasonable too that I should set forth to the world, where fashioning and art have so much credit and authority, some crude and simple products of nature, and of a very feeble nature at that?' (Montaigne 2003: 741 ['Of repentance']). But then, tentativeness was the touchstone of his entire project: 'If my mind could gain a firm footing, I would not make essays, I would make decisions; but it is always in apprenticeship and on trial' (Montaigne 2003: 740 ['Of repentance']). The thorough self-presentation of his inner character within the narrative was a thorough presentation of *ethos*, as persuasive as scepticism allowed: 'Authors communicate with the people by some special extrinsic mark; I am the first to do so by my entire being, as Michel de Montaigne, not as a grammarian or a poet or a jurist' (Montaigne 2003: 741 ['Of repentance']; and see Cave 1979: 273; Struever 1989: 244, 247–8). As *ethos* slipped away from the prologue, Montaigne even sought the audience's goodwill in a remarkably exordial section of the narrative:

> There is no place where the faults of workmanship are so apparent as in material which has nothing in itself to recommend it. Do not blame me, reader, for those that slip in here through the caprice or inadvertency of others: each hand, each workman, contributes his own. (Montaigne 2003: 895 ['Of vanity'])

Montaigne had pioneered a new form of *ethos*, avowedly anti-rhetorical yet still intent on persuasion.

Ethos could slip fairly easily from prologue to narrative where author and subject were identical, but what if the subject were a fictitious character? The transfer of *ethos* within prose fiction followed Montaigne's example, but by a more complicated path. First, *auctoritas*, authorial *ethos*, lost its central role with the emergence of an autonomous narrator detached from and independent of authorial support. This was a pioneering development:

> It is not until the last decade of the sixteenth century that clearcut, unmistakable narrators first make their appearance in English prose works. Before 1590, all prose narratives originally written in English could still be analyzed using the categories provided by Plato in the *Republic*. Even a work as sophisticated as More's *Utopia* (1516) still falls within the purview of these categories . . . Raphael Hythloday, the speaker of Book Two, may appear at first to be a narrator, but he is in fact only a character who has been introduced into the narrative by the main speaker or author. (Rothschild 1990: 24)

In English prose fiction, the pioneering of the autonomous narrator took place in Elizabethan cony-catching pamphlets and rogue literature. Cony-catching pamphlets engaged in a clear progression from Thomas Harman, whose *A Caveat for Common Cursitors* (1566) contained 'an undifferentiated narrative and authorial voice . . . [and was unwilling] to acknowledge any overt contradiction between the implications of his narrative for himself (the author who is betraying many years of confidences) and the narrator who is educating the Elizabethan populace', to Robert Greene (1558–92), whose works in the early 1590s displayed a complete disjunction between narrator and author. Greene's 'Conversion of an English Courtezan', in his *A Disputation between a He Conny-catcher and a She Conny-catcher* (1592), was apparently the earliest work of English prose to deploy a thoroughly detached narrator (Relihan 1994: 61–76; Rothschild 1990: 25). Nashe, *quondam* anti-Martinist pamphleteer, published *The Unfortunate Traveler* (1594), a work of roguery that was 'the first extended narrative in English to employ a narrator' (Rothschild 1990: 26–7). By the early eighteenth century Daniel Defoe (1660–1731) could write in *Roxana* (1724) that 'it is not always necessary that the names of persons should be discovered', and the preface of *Moll Flanders* (1722) blandly asserted the unimportance of anonymity:

> The author is here supposed to be writing her own history, and in the very beginning of her account she gives the reason why she thinks fit to conceal her true name, after which there is no occasion to say any more about that. (Defoe 1881c: vi–vii; 1950: v)

The Marprelate Tracts registered the moment when the narrator could be conceived of but could not yet persuade: a few short years later, the narrator of English prose fiction began to sustain himself without an author (but see Rothschild 1990: 27–31).

Second, the prose fiction prologue further decayed as a site of persuasive authority. This was a slow and uneven process: Samuel Richardson (1689–1761) and Henry Fielding (1707–54) wrote quite traditional prefaces for their works. Defoe's preface to *Colonel Jack* (1722), however, scoffed at the whole idea of prologues, characterising them generally as customary rather than useful and calling itself (in what was not merely a trope of modesty) virtually superfluous:

> *It is so customary to write Prefaces to All Books of this Kind to introduce them with the more Advantage into the World, that I cannot omit it, tho' on that Account, 'tis thought, this Work needs a Preface less than any that ever went before it.* (Defoe 1965: 1)

Eliza Haywood (c. 1693–1756) wrote in the preface of *The Injur'd Husband* (1723) that 'Troubling the Reader with any thing of this Kind, is generally so little to the Purpose, that I have often thought the Authors made Use of such Introductions more to swell the Bulk of their Book, than any other Reason' (Haywood 1723: [v] ['Preface']; Bartolomeo 1994: 33). By 1766 Henry Brooke (1703–83) had written in the preface of *The Fool of Quality* that 'I hate prefaces. I never read them, and why should I write them?' (Henry Brooke 1767: I, xxix; Bartolomeo 1994: 89; and see Marivaux 1714: viii–xiii, translated in Russo 2007: 74–5).[5]

The narrative came to replace the prologue as the site of persuasive authority. In *The Compleat Mendicant* (1699) Defoe recognised that 'the first great objection against him [the mendicant, the narrative] will be, that he's an absolute stranger, and comes into the World without the assistance of a Name, Place, or Recommendation; and so consequently may be an Imposter' (Defoe 1699: sig. A7r). In response, Defoe shifted authority into the narrative:

> the whole Narrative is exactly of a piece, all regular, natural and familiar, and withal confirm'd by such a multitude of concuring Circumstances, that in my sence he must be a Person that nothing will go down with, but flat Demonstrations that will object against it.(Defoe 1699: sig. A8r–v)

In the preface to *Memoirs of a Cavalier* (1720), having constructed a spurious web of authority for its historicity, Defoe concluded that

> it is enough, that we have the authorities above to recommend this part to us that is now published; the relation, we are persuaded, will recommend itself, and nothing more can be needful, because nothing more can invite than the story itself, which, when the reader enters into, he will find it very hard to get out of, until he has gone through it. (Defoe 1881b: xvi)

In *Roxana* (1724) Defoe wrote that 'The history of this beautiful lady is to speak for itself' (Defoe 1881c: vi).

Third, the *ethos* of a character came to address the reader independent of the authorial voice. Characters had traditionally displayed a variety of *ethos*: they used *ethos* in their (oratorical) addresses to other characters, and they displayed their *ethos* to the audience. Aristotle wrote in the *Poetics* that 'character [*ethos*] is the kind of thing which discloses the nature of a choice; for this reason speeches in which there is nothing at all which the speaker chooses or avoids do not possess character' (Aristotle 1996: 12 [6]). But this conception of *ethos*, still strong in Renaissance poetics, differed from authorial *ethos*; the display of *ethos* in a character was not to gain an audience's goodwill but to provide an object for emulation. *Ethopoeia*, the drawing of character, itself 'most likely modeled on the techniques of the [Greek] poets', remained in essence a subset of epideictic rhetoric (Aristotle 2004: 129–30, 151 [3.7.1408a, 3.16.1417a]; J. May 1988: 3). A character was praised for his virtues and blamed for his vices so as to stimulate a passion in the audience (*pathos*) to emulate or to avoid emulation of that character (Vickers 1983: 510–11). Minturno wrote in *De poeta* that

> emulation spurs good men to virtue that they may attain the praise and glory which they seek . . . whoever hears it [praise of virtue] is excited to emulate him who merits so much praise, since both men believe that praise is the highest reward of virtue . . . [lyric] stimulates men to honorable and excellent acts. (Minturno 1559: 222, 381–2, translated in Hardison 1962: 37–8, 95–6; Vickers 1983: 511)

Philip Sidney's (1554–86) *An Apology for Poetry* (1595) likewise strove to inculcate virtue in the reader:

> Who readeth Aeneas carrying old Anchises on his back, that wisheth not it were his fortune to perform so excellent an act? . . . as virtue is the most excellent resting place for all worldly learning to make his end of, so Poetry, being the most familiar to teach it, and most princely to move towards it, in the most excellent work is the most excellent workman. (Sidney 2002: 95–6; Delehanty 2013: 13)

Tommaso Campanella (1568–1639) wrote in *Rationalis philosophiae pars quarta* (1638) that

> Since some outstanding men were worthy of praise on account of excellent benefits to the people and virtue shown at death or in some outstanding deed – as in the case of saints and heroes – therefore hymns and odes were invented and the songs which we sing to the lyre. (Campanella 1638: 161, translated in Hardison 1962: 95)

The rules of poetry in seventeenth-century France likewise aimed at the continuing goal of moving the passions towards virtue; so Jean Racine (1639–99) wrote in his Preface to *Phaedra* (1677) that

> no play of mine so celebrates virtue as this one does. The least faults are here severely punished. The mere thought of crime is seen with as much horror as the crime itself. Weaknesses begot by love are treated

> here as real weaknesses; the passions are here represented only to show all the disorder which they bring about; and vice is everywhere painted in colors which make one know and hate its deformity. To do thus is the proper end which every man who writes for the public should propose to himself; and this is what, above all, the earliest tragic poets had in view. Their theatre was a school in which virtue was taught no less well than in the schools of the philosophers. Therefore Aristotle consented to establish rules for the dramatic poem; and Socrates, the wisest of philosophers, deigned to have a hand in the writing of Euripides' tragedies. (Racine 1987: 5 [Preface]; Delehanty 2013: 13–15; Lyons 1999: 122–39)

In a late, ironic rendition of the ambition to forward virtue, Defoe wrote in the preface of *Dickory Cronke* (1719) that

> Here is a dumb philosopher introduced to a wicked and degenerate generation, as a proper emblem of virtue and morality; and if the world could be persuaded to look upon him with candour and impartiality, and then to copy after him, the editor has gained his end, and would think himself sufficiently recompensed for his present trouble. (Defoe 1881a: 468)

The author displayed his creations' characters; they did not speak to the audience themselves.

But the fading of the author's *ethos* also reduced his ability to speak on his characters' behalf. As a result, this traditional conception of the function of a character's *ethos* shifted radically in the eighteenth century. In her preface to *The Secret History of Queen Zarah* (1705)[6] Mary de la Rivière Manley (1663–1724) retained the Aristotelian goal of inducing identification and catharsis in an audience but dislocated the explicit epideictic frame of characterisation (Manley 1705: sig. a3v; and see Fénelon 1722: 128). The traditional goal of characterisation, the instruction of virtue, was still sought, but the means of instruction had changed:

> To make proper judgments, the reader requires no evaluative statement imbued with the authority of the novelist's own voice. Instead, properly discriminated and detailed descriptions will lead the reader to pity the virtuous characters (and to admire virtue) while despising the vicious ones (and, hence, vice). (Bartolomeo 1994: 27)

The character no longer merely displayed his *ethos* to the spectators for their emulation but, unprecedentedly, addressed it directly to the reader, as the author had once done (Ong 1975: 14). This address acknowledged the essential mutual unknownness of speaker and audience but sought thereby to create (as Warner puts it) an intimate relationship among strangers from an address of public speech both personal and impersonal (Warner 2002: 74–87). The invisible figure of Mr Spectator, unknown to his readers but able to address them with knowing familiarity, was an icon of this rhetoric (Bond 1965: I, 1–6 [No. 1, 1 March 1711]). Disembodied character would make its own argument to the reader.

Montaigne's sincere presentation of inner character within the narrative now found its counterpart in the poetics of a prose fiction in which *auctoritas* had decayed, authority had shifted from the prologue to the narrative, and characters directly addressed readers: the author now persuaded by revealing to the reader the interiority of his characters in the narrative. Jane Austen's (1775–1817) *Persuasion* (1818) embodied, not least in its metonymic title, the culmination of this transformation (Swanson 1981; and see Rigberg 1999: 193–235). To convey Austen's *ethos*, the novel possessed a preface – but only because Austen's untimely death led her brother Henry (1771–1850) to write a posthumous biographical sketch (Austen 2013: 202–7). The emotional weight of the novel depended on revelations of interior *ethos*; for example, Wentworth's perceived value by the reader as Anne Elliot's beloved depended upon his disclosing to the audience his quiet sympathy towards Mrs Musgrove when she speaks of her dead son, rather than on his show of flash and his gab (Austen 2013: 49 [8]; Tave 1973: 261). The general judgement of the novel balanced among the condemnation of the Elliots and (to an extent) Lady Russell, possessed of public manners but not the inner feelings that allow for true propriety; the mild disapproval of the Musgroves, possessed of inner feelings without public manners; and esteem for the navy group, the Crofts and Captain Harville, who embodied most harmoniously (if not perfectly) public manners and inner feelings (Nardin 1973: 133–8). Most important, Austen made Anne address her *ethos* as much to the reader as to any other character:

> How eloquent could Anne Elliot have been, – how eloquent, at least, were her wishes on the side of early warm attachment, and a cheerful confidence in futurity, against that over-anxious caution which seems to insult exertion and distrust Providence! – She had been forced into prudence in her youth, she learned romance as she grew older – the natural sequel of an unnatural beginning. (Austen 2013: 22–3 [4])

The power of the novel depended on the contrast between the silent decorum Anne displayed towards the other characters and the presentation of her inner self to the reader (Swanson 1981; Tave 1973: 256, 258–9). Where in traditional rhetorical poetics the author had persuaded by presenting his *ethos* to his audience, Austen persuaded by addressing Anne's inner character to the unknown reader. Where once the author's character persuaded, now her characters would persuade. The persuasive address of a sincerely self-revealing character to an unknown audience of readers now characterised the Enlightenment's literary discourse (cf. Booth 1961).

Conclusion

Several intertwining narratives govern this millennial history of the fine arts and poetics. One narrative concerns the steady application of rhetoric to these various genres: the offhand strictures of Quintilian, the medieval endurance of scattered fragments of rhetorical thought, the Renaissance reconception of these several genres as coherent modes of rhetoric, and the explicit theorisation of these several genres in rhetorical terms (as early as Alberti for art, as late as Burmeister for music). Another narrative touches upon the conversationalisation of these various genres – the inexorable application of conversational aesthetics to every branch of the *beaux arts* and *belles lettres*, as registered in emphases on naturalness, the imitation of nature, *sprezzatura*, the communication of inner character, and a reconception of communication from a foundation on reason to a foundation on passion or sentiment. A third narrative concerns the slow dwindling of rhetoric as an explicit frame, while at the same time a universalisation of the rhetorical framework preserves rhetoric in the guise of such concepts as taste and aesthetics. A fourth narrative concerns the further universalisation as rhetoric is dislocated from explicit reference to and reliance on the word, and reconceived as applying with equal validity to art and architecture (from the *quattrocento*), music and dance (not fully until the Enlightenment). The Enlightenment culmination of these several narratives produced a rhetoric of the fine arts and poetics that had a theoretical knowledge of its practices, was conversational in its structure and its subject matter, had sublimated into conceptions of taste and aesthetics, and had universalised itself from the narrower realm of words to apply to picture, building, landscape, music and dance. Conversation was always meant to inspire new conversations; here the very genre of verbal conversation had inspired conversations in new modes, granted the liberty to continue independent of the word. The universality of conversation in the Enlightenment may be measured precisely by the fact that it had come to be conducted in a daub of paint, an antiphony between violin and viola, an expressive fall of the hand.

These modes had now become autonomous conversations – but they remained united by conversational taste, by conversational aesthetics, by universal faculties of the mind. Rhetoric, in the form of taste and aesthetics, had re-emerged as a subject of philosophy, among whose central concerns had always been the mind and its faculties. Rhetorical inquiry, indeed, would be reformulated in the Enlightenment as philosophical inquiry, the vocabulary of rhetoric translated into the vocabulary of philosophy, and the conversational mode in particular would generate a philosophy of conversation. The apparent dichotomy of philosophy and rhetoric disguised a large overlap between the two, fixed not least upon the hinge of conversation.

Notes

1. For the conversational aesthetic of eighteenth-century English garden design, see also Batey 2005; J. Hunt and Willis 1988: 268–72, 289–97, 301–7, 351–7; Williamson 1995: 48–50, 58–9, 65–75, 111–13.
2. For the previous two paragraphs, see Hanning 1989; Keefe 2001: 15, 27; Maniates 1969: 132; Parker 2002: 49–51; Vial 2008: 78–89.
3. For the previous two paragraphs, see Bonds 1991: 64–6; Keefe 2001: 10, 15, 18–21, 45–100, 146–85; Parker 2002: 52-278; Vial 2008: 81–3, 169–70, 175–6; Wheelock 1992: 90–4; and see Keefe 2001: 24–41.
4. I have cited De Pure above describing dance as oratorical. I take him to represent a transitional moment, where dance was beginning to shift from an oratorical to a conversational mode.
5. For eighteenth-century French literary explorations of character and dialogue that work out the implications of conversational aesthetics, see Russo 2007.
6. Manley translated and plagiarised Bellegarde's *Lettres curieuses de littérature et de morale* (1702), itself a paraphrase of a section of the Sieur du Plaisir's *Sentimens sur les lettres et sur l'histoire* (1683). Bellegarde 1702: 79–104; Bartolomeo 1994: 23; J. Sutton 1984.

Chapter 4

The Philosophy of Conversation

Introduction

The universalisation of rhetoric (especially the conversational mode), the transformation of rhetoric and conversation into attributes of natural law and/or a faculty of the mind, and their extension into the realms of aesthetics and taste led to an interpenetration of rhetoric, conversation and philosophy. Seventeenth- and eighteenth-century philosophers – especially eighteenth-century philosophers in Britain – now began to translate rhetorical and conversational concepts into the vocabulary of philosophy. Rhetoric and conversation thus re-emerged within the genre of philosophy, rhetoric's sociological framework rearticulated in the languages of epistemology, morals and aesthetics.[1]

This incorporation of rhetoric and conversation into philosophy was less startling to contemporaries than it is to modern scholars. The retrospective creation of a history of philosophy around a putative mainstream of (say) Hobbes, Locke, Descartes, Baruch Spinoza (1632–77) and Kant tended to shear rhetoric out of the picture, to make it an other to be rejected by proper philosophers. The rhetorical background and concerns of the Earl of Shaftesbury (1671–1713), Hume and Smith – and the anxious ambivalence regarding rhetoric of the so-called philosophical mainstream – were largely forgotten, only to be recuperated in a serious fashion in the last few generations. To trace rhetoric and conversation in the philosophy of the Enlightenment is in many ways simply to draw out the broad intellectual context that was obscured for too much of the nineteenth and twentieth centuries (Rée 1978: 31–2; and see Tuck 1987).

That said, the rhetorical and conversational strains of Enlightenment philosophy were emphatically not the whole of that century's philosophy – or identical to one another. Kant can be no more than lightly rhetoricised; Hume is a far more rhetorical philosopher, and his relative acceptance of rhetoric is a useful category by which to distinguish the two. Contrariwise, Giambattista Vico's (1668–1744) rhetorical philosophy (Grassi 1990; Marshall 2010; J. Schaeffer 1990) is not greatly amenable to the conversational strains that characterised Shaftesbury: the difference between the two is the old difference between oratory and conversation, rendered into philosophy. This chapter focuses upon the conversational tradition in particular, not the whole of Enlightenment philosophy. I take for granted, and leave largely undescribed, the rival philosophical traditions to the conversational *via media*.

It is worth underscoring that this chapter provides an alternative to Habermas' lineage of philosophers leading to Kant, whose thought he takes both to characterise the age and to make transhistorically true arguments. We may recollect that Habermas' conception of the early modern public sphere derived in good part from a Kantian epistemology, and the corollary Kantian theory of communication. In *Structural Transformation*, Habermas made extended reference to Kant as the centrepiece of his crucial chapter 'The Bourgeois Public Sphere: Idea and Ideology', and the following quotation from Kant, selectively cited by Habermas, may be taken as the inspiration of Habermas' public sphere theory:

> Persuasion is a mere illusion; for the judgment's basis, which lies in the subject, is regarded as objective. Hence such a judgment also has only private validity, and the assent cannot be communicated. Truth, however, rests on agreement with the object; consequently, in regard to the object the judgments of every understanding must be in agreement (consentientia uni tertio, consentiunt inter se). Thus, whether assent is conviction or mere persuasion, its touchstone externally is the possibility of communicating assent and of finding it to be valid for every human being's reason. For then there is at least a presumption that the agreement of all the judgments, despite the difference among the subjects, will rest on the common basis, viz., the object, and that hence the judgments will all agree with the object and will thereby prove the truth of the [joint] judgment. (Kant 1996: 748 [A820–1; B848–9]; Habermas 1991: 108)

For Kant, true knowledge depended on reason, and true communication on this true knowledge underpinned by reason – where 'true' is also a rough synonym for 'normative, moral ideal'. Habermas associated this Kantian epistemology and theory of communication with the practice of the early modern public sphere; his own more general theory of communicative rationality also derived from this Kantianism – albeit with a swerve away from Kant's transcendentalism (Habermas 1979: 42–6; 1998: 240; Bernstein 1983: 194).

We may also recollect at this point that in the Kantian passage cited above, Habermas drew upon one of the passages where Kant's hostility to rhetoric was clearest: 'Persuasion is a mere illusion.' Kant expressed this hostility even more explicitly in his *Critique of Judgment* (1790), where he savaged rhetoric at length as unserious, ornamental, deceptive, insidious and essentially incompatible with the autonomy of human reason (Kant 1952: 184–5, 192–3 [II.1.51, 53: 321, 327]; Dostal 1980: 225; but see Gehrke 2002; Stroud 2005; 2006).

This chapter partly consists of a rereading of Enlightenment philosophy, by way of rehabilitating rhetoric, and demonstrating that Kant's judgement of rhetoric was neither characteristic of the age nor (I would submit) entirely just. The chapter also consists of supplying a conversational tradition that can fulfil a parallel historical-philosophical function to Habermas' sketched pre-Kantian lineage – not to supplant that lineage, but to demonstrate the existence of a robust alternative. The argument here combines the historical and the philosophical, as does my Habermasian model.

So in this chapter I will first describe the challenges to rhetoric in the philosophical tradition, which form the background for Habermas' conception of philosophy shorn of rhetoric. I will then narrate how rhetoric in general survived in Enlightenment philosophy, describe the specifically conversational aspects of Enlightenment philosophy, focus upon those private, inner conversations that established the self and conscience as capable of making autonomous moral judgements, and finish with a discussion of the creation of a standard of taste, of judgement, within the strictures of conversational philosophy. This last provides the fundamental basis for conversational philosophy as a whole, then and now, and thus provides the culmination of this chapter.

The Philosophical Challenge to Rhetoric

As the European rhetorical tradition received its classical formulation from Aristotle's *Rhetoric*, that tradition therefore also derived its epistemological underpinnings from Aristotle. Aristotle believed that human knowledge depended in part upon *phantasia*, imagination, the reception and retention of sensory images, and in part upon *nous*, direct, rational intuition of the world, and in particular of universals and forms. Sense and reason were not mutually exclusive, but moved in natural complement: the animal part of men was limited to sense, the rational part of man transcended those limits, and man as rational animal synthesised both modes of knowledge (Aristotle 1984: I, 685–7 [*De anima* 3.7–8]; J. Randall: 1960: 94–7). Language, in turn, represented man's knowledge: 'Words spoken are symbols or signs of affections or impressions of the soul; written words are the signs of words spoken' (Aristotle 1962: 115 [1]). Rhetoric, the art of persuasion, aimed at the skilful communication of both modes of knowledge from one man to another, so as to instil belief. Rhetoric's concern with *logos* communicated reason; the passions, the product of the senses, were communicated by *pathos*. The concern with *ethos*, character, derived from the limitations of knowledge derived from sensation: sensations were not universally perceived, and therefore not all knowledge could be acquired directly. Since reason could not replace sensation, knowledge depended upon the testimony of others – hence, the reliance on the *ethos* of the testifiers.

Aristotle was not the sole philosophical influence on the rhetorical tradition: Quintilian, for one, incorporated large portions of Platonism into his conception of the *vir bonus dicendi peritus* (Quintilian 1920–2: IV, 355–73 [12.1.1–32]; Brinton 1983: 167–84). But as the practice of rhetoric in the West generally followed Aristotle's precepts (though often they came with (Cicero's) Latin garb and attribution), so rhetoric's assumed epistemology and philosophy of language remained generally Aristotelian, and remarkably unaffected by the innovations of classical, medieval and early Renaissance philosophy. Indeed, the reintroduction of Aristotelian philosophy from c. 1200 onwards strengthened the Aristotelian epistemological underpinnings of rhetoric (and see Nelson 1933: 120). As late as the sixteenth century, the philosophy of rhetoric remained recognisably in the Aristotelian mould.

The sixteenth and seventeenth centuries, however, saw unprecedented challenges to the philosophical bases of rhetoric. In the sixteenth-century, Petrus Ramus (1515–72) proselytised an autonomous heuristics, wherein 'the arrangment of various things [is] brought down from universal and general principles to the underlying singular parts' (Ramus 1546: 83, cited and translated in Ong 2004: 245). In Garver's summary analysis, 'universal logical method . . . [provided] a substitute for knowledge of any particular subject' (Garver 1987: 14; and see Ong 2004). The implications for rhetoric were profound, for Ramus (and Omer Talon (c. 1510–62)) eviscerated rhetoric by reassigning the functions of invention, disposition (arrangement) and memory from rhetoric to logic (Talon 1577: 22; Howell 1961:

148–9). In so doing, Ramus restricted reason to scientific knowledge (Ramus 1555: 3–4, translated in Howell 1961: 154). Where reason was no more than a matter of scientific proofs, rhetoric had no essential communicative role: language was to be organised by logic alone. The purpose of rhetoric, reduced to style and delivery,

> serve[s] no other purpose than to lead this vexatious and mulish auditor, who is postulated to us by this [i.e., the prudential] method; and . . . [has] been studied on no other account that that of the failings and perversities of this very one. (Ramus 1555: 134; translated in Howell 1961: 164)

Rhetoric, for Ramus, was strictly ornamental.

Ramus' own system of thought had a strictly limited influence: while it was very influential throughout much of Europe from the mid-sixteenth to the early seventeenth centuries, particularly (since Ramus turned Protestant and ended up a victim of the St Bartholomew's Day massacre) in the Reformed tradition, Ramism swiftly receded thereafter outside the Puritan backwater of New England (P. Miller 1961: 300–62). So far as rhetoric was concerned, Ramism's long-term influence lay not in establishing a viable philosophy to oppose to Aristotle's, but in publicising and strengthening the conception that scientific, rationalising philosophy could dispense with rhetoric as the essence of communication, and reduce it to the status of mere decoration.

In the seventeenth century, the next great challenge to rhetoric proceeded from Descartes' philosophy, focused upon the autonomy of theoretical reason, and therefore concerned centrally with inquiry rather than with communication (Descartes 2006; Garver 1987: 13; Howell 1961: 347). Although the Cartesian tradition did in important ways align with the conversational tradition (Arnauld and Nicole 1662: 298; Nicole 1677: I, 214, 218; H. Davidson 1965: 50, 79–82, 100; D. Randall 2018: 81–2), the concern with inquiry also led Cartesian thinkers to conceive of rhetoric as a crafty means to convey the one, logically discovered truth to auditors of limited or prejudiced understanding, and manipulate them into agreement with the truth without their awareness (France 1972: 40–67; Warnick 1993: 29). So Bernard Lamy argued in *La Rhétorique ou l'art de parler* (1675)

> that to perswade, we need but one Argument, if it be solid and strong, and that Eloquence consists in clearing of that, and making it perspicuous. All those feeble Arguments . . . deriv'd from Commonplaces, are like ill Weeds that choke the Corn. (Lamy 1676: third pagination, 106 [1.5]; Howell 1961: 381; see also Warnick 1993: 25)

Furthermore, Lamy wrote, with pronounced Cartesian accent, that

> when things are propos'd contrary to the interest or inclination of the Hearer, then is address most necessary: There is no way to insinuate with him but by ambages, and fetches so cunningly introduc'd, that he is not to perceive the truth to which we would perswade him, till he be throughly convinced, otherwise his ears will be shut, and the Orator reckon'd an Enemy. (Lamy 1676: second pagination, 117–18; Warnick 1993: 29; and see also Lamy 1676: first pagination, 138–9 [2.4.3]; Fénelon 1722: 68; Howell 1971: 511)

Since Descartes emphasised sensory stimulation as the source of cognition, Cartesian rhetoric emphasised verisimilitude, vivacity and clarity not least as ways to convey sensory information most effectively (Lamy 1676: third pagination, 7–8 [4.1.2]; Warnick 1993: 8–10, 31–2). All this, to repeat, in some ways contributed to the expanding conversational tradition of rhetoric – but Cartesian rhetoric, as Ramist rhetoric, also supported an understanding of language as subordinate to a narrowly defined reason, and rhetoric as essentially ornamental. Moreover, Descartes' epistemology, by its emphasis on the senses as a source of knowledge, directly challenged Aristotelian epistemology. Together Ramus and Descartes, and the rhetoricians who followed them, had presented a grave challenge to both Aristotelian epistemology and rhetoric.

But the toppling blow to the traditional formulations of Aristotelian rhetoric and epistemology came from Lockean empiricism. Locke argued that human knowledge of the particulars of the world and of ideas in the mind both derived exclusively from the senses: the source of knowledge was 'Our observation employ'd either about *external, sensible objects; or about the internal operations of our minds*' (Locke 1997: 109 [2.1.2]). His philosophy denied intuitive knowledge and thereby shattered the Aristotelian epistemology underlying traditional rhetoric. Language, moreover, although derived from an intention to represent sensible ideas, Locke took to have no necessary correspondence to anything outside of our minds: '*words in their primary or immediate signification, stand for nothing, but the ideas in the mind of him that uses them*' (Locke 1997: 364 [3.2.2]). Aristotle's intuitive knowledge had implied intuitive communication, itself the basis of rhetoric; Locke's decoupling of word and thing thus also directly upended rhetoric (Law 1993: 44–5). Ramus and Descartes had challenged Aristotelian rhetoric; Locke swept it away.

Unsurprisingly, Locke expressed a quite hostile attitude towards rhetoric. This hostility was not due to epistemological differences alone: Locke's preference for reason and logic as the guiding forces for language, in many ways akin to that of Ramus and Descartes, contributed heavily to his negative attitude:

> [A]ll the artificial and figurative application of words eloquence hath invented, are for nothing else but to insinuate wrong ideas, move the passions, and thereby mislead the judgment; and so indeed are perfect cheats: and therefore however laudable or allowable oratory may render them in harangues and popular addresses, they are certainly, in all discourses that pretend to inform or instruct, wholly to be avoided; and where truth and knowledge are concerned, cannot but be thought a great fault. (Locke 1997: 452 [3.10.34])

The post-Lockean empirical tradition inherited Locke's anti-rhetorical attitude. George Berkeley (1685–1753) preferred ideas naked of the 'dress and encumbrance of words which so much contribute to blind the judgment and divide the attention' (Berkeley 1996: 22). Hume on occasion expressed a restrained disapprobation of rhetoric: 'In all abstract reasonings, there is one point of view, which, if we can happily hit, we shall go farther towards illustrating the subject than by all the eloquence and copious expression in the world' (Hume 1996: IV, 90 [7.2] [*An Inquiry Concerning the Human Understanding*]). Kant himself, no matter how severe his critique of other aspects of empiricism, adopted empiricism's critique of rhetoric wholeheartedly. Habermas can scarcely be blamed for believing that he had no need to consider rhetoric in his conception of the public sphere; it had been disposed of roundly as far back as Locke.

The Rhetorical Recrudescence

But this brief sketch was not the entire story: rhetoric survived into the Enlightenment (Howell 1971, esp. 74–142; Struever 1985). The avowed hostility of Lockean empiricism to rhetoric disguised significant areas of alignment between the two intellectual traditions (and for rhetorical thought in Hobbes, see Kahn 1985: 152–81; and Skinner 1996). Locke and Aristotle shared a common emphasis on sense as a source of knowledge, and likewise their theories of language were by no means totally opposed. Rhetoric lurked, sublimated, in empirical thought, and the empirical philosophers were scarcely consistent in their condemnation of rhetoric. This rhetorical mode of empiricism led directly to the British New Rhetoric, the explicit reconceptualisation of rhetoric in terms of Lockean empiricism.

Locke's inheritance certainly included the anti-rhetorical tradition that led to Kant – but it also included the rhetorical tradition that led to George Campbell.

This lurking use of the rhetorical mode was present in Locke's own writings. Locke used that most rhetorical concept of 'persuasion' not only to refer to opinion and probable knowledge, the traditional domains of rhetoric, but also, notably in *A Letter Concerning Toleration* (1689), to strong (religious) belief itself: 'All the life and power of true religion consists in the inward and full persuasion of the mind; and faith is not faith without believing' (Locke 2003: 219). Since Locke had also previously defined knowledge as compellingly strong belief, his argumentation aligned with, and implicitly identified, knowledge itself as persuasion. Locke reinforced this identification by his recommendation that religious belief should be the subject of persuasion – of eloquence, argument and oratory.

> Oh that our ecclesiastical orators, of every sect, would apply themselves, with all the strength of argument that they are able, to the confounding of men's errors! . . . Any one may employ as many exhortations and arguments as he pleases, towards the promoting of another man's salvation. (Locke 2003: 228, 241–2; W. Walker 1994: 112–15)

Locke prescribed such persuasion as an uncoercive alternative to compulsion – but still acknowledged its efficacy.

Furthermore, Locke's account of the origin of language was an empiricist generalisation of the traditional account of the origin of trope and metaphor. To say that men 'were fain to borrow words from ordinary known ideas of sensation, by that means to make others the more easily to conceive those operations they experimented in themselves, which made no outward sensible appearances', was to restate Cicero's claim that

> the metaphorical employment of words was begun because of poverty . . . when something that can scarcely be conveyed by the proper term is expressed metaphorically, the meaning we desire to convey is made clear by the resemblance of the thing that we have expressed by the word that does not belong. (Locke 1997: 362 [3.1.5]; Cicero 1967: II, 123 [3.38.155–6]; W. Walker 1994: 115–18)

Finally, Locke's hostility to the figures of rhetoric was by no means unremitting. The '*ends of language*' itself were '*first, to make known* one man's thoughts or ideas to another. *Secondly*, to do it *with* as much ease and *quickness*, as is possible; and *thirdly*, thereby *to convey* the *knowledge* of things' (Locke 1997: 449 [3.10.23]). The second end, 'ease and quickness', opened the door to rhetoric. Subsequently, Locke provided a far more explicit justification of rhetoric. In his posthumously published *Of the Conduct of the Understanding* (1706), he granted that

> figured and metaphorical expressions do well to illustrate more abstruse and unfamiliar ideas which the mind is not yet thoroughly accustomed to; but then they must be made use of to illustrate ideas that we already have, not to paint to us those which we yet have not. Such borrowed and allusive ideas may follow real and solid truth, to set it off when found, but must by no means be set in its place and taken for it. (Locke 1966: 101 [32]; W. Walker 1994: 118)

In this passage, Locke closely delimited and subordinated rhetoric, while conceiving of it more as an aid to exposition than as a means to persuasion (Howell 1971: 501). Yet the shackles he placed on rhetoric here were ultimately of secondary importance. What mattered more was that Locke now had provided a role for, and legitimated, both the rhetorical function of language in general and specific elements of the rhetorical tradition in particular.

If rhetoric was to have a role, however, it would have to follow the strictures of Lockean epistemology and philosophy of language. Most relevant for rhetoric was Locke's conception that words, even if they only represented ideas in the mind, excited those ideas in the same manner as sensory impressions:

> *there comes by constant use*, to be such *a connexion between certain sounds, and the ideas they stand for*, that the names heard, almost as readily excite certain ideas, as if the objects themselves, which are apt to produce them, did actually affect the senses. (Locke 1997: 365 [3.2.6])

Words, therefore, had the power to affect the mind of an auditor, even if speaker and auditor shared no common understanding of their meaning (W. Walker 1994: 119). Furthermore, some such sensory knowledge – e.g., distinction of colour, shape and number – was compelling: 'This part of knowledge is irresistible, and like the bright Sunshine, forces itself immediately to be perceived, as soon as ever the mind turns its view that way; and leaves no room for hesitation, doubt, or examination' (Locke 1997: 472 [4.2.1]). In consequence, the compelling power of words depended upon the clear exposition of such compelling knowledge: to display 'the naked ideas on which the force of the argumentation depends, in their due order, in which position the mind taking a view of them, sees what connexion they have' (Locke 1997: 597 [4.17.4]). Such words could also deceive, since metaphor's relationship to idea remained loose (Locke 1997: 597 [4.17.4]). The rhetoric that aimed to trick the senses could not rely upon the senses, and hence was less compelling: deceptive rhetoric was weak rhetoric. But this was not an argument against the use of rhetoric or evocative language per se, but rather an argument for the use of language correctly tied to sense and ideas. Language should use right reason and perspicuity to express sense and ideas correctly: 'Perspicuity, consists in the using of proper terms for the ideas or thoughts, which he would have pass from his own mind into that of another man's' (Locke 1720: 234 ['Some Thoughts Concerning Reading and Study for a Gentleman']; Howell 1971: 500). Rhetorical power derived from the skilful communication of compelling sensory knowledge.

It is worth emphasising that here, as above, Locke provided a universalising, empirical rendition of aspects of classical rhetorical theory. *Enargeia* (vivid illustration, palpability) and *energeia* (liveliness, actuality) were well-established (and often conflated) parts of rhetorical theory, promoted by Aristotle, Cicero, Longinus and Quintilian.[2] The very philosophical vocabulary of empiricism – *force*, *liveliness*, *vivacity* – derived from classical rhetorical theory, notably paralleled in the work of neoclassical French rhetoricians such as César Chesneau, Sieur Dumarsais (1676–1756). Campbell's later reintegration of rhetoric and empiricism was made easier by the fact that many of empiricism's concepts were themselves rhetorical in origin (Dumarsais 1757: 9; Potkay 1994: 183–4). In the guise of vivacity and perspicuity, Locke had promoted specific rhetorical tropes to general attributes of language itself (W. Walker 1994: 121). Likewise, Locke's subordination of language to common use – common apprehension – preserved rhetoric's traditional concern with shaping speech to suit the nature of an audience.

> [Men] *must* also take care to *apply their words*, as near as may be, *to such ideas as common use has annexed them to*. . . . Men's intentions in speaking are, or at least should be, to be understood; which cannot be without frequent explanations, demands, and other the like incommodious interruptions, where men do not follow common use. (Locke 1997: 457 [3.11.11]; W. Walker 1994: 121–2)

'Common use' implied a sharp distinction between the traditional rhetorical conception of particular audiences and the Lockean conception of a universal audience (which Lockean conception, not incidentally, was a vital prerequisite for the idea of a public sphere). But the simple acknowledgement that language use should take into account the nature of the audience, whether general or particular, further aligned Locke's theory of language with that of rhetoric.

Locke's philosophy of language retained many of the communicative assumptions of rhetoric. Indeed, Locke's sustained, if minor-key, approbation of rhetoric provided the sanction for his own extensive use of metaphor and figural language to forward the persuasive purposes of his philosophical writings (Locke 1997: 58 [1.1.6]; W. Walker 1994: 125; Richetti 1983: 75–9). The later resurgence of rhetoric within the empirical tradition, therefore, was not a clumsy and retrospective attempt to splice two dissimilar intellectual traditions. Rather, it developed naturally from later philosophers' accurate perception that Locke had embedded rhetorical thought and practice in the wellspring of empirical thought.

Hume, as much as Locke, also resurrected large portions of rhetorical thought in his empirical philosophy. In the first place, the metaphors by which Hume conceived the operations of the human mind were drawn from the political world animated by oratorical rhetoric:

> I cannot compare the soul more properly to any thing than to a republic or commonwealth, in which the several members are united by the reciprocal ties of government and subordination, and give rise to other persons, who propagate the same republic in the incessant changes of its parts. (Hume 1996: I, 322–3 [*Treatise*, 1.4.6]; Potkay 1994: 185)

Furthermore, Hume's own philosophy also aligned with rhetoric in many particulars. Following Locke, he derived knowledge from sensory ideas; he therefore also conceived of rhetoric – eloquence, discourse – as aimed to promote the communication of these ideas. Sympathy was a handmaiden to such communication: 'Sympathy being the conversion of an idea into an impression, demands a greater force and vivacity in the idea than is requisite to comparison' (Hume 1996: II, 377 [*Treatise* 3.3.2]; see also Potkay 1994: 48). Indeed, vivacity in turn forwarded the persuasion that constituted belief:

> It is difficult for us to withhold our assent from what is painted out to us in all the colours of eloquence; and the vivacity produced by the fancy is in many cases greater than that which arises from custom and experience. (Hume 1996: I, 116 [*Treatise* 1.3.5], 160 [*Treatise* 1.3.10]; Potkay 1994: 182–3; Townsend 2001: 86–136)

Moreover, Hume also retained Locke's conception of a universal audience – now called a 'public' – and explicitly associated it with rhetoric. Indeed, Hume emphasised the essential universality of rhetoric (with implicit contrast to science), since rhetoric's excellence, uniquely among the arts, consisted essentially in the popular success of its appeal: 'eloquence; which, being merely calculated for the public, and for men of the world, cannot, with any pretence of reason, appeal from the people to more refined judges, but must submit to the public verdict without reserve or limitation' (Hume 1996: III, 115–16 ['Of Eloquence']).

Finally, Hume's attitude towards rhetoric was hardly one of universal condemnation: if on occasion he expressed nuanced disapprobation, he also on occasion expressed nuanced approval of 'modern eloquence; that is . . . good sense, delivered in proper expressions' (Hume 1996: III, 111 ['Of Eloquence']). In general, his attitude towards rhetoric was one of sober evaluation, and as much analytical as normative (e.g., Hume 1996: III, 104–18 ['Of Eloquence']). If he did not embrace rhetoric with open arms, neither did he conceive of his thought as essentially opposed to rhetoric's assumptions.

In much of this above consideration of rhetoric, Hume echoed Locke. Yet Hume's thought also differed significantly from Locke's, not least in the emphasis he placed on the passions, and on the positive moral valence he gave to them. Among the many effects of this emphasis was a particular impact upon Hume's approach to language and to rhetoric. Hume's rhetoric, far more than Locke's, was a rhetoric of the passions. Hume, as had Locke, took passions to be ideas: 'Every lively idea is agreeable, but especially that of a passion, because such an idea becomes a kind of passion, and gives a more sensible agitation to the mind than any other image or conception' (Hume 1996: II, 94 [*Treatise* 2.2.4]). In consequence, he believed that rhetoric should aim to excite the passions:

> Nothing is more capable of infusing any passion into the mind, than eloquence, by which objects are represented in their strongest and most lively colours. We may of ourselves acknowledge, that such an object is valuable, and such another odious; but till an orator excites the imagination, and gives force to these ideas, they may have but a feeble influence either on the will or the affections. (Hume 1996: II, 180 [*Treatise* 2.3.6])

Indeed, passion was central to Hume's philosophy and rhetoric. Reason had limited power to move men: 'Reason is, and ought only to be, the slave of the passions, and can never pretend to any other office than to serve and obey them' (Hume 1996: II, 166 [*Treatise* 2.3.3]).

Sympathy united different, particular groups but could not easily transcend the bounds of communal particularity; indeed, the very sympathetic process that transcended individuality at the same time reinforced the distinction of communities:

> The propensity to company and society is strong in all rational creatures; and the same disposition, which gives us this propensity, makes us enter deeply into each other's sentiments, and causes like passions and inclinations to run, as it were, by contagion, through the whole club or knot of companions. (Hume 1996, III, 222–3 ['Of National Characters']; Potkay 1994: 50)

What reason and sympathy could not do, passion did. Passion, *because it was universal*, was the necessary means by which any one human being could persuade any other (Hume 1996: II, 355 [*Treatise* 3.3.1]). Rhetoric was therefore truly universal not only because it appealed to public judgement but also precisely because it appealed to passion. Indeed, Hume's passionate eloquence appealed to, and sought to create, a public constituted at least as much by the concordance of hearts as by the common sense of reason:

> In general, it is certain, that wherever we go, whatever we reflect on or converse about, every thing still presents us with the view of human happiness or misery, and excites in our breast a sympathetic movement of pleasure or uneasiness. In our serious occupations, in our careless amusements, this principle still exerts its active energy. (Hume 1996: IV, 285 [*Enquiry Concerning the Principles of Morals*, 5.2]; Potkay 1994: 48)

Only rhetoric could properly move the passions, and only passion could assemble a universal public.

Humean philosophy directly inspired the British school of New Rhetoric: indeed, the exemplar of that school, George Campbell, clearly aimed to provide in his culminating synthesis, *The Philosophy of Rhetoric* (1776), a system of rhetoric based firmly on Lockean and Humean philosophy (Campbell 1963: ix–xxix; Bitzer 1969; but see Warnick 1993; cf. A. Smith 1985). Campbell's influential synthesis (Campbell 1963: ix; Kennedy 1999: 282, 285–6; and see Abbott 1998; Kennedy 1999: 285) was not merely a sublimation of rhetoric: where Locke grudgingly accepted the necessity of rhetorical thought, and Hume, by cool nuance, avoided a wholehearted embrace, Campbell, without apology, reiterated rhetoric's traditional format and claims:

> In speaking there is always some end proposed, or some effect which the speaker intends to produce on the hearer. The word *eloquence* in its greatest latitude denotes, 'That art or talent by which the discourse is adapted to its end'. (Campbell 1963: 1 [I.1]; see also Blair 2005: 264–5 [25])

His consideration of rhetoric, moreover, preserved classical rhetoric's sense of the specificity of speaker, auditor and subject: 'Eloquence not only considers the subject, but also the speaker and the hearers, and both the subject and the speaker for the sake of the hearers, or rather for the sake of the effect intended to be produced in them' (Campbell 1963: 33 [I.4]; and see 95–6 [I.8]). Campbell's defence of rhetoric harked back to all the similar defences over the millennia:

> If the orator would prove successful, it is necessary that he engage in his service all these different powers of the mind, the imagination, the memory, and the passions. These are not the supplanters of reason, or even rivals in her sway; they are her handmaids, by whose ministry she is enabled to usher truth into the heart, and procure it there a favourable reception. As handmaids they are liable to be seduced by sophistry in the garb of reason, and sometimes are made ignorantly to lend their aid in the introduction of falsehood. But their service is not on this account to be dispensed with; there is even a necessity of employing it, founded on our nature. (Campbell 1963: 72 [I.7]; see also Blair 2005: 265–6 [25]; and cf. Lawson 1758: 127)

At the same time, Campbell integrated his rhetoric very tightly with the new philosophy: 'As men in general, it must be allowed there are certain principles in our nature, which, when properly addressed and managed, give no inconsiderable aid to reason in promoting belief' (Campbell 1963: 71 [I.7]). Lockean senses and ideas once more provided the source of knowledge: 'The senses, both external and internal, are the original inlets of perception' (Campbell 1963: 47 [I.5]). Memory consisted of ideas that were, essentially, 'the prints that have been left by sensible impressions', while experience resulted from the repetition of similar ideas, which associated them with one another (Campbell 1963: 47–8 [I.5]). The passions, in turn, were also 'most strongly excited by sensation' (Campbell 1963: 81 [I.7]). Certainty was nothing more than a Lockean concatenation of probabilities: 'Probability results from evidence, and begets belief. Belief invigorates our ideas. Belief raised to the highest becomes certainty' (Campbell 1963: 81 [I.7]). And, where empiricism failed to provide answers, Campbell, like Locke and Hume, relied on the *a priori*s of common sense (Campbell 1963: 40 [I.5]).

Campbell's rhetoric aimed to use words so as to excite the ideas of sense, memory and passion into a state of highly probable belief. Perspicuity, the clear expression of ideas, was therefore a primary goal of his rhetoric – particularly when the goal was information rather than persuasion (Campbell 1963: 2 [I.1]). But perspicuity was a general goal: perspicuity 'being to the understanding what light is to the eye, [it] ought to be diffused over the whole performance' (Campbell 1963: 216 [II.6]). Since abstraction and metaphor arose from particular ideas, it was important that abstraction and metaphor not stray too far from their sensory origins (Campbell 1963: 261 [II.7]). Furthermore, since memory was nothing more than the fading imprint of sense, 'care must be taken by the orator that, in introducing new topics, the vestiges left by the former on the minds of the hearers may not be effaced'. Orderly composition, since easier to remember, fitted speech to the inescapable decay of memory (Campbell 1963: 75–6 [I.7]).

Vivacity, the lively expression of ideas, was perhaps the most important aim of rhetoric:

> I will not say with a late subtle metaphysician [Hume], that 'Belief consisteth in the liveliness of our ideas.' Thus much however is indubitable, that belief commonly enlivens our ideas; and that lively ideas have a stronger influence than faint ideas to induce belief. (Hume 1996: I, 127–8 [*Treatise* 1.3.7]; Campbell 1963: 73 [I.7])

Vivacity was especially important when the goal *was* persuasion. 'Lively signatures of memory . . . command an unlimited assent', 'vivid ideas are . . . more easily retained', and so vivid words were prescribed to stimulate the belief that accompanied vivid memory (Campbell 1963: 41 [I.5], 75 [I.7]). But belief also derived from passion: 'If it is fancy which bestows brilliancy on our ideas, if it is memory which gives them stability, passion doth more, it animates them. Hence they derive spirit and energy' (Campbell 1963: 77 [I.7]). Vivacity was doubly persuasive because it moved the passions as much as the memory: 'to excite some desire or passion in the hearers . . . is effected by communicating lively and glowing ideas of the object' (Campbell 1963: 77–8 [I.7]). Vivacity also engaged the imagination, and so excited belief to an even higher pitch (Campbell 1963: 73 [I.7]).

But aside from these emphases, concepts collectively rehearsed in Locke and Hume, Campbell also engaged in an extensive translation of the elements of classical rhetoric into an eighteenth-century vocabulary. Campbell gave explicit commendation to the rhetorical power of *ethos*, character:

> it hath become a common topic with rhetoricians, that, in order to be a successful orator, one must be a good man; for to be good is the only sure way of being long esteemed good, and to be esteemed good is previously necessary to one's being heard with due attention and regard. (Campbell 1963: 96–7 [I.9])

Moreover, Campbell translated *ethos* into concepts of sympathy and testimony. Sympathy derived very largely from the audience's estimation of the speaker's character, and, just as *ethos* acted upon *pathos*, so 'sympathy is one main engine by which the orator operates on the passions' (Campbell 1963: 96–7 [I.9]; see also E. Burke 1958: 22 [Introduction on Taste]; 44 [I.13]; 173–6 [V.7]). The rhetorical force of testimony also derived very largely from character: 'the reputation of the attester hath a considerable power' (Campbell 1963: 96 [I.9]; and see 54–6 [I.5]; cf. Blair 2005: 267 [25]). *Pathos*, in turn, found its equivalent in Campbell's extensive treatment of the passions – an equivalence that he made explicit (Campbell 1963: 80 [I.7]). Persuasion depended upon moving the passions: 'The coolest reasoner always in persuading addresseth himself to the passions some way or other . . . So far therefore it is from being an unfair method of persuasion to move the passions, that there is no persuasion without moving them' (Campbell 1963: 77 [I.7]; see also Blair 2005: 265–7 [25]). *Logos*, rational argument, the final component of the trinity of rhetoric, also retained its place. Campbell defined its scope to include

> moral evidence . . . founded on the principles we have from consciousness and common sense, improved by experience; and as it proceeds on this general presumption or moral axiom, that the course of nature in time to come will be similar to what it hath been hitherto, it decides, in regard to particulars, concerning the future from the past, and concerning things unknown from things familiar to us. (Campbell 1963: 43 [I.5]; see also 62 [I.6])

This definition paralleled the definition of *phronesis*, prudence, that form of reason traditionally associated with rhetoric (Aristotle 1984: II, 1799–1801 [6.4–5]; Kahn 1985: 9–10). Furthermore, Campbell gave to reason much the same role in persuasion that Aristotle had to *logos* – necessary, but not sufficient. Reason's consideration of moral evidence could not persuade by itself:

> In order to evince the truth considered by itself, conclusive arguments alone are requisite; but in order to convince me by those arguments, it is moreover requisite that they be understood, that they be attended to, that they be remembered by me; and in order to persuade me by them to

> any particular action or conduct, it is further requisite, that by interesting me in the subject they may, as it were, be felt. It is not therefore the understanding alone that is here engaged. (Campbell 1963: 71–2 [I.7])

But reason remained indispensable when considering such moral evidence: once passion had been excited, the orator had to convince his audience

> that there is a connexion between the action to which he would persuade them, and the gratification of the desire or passion which he excites . . . the latter . . . [is effected] by presenting the best and most forcible arguments which the nature of the subject admits. (Campbell 1963: 77–78 [I.7])

Ratio and *oratio* remained twined in Campbell's scheme; *ethos*, *pathos* and *logos* continued their long association as sympathy, passion and moral evidence. The most persuasive rhetoric combined these separate methods: it was 'an artful mixture of that which proposes to convince the judgment, and that which interests the passions, its distinguished excellency results from these two, the argumentative and the pathetic incorporated together' (Campbell 1963: 3–4 [I.1]; cf. Blair 2005: 265 [25]; Box 1990: 57).

Campbell also explicitly addressed the claims of science. He largely separated demonstrative evidence – scientific reason – from rhetoric. Yet while demonstrative evidence, 'built on pure intellection, and [which] consisteth in an uninterrupted series of axioms', had little to do with rhetoric, rhetoric was not entirely absent from demonstrative argument (Campbell 1963: 43 [I.5]). Still, in this realm rhetoric was supposed to have a light touch:

> In explanatory discourses, which are of all kinds the simplest, there is a certain precision of manner which ought to pervade the whole, and which, though not in the form of argument, is not the less satisfactory, since it carries internal evidence along with it. (Campbell 1963: 33 [I.4]; see also 43 [I.5])

But just as Campbell made sure that rhetoric was not to infringe upon the realm of science, he also made sure not to allow science to infringe upon the realm of rhetoric. He carefully delimited the scope of demonstrative reasoning:

> The sphere of Demonstration is narrow, but within her sphere she is a despotic sovereign, her sway is uncontrollable. Her rival [moral evidence], on the contrary, hath less power but wider empire. Her forces, indeed, are not always irresistible; but the whole world is comprehended in her dominions. (Campbell 1963: 46 [I.5])

Furthermore, fallible human capacities and memory rendered the claims of science suspect even within their own sphere: therefore, 'demonstration itself doth not always produce such immovable certainty, as is sometimes consequent on merely moral evidence' (Campbell 1963: 58–61 [I.5]). In a sense, Campbell had reversed Locke's emphases: where Locke had provided a strictly constrained role for rhetoric, now Campbell provided a strictly constrained role for science. Here, indeed, was also an answer to the successive challenges of Ramus, Descartes and Locke, each of whom had to some extent opposed some form of necessary logic against the uncertainties and persuasions of rhetoric. The answer was no more than a restatement of Aristotle – but it was an Aristotelian conclusion built upon the philosophy of Locke and Hume. And this, of course, was Campbell's accomplishment writ large: to pour new wine back into an old bottle, to construct from empirical premises a philosophically sound rhetoric.

Shaftesbury's Conversational Philosophy

On this Lockean world of overlapping rhetoric and empiricism, the Third Earl of Shaftesbury brought conversation to bear, and made conversation central to his philosophy. We must here address Shaftesbury's philosophy at length, for he married the model and practices of conversation to Lockean empiricism. Shaftesbury out of Locke would provide the matrix for the following century of this strand of British philosophy.

Shaftesbury, drawing heavily upon the seventeenth-century French conversational tradition, formed a great deal of his philosophy around the model and means of conversation:

> 'Tis the Habit alone of reasoning, which can make *a Reasoner*. And Men can never be better invited to the Habit, than when they find Pleasure in it. A Freedom of Raillery, a Liberty in decent Language to question every thing, and an Allowance of unravelling or refuting any Argument, without offence to the Arguer, are the only Terms which can render such speculative Conversations any way agreeable. (Shaftesbury 1999: 33 ['Sensus Communis']; L. Klein 1994: 98–9, 119)

The Shaftesburian project was to marry politeness to philosophy:

> To philosophize, in a just signification, is but to carry good breeding a step higher. For the accomplishment of breeding is to learn whatever is decent in company or beautiful in arts, and the sum of philosophy is

> to learn what is just in society and beautiful in nature and the order of the world. (Shaftesbury 1999: 407 ['Miscellany III']; L. Klein 1984–5: 198–200; cf. Descartes 1985: II, 399–420)

Philosophy was to be elaborated by polite means, meant to forward the larger goal of a polite culture, and conducted by polite people in polite places. In so doing, Shaftesbury updated old themes: in his polemics against the pedantries of the unsociable university (Shaftesbury 1999: 148–9, esp. note 82 ['Soliloquy'], 232 ['Moralists']; and see L. Klein 1984–5: 202–5; Watts 1743: 44; Mee 2011: 71), and in his advocacy of philosophy as an activity of gentle leisure, he recapitulated the self-definition of the Italian academies, and indeed of Ciceronian conversation.

Philosophical writings themselves were to use both the style of polite conversation – familiar, plain and eschewing the assumption of authority – and the forms of the dialogue and letter, so as to provoke further thought in a common audience. Shaftesbury embodied these prescriptions in his own philosophical writings: 'We might now perhaps do best to lay aside the gravity of strict argument and resume the way of chat, which, through aversion to a contrary formal manner, is generally relished with more than ordinary satisfaction' (Shaftesbury 1999: 380 ['Miscellany II'] and *passim*; L. Klein 1994: 107–12, 114–19, 205; but see Prostko 1989: 58–61; and see Valenza 2009). In pursuit of these larger goals, Shaftesbury also advocated conversation as a means of inquiry into truth, whether in the spheres of politics, art or the rest. Palemon in 'The Moralists' (1709), iconically, was a 'well-bred man' who took a 'fancy to talk philosophy in such a circle of good company as we had round us yesterday, when we were in your coach together in the park' (Shaftesbury 1999: 231 ['Moralists']). In all this, Shaftesbury took himself to be following the precedent of Athenian philosophy, which Socrates had brought before a public audience, in the city. Socrates' comportment, after all, was 'of a more open free & polite Conversation' (P.R.O. 30/24/27/14, p. 91 [f. 50r], cited in L. Klein 1994: 42; 1994: 34–43; 1984–5: 209–12). Conversation was the means by which to bring forth philosophy to the world.

For our narrative here, certain aspects of Shaftesbury's thought are worth emphasising. The natural state of human beings as sociable men embedded in society – and not, *contra* Hobbes and Locke, atomised individuals – made the individual self peculiarly susceptible to melting into society (Shaftesbury 1900: 232–4; L. Klein 1994: 68, 76–8). As neither isolation nor such uncontrolled susceptibility was acceptable, Shaftesbury prescribed a rational sociability to provide a middle course between the two that would allow for both autonomy and sociability:

> The Perfection of Carriage & Manners, is between the Ruggedness of one who cares not how he gives offense, and the Suppleness of one who only studdyes how to please. And this is Simplicity. for, Affectation is as well on the one side as on the other. (P.R.O. 30/24/27/10, p. 67 [f. 35r], cited in L. Klein 1994: 96; 1994: 79–85, 96)

Polite conversation articulated this rational sociability, formed a habit of free reasoning among its participants, and sparked further polite conversations; it was therefore prerequisite for all goods formed by rational sociability, whether personal, political or philosophical (Shaftesbury 1999: 33, 37 ['Sensus Communis']; L. Klein 1994: 96–8).

Shaftesbury also provided an explicit link between the liberty of conversation and political liberty. Liberty was prerequisite for polite, reciprocal and rational conversations:

> All politeness is owing to liberty. We polish one another and rub off our corners and rough sides by a sort of amicable collision. To restrain this is inevitably to bring a rust upon men's understandings. It is a destroying of civility, good breeding and even charity itself, under pretence of maintaining it. (Shaftesbury 1999: 31 ['Sensus Communis']; L. Klein 1994: 196–7; and see L. Klein 1989: 597).

The future therefore augured well for British politeness, since, although still unpolished, their liberty naturally disposed them to it: 'It is easy . . . to apprehend the advantages of our Britain in this particular and what effect its established liberty will produce in everything which relates to art, when peace returns to us on these happy conditions.' The French, by contrast, had made progress in politeness by dint of 'truer pains and industry', but their authoritarian politics had ultimately stunted the arts that should be the natural fruit of such politeness, and would continue to do so (Shaftesbury 1999: 98 ['Moralists']; L. Klein 1994: 206–10). Shaftesbury precisely reversed the French polemic that disparaged licentious British liberty (see below).

This argument associating liberty and conversation required some elaboration, however, for the historical development of liberty was famously associated with the development of oratory rather than with conversation. Shaftesbury's reply to this was that the general knowledge of rhetoric led the orator's auditors to both a critical knowledge of and a taste applied to rhetoric, and hence to the superior rhetoric of conversation: 'When such a race as this was once risen, it was no longer possible to impose on mankind by what was specious and pretending. The public would be paid in no false wit or jingling eloquence' (Shaftesbury 1999: 108 ['Soliloquy']; L. Klein 1994: 201). Rather, they would prefer the artful artlessness of conversational style – the old *sprezzatura* – required by an audience capable of fine judgement:

> the satiric or miscellaneous manner of the polite ancients required as much order as the most regular pieces. But the art was to destroy every such token or appearance, give an extemporary air to what was written, and make the effect of art be felt without discovering the artifice. (Shaftesbury 1999: 348 ['Miscellany I']; L. Klein 1994: 114)

This style Shaftesbury recognised elsewhere as Attic (Shaftesbury 1999: 105 ['Soliloquy']). In effect, he paralleled the Machiavellian shift from *The Prince* (1532) to the *Discourses on Livy* (1531): as the transformation from one prince acting to many citizens acting resulted in republicanism, so the shift from one orator persuading to many orators persuading resulted in conversation.

Shaftesbury did not by this argument claim that conversation had superseded rhetoric: rhetoric and politeness worked in tandem to promote liberty:

> where persuasion was the chief means of guiding the society, where the people were to be convinced before they acted, there elocution became considerable, there orators and bards were heard, and the chief geniuses and sages of the nation betook themselves to the study of those arts by which the people were rendered more treatable in the way of reason and understanding, and more subject to be led by men of science and erudition. The more these artists courted the public, the more they instructed it. In such constitutions as these, it was the interest of the wise and able that the community should be judges of ability and wisdom. (Shaftesbury 1999: 107 ['Soliloquy']; L. Klein 1994: 201–2)

Yet the formulation that rhetoric and politeness worked in tandem obscured some tension. On the one hand, Shaftesbury thought the liberty of conversation more attractive than the monologic and fundamentally unpersuasive compulsions of oratory and dogmatic sermonising (Shaftesbury 1999: 34 ['Sensus Communis']; L. Klein 1994: 99, 104, 106; and see also Shaftesbury 1999: 380 ['Miscellany II']; L. Klein 1994: 99 (note 29)). On the other hand, Shaftesbury expected conversation to defer to the opinions of the public, to reserve certain topics for private discussion so as to encourage the broadest possible discussion:

> To start questions or manage debates, which offend the public ear, is to be wanting in that respect which is due to common society. Such subjects should either not be treated at all in public or in such a manner as to occasion no scandal or disturbance. The public is not, on any account, to be laughed at to its face or so reprehended for its follies as to make it think itself contemned. And what is contrary to good breeding is in this respect as contrary to liberty. It belongs to men of slavish principles to affect a superiority over the vulgar and to despise the multitude. The lovers of mankind respect and honour conventions and societies of men. And in mixed company, and places where men are met promiscuously on account of diversion or affairs, it is an imposition and hardship to force them to hear what they dislike and to treat of matters in a dialect which many who are present have perhaps been never used to. It is a breach of the harmony of public conversation to take things in such a key as is above the common reach, puts others to silence, and robs them of their privilege of turn. (Shaftesbury 1999: 36 ['Sensus Communis'])

Shaftesbury here was partly critiquing the resort by the educated to jargons that would perplex and silence the multitude, and thus stop discourse – but partly he was recapitulating the old, terrified deference of the courtier to the prince: *The public is not, on any account, to be laughed at to its face or so reprehended for its follies as to make it think itself contemned.*

It is worth emphasising here that for all that oratory remained necessary to liberty, it also remained problematic: 'Orations are fit only to move the passions, and the power of declamation is to terrify, exalt, ravish or delight rather than satisfy or instruct' (Shaftesbury 1999: 34 ['Sensus Communis']; L. Klein 1994: 99, 104, 106). Yet with all these weaknesses of the public and of oratory clearly delineated, conversation still needed to engage in self-censorship, as part of the generative conditions for public discussion. Relatedly, Shaftesbury conceived of conversational liberty as distinct from licence in that a mutual decency in both speakers and listeners restrained all participants from giving or taking unnecessary offence in the course of the conversation (Shaftesbury 1999: 33 ['Sensus Communis']; L. Klein 1994: 98, 98 (note 25)). Shaftesbury evidently considered these limitations on conversation to be justified, but he did not deny their existence.

Such self-censorship encouraged a shift of much of the focus of polite, conversational liberty from the political realm to the cultural realm. Shaftesbury grandiloquently labelled the exercise of 'taste or judgment' in the realm of literature and '*the common cause of author and reader, the interest of letters and knowledge*' as '*the chief liberty, privilege and prerogative of the rational part of mankind*' (Shaftesbury 1999: 444 ['Miscellany V']; L. Klein 1994: 197–8; and see Struever 1985: 84–5, 88). But this transposition to culture was a cause for optimism. As in other realms of polite culture, British liberty augured well for the nation's progress in arts, for liberty would improve the taste in arts as well: 'When the *free* Spirit of a Nation turns it-self this way, Judgments are form'd; Criticks arise; the publick Eye and Ear improve; a right Taste prevails, and in a manner forces its way' (Shaftesbury 1732: 402–3 ['A Letter Concerning the Art, or Science of Design']). Polite conversation could extend itself in this sphere, foster the polite culture that would in turn foster liberty, but simultaneously keep conversation from intruding on the political subject matter central to the realm of oratory.

This deference also encouraged a shift back to the realm of virtue – albeit this shift also had other sources. The Shaftesburian project of politeness was working to establish itself in rivalry with a neo-Machiavellian tradition that contrasted the rude simplicities of civil virtue with the corrupting luxuries of politeness; against this thesis, Shaftesbury had to argue that civilisation and virtue were complements. This question was particularly acute because, since the middle of the seventeenth century, the vocabularies both of republican virtue and of courtly manners had come to be applied to the same class of English gentlemen, who took as sharply relevant the question of how best to accommodate these two vocabularies, and their competing values (L. Klein 1989: 585; and see 590–1).

Shaftesbury based his argument on the alignment of sociability and morality – although the passions had to be educated properly to make sure that disordered affections did not snap that link. He wrote in *An Inquiry Concerning Virtue* (1699) that,

> If the Affection be equal, sound, and good, and the subject of the Affection such as may with advantage to Society be ever in the same manner prosecuted or affected; this cannot but be right. . . . yet if through Superstition or strange Custom and Vogue, or through any wildness or extravagancy of Opinion, there come to be very gross mistakes in the assignment or application of the Affection . . . this cannot but be wrong and vitious. (Shaftesbury 1699: 29, 33; L. Klein 1994: 57–9)

Furthermore, the sociable and conversational aspects of politeness rendered it a superior means of inculcating proper *mores* in England's ruling elite:

> The mere amusements of gentlemen are found more improving than the profound researches of pedants. And, in the management of our youth, we are forced to have more recourse to the former as an antidote against the genius peculiar to the latter. (Shaftesbury 1999: 149 ['Soliloquy'], 148–9, 148 (note 82); L. Klein 1994: 45–6)

Conversation, moreover, could address itself to the judgement of morals as much as to any other serious subject:

> An easier method of treating those subjects will make them more agreeable and familiar. To dispute about them will be the same as about other matters. They need not spoil good company or take from the ease or pleasure of a polite conversation. And the oftener these conversations are renewed, the better will be their effect. (Shaftesbury 1999: 37 ['Sensus Communis'])

In Shaftesbury we thus see a significant assimilation of conversation to the question of moral judgement. Indeed, we see his philosophy of conversation assimilate into the question of judgement, period – and hence into the concepts of self, conscience, aesthetics and taste.

Internal Conversation: Privacy and Conscience

Conscience had been a subject matter of Augustine, and hence of Petrarch's partially Augustinian dialogue. The Montaignean examination of self drew loosely on this tradition, although with the desire for redemption shifted into the framework of self-knowledge as inquiry into a secularised *humaine condition* (Petrarca 2003; Auerbach 1953: 285–311, esp. 300; Marsh 1980: 3–4; D. Randall 2018: 49–50). Very broadly speaking, Augustinian conscience and Montaignean self-knowledge partook of a tradition that made *ethos* the subject matter of conversation and hence constituted to some extent by conversation. When Shaftesbury made the inner self explicitly the creation of internal conversation, he drew, at least loosely, upon this long tradition.

Shaftesbury's innovation derived from his stipulation, noted above, that the individual self was susceptible to melting into society. Polite conversation with other people was an insufficient answer to this danger, as it partook of that very sociability that threatened the self. Shaftesbury's solution was to form another species of dialogue, an internal conversation seeking truth that could both steady and constitute the autonomous moral self:

> Let me learn to reason and discourse thus with my own mind, that I may be no longer inconsistent with myself and my own reason, and live in

> perpetuall disorder and perplexity. Let me examine my ideas, challenge and talk with them thus, before they be admitted to pass. (Shaftesbury 1900: 167; 1999: 75, 77, 87, 89 ['Soliloquy']; L. Klein 1994: 86–90; Mee 2011: 45)

As the Italian humanists' ideal woman was to look into a mirror, so now all mankind was to engage in internal dialogue.

This internal conversation, moreover, was necessary for the proper philosophical search for knowledge. A proper philosopher needed to engage in such inner discourse so as to acquire that modicum of self-knowledge prerequisite for his avocation: 'This was, among the ancients, that celebrated Delphic inscription, "Recognize yourself!", which was as much as to say, "Divide yourself!" or "Be two!"' (Shaftesbury 1999: 77 ['Soliloquy']). It was also necessary for the philosopher so as to instil into his character and practice the conversational mode that sought to spark philosophising in others, in aid of the mutual search for truth, rather than to assume unwarranted authority and utter, in monologue, philosophical *dicta*.

> And this, in our default, is what the moralists or philosophers endeavour to do, to our hand, when, as is usual, they hold us out a kind of *vocal* looking-glass, draw sound out of our breast and instruct us to personate ourselves in the plainest manner. (Shaftesbury 1999: 78 ['Soliloquy']; L. Klein 1994: 102–7; and see Shaftesbury 1999: 35 ['Sensus Communis']; L. Klein 1994: 188–91, 198–200; Prostko 1989: 43–4; cf. Struever 1985: 85; Thweatt 1980: 43, 243).

Both a self capable of knowledge and the pursuit of such knowledge depended on conversation with oneself.

These internalised conversations rendered potentially universal the locales for conversation in previous iterations of the conversational tradition: the Ciceronian villa, the Guazzian closet, the Parisian *salon*. Montaigne, for example, had given an internalised twist to conversational solitude:

> We must reserve a back shop [*arrière-boutique*] all our own, entirely free, in which to establish our real liberty and our principal retreat and solitude. Here our ordinary conversation must be between us and ourselves, and so private that no outside association or communication can find a place. (Montaigne 2003: 214–15 ['Of solitude'])

Pierre Charron (1541–1603) had made a similar point in *Of Wisdome* (1601), emphasising that this interiority could be preserved even in the bustle of private affairs (Charron n.d. [after 1612]: 450 [III.6]). Shaftesbury's latter-day internalisation therefore significantly deepened the tradition that valued *privacy*, the psychological equivalent of the villa, the closet and the *salon*, as prerequisite for the formation of both the autonomous moral self capable of rational sociability and the philosophical character capable of inquiry into truth. Privacy, in other words, was an internalised abstraction of the *oikos*, and of all those architectural correlates of the *oikos* listed above, a home for the soul that allowed for the development of individuality, of character and style (and see Peterman 1993; Rosen and Santesso 2013: 108–56; Spacks 2003).

Privacy was also the necessary and therapeutic counterpart of the endless, wearying civilities required by the sociable life. More writers of the age, perhaps, prized the therapeutic value of conversation, and endorsed sociability's critique of solitude (Nicole 1677: 174–5, 211; A. Smith 2002: 28 [1.1.4.10]; Kerry 2008: 81–2; L. Klein 1997b; Mee 2011: 74–5). Yet a swelling crowd of eighteenth-century writers praised rather the relaxations of privacy. So Alexander Pope (1688–1744) wrote in his imitation of Horace's Epistle 2.2 (1737):

> 'Oh but a wit can study in the Streets,
> And raise his Mind above the Mob he meets.'
> Not quite so well however as one ought;
> A Hackney-Coach may chance to spoil a Thought, . . .
> Soon as I enter at my Country door,
> My Mind resumes the thread it dropt before;
> Thoughts, which at Hyde-Park-Corner I forgot,
> Meet and rejoin me, in the pensive Grott.
> There all alone, and Compliments apart,
> I ask these sober questions of my Heart.
>
> (Pope 1963: 652, 655 [ll. 98–101, 206–11])

William Cowper (1731–1800) in *The Task* (1785) likewise wrote

> Oh blest seclusion from a jarring world
> Which he, thus occupied, enjoys! Retreat
> Cannot indeed to guilty man restore
> Lost innocence, or cancel follies past,
> But it has peace, and much secures the mind
> From all assaults of evil.
>
> (Cowper 1994: 134 [ll. 675–6])

The British poets set the tone for the growing preference for privacy as tonic (Spacks 2003, esp. 196–216).

Shaftesbury's concern to establish the preconditions for those internal conversations that constituted the self capable of further conversational inquiry led towards the tradition of privacy; his concern to estabish a conversational moral self capable of maintaining its independence from society led towards Smith's notion of the impartial spectator, in his appearance as conscience (cf. Habermas 1991: 90–2). Francis Hutcheson (1694–1746) in his *Illustrations upon the Moral Sense* (1728) provided one link in this narrative that connected Shaftesbury to Smith, with his conception of the moral sense deriving from spectatorial approbation (Hutcheson 1756: 229, 285, 290–1; Raphael 2007: 27–9). Hume's philosophy of sympathy likewise had a spectatorial basis: 'The hypothesis which we embrace . . . defines virtue to be *whatever mental action or quality gives to a spectator the pleasing sentiment of approbation*; and vice the contrary' (Hume 1996: IV, 357 [*Enquiry Concerning the Principles of Morals*, Appendix 1]; Raphael 2007: 29–30).

In Smith, the impartial spectator (in the later editions of *The Theory of Moral Sentiments*) who became reflexive and internal in his judgements was the result of an imaginative evocation of such internal dialogue, an imagined audience the proper object of rhetorical/conversational practice, applied to the judgement of our own actions (A. Smith 2002: 131 [3.1.6]; McKenna 2006: 111–32; 2011: 62; Raphael 2007: 31, but see 32, 36–9, 42; cf. Astell 1697: Part II, 184). This impartial spectator of conscience, knowing one's insides more fully than any outsider could, reoriented one from seeking to be praised to seeking to be praiseworthy (Raphael 2007: 45). Sociologically, this effect was associated with the commercial society, which was a society of strangers rather than friends, from whom one could expect less sympathy; the conscience of the impartial spectator was developed more easily, and was more imperative, in a commercial society (A. Smith 2002: 27 [1.1.4.7]; Berry 2013: 135–7). Smith wavered somewhat in whether the impartial spectator was to be conceived of primarily as the universal audience of society, that world of strangers substituting for God, or as inner conscience. The double image, however, did ensure that the rhetorical framework that Smith explored in *Lectures on Rhetoric and Belles Lettres* (1762–3) applied very nicely to his presentation of the impartial spectator in *Theory of Moral Sentiments* (1759) (McKenna 2011: 62).

A notable consequence of this was that the *ethos*, the character, that one presented towards the impartial spectator was presented as towards an audience of strangers. The proper style, therefore, was toned down, as one was communicating one's sentiments to strangers, who could not sympathise with one with the same intensity as one did oneself, or as would one's friends and family:

> But he can only hope to obtain this by lowering his passion to that pitch, in which the spectators are capable of going along with him. He must flatten, if I may be allowed to say so, the sharpness of its natural tone, in order to reduce it to harmony and concord with the emotions of those who are about him. (A. Smith 2002: 27 [1.1.4.7]; McKenna 2006: 114–22; cf. Faret 1632: 252–4)

Smith also prescribed the stylistic precepts of conversation: we were to govern ourselves so as to communicate our character with propriety, naturally and agreeably, plainly and clearly, so as to elicit sympathy from this imagined audience (McKenna 2011: 51, 55–6, 58, 60; Phillipson 2010: 93; cf. Mandeville 1988: 291–2 [345–6]). This style would aid us in lowering our pitch:

> A wise man too in conversation and behaviour will not affect a character that is unnaturall to him; if he is grave he will not affect to be gay, nor if he be gay will he affect to be grave. He will only regulate his naturall temper, restrain within just bounds and lop all exhuberances and bring it to that pitch which will be agreable to those about him. (A. Smith 1985: 55 [i.35])

Sprezzatura and self-command combined in conveying a version of the sincere inner character to the audience of the world and to one's own conscience, so as to make of oneself not merely a stable self, as in Shaftesbury, but a virtuous one. Conscience was addressed in that conversational style both intimate and chaste with which one would address an audience of strangers.

Privacy allowing internal conversation made possible a conversational self, and internal conversation also made possible the conscience; self and conscience combined to create a being capable of making autonomous moral judgements. Each person would be embedded in external conversations – and, as we shall see below, would seek out norms of judgement by means of these exterior discourses. Yet internal conversation, by way of privacy and conscience, would preserve each individual from mental or moral dissolution into the larger world of conversation. These internal conversations would thus provide an essential pendant to the conversational process that would establish a universalising standard of taste.

The Standard of Taste: Rhetoric

As noted above, the quotation from Kant immediately below underpins Habermas' conception of the public sphere and communicative rationality as derived from the discourse of reason:

> the judgments of every understanding must be in agreement (*consentientia uni tertio, consentiunt inter se*). Thus, whether assent is conviction or mere persuasion, its touchstone externally is the possibility of communicating assent and of finding it to be valid for every human being's reason. (Kant 1996: 748 [A820–1; B848–9])

These sentences include the word 'judgment' in close proximity to 'reason'. This proximity was at the heart of both Kantian philosophy and Habermas' public sphere theory. Kant, although quite aware of the objections that could be proffered to his stance, ultimately resolved the Antinomy of Taste by a recourse to the normative laws of reason (Costelloe 2007: 37–52), and so derived first an aesthetics, and then a teleology, based upon reason's sharply demanding and monist strictures:

> when he [a man] puts a thing on a pedestal and calls it beautiful, he demands the same delight from others. He judges not merely for himself, but for all men, and then speaks of beauty as if it were a property of things. Thus he says the *thing* is beautiful; and it is not as if he counted on others agreeing in his judgment of liking owing to his having found them in such agreement on a number of occasions, but he *demands* this agreement of them. He blames them if they judge differently, and denies them taste, which he still requires of them as something they ought to have; and to this extent it is not open to men to say: Every one has his own taste. This would be equivalent to saying that there is no such thing as taste, i.e. no aesthetic judgment capable of making a rightful claim upon the assent of all men. (Kant 1952: 52 [I.7: 212–13])

Reason's demanding standard of judgement was bound up in Habermas' thought: the discourse of reason necessarily impelled its participants towards the positively valenced teleology of a rationalist Utopia. The rhetorical empiricism of Hume, however – and of Kames, Blair and (to a more limited extent) Edmund Burke (1729–97), whom I will largely cite hereafter as exponents of quasi-Humean thought – was associated with a very different standard of judgement, a very different aesthetics, and therefore a very different approach to teleology (see also Costelloe 2004; 2007; P. Jones 1976; Kivy 1967; 1983;

Kulenkampf 1990; Shusternan 1989; Townsend 2001).[3] Within this rhetorical aesthetics, conversation (and not a Kantian reason) was the means by which to unite the judgements of mankind so as to form a standard of taste. Hume's standard of taste united Locke's rhetorical empiricism and Shaftesbury's philosophy of conversation.

The rhetorical aspect of Hume's aesthetics derived not least from the fact that the concept of taste, and hence the discipline of aesthetics, itself descended from rhetorical thought (cf. Poulakos 2007). Taste originated in Aristotle as a form of judgement constituted by common sense – where 'common sense' meant 'what is sensed in common by the various senses', although not a separate sense itself (Aristotle 1984: I, 676–7 [*De anima* 3.1]; Summers 1987: 78–86, 103–4; Townsend 2001: 47–51). Taste, therefore, by its association with 'common sense' (albeit in a somewhat different usage from its primary signification) and judgement, was linked loosely with prudence, opinion and a rhetorical mode of thought from its Greek beginnings (Kahn 1985: 33).

This loose association of taste with rhetorical thought was greatly strengthened in the Renaissance, when proto-aesthetic thinkers such as Leon Battista Alberti, by means of (possibly inaccurate) readings of the classical rhetoricians, began to reconceive of taste as a faculty of judgement (Quintilian 1920–2: II, 515 [6.5.1–2]; Alberti 1988: 157 [6.2]; Curtius 1963: 296–301; Townsend 2001: 52). By the sixteenth century, the association of *giudizio* (judgement) and *gusto* (taste) was a commonplace. Giorgio Vasari (1511–74) united the two concepts in his description of Michelangelo in his *Lives* (1550, expanded 1568): 'ebbe giudizio e gusto in tutte le cose' (Vasari 1881: 272). Giovanni Paolo Lomazzo (1538–92) in *Idea of the Temple of Painting* (1590) likewise wrote of 'giudizio, ò sia gusto della belleza' (Lomazzo 1590: 87; 2013: 115 [26]).

The equation of taste with judgement highlighted taste as a *personal* quality – a mark of individual character (*ethos*), and hence of style, now become the external expression of character and taste. Anton Francesco Doni (1513–74) wrote in *Disegno del Doni* (1549), of drapery in painting, that 'questi panni sie no tutta gratia & maniera, che s'acquista per studiare una materia fatta d'altro maestro, che più t'è ito a gusto che alcuno altro' (Doni 1549: fol. 16v). Lomazzo stated in *Idea of the Temple of Painting* that

> The artist succeeds, by means of this science [practice], in so sharpening and refining his judgment . . . excellences differ according to the different nature granted each man: the better we know how to recognize our own

> nature, and respectively apply the proper art and instruction, the more it will operate in us and raise us to a higher level of perfection. . . . he who knows his nature, and follows it, easily reaches the supreme excellence in that part for which he is predisposed. (Lomazzo 2013: 50–1 [2]; and see Poussin 1964: 171; R. Klein 1979: 167; Townsend 2001: 52–3)

The man who possessed such artistic judgement now became the man of taste, the *huomo di gusto* (Mancini 1956: 109, 140).

Such judgement (*giudizio*), diversely varying with individual temperament and acting upon the contingent particulars of artistic subject matter, was the analogue of *discrezione* – a key component of prudence. Paolo Pino (1534–65) wrote in *Dialogo di pittura* (1548), 'Ma qui ci concorre la discrezione, ch'è intesa da me per buon giudicio' (Pino 1960: 104). Lodovico Dolce (1508–68) wrote likewise in his *Dialogo della Pittura* (1557): 'Aviene anco che le figure, o tutte o alcuna parte di esse, scortino. La qual cosa non si può fare senza gran giudicio e discrezione' (Dolce 1960: 180). Judgement was also closely associated with *ingegno* (wit or genius), the virtuosic exercise of such individual judgement (Armenini 1977: 115 [1.5]; Aretino 1957: I, 101–2, 102 (note 1) [LXIII, letter to Fausto da Longiano, 17 December 1537]); R. Klein 1979: 162–5; Townsend 2001: 57–8; and see Summers 1987: 266–82). *Ingegno*, since rooted in individual judgement rather than in beauty immanent in external reality, was the aesthetic equivalent of Niccolò Machiavelli's (1469–1527) equally rhetorical, prudentialist notion of *virtù* (Garver 1987: 11, 13–14; Hirschman 1977: 12–13; Kahn 1994: 37–8; cf. Garver 1987: 20).

The Italian mannerist notion of 'productive taste' further emphasised this rhetorical, virtuosic definition of taste and brought it ever closer towards being a sense in and of itself. Pino wrote in *Dialogo di pittura* that

> Circa alla prima, detta da me giudicio, in questa parte ci conviene aver la natura et i fati propizii, e nascere con tal disposizione, come i poeti; altro non conosco, come tal giudizio se possi imparare. E ben vero ch'isercitandolo nell'arte, egli divien più perfetto, ma, avendo il giudicio, voi imparerete la circonscrizzione. (Pino 1960: 113–14)

Giovanni Battista Armenini (1530–1609) likewise stated in *De veri precetti della pittura* (1587) that 'if Zeuxis had not possessed an unique personal style in addition to his great diligence, he would never have been able to harmonise the beautiful individual parts he copied from so many virgins and would never have given form to the perfect work he had envisioned' (Armenini 1977: 160 [2.3]; R. Klein 1979: 165, 167; Townsend 2001: 60; and see Aretino 1957: I, 88 [LV, letter to Francesco Pocopanno, 24 November 1537]). The Spanish mannerist writers, and especially Baltasar Gracián (1601–58), finally articulated taste as a sixth sense, a mental faculty in itself:

> You may know a noble spirit by the elevation of his taste: it must be a great thing that can satisfy a great mind. . . . Things of the first importance are few; let appreciation be rare. Taste can be imparted by intercourse: great good luck to associate with the highest taste. (Gracián 1945: 37; Townsend 2001: 61; cf. Dubos 1748: II, 239)

This faculty remained deeply rhetorical: Gracián's articulation of the concept of a faculty of taste was embedded within his prudentialist maxims, and he explicitly cautioned that taste should be exercised according to the principles of prudence (Gracián 1945: 160; Kivy 1976: 5; Townsend 2001: 61). And taste retained a virtuosic aspect: 'You can train it like the intellect' (Gracián 1945: 37).

This seventeenth-century reconception of taste as a sense (and see Croce 1968: 189–203) paved the way for taste's assimilation by eighteenth-century British philosophers into a Lockean, sense-based epistemology (see also Stolnitz 1963; Townsend 1987; 1991). Within the framework and vocabulary of Lockean empiricism, taste re-emerged as 'perception'. Shaftesbury had attributed both judgements of beauty and morals to a natural sense independent of reason (Shaftesbury 1999: 172–3 [*Inquiry*, 2.3]; Tuveson 1974: 53–4), and Joseph Addison had sharpened the idea of an imagination independent of rational understanding: 'We are struck, we know not how, with the Symmetry of any thing we see, and immediately assent to the Beauty of an Object, without enquiring into the particular Causes and Occasions of it' (Bond 1965: III, 538 [No. 411, 21 June 1712]; Tuveson 1974: 92–131). Francis Hutcheson had provided in *An Inquiry into the Original of our Ideas of Beauty and Virtue* (1726) the phrase 'moral sense' (Hutcheson 1753, *passim*, esp. 111–14), and Alexander Gottlieb Baumgarten (1714–62) in 1735 had defined this new 'science of perception' as *aestheta* – aesthetics (Baumgarten 1954: 78 [§116]). Judgements of beauty and judgements of morals, not yet necessarily regarded as a unity, both increasingly came to be regarded as matters of perception during the eighteenth century.

This new formulation at first received a more extensive articulation with regard to judgements of beauty. The new centrality of perception gave rise to a reformulation of the concept of artistic genius – and to a sense of judgement derived from perception and aesthetics (Tuveson 1974: 132–63; and see Blair 2005: 10–25 [2–3]; cf. Raphael 2007: 28). In Lord Kames' words, 'Beauty, in its very conception, refers to a percipient; for an object is said to be beautiful, for no other reason but that it appears so to a spectator' (Kames 1967: I, 260–1 [3]). Aesthetic judgement increasingly resolved itself into mere perception. But neither the old concepts nor the old vocabulary disappeared. Taste not only survived but flourished as the age's denomination for this judgement of beauty. Taste was, as Burke wrote, 'that faculty, or those faculties of the mind which are affected with, or which form a judgment of the works of imagination and the elegant arts' (E. Burke 1958: 13 [Introduction on Taste]; cf. J. Reynolds 1959: 99).

But if judgement derived solely from individual perception, and not from intuition or reason, what then provided the standard of judgement? Lord Kames thought that aesthetic judgement, unlike moral judgement, could not be given a definitive standard: were aesthetic judgement

> strong and lively, it would usurp upon our duty, and call off the attention from matters of greater moment. Were it more clear and authoritative, it would banish all difference of taste: a refined taste would not form a character, nor be intitled to esteem. (Kames 1967: III, 368 [25])

Similarly, Blair could not determine one absolute standard: 'Taste is not resolveable into any such operation of Reason. . . . Truth, which is the object of reason, is one; Beauty, which is the object of Taste, is manifold' (Blair 2005: 10, 16 [2]). Hume could only say that such a standard must be assumed to exist, but that men would always differ with one another about its precise character.

> Whether any particular person be endowed with good sense and a delicate imagination, free from prejudice, may often be the subject of dispute, and be liable to great discussion and inquiry: but that such a character is valuable and estimable, will be agreed in by all mankind. Where these doubts occur, men can do no more than in other disputable questions which are submitted to the understanding: they must produce the best arguments that their invention suggests to them: they must acknowledge a true and decisive standard to exist somewhere, to wit, real existence and matter of fact; and they must have indulgence to such as differ from them in their appeals to this standard. (Hume 1996: III, 266 ['Of the Standard of Taste'])

Yet this modest refusal to answer did not satisfy: these same philosophers continued to search for a more certain standard of judgement. Unsurprisingly, and despite the qualms stated above, recourse was made to reason. For Burke, taste might vary, but good taste relied upon reason:

> wherever the best Taste differs from the worst, I am convinced that the understanding operates and nothing else; and its operation is in reality far from being always sudden, or when it is sudden, it is often far from being right. (E. Burke 1958: 26 [Introduction on Taste])

Blair thought that reason improved taste, even if taste did not derive from reason: 'Though Taste, beyond doubt, be ultimately founded on a certain natural and instinctive sensibility to beauty, yet Reason, as I shall shew hereafter, assists Taste in many of its operations, and serves to enlarge its power' (Blair 2005: 11 [2]; cf. Dubos 1748: II, 237–43). But in the end, reason did not suffice as a standard of aesthetic judgement. Blair wrote that reason must 'refer at last to sense and perception. . . . It is from consulting our own imagination and heart, and from attending to the feelings of others, that any principles are formed which acquire authority in matters of Taste' (Blair 2005: 18 [2]). Blair did not think too much fuss should be made over this distinction: in practice, he thought taste based on reason and taste based on common sentiment came to similar conclusions (Blair 2005: 18 [2]). Yet it still mattered that, as Hume wrote, 'it is evident that none of the rules of composition are fixed by reasonings *à priori*' (Hume 1996: III, 253 ['Of the Standard of Taste']; and see J. Reynolds 1959: 230).

The only standard available, in the end, was what Hume had identified as the essence of rhetoric: the appeal to the public, universal human judgement, shorn of any reference to beauty immanent in external reality. As Kames wrote, 'However languid and cloudy the common sense of mankind may be with respect to the fine arts, it is yet the only standard in these as well as in morals.' Granted, he excluded the labouring many, who had never learned taste, and also excluded those among the educated whose tastes he judged had become corrupted, but this was still a powerful statement of trust in universal judgement (Kames 1967: III, 369–71 [25]). Blair could imagine the existence of a perfect judge, 'whose internal senses were in every instance exquisite and just, and whose reason was unerring and sure, the determinations of such a person concerning beauty, would, beyond doubt, be a perfect standard for the Taste of all others'.

Such a person, however, did not, and would never, exist; therefore, 'to the sense of mankind the ultimate appeal must ever lie, in all works of Taste' (Blair 2005: 17 [2]). Hume, who could imagine a perfect judge as well as Blair, gave this sense of mankind a temporal aspect: 'Just expressions of passion and nature are sure, after a little time, to gain public applause, which they maintain for ever' (Hume 1996: III, 267 ['Of the Standard of Taste']; Warnick 1993: 99–101; and see J. Reynolds 1959: 133).

This universality of judgement did retain a possibility of consensus, because it in turn rested on the universality of emotion, feeling, passion. As Kames wrote,

> a wonderful uniformity is preserved among the emotions and feelings of different individuals . . . . Every doubt with relation to this standard [of taste] occasioned by the practice of different nations and different times, may be cleared by applying to the principles [the passions] that ought to govern the taste of every individual. (Kames 1967: III, 373–4 [25])

Burke wrote that, 'by the contagion of our passions, we catch a fire already kindled in another, which probably might never have been struck out by the object described' (E. Burke 1958: 175–6 [V.7]). Blair, in turn, wrote that human taste 'is built upon sentiments and perceptions which belong to our nature; and which, in general, operate with the same uniformity as our other intellectual principles' (Blair 2005: 19 [2]). Hume had more faith in the stability and universality of passionate judgement than he did in the stability and universality of any science (Hume 1996: III, 266–7 ['Of the Standard of Taste']). And, crucially, Hume provided the obvious corollary and put moral judgement onto the same basis as aesthetic judgement: virtue was '*whatever mental action or quality gives to a spectator the pleasing sentiment of approbation*' (Hume 1996: IV, 357 [*Enquiry Concerning the Principles of Morals*, Appendix 1]). Moral judgement could found itself on no standard more secure than that of the passions of the public.

And no less secure. Such passions – sentiments – were not irrational. Sentiments were not facts subject to scientific reasoning, but they were ideas properly subject to moral reasoning – prudentialist (rhetorical) reasoning under another name. Hume put it that

> in many orders of beauty, particularly those of the finer arts, it is requisite to employ much reasoning, in order to feel the proper sentiment; and a false relish may frequently be corrected by argument and reflection. There are just grounds to conclude that moral beauty partakes much of this latter species, and demands the assistance of our intellectual faculties, in

> order to give it a suitable influence on the human mind. (Hume 1996: IV, 233 [*Enquiry Concerning the Principles of Morals*, 1.1]; Costelloe 2003: 174–6; and see Kivy 1983: 199, 201; Townsend 2001: 137–57)

But the passions of the public were not themselves unrelated to the aesthetic judgements of men of taste. The Renaissance conception of taste had been virtuosic – taste as an exercise of rhetoric – and Hume's rhetorical conception of taste yoked this virtuosity to the appeal to public judgement. While a pretender to the status of a man of taste simply echoed the existing standard of taste – engaged in a hollow exercise of promptuary rhetoric (rhetoric without invention; see Garver 1987: 70) – the true man of taste submitted his inventive aesthetic judgement to public judgement as an act of *virtù* and, by this rhetorical exercise, contributed towards the constitution of both that self-same public judgement and the standard of taste (P. Jones 1976: 337–9; cf. L. Brown 1995). As Hume wrote:

> they [men of taste] must produce the best arguments, that their invention suggests to them . . . The ascendant, which they acquire, gives a prevalence to that lively approbation with which they receive any productions of genius, and renders it generally predominant. Many men, when left to themselves, have but a faint and dubious perception of beauty, who yet are capable of relishing any fine stroke which is pointed out to them. (Hume 1996: III, 266–7 ['Of the Standard of Taste'])

The virtuosic element of this taste could be seen also in that it was improvable by practice:

> But though there be naturally a wide difference, in point of delicacy, beween one person and another, nothing tends further to increase and improve this talent [taste], than *practice* in a particular art, and the frequent survey or contemplation of a particular species of beauty. (Hume 1996: III, 260 ['Of the Standard of Taste'])

Moreover, just as the aim and proof of the exercise of *virtù* was the creation of stable power over successive moments of contingent time, so the aim and proof of the exercise of taste was the creation of stable taste upon the vicissitudes of popular judgement (Garver 1987: 11, 16, 28, 71, 76; cf. Erasmus 1965: 98; Hume 1996: III, 362 [*Treatise* 3.3.1]). Enduring judgement, therefore, was the great proof of virtuosic taste: 'Just expressions of passion and nature are sure, after a little time, to gain public applause, which they maintain for ever' (Hume 1996: III, 267 ['Of the Standard of Taste']; and see

J. Reynolds 1959: 122–3; cf. Bracciolini 1978: 128–9; Charron n.d. [after 1612]: 277 [II.3]). The ambition of the man of taste was to invent a new judgement that would contribute to the standard of taste and that would likewise endure in the judgements of mankind. Finally, just as for Machiavelli the rule of a republic, rooted upon the collective exercises of *virtù* by its citizenry, was more stable than the rule of a single prince, so for Hume the collective exercise of aesthetic judgement by men of taste, at any time and over the centuries, was more stable than the judgement of a single man of taste: hence Hume's verdict that the 'joint verdict of such [men of taste], wherever they are to be found, is the true standard of taste and beauty' (Machiavelli 2003: 282 [3.9]; Hume 1996: III, 265 ['Of the Standard of Taste']; Gurstein 2000: 215; Kahn 1994: 40). By means of a rather Machiavellian and rhetorical aesthetics, Hume bound together the judgements of men of taste, reliance on the diverse judgements of the plural public, and a means by which to establish both the identities of the true men of taste and a standard of taste and judgement (cf. P. Jones 1976: 340; and see Townsend 2001: 180–216).

Hume's reliance on both the joint verdicts of men of taste and the diverse passions of the public to provide the standard of judgement implied that an irreducible plurality would remain in the standard of judgement: in 'the different humors of particular men . . . [and] the particular manners and opinions of our age and country . . . a certain degree of diversity in judgment is unavoidable' (Hume 1996: III, 268 ['Of the Standard of Taste']). Where Kant's aesthetics, based exclusively on the standard of judgement provided by reason, was sharply normative and demanding – inherently teleological – the aesthetics of Hume, Kames and Blair, since it based itself on a pluralist standard of judgement, was not monist, not demanding – and therefore not, strictly speaking, teleological. The rhetorical exercise of judgement attempted nothing more than to establish as stable a standard of judgement as the diverse nature of mankind would allow.

In this Humean framework, the autonomy of judgement was key, not the autonomy of reason; the discourse of the public sphere was constituted by a universal, virtuosic use of rhetoric that aimed more to acquire the free consent of the passions than the free consent of reason; and all mankind possessed both the right to persuade and the duty – to judge with an open heart, and always be willing to be persuaded. If there were any normativity implied in this Humean standard of judgement – any transmutation from 'is' to 'ought' in this rhetorical public sphere – it lay in the desire to constitute an enduringly stable standard from the irreducibly diverse passions of the universal public (and see Costelloe 2007: 98; MacIntyre 1959:

463–6; Struever 1985: 91–2). If the instability of the standard of taste derived in the last analysis from the diversity of human passion, then the search for stability implied a search for a way to evoke a union of passion from mankind's diversity. Rhetoric provided the means by which to appeal to mankind's universal judgement, for that appeal was itself the essence of rhetoric. As Hume wrote, 'General language therefore, being formed for general use, must be moulded on some more general views, and must affix the epithets of praise or blame, in conformity to sentiments which arise from the general interest of the community' (Hume 1996: IV, 293 [*Enquiry Concerning the Principles of Morals*, 5.2]). As the ultimate act of *virtù*, the collective exercise of judgement by men of taste could address the disparate human passions and move them towards that universal harmony of sentiment that would in turn generate at last a stable standard of judgement. As Hume argued, 'If . . . there be an entire or a considerable uniformity of sentiment among men, we may thence derive an idea of the perfect beauty' (Hume 1996: III, 256 ['Of the Standard of Taste']). The Humean public sphere's telos of passionate judgement, and of the virtuoso exercise of rhetorical aesthetics, if it existed at all, lay beyond the ken of Kantian reason, in this creation of the longed-for unison of the hearts of all mankind (cf. Habermas 1973: 147–8, 163–4).

The Standard of Taste: Conversation

Yet it is important also to consider that Hume's philosophy was not only generally rhetorical, but specifically articulated the antinomy between conversation and oratory. He faced a culture that opposed politeness to rhetoric and was therefore hostile towards the latter; Hume, however, also valued rhetoric and wished to combine the two harmoniously in his philosophy of character and taste (Hanvelt 2012: 128). He broadly endorsed a rhetorical aesthetics and standard of taste – but within the realm of rhetoric, he desired a conversational aesthetics and standard of taste.

Hume's conversational aesthetics derived from a broad incorporation of conversation throughout his philosophy. To begin with, he took all processes of the mind to pertain to the passions, best moved by rhetoric, but he distinguished between different sorts of passion.

> Now it is certain there are certain calm desires and tendencies, which, though they be real passions, produce little emotion in the mind, and are more known by their effects than by the immediate feeling or sensation.

> These desires are of two kinds; either certain instincts originally implanted in our natures, such as benevolence and resentment, the love of life, and kindness to children; or the general appetite to good, and aversion to evil, considered merely as such. When any of these passions are calm, and cause no disorder in the soul, they are very readily taken for the determinations of reason, and are supposed to proceed from the same faculty, with that, which judges of truth and falshood. Their nature and principles have been supposed the same, because their sensations are not evidently different. . . . What we call strength of mind, implies the prevalence of the calm passions above the violent; though we may easily observe, there is no man so constantly possessed of this virtue, as never on any occasion to yield to the solicitations of passion and desire. From these variations of temper proceeds the great difficulty of deciding concerning the actions and resolutions of men, where there is any contrariety of motives and passions. (Hume 1996: II, 169–70 [*Treatise* 2.3.3]; Hanvelt 2012: 129)

These calm passions were to the violent ones as conversation was to oratory – and calm conversation was the appropriate genre of rhetoric to motivate these gentler passions. Hume, closely following Cicero, consequently associated such gentle sentiments with conversation:

> Any question of philosophy, on the other hand, which is so *obscure* and *uncertain*, that human reason can reach no fixed determination with regard to it; if it should be treated at all, seems to lead us naturally into the style of dialogue and conversation. Reasonable men may be allowed to differ, where no-one can reasonably be positive: Opposite sentiments, even without any decision, afford an agreeable amusement: And if the subject be curious and interesting, the book carries us, in a manner, into company; and unites the two greatest and purest pleasures of human life, study and society. (Hume 2013a: 96; Gordon 1994: 165)

Hume also discriminated between high and low rhetorics, where high rhetoric was polite, conversational in style, rational and undogmatic, and promulgated a mode of persisting inquiry among the audience. He allowed that ancient eloquence must be superior to the modern, despite its impolite character, since the audience's approbation was the only relevant judgement. Yet still he provided a place for the modern, conversational style of oratory, 'which ancient critics denominated Attic eloquence, that is, calm, elegant, and subtile, which instructed the reason more than affected the passions, and never raised its tone above argument or common discourse' (Hume 1996: III, 116 ['Of Eloquence']; Hanvelt 2012: 129–30). Hanvelt argues, persuasively, that Hume took this modern, conversational style of polite rhetoric to be the animating discourse for his preferred polity (Hanvelt 2012: 78–9, 124–44).

Conversation was thus prominent throughout Hume's thought – and not least in his philosophy of the mind. To begin with, Hume took conversation in *A Treatise of Human Nature* (1738–40) to be 'a transcript of the mind' and a means to convey testimony about particulars of the world; in 'Of Essay Writing' (1742) he took it also as a medium of 'experience' (Hume 1996: II, 396 [*Treatise* 3.3.4]; 1998: 2 ['Of Essay Writing']; Dickins 2008: 21). Conversation, moreover, was the means of communication of sentiments, which by fostering sympathy and sociability offered a means to overcome those passions that encouraged partial and variable moral judgements.[4] Conversation, sympathy and sociability allowed for the development instead of a more acute and more stable standard of moral judgement.

> In like manner, though sympathy be much fainter than our concern for ourselves, and a sympathy with persons remote from us much fainter than that with persons near and contiguous; yet we neglect all these differences in our calm judgments concerning the characters of men. Besides, that we ourselves often change our situation in this particular, we every day meet with persons who are in a different situation from ourselves, and who could never converse with us on any reasonable terms, were we to remain constantly in that situation and point of view, which is peculiar to us.
>
> The intercourse of sentiments, therefore, in society and conversation, makes us form some general inalterable standard, by which we may approve or disapprove of characters and manners. And though the *heart* does not always take part with those general notions, or regulate its love and hatred by them, yet are they sufficient for discourse, and serve all our purposes in company, in the pulpit, on the theatre, and in the schools. (Hume 1996: II, 387 [*Treatise* 3.3.3]; Dickins 2008: 24–9; and see: Hume 1996: IV, 292 [*Enquiry Concerning the Principles of Morals*, 5.2]; cf. Gracián 1945: 37; Saint-Évremond 1700: I, 170; Watts 1743: 32; and with some qualification, J. Millar 1803: 246–7 [II.6.2]; but see Mee 2011: 75–6; Raphael and Macfie 1976: 15–16)

Thus Hume tied together dialogue, sentiment and the formation of opinion (Krause 2008a: 112–13; and see 2008b: 139, 142). Judgement and taste, in consequence, were not only generally passionate in nature but also specifically conversational (Bennett 1996: 39; cf. Struever 1985: 81–3). Conversationally, the exercise of taste was meant to inspire taste in others: to repeat and continue the quotation above, '[m]any men, when left to themselves, have but a faint and dubious perception of beauty, who yet are capable of relishing any fine stroke, which is pointed out to them. Every convert to the admiration of the real poet or orator, is the cause of some new conversion' (Hume 1996: III, 267 ['Of the Standard of Taste']). Just as conversation in the commonwealth fostered the commonwealth's continuance, so conversational judgement fostered the continuance of judgement.

Hume thus combined an argument for a rhetorical standard of taste with an argument for a conversational standard of taste. Rhetoric was meant to form taste, and the standard of taste, as an act of *virtù*, and such taste was still meant to be submitted to popular judgement. Conversation tried to enlarge and enlighten the public's opinions, but always with the stipulation of finally deferring to oratory, to passion, to the multitude, to opinion. Rhetoric sought a taste, an aesthetic, a virtue, a norm, that would elicit assent from the hearts of all mankind (cf. Habermas 1991: 98). Conversation sought this as an indefinite topic, not seeking too prompt a settled consensus or an end of dialogue, always seeking to elicit further judgements, so as to make the standard of taste not simply a transhistorical unison, but a unison perpetually constituted and reconstituted by mankind's continuing judgements, which conversation would never cease to elicit.

Conclusion

An ensemble of eighteenth-century British philosophers grounded post-Lockean philosophy broadly on rhetoric and more narrowly on conversation. To begin with, Locke sublimated key aspects of rhetoric in his empiricism, Hume constructed a thoroughly rhetorical innovation upon Lockean philosophy, and Campbell provided a new rhetoric built essentially upon Humean grounds. In a slightly different philosophical lineage, Shaftesbury formulated a philosophy of conversation, continued notably by Smith, by which exterior conversation between individuals placed conversation at the heart of moral philosophy, while private interior conversation within individuals constituted selves and consciences capable of judgement. Hume then defined the standard of taste as formed dialogically, by the rhetorical submission of individual judgements to the joint verdicts of mankind – where those joint verdicts were best formed by conversation, which refined the passions that were the irreducible basis of judgement. Rhetoric and conversation were the warp and woof of this philosophy – and constituted those key concepts of self, conscience and the standard of taste.

Conversation thus had permeated not only the culture of the Enlightenment but also its philosophy. This was another register of the universalisation of conversation, for now conversation was taken to constitute each self and conscience, as well as to provide those aspirations to universal judgement, the norms of mankind. Those who judged, and their standards of judgements, had both become conversational.

This conversationalisation left one realm yet to be universalised – the subject matter of such judgements. Renaissance developments had hinted strongly that conversation should aspire to a universal subject matter, including the public world, and this would now come to fruition in the Enlightenment. *Public opinion* became that universal conversation. It assumed both interior and exterior conversational selves among its participants and it adopted conversational means of achieving standards of judgement. The conversation of public opinion was to be conducted between all mankind (at least in aspiration), and was to encompass every conceivable subject.

Notes

1. Part of this chapter previously appeared in D. Randall 2011a and 2011b.
2. Aristotle 2004: 135–41 [3.10–11]; Cicero 1967: II, 161 [3.53.202], 327 [*De partitione oratoria*, 6.20], 351 [*De partitione oratoria*, 15.53]; Longinus 2000: 133 [15]; Quintilian 1920–2: II, 83–5 [4.2.63–5], III, 261 [8.3.89], 363 [9.1.27], 397 [9.2.40]; Bussels 2012: 71–3; W. Walker 1994: 120–1.
3. The leap from aesthetic judgement to moral judgement should not be assumed. As Kivy notes, unlike Hutcheson, Hume makes no formal progression in his work from the one to the other. Kivy 1983: 198. Costelloe, however, provides warrant for such a leap, by demonstrating at length Hume's parallel treatment of moral and aesthetic beauty, and moral and aesthetic judgement. Costelloe 2007: 23–36.
4. For conceptions of sympathy from the ancient rhetoricians to the eighteenth century, see Fairclough 2013: 25, 42, 50, 52, 57, 59–121; Mullan 1988: 26–30, 33–4, 36–9, 43–51; Rebhorn 1995: 87–8, 92–3; Schmitter 2012: 258–61, 263–71, 274–6; Shaftesbury 1999: 10 ['A Letter Concerning Enthusiasm to My Lord *****'].

Chapter 5

Public Opinion

Introduction

Conversation, the discourse that united passion with reason, became a universal discourse in the Enlightenment, whose reasonable judgement judged all things. This formation of public opinion occurred in France, drawing directly upon the *salonnier* traditions of conversation, sociability and free judgement upon set topics. Yet in its moment of triumph, this universal conversation of public opinion continued to reflect conversation's old instability. So, just as conversation oscillated between its neighbours of oratory and philosophical dialogue, public opinion oscillated between variations constituted more by oratory – the British example – and more by philosophical dialogue – the public opinion of the *philosophes* and the Physiocrats. In the last generation of the *ancien régime*, the major stream of French thought shifted into the channel of the *philosophes*, and settled upon an imperious version of public opinion, a conversation that assumed sovereignty and command. It was a conversation that had thereby abandoned the old characteristics of *sermo* for a hollow throne.

Yet a minority report of the French Enlightenment, articulated above all by Gabriel Bonnot de Mably and Jacques Peuchet, preserved the conception of public opinion that (as Humean reason submitted itself to the passions) submitted its judgement to the people rather than aspired to command them.[1] This minority report echoed across the Atlantic, to the receptive mind of James Madison, who recapitulated this minority opinion and, translating it into the structure of the American polity, made it an essential component of the new American republic. Madisonian public opinion, submitting itself to Madisonian dispersed prudence, became the keystone of American political practice. Conversational public opinion, a refugee from France, would flourish in the Great Republic's political order – the avatar of the conversational public sphere.

Opinion

Opinion was popular judgement that judged reputation. Now, what was reputation? Reputation was character, that material of trustworthiness and persuasion which the orator would convey in speech as *ethos* – and perhaps constituted itself by speech. So Aristotle:

> Persuasion is achieved by the speaker's personal character when the speech is so spoken as to make us think him credible. . . . This kind of persuasion, like the others, should be achieved by what the speaker says, not by what people think of his character before he begins to speak. (Aristotle 2004: 7 [1.2.1356a]; Garver 2004: 144; G. Kennedy 1999: 82)

Opinion, of course, was a creature of *pathos*, passion, the traditional subject of *ethos*. Reputation and opinion were a linked dyad, the means of persuasion and the subject of the persuasion.

In the political realm – and to begin with, the reputation that was judged was, above all, political – opinion's divorce from both the perduring stability and the free exercise of reason gave to this dyad an essential weakness that rendered them liable to perpetual critique. Opinion (as any passion) was mutable and compulsive, a thing so light in substance and tyrannical in operation as to argue its worthlessness and its perniciousness. Stefano Guazzo wrote in the *Civile Conversation* (1574) 'that our name dependeth of the general opinions, which have such force, that reason is of no force against them' (Guazzo 1967: I, 61 [Bk 1]). Pierre Charron in his *Of Wisdome* (1601) provided an extended denunciation:

> opinion . . . is a vaine, light, crude and imperfect judgement of things drawen from the outward senses, and common report, feeling and holding itself to be good in the imagination, and never arriving to the understanding, there to be examined, sifted, and labored; and to be made reason which is a true, perfect and solide judgement of things: and therefore it is uncertaine, inconstant, fleeing, deceitfull, a very ill and dangerous guide, which makes head against reason, whereof it is a shadow and image, though vaine and untrue. It is the mother of all mischiefs, confusions, disorders: from it spring all passions, all troubles. It is the guide of fooles, sots, the vulgar sort, as reason of the wise and dexterious. (Charron n.d. [after 1612]: 69–70 [I. 16])

Pierre Le Moyne (1602–72) in *Les Peintures morales* (1640) referred to the 'Tyrannie des opinions' to which mankind was subject (Le Moyne 1640: 214 [2.5.1], 308 [3.4.1]; Gunn 1995: 32). A persisting image was of a torrent. Guazzo wrote of Custom, which he used as a synonym for opinion, that

> as the river Po, king of rivers, being over neere unto us, for that there hath beene no resistance made against it, is within this sixe yeeres come so farre forward, and hath wonne so much grounde upon this Citie, that at length it hath broken the walles, and nowe threatneth to overthrow them: so in like manner, the violence of custome, for that wee have too much suffered it, hath at this day in manner vanquished reason. (Guazzo 1967: I, 62 [Bk 1])

Nicolas Caussin (1583–1651) in *La Cour Sainte* (1624) described opinion by the overlapping images of a torrent, a yoke and a tyranny (Caussin 1678: 39–40 [1.2.3]; Gunn 1995: 72; see also Gunn 1993: 26). François de La Mothe Le Vayer (1588–1672) likewise referred in *Dialogue de la diversité des religions* (1671?) to 'la Tyrannique opiniastreté des opinions communes' as the 'torrent de la multitude' (La Mothe Le Vayer 1671: 269; Gunn 1995: 36; cf. Boyer 1702: [A3], 125).

Above all, opinion was the Queen of the World – an image almost certainly inherited from that of Lady Rhetoric. The Greeks took persuasion to be a goddess, Peitho; Cicero called rhetoric an *imperator* and, quoting Pacuvius (220–c. 130 BC), 'soulbending sovereign [*regina*, queen] of all things' (Cicero 1967: I, 332–3 [2.44.187]). Tacitus (AD 58–117) in his *Dialogus de oratoribus* (AD 102) recollected that eloquence had once been the *domina* of Rome (Tacitus 1925: 101 [32.4]); and Quintilian also cited Pacuvius: 'But he that has enough of the divine spark to conceive the ideal eloquence, he who, as the great tragic poet says, regards "oratory" as "the queen of all the world"' (Quintilian 1920–2: I, 199 [1.12.18]; Rebhorn 1995: 38). This image had been elaborated in late antiquity by Martianus Capella (*fl.* c. 410–20) as Lady Rhetoric:

> The garment under her arms was covered by a robe wound about her shoulders in the Latin fashion; this robe was adorned with the light of all kinds of devices and showed the figures of them all . . . When she clashed her weapons on entering, you would say that the broken booming of thunder was rolling forth with the shattering clash of a lightning cloud; indeed it was thought that she could hurl thunderbolts like Jove. For like a queen with power over everything, she could drive any host of people where she wanted and draw them back from where she wanted;

> she could sway them to tears and whip them to a frenzy, and change the countenance and senses not only of cities, but of armies in battle. She was said to have brought under her control, amongst the people of Romulus, the senate, the public platforms, and the law courts, and in Athens had at will swayed the legislative assembly, the schools, and the theaters, and had caused the utmost confusion throughout Greece. (Martianus Capella 1977: 156; Rebhorn 1995: 64)

That queenly image had become widespread in Renaissance Europe: so Cesare Ripa's (1555–1622) *Iconologia* (1625) described Eloquenza as follows:

> A beautiful young woman with her breast armored and her arms bare will have on her head a helmet surrounded by a crown of gold and at her flank a staff, in her right hand a rod, in her left a lightning bolt, and she will be dressed in purple. . . . she holds dominion over human spirits. (Ripa and Orlandi 1765: 318–19, translated in Rebhorn 1995: 64; 1995: 64–5)

The overlapping masculine imagery of Hercules Gallicus, which equally yoked rhetoric and sovereignty, likewise spread throughout the continent. Thomas Wilson (1524–81) wrote in *The Arte of Rhetorique* (1553) that

> the Poetes do feyne that *Hercules* being a man of greate wisdome, had all men lincked together by the eares in a chaine, to draw them and leade them even as he lusted. For his witte was so greate, his tongue so eloquente, and his experience suche, that no one man was able to withstand his reason, but everye one was rather driven to do that whiche he woulde, and to wil that whiche he did, agreing to his advise both in word and worke, in all that ever they were able. (T. Wilson 1553: sigs. aiii^{v}–aiii^{r} [*sic*: sig. aiii repeats]; Rebhorn 1995: 66–73)

Now, female personifications were common enough in early modern Europe. Lady Philosophy was also a queen, and Gunn wisely warns us that

> [w]e must, of course, recognise that early modern French was a language peculiarly well supplied with resources for invoking moral forces in reified or personified form. To write of the 'empire' exercised by one sector of existence on others was a normal way of expressing one's self in discourse where allegory was standard fare. (Gunn 1993: 20)[2]

Nevertheless, the continuities between the imagery of Lady Rhetoric and of Queen Opinion were remarkably strong. In the sixteenth century, Pierre de Ronsard (1524–85) and Amadis Jamyn (1538–92), among others, had pictured opinion as a sometimes-divine female figure. For Jamyn, Opinion was 'fille du Ciel et de la Terre, *Gouvernante des affaires humaines*'; for Ronsard, Opinion was a child of Jupiter and Dame Presumption (Jamyn 1887: 306–7; Ronsard 1563: 4r–v; Vianey 1903; Gunn 1995: 71). Nicolas Faret (1596–1646) in *L'honnête homme* (1630) stated that opinion 'makes the minde of man to yeeld at her Pleasure, and gouernes the will with such an absolute command, as if shee had reason for her guide' (Faret 1632: 223).

In his *De l'autorité des roys* (1631), François de Cauvigny, Sieur de Colomby (1588–1648), conceived of opinion as a queen absolutely sovereign over the human will: '*Ce quon a dit autresfois est bien veritable, qu'il n'est rien de si puissant entre les hommes que l'opinion. Ceste Reyne domine sur nos volontez auec vn empire si absolu*' (Colomby 1631: sig. ă r; Gunn 1995: 19). Gabriel Naudé's (1600–53) *Considérations politiques sur les coups d'estat* (1639) popularised the saying, attributed by Naudé to the sixteenth-century Italian Gerolamo Cardano (1501–76) (apparently wrongly; Naudé may have coined it himself), that 'L'Estime & l'opinion sont les Reines de toutes les choses humaines' – and hence to be intelligently manipulated by a prudent prince (Naudé 1667: 81, 81 (note 2); Gunn 1995: 21–2). A generation later, Blaise Pascal (1623–62) would also write in his *Pensées* (1670), very influentially, of opinion as queen of the world (Pascal 1846: 96 [6.3]; Gunn 1995: 70–84). Ancient and Renaissance writers alike had conceived that passions rule and compel: Quintilian wrote that, 'it is this emotional power that dominates [*dominetur*] the court, it is this form of eloquence that is the queen of all [*haec eloquentia regnat*]' (Quintilian 1920–2: II, 419 [6.2.4]; Tinkler 1991: 68–9). Passionate opinion was naturally a queen.

But what did opinion judge? As far back as the *quattrocento*, Poggio Bracciolini (1380–1459) in 'On Nobility' (1440) had made explicit the particular link between noble reputation and opinion, and the unsettling possibility that 'I [Niccolò] am forced to doubt, on this account, that the common everyday word, "nobility", is more than an empty name' (Bracciolini 1978: 124–5). In the judgement of reason, reputation was nothing; it was only a hollow mask framed to delude the passions. Yet while Bracciolini provided due space for Niccolò's argument – the argument of the humanist, the scholar, that nobility was a form of virtue – Lorenzo's riposte would be enduringly persuasive:

> For what is the nobility of a philosopher, content with his studies, living obscurely in a library where even he hardly hears of himself, or of a man

> who lives moderately, uprightly, chastely and wisely in a hidden villa, while no one talks about him or praises him. Virtue I would concede to them, but not nobility. I would call them lovers of virtue but not noblemen. (Bracciolini 1978: 143–6; and see Skinner 1987: 135–40)

Sixteenth- and seventeenth-century Italian and French writers, the latter with increasing emphasis in the reign of Louis XIV, continued to stress that a very large portion of the reputation of the aristocrat – his nobility and glory – was a matter of other people's opinions (Gunn 1995: 49–84; but see Peacham 1622: 3; L. Klein 1984–5: 193–4). So Torquato Tasso (1544–95) wrote in 'Il Forno, o Vero de la Nobiltà' (1581) that 'fama . . . altro non è che opinione universale, e divolgata per tutto'; in the French translation *De la noblesse* (1633), such glory was rendered as 'une constant et perdurable opinion de la valeur d'autruy, qui se publie de toutes les parts' (Tasso 1858: II, 155; 1633: 325–32, 334, 779–80, cited in Gunn 1995: 54). Marc de Vulson, Sieur de La Colombière (d. 1658), in turn wrote in *Le Vray théâtre d'honneur et de chevalerie* (1648) that 'l'honneur est vn certain signe & demonstration que celuy qui honnore, rend à celuy qui est honnoré, & la Renommée ne consiste qu'en l'opinion d'autruy' (Vulson 1648: II, 635; Gunn 1995: 55).

This conception of noble honour would in time make the noble order itself a hostage to the fortunes of (public) opinion. If nobility was no more than reputation, then, when the nobility lost the support of (public) opinion – as they did so rapidly at the end of the eighteenth century, in the plummet towards Revolution – their status in general, legal, political and social, would disintegrate (Gunn 1993: 30–3). Irrationality of opinion enduringly rendered reputation a nullity in the eyes of reason.

This nullity of reputation had no small implication for the Machiavellian tradition's emerging link between reputation and the prince's power – or in a later, Hobbesian rendition, between reputation and the power of the abstracted state (D. Randall 2011c). Writers in the reason-of-state tradition such as Giovanni Botero (c. 1544–1617) linked political reputation, especially a prince's reputation, to prestige, which ultimately depended upon the opinion of the people: 'la reputation d'vn Prince est posee aux opinion, & conceps que le peuple s'imagine de luy' (Botero 1606: 384; Gunn 1995: 16–18; cf. Habermas 1991: 267 (note 3)). The prince's reputation was thus delicate, as opinion was essentially unsteady. In his *De l'autorité des roys* (1631), the Sieur de Colomby took the people, subject to 'fureur' and 'imagination', as susceptible to rebellion. The prince's reputation could collapse once nicked:

> *Car que sont proprement les reuoltes, que des effects de l'oubly du deuoir à quoy les subjects sont obligez? Ce sont des fureurs où les hommes n'entrent samais que par l'imagination qu'on leur donee que leurs Princes prennent plus d'autorité qu'ils ne doiuent.* (Colomby 1631: sig. ăii[v]; Gunn 1995: 19)

Guez de Balzac (to piece together several of his disparate writings) took opinion to be both the object of the prince's appeal, and sovereign: 'It is not now onely that opinion governes the world; there hath beene disputing against Reason in al ages' (Guez de Balzac 1638: 96 ['To Mounsieur *Maynard*. Letter XXX']; Gunn 1995: 23–4). The Machiavellian tradition's emphasis on reputation brought with it as a corollary a dependence on opinion – fearfully powerful, yet unstable and fragile.

The Machiavellian tradition's dependence upon uncertain, hollow opinion in consequence made that very opinion a central subject of the exercise of *virtù*, which quite deliberately endeavoured to produce the proper reputation, and power, of the prince and state. In other words, it was the task of the ruler, informed perhaps by reason (of state), to govern opinion, whether by an appeal to love or to fear (Gunn 1995: 43–5). So the Duc de Rohan (1579–1638) ascribed reputation to popular opinion, and wrote of both as components of political power and, therefore, objects of political technique: 'From all these things results the reputation of *Spaine*. Her *Interest* is, to manage well *this pietie*. . . . all *Princes* hold for a generall maxime, that they should carefully conserve their reputation' (Rohan 1641: 13–15; Gunn 1995: 22–3, 44–5). Such endeavours, however, did not (at first) partake of sweet reason: Naudé, typically, took the populace to be brutish and their credulous imaginations susceptible to deception: he wrote in *Considérations politiques sur les coups d'estat* (1639) that

> cette populace est comparée à une mer sujette à toutes sortes de vents & de tempestes: au Cameleon qui peut recevoir toutes sortes de couleurs excepté la blanche; & à la sentine & cloaque dans laquelle coulent toutes les ordures de la maison. (Naudé 1667: 236; Gunn 1995: 19–20)

Such a conception of the populace naturally encouraged a resort to deceit, and all the manipulations appropriately to be used upon a great beast incapable of reason.

This conception also encouraged a distinct emphasis on unanimity, to which we will return later: both Italian and French writers generally argued that good reputation required unanimity, since a reputation lost could not be regained (Gunn 1995: 45–6). So Virgilio Malvezzi (1595–1634) wrote in *Considerations upon the lives of Alcibiades and Corialanus* (1648) that 'Reputation is not diminished by degrees, nor cannot be broken piece-meale: if it be not reserved intire, it quite abandoneth one' (Malvezzi 1650: 149). Daniel de Priezac (1590–1662) added in *Discours politiques* (1652) that 'la Reputation est vn consentement vniuersel de tous les Peuples, & vn bien public dont chacun peut vser à sa volonté, & mesme le dispenser à qui bon luy semble' (Priezac 1652: 171–2). Opinion's focus on reputation inclined it thus early (and persistingly) towards a demand for unanimity (Robespierre 1828: 15; Gunn 1995: 389–90; but see 1993: 22), as a means of persuasion of the multitude (and see Fumaroli 1983: 272).

Yet the distaste that reputation and opinion aroused in so many European thinkers by dint of their essential nullity led directly to dreams of some alternative mode, by which one could ground reputation – authority, sovereignty itself – in reason. So although Jean de Silhon (1596–1667) also related opinion to reputation, particularly in his *Le Ministre d'estat, seconde partie* (1643), he added to this equation in his later work the claim that one could escape the uncertainties of deluded opinion for some mode of certain knowledge that could dissolve the deceptive appearances of the world: 'aprés la description que nous y auons, donnée de cét autre genre de Connoissance, qu'on appelle *Opinions*; il nous faut rechercher la nature & les conditions d'vne autre maniere de raisonner & d'aller à la queste de la verité' (Silhon 1643: 68; 1661: 555, and see 64, 559–60, 562–3; Gunn 1995: 26–30). The later history of opinion consisted very largely of a search for a mode of certain knowledge, so as to ground opinion (hence reputation, hence sovereignty) in the enduring strength of rational substance.

From Conversation to Public Opinion

We will first consider the search for a mode of certain knowledge that could be applied to opinion – in effect, a way to apply reason to opinion. One mode was via the power of *interest* in people – including not least economic self-interest – since *interest* was susceptible to reason, as *opinion* was not (Hirschman 1977: 9–66). In seventeenth-century France, however, the pursuit of *interest* applied to individuals, *opinion* to the multitude (Gunn 1993; 1995: 45). Interest could make the individual man reasonable, but not mankind. How could mankind, collectively, come to judge reasonably?

Conversation provided that judgement of reason. The realm of conversation was a realm where one submitted one's arguments to a common judgement informed by the common search for truth by means of reason. Indeed, it was crucial that conversation sought rational assent: only speech that sought rational assent could elicit it. By the late seventeenth century in France, conversation had expanded sufficiently in scope that it could apply itself to the realm of opinion. Madeleine de Scudéry could write in 'On Conversation' that 'we may affirm without falsehood that there is nothing that cannot be said in conversation' (Scudéry 2002: 89). Pierre d'Ortigue, Sieur de Vaumorière (1610–93), connected conversation explicitly to opinion when he wrote in *The Art of Pleasing in Conversation* (1691) that in conversation 'We may speak our opinions touching the Government of other Nations with as much boldness as *Belise* does' (Vaumorière 1691: 314). At the same time, he indicated conversation's limitations: 'But when we are pleased to discourse on the State under which we live, we should never extend our conjectures too far, nor affect to appear too penetrating' (Vaumorière 1691: 314). But conversation's rational judgements and the judgements of opinion were already linked by the end of the Sun King's reign – conversation's audacious aspirations limited in their exercise only by a prudential wariness of the sanctions of the state. The later development of public opinion as a forum by which mankind in common could render judgements upon the *moeurs* and *police* of France paid explicit homage to its roots in the conversations of the *salonnières* as they judged in the narrower realm of the arts and letters (D. Goodman 1994: 235–40). So Charles Pinot Duclos (1704–72) wrote in *Considérations sur les moeurs de ce siècle* (1751) that,

> Men having become polite and enlightened, those whose souls were the most *honnête* have supplemented the laws with morality in establishing, by a tacit convention, procedures to which usage has given the force of law among *honnêtes gens*, and which are the supplement of positive laws . . . public opinion, which exercises justice in this regard, metes it out in exact proportions, and makes very fine distinctions. . . . public opinion being itself the punishment of the actions of which it is the judge, cannot fail to be severe concerning those things which it condemns. There are such actions of which suspicion is the proof, and publicity the chastisement. (Duclos: 1751: 69–72, translated in D. Goodman 1994: 236)

Public opinion, forged from the conversational severities of the *salons*, would judge with a certainty derived precisely from its reliance on rational assent.

Yet the development of conversation as a forum of judgement did not depend solely on arguments of *logos*, but embedded them (as all rhetoric) in *ethos* and *pathos*. *Ethos*, character, was among other things reputation argued in speech (Garver 2004: 144; G. Kennedy 1999: 82) – argued above all in oratory. In conversation, however, what now conveyed trustworthiness was a transformed *ethos*, the sincere revelation of interiority (see the discussion of eighteenth-century conversational poetics above; and D. Randall 2018: 21, 86, 92, 112–13, 127, 159, 161, 194, 199). The application of this mode to public speech allowed the trustworthiness of conversation likewise to be applied to the public realm. A second prerequisite was a belief that reason could harmonise with passion – that conversation, which appealed to sentiment and was accessible to reason, had the capacity to supplant oratory, which appealed solely to passion and provided reason with no purchase (see the discussion of conversational philosophy above; and cf. Tinkler 1991: 63, 69). The collective and dialogic rational judgement of conversation, drawn from the mutual and sincere revelation of interiority and applied to the world of politics, could form *among those capable of such conversation* the latest iteration of the old humanist belief in dialogue as the suturing mode of inquiry by which to elicit guidance from the world of eternal truth so as to inform our actions in the mutable world of power. This latest iteration of such conversational inquiry would come to be known as *public opinion*.

The phrase *l'opinion publique* existed long before it acquired this precise connotation. It was present in France as early as in Montaigne's essays, where – as opinion did without the modifier – it referred to the judgement of individual reputations; scattered usage continued over the following century (Montaigne 2003: 102 ['Of custom, and not easily changing an accepted law'], 984 ['Of physiognomy']; Gunn 1995: 12–13, 121–5). Use of the phrase began to increase both in frequency and in the value placed on it during the latter part of the reign of Louis XIV; it referrred particularly to a writer's audience, presumptively possessed of some minimal competence to undergird its opinions. So Charles Rivière Dufresny (1648–1724) wrote in 'Le Public' (1699) that

> Le Public est un souverain, duquel relevent tous ceux qui travaillent pour la reputation, ou pour le gain. . . . Le droit qu'il a de juger de tout, a bien produit des vertus, & bien étouffé des crimes. . . . Le public est le plus severe & le plus fin critique du monde. (Dufresny 1699: 126, 129)

L'opinion publique judged in the non-political realm of conversation, and was constituted by an audience that overlapped with the *salonnières*. Pierre-Jacques Brillon (1671–1736) specified in *Apologie de monsieur de La Bruyère* (1701) that he meant *le peuple* in a special sense: not 'un nombre d'hommes peu instruits, peu civilisez, esprits mediocres, Juges prevenus, & par consequent mauvais Juges', but rather 'personnes qui s'elevent, montrent des talens, produisent leur sçavoir, sont éclatter du merite . . . il perd ce tître méprisable, cette vile qualité, par un juste discernement & par une estime legitimement accordée' (Brillon 1701: 300–1; Gunn 1995: 85–100).

At this early stage *l'opinion publique* was often invoked by political and literary conservatives. In the battle of the ancients and the moderns, for example, Bellegarde in his *Lettres curieuses de littérature et de morale* (1702) invoked the public on the side of the ancients: 'On sait de quoi la prévention est capable, & que l'opinion publique n'est pas toujours une preuve assurée d'un veritable merite; mais un consentement si general confirmé durant tant de siècles, ne peut être fondé, que sur la vérité' (Bellegarde 1702: 181). Anne Lefévre Dacier (1654–1720) likewise argued in *Des causes de la corruption du goût* (1714) against Antoine Houdar de la Motte's (1672–1731) contention, used to support his critique of Homer's imperfections, that '*Nostre raison est l'arbitre naturel de tout ce que les hommes nous proposent.*' Dacier invoked the more durable opinion of the centuries:

> Cela est vray, quand ce qu'ils nous proposent est particulier ou nouveau, & qu'il n'est pas revestu de l'authorité d'une approbation generale. Mais quand une fois une opinion a esté authorisée par le consentement de tous les siecles & de tous les hommes, ou de la plus grande & de la plus faine partie des hommes, les sages y soumettent leur raison, & il n'y a que les fous qui s'y opposent. (Dacier 1714: 53–4)

The quality of enduring judgement attached to public opinion still had a traditionalising resonance (Gunn 1995: 100–4).

The public's association with a specialised audience introduced the notion of the *gens de lettres* as a distinctive public. Jean-Baptiste Dubos (1670–1742) (to whose broader conception of public judgement we will return shortly) wrote in *Réflexions critiques sur la poësie et sur la peinture* (1719) that

> I do not mean the lower class of people by the public capable of passing judgment on poems or pictures, or of deciding the measure of their excellence. The word *public* is applicable here to such persons only, as have acquired some lights, either by reading or by being conversant with the world.

It also introduced the idea of multiple, specialised publics. Even within Dubos' capable public, 'every one that is able to pass a sound judgment on a French tragedy, is not equally capable of forming a right opinion of the Aeneid, or of any other Latin poem' (Dubos 1748: II, 245–6 [Ch. 22]; Gunn 1995: 104–10; and see Crow 1985; Dejean 1997: 31–77; Guichard 2012; Ray 2004; Weber 1980). Neither of these associations was entirely new: Descartes in his *Discourse on Method* (1637) spoke of 'communicating to the public' (Descartes 1985: I, 143 [6.63]; Fumaroli 1988: 135–6), and Descartes approved, in Étienne de Courcelles' (1586–1659) Latin translation of 1644, the rendition of 'public' as '*Respublica literaria*' (Descartes 1644: 55; 1985: I, 142 [6.61]; Fumaroli 1988: 136). Yet these associations now became stronger, and more explicitly articulated. To add *publique* to *l'opinion* was to align with it one or the other of the overlapping elites capable of reason, of conversation and of judgement (but see Gunn 1995: 329–86; Ozouf 1988: S1–S4, S18, S21).

To these attributes of public opinion, we must add, and emphasise, those given by Louis de Sacy (1654–1727) in his *Traité de la gloire* (1715). Sacy ascribed (public) opinion's value in its estimation of glory (i.e., reputation) to its constancy and its unanimity: 'Car la gloire ne consiste point dans une acclamation momentanée, mais dans la constant & unanime admiration meslée d'amour, que tout le monde temoigne pour les actions vertueuses, & pour les talents rares.' Such unanimity was a sign of truth: 'La verité est le premier fondement de l'opinion publique. On ne voit point d'homme generalement estimé pour un talent, pour une vertu qu'il n'a pas' (Sacy 1715: 50, 55; Gunn 1995: 112–13). Sacy thus articulated what made public opinion so attractive: unlike the torrential mutability of opinion, it could be relied upon because it was a durable consensus (but see Ozouf 1988: S3). Public, reasoned opinion that was capable of such constancy and unanimity thus emerged as a superior replacement of the passionate opinion of old.

In the early eighteenth century, public opinion began to be associated more and more closely with conversationalists and the world of conversation. The judgement of a man's politeness and merit, shorn of reference to hierarchy and status, now came from *le publique*, a collectivity of the conversationalists of the *monde* – disjunct from the court, fuzzily associated with the *salons*, but more generally associated with a mode of sociable behaviour than with a particular social space. As Bellegarde put it in *Reflexions sur le ridicule et sur les moyens de l'éviter* (1696), 'Laissez au Public la liberté de son suffrage, c'est à lui à décider de la gloire que vous meritez' (Bellegarde 1697: 138; Gordon 1994: 99–100).

This emphasis on public judgement became more explicit at the beginning of the eighteenth century. La Motte wrote in *Réflexions sur la critique* (1716) that 'It is a natural right of the Public to judge the writings that are exposed to it' (La Motte 1716: 21, translated in Kaiser 1989–90: 184). Nicolas Boileau-Despréaux (1636–1711), meanwhile, wrote that, 'There are no readers who do not give their opinion on the writings one has printed . . . In effect, what is it to publish a work? Is it not in some measure to say to the Public "Judge me"?' (Boileau-Despréaux 1966: 6 ['Preface'], translated in Kaiser 1989–90: 184) There were qualms about this new mode of public judgement: Jean Mabillon (1632–1707) wrote in *Traité des études monastiques* (1691) that 'Les siecles precedens ont peché par un excés de simplicité & de credulité: mais dans celui-cy les pretendus esprits forts ne reçoivent rien qui n'ait passé par leur tribunal' (Mabillon 1691: 290–1). Yet such sceptics of the new turn to public judgement also, perforce, had to acknowledge that it was the mode of the times. Mabillon continued, 'Le pays des lettres est un pays de liberté, où tout le monde presume avoir droit de bourgeoisie' (Mabillon 1691: 293; Kaiser 1989–90: 184–5).

Jean-Baptiste Dubos wrote at length of public judgement in his *Réflexions critiques sur la poësie et sur la peinture* (1719), especially as regarded the arts and letters, but also (in a telling extension of the term) of politics as well. He ascribed to the public a sentimental knowledge of the world: 'The decision of the question does not belong to the jurisdiction of reason: This ought to submit to the judgment pronounced by sense, which is the competent judge of the question' (Dubos 1748: II, 237–9, 243–4 [Ch. 22]). The multiplicity of judges in the public gave it the advantage of disinterest:

> I do not pretend to affirm that one does not meet with some whom friendship engages in favour of authors, and others who are prejudiced against them by a particular aversion. But these are in so small a number, that their prevention hath no great influence in the general suffrage. (Dubos 1748: II, 236 [Ch. 21]).

If the public was less accurate in its judgement of politics, it was because it knew fewer of the facts in question than it did of arts and letters (Dubos 1748: II, 259–62 [Ch. 24]). Implicitly, though, greater knowledge of political affairs would remedy that relative deficiency.

Dubos, however, gave a conservative twist to his notions by emphasising that the test of worth was not only by one public, but by many through the years and miles of the world: an enduring judgement, endorsed by the scattered nations.

> [T]he public continues frequently for some time in a state of uncertainty or error . . . This first time being elapsed, the public appraises a work to its full value, and gives it a rank due to its merit, or condemns it to oblivion. (Dubos 1748: II, 235–6 [Ch. 21]; and see 247 [Ch. 22], 258 [Ch. 23], 273 [Ch. 26], 307, [Chs. 30–1])

As noted above, Dubos retained against this traditionalising universality a somewhat elite conception of the public – one, in essence, properly educated, as sentiment was a matter not only of the universal passions but also of the intellect, which only a few possessed (Dubos 1748: II, 245–6 [Ch. 22]). But Dubos thought the public had increased in historic time:

> A particular rank of citizens, who have not the advantage of these lights in a country town, have them in a metropolis. A rank that was deprived of them at the commencement of the sixteenth century, is favoured with them at the close of the seventeenth. For instance, since the establishing of operas, the number capable of giving their judgment on music, is considerably increased at Paris. (Dubos 1748: II, 246 [Ch. 22])

The public, in other words, was a historicised subject: 'The word *public* is likewise limited more or less, according to the times and places spoken of' (Dubos 1748: II, 246 [Ch. 22]). Historicised, it could be changed by historical processes – itself a very important conceptual innovation – and Dubos set no limit to the future increase of the public (Kaiser 1989–90: 193–4; and see also Delehanty 2013: 145–68).

As Dubos' example indicates, 'public opinion' had political connotations by the first decades of the eighteenth century. The anonymous *Première requête présentée au Roy par les pairs de France* (1716), possibly written by Sacy, took the quarrel for precedence between the peers and the Presidents of the Parlement of Paris to include as a goal the establishment of 'une espèce de possession dans l'opinion publique' (*Recueil* 1716: 10; Gunn 1995: 121–5). Whatever the phraseology, the existence of what we now (in the broadest sense) call public opinion predated the actual use of the phrase in the political field by centuries or millennia.

Yet something more like public opinion in the narrower sense was emerging in practice in France during the eighteenth century: in 1745, for example, the French government investigated public reactions to a proposed increase in taxes – in effect, attempted to determine the state of public opinion (Ozouf 1988: S8). This incident may be significant in its chronology: the use of public opinion in the political sense exploded in use from the late 1740s. Montesquieu's *The Spirit of the Laws* (1748) popularised a variety of concepts associated with public opinion – *moeurs*, prejudice, honour (Montesquieu 1989: *passim*, but notably xliii–xliv [Preface], 26–8 [1.3.6–8], 308–33 [3.19]). Immediately thereafter, from about 1749, the *parlementaires* grew more daring and began to invoke public opinion and related concepts against the crown (Gunn 1995: 126–78; Ozouf 1988: S6; see also S2–S3). In 1762, Charles de Brosses (1709–77) and Maleteste de Villey (1709–85) [?] quoted Montesquieu directly in *Nouvelles remontrances du parlement de Bourgone au Roi*:

> Dans notre Monarchie (1) [Esp. des Lois. XII. 25.] *toute la félicité consiste dans l'opinion que le Peuple a de la douceur du gouvernement . . . il y a une certaine facilité dans le commandement; il faut que le Prince encourage, & que ce soit les Loix qui menacent.* [Paragraph] Heureusement, SIRE, ce sentiment, si digne de vous & de la nation, est dans votre coeur comme dans ceux de vos sujets. ([De Brosses and Villey] 1762: 79; Gunn 1995: 161)

In 1766, Pierre-Louis Chaillou (1740–1806) [?] wrote in *Des commissions extraordinaires en matière criminelle* of that ultimate tribunal 'que le principe naturel de la Monarchie, l'honneur, répand dans tous les Ordres de l'État; & d'où se forme l'opinion publique que les Rois même se font gloire de respecter' ([Chaillou] 1766: 4–5; Gunn 1995: 161). We will return to this image of public opinion as a tribunal a little below.

The *gens de lettres*, the *philosophes*, also began to claim public opinion as uniquely their own; Voltaire, for example, argued in *La Voix du sage et du people* (1750) that 'Les Philosophes n'aïant aucun interêt particulier, ne peuvent parler qu'en faveur de la raison & de l'interêt public' (Voltaire 1750: 12; Gunn 1995: 170). This mid-century tranformation also saw the development of the concept of *prejudice*, a darkly limned redescription of opinion, which needed to be corrected by the enlightened – and could be. Baron d'Holbach (1723–89) [?] wrote in *Essai sur les préjugés* (1770),

> Pourquoi renoncerions-nous à l'espérance de trouver des coeurs droits revêtus du pouvoir écouter la vérité, dessiller les yeux des peuples & bannir ces vains préjugés qui depuis tant de siecles ont infecté les nations? La vérité, armée de la puissance souveraine, a des forces invincibles; il

> n'est point d'erreur qui puisse résiser au coups d'un Monarque équitable, magnanime, biensaisant, dont les soins ont acquis des droits sur tous les coeurs. Malgré le prestige de l'opinion, la superstition elle-même sera forcée de plier devant un Prince que ses vertus réelles rendront cher à ses peuples. (Holbach 1770: 79–80; Gunn 1995: 216–45)

In general, remarkably swiftly, public opinion became especially associated both with men of letters – particularly by the men of letters themselves – and with the *parlements* (Ozouf 1988: S6–S7).

The Tribunal of Public Opinion

The judgement of *le publique* also became associated with the image of the tribunal (Chartier 1991: 30–7; D. Goodman 1994: 118; and see Beasley 2006: 28). This imagery associated public opinion not simply with judgement in the abstract, but with judgement as an institution of judicature and government. The concept of the *tribunal of public opinion* greatly facilitated the transference of public opinion to the political realm – and public opinion's culminating claim to sovereignty itself.

As early as 1701, the *Dictionnaire universel* provided two examples of 'public' that used judicial imagery: 'Quelque decrié que soit le *public*, il n'y a pas de Juge plus incorruptible, & tôt ou tard il rend justice. . . . Le *public*, qui est le Juge souverain, se laisse prevenir comme les particuliers' (*Dictionnaire universel* 1701: III, *s.v.* 'Public'; Ozouf 1988: S2; and see Boyer 1702: 219). In the 1730s, Abbé Prévost (1697–1763) likewise associated the opinion of the readers of his newspaper *Le Pour et contre* with judgement, often explicitly associated with the imagery and subject matter of the law court. So, defending himself to his readers against the slanders of Abbé Lenglet-Dufresnoy (1674–1755), Prévost addressed them as if they were judges in a court: 'Voilà le Procez tout instruit' (Prévost 1967: 285 [IV, 47 (1734), p. 35]; Bloom 2009: 100; and see Chartier 1991: 34–5). As a general matter, he put it that, 'Nothing has so much power over a writer than [*sic*] the opinion of his readers, that is to say his judges' (Prévost 1967: 367 [V, 61 (1734), p. 5]), translated in Bloom 2009: 98; 2009: 98–101).

This conception of public opinion broadened in the later eighteenth century into a collective judgement of all matters discussed by *le monde* – which, as the scope of such matters increased, came to have a very broad remit indeed (see also Crow 1985). In 1775, Malesherbes (1721–94) wrote in his *Discours prononcé dans l'Académie française le jeudi 16 février* that,

> A tribunal has been raised independent of all powers and respected by all powers, which evaluates all talents, and pronounces on all people of merit. And in an enlightened century, in a century in which each citizen can speak to the entire nation by means of print, those who have the talent for instructing men and the gift of moving them – men of letters, in a word – are, among the dispersed public, what the orators of Rome and Athens were in the midst of the public assembly. (Malesherbes 1808: 151, translated in Ozouf 1988: S9)

By the 1780s, the association of public opinion with the concept of a tribunal was very strong. Jacques Necker (1732–1804) referred to public opinion in *De l'administration des finances de la France* (1785) as 'a tribunal before which all men who attract attention are obliged to appear' (Necker 1785: 165; Baker 1990: 193); while Jacques Peuchet (1758–1830) referred to public opinion in 'Discours préliminaire' (1789) 'as grounds for the judgements made by a nation on matters submitted to its tribunal' (Peuchet 1789: ix; Baker 1990: 193–4). Necker's formulation, in particular, gave sovereign attributes to that 'tribunal before which all men who attract attention are obliged to appear: There, public opinion, as if from the height of a throne, awards prizes and honors, makes and unmakes reputations' (Necker 1785: 165; Baker 1990: 193).

Necker's association of public opinion with both the tribunal and the throne was not accidental, for the tribunal in ancient Rome (about whose history the *philosophes* were usually formidably informed) had been both judicial and sovereign in character.[3] The *tribunus plebis* – the tribune – had been given the power to protect Roman citizens, especially plebeians, from the arbitrary exercise of power by other (patrician) magistrates, by the exercise of a veto. In the exercise of his protective power, the tribune had also acquired the power to prosecute misbehaving magistrates in the plebeian assembly. The tribune's own person had been sacrosanct, inviolate. With the coming of the Empire, Octavian (63 BC–AD 14) had given himself tribunal power – *tribunicia potestas*. This acquisition had been renewed among the early emperors, until it became absorbed among the Imperial attributes. That 'tribune' also referred to military officers further identified the concept with sovereign force. The identification of public opinion with the tribunal, therefore, also identified it with sovereign power (A. Collins 2002: 82; Loewenstein 1973: 69–74, 182–3, 347; Mousourakis 2007: 27, 84, 100, 103–4, 106, 228 (note 22); Rowe 2002: 41–66; and see F. Millar 1977: 3–4, 228–40, 465–7, 507).

Whether in its Republican guise as *tribunus plebis* or in its Imperial guise as *tribunicia potestas*, this conception of the tribunal encompassed a shift in meaning from the tribunal to the tribune – the active magistrate who embodied the tribunal powers. To speak of public opinion as a tribunal was to speak of the possibility of a tribune of public opinion – on the one hand, a liberating Gracchus (c. 165–133 BC); on the other, a sovereign Augustus. Rousseau's Tribunate in *The Social Contract*, which also had a veto on governmental actions, was sacrosanct and drew its authority from beyond the will of the sovereign, reflected one Enlightenment meditation on the image of the tribune (Rousseau 1994: 211–12 [4.5]; Bates 2012: 201; Sabl 2002: 208–9; Thom 1995: 158). Necker's tribunary imagery reflected another: the conceptual association that allowed the concept of public opinion to migrate from judgement to sovereignty.

The Public Opinion of the *Philosophes*

The emergence of public opinion – political in its scope, tribunary in its imagery, sovereign in its ambitions – coincided with another momentous shift: the re-emergence of the old Republic of Letters, in the guise of *philosophes*, to challenge their incorporation within the larger category of the world of conversation and the *salons*. For a generation and more, the *philosophes* had, as much as they ever would, submitted their judgement to that of a *monde* and *publique* defined around the *salonnières*. Even this submission had been uneasy. Pierre-Daniel Huet (1630–1721), for example, although generally favourable to *salons* and *salonnières*, had been uncomfortable about the exercise of female taste (Huet 1722: 175–6, translated in Beasley 2006: 42). After about 1750, the *philosophes*, increasingly self-confident, began to elevate their own judgement, as that of the properly enlightened and educated, over the *salonnières*' amateur judgement. Rather than rely upon the judgement of the *salons*, aristocratic in tone and open to women, the *philosophes* set up their own associations, masculine and democratic – *musées*, clubs, *lycées*, *sociétés* – from which to form their own public, conversation, opinion and judgement. *Le Club des dames* (1784) (anonymous, probably written by a female author) articulated the masculinising shift so:

> In order to be a real philosophe, one must not live with women; this noble character would be weakened with us: our virtues hold too much to nature. . . . To betray with audacity, to be enterprising, bold, in short, to wish to dominate; this is what is called being a man. (*Le Club* 1784: 3, translated in D. Goodman 1994: 241)

'Monsieur le Public' came to be gendered male (Mercier 1782–8: VI, 303), and if the *philosophes* submitted themselves to public opinion's tribunal, they were also its self-appointed arbiters (Beasley 2006: 30, 41, 43–9, 76–88; D. Goodman 1994: 40, 233–80; Lougee 1976: 70–84; and see Pekacz 1999b). Rousseau, for his part, praised the masculine conversation of the *cercles* of Geneva, where

> [t]hey do not humor one another in dispute: each, feeling himself attacked by all the forces of his adversary, is obliged to use all of his own to defend himself; it is thus that the mind gains precision and vigour. (Rousseau 2004: 328; Mee 2011: 78)

This shift to *philosophe* judgement was allied with a recrudescence of the Baylean tradition of criticism and critique. The Baylean tradition harmonised badly with the conversational tradition, for it derived from humanist philological analysis, which aimed to supersede mere opinion by resort to judgement based on reason in a dialectic mode (*pour et contre*; the heir of the *sic et non* and the disputation) rather than a dialogic one (*in utramque partem*). As opposed to the conversational pursuit of truth, critique sought universal truth via polarising arguments, where one argument conquered the other. Pierre Bayle (1647–1706) had set the tone in his description of the Republic of Letters:

> Every body there [in the Republic of Letters] is both Sovereign and under every-body's Jurisdiction. The Laws of the Society have done no Prejudice to the Independency of the State of Nature, as to Error and Ignorance: in that respect, every particular Man has the Right of the Sword, and may exercise it without asking leave of those who govern. (Bayle 1735: 389; Koselleck 1988: 103–18; D. Randall 2018: 162–3).

Indeed, although critique shared with conversation a basis in the joint and democratic exercise of speech, its conquering aspect rendered it in many ways an imperious continuation of the *ancien régime*, whose judgement spoke with sovereign finality. Jean-François Marmontel wrote in 'Critique' for the *Encyclopédie Methodique* that

> il faut juger les hommes en homme vertueux, mais en homme; se connoître, connoître ses semblables, & savoir ce qu'ils peuvent avant d'examiner ce qu'ils doivent; concilier la nature avec la société, mesurer leurs droits & en marquer les limites, raprocher l'intérêt personel du bien général, être enfin le juge non le tyran de l'humanité . . . Par-là l'Histoire, dans sa partie morale, est un espece de labyrinthe où l'opinion du lecteur ne cesse de s'égarer; c'est un guide qui lui manque: or ce guide seroit un *Critique* capable de distinguer la vérité de l'opinion, le devoir de l'intérêt, la vertu de la gloire elle-même, en un mot de réduire l'homme, quel qu'il fût, à la condition de citoyen: condition que est la base des loix, la regle des moeurs, & dont aucun homme en société n'eût jamais droit de s'afranchir. (Marmontel 1786: 557; Koselleck 1988: 110, 118)

The critique of the *philosophes*, self-assured and severe, a judge that protested perhaps too strongly that it was not a tyrant, now began to compete with the conversation of the *salonnières* as the mode by which best to articulate public opinion.

Critique's increasing success would, among other effects, make it increasingly difficult for participants in public debates to refrain from impoliteness that cracked the conversational bounds. André Morellet's critique in *Réfutation de l'ouvrage* (1770) of Ferdinando Galiani's *Dialogues sur le Commerce des Blés* (1770) was discourteous in the last analysis because Morellet was a disputatious soul who relished an argy-bargy, but Morellet transformed such impoliteness into a matter of methodological principle by arguing for the superiority of critique over dialogue:

> I believe I see in the Dialogues little attachment to what the Author himself regards as the truth: indifference, lightness concerning a matter that is serious and of interest; an affected respect for all received opinions; constant flattery for the authority of all times and all places; a very marked taste for despotism; a dogma of infallibility concerning those who govern. (Morellet 1770: 3, translated in D. Goodman 1994: 205)

Morellet's *Réfutation* owed its success in good measure to state support – his loudly independent-minded critique doubled as hack work for the government – but also to its articulation of the burgeoning claims of critique (D. Goodman 1994: 183–232). Such relentless critique, indeed, was forming a political culture in its own image, the sword of reason soon to seek more palpable swords (cf. Schama 1990).

This is to anticipate. While the tradition of critique was gaining ground, further transformations rapidly altered the concept of public opinion in the last decades of *ancien régime* France (see also Gunn 1995: 282–328). Jean-Baptiste-Antoine Suard (1732–1817), in a speech in 1774, stated that public opinion 'governs the world', and that its power exceeded 'the public force charged with the execution of the laws' (Suard 1774: 16, translated in Gordon 1994: 174). Public opinion was now taken to govern the political realm – but the exact means by which this governance occurred was specified; Suard described an automatic process by which government submitted to the consensual opinions of civil society. This process now sublimated into the historical process: historical progress consisted of the intensification of civility, public opinion and self-government, until such time as the coercions of government, fit for savages rather than civilised, reasonable men, withered away. Suard was somewhat hazy about the precise mechanisms of this transformation (Suard 1774: 16), but the happy conclusion of *le progrès des lumières* was clear enough. Force – politics – would fall away, without the need for *le publique* to assume its responsibilities: the *philosophes* would become free, but without acquiring the attributes and responsibilities of sovereignty (Gordon 1994: 174; see also Baker 1990: 193).

Parallel shifts occurred from the late 1760s onwards, as Frenchmen began to give the tribunal of public opinion, especially as exercised via the medium of print, a governing role over government itself – or, more precisely, an enlightening and revolutionary role against the tyrannies of despots (Baker 1990: 187–8). Charles Pinot Duclos wrote in his revision of *Considérations sur les moeurs* in 1767 that

> Of all empires, that of *gens d'esprit*, without being visible, is the most extensive. The powerful command, but the *gens d'esprit* govern, because in the long run they form public opinion, which sooner or later subjugates or overthrows every kind of despotism. (Duclos 1772: 217, translated in Baker 1990: 187)

Louis-Sébastien Mercier (1740–1814) added in *Tableau de Paris* (1782) that

> In the last thirty years alone, a great and important revolution has occurred in our ideas. Today, public opinion has a preponderant force in Europe that cannot be resisted. Thus in assessing the progress of enlightenment and the change it must bring about, we may hope that it will bring the greatest good to the world and that tyrants of all stripes will tremble before this universal cry that continuously rings out to fill and awaken Europe. (Mercier 1782–8: IV, 169, translated in Baker 1990: 187–8)

André Morellet took public opinion to be a means by which to instruct the ruler, to steer the state, without particular consideration of *douceur*. Public opinion acquired sovereign attributes: 'We act upon public opinion and public opinion will eventually subjugate fanatics and even tyrants' (Morellet 1991: 59 [André Morellet to Cesare Beccaria, July (day unknown) 1766, translated in Gordon 1994: 182]; Gordon 1994: 181–2). Morellet preserved a conception of consensual public opinion, even though the disputes of the *philosophes* (not least Morellet himself) were already fracturing that putative consensus (Gordon 1994: 182–9). He derived his conception of public opinion from conversation, which he continued to regard as a means by which to produce knowledge (Gordon 1994: 199–208). Morellet wrote in *Réflexions sur les avantages de la liberté d'écrire et d'imprimir sur les matières de l'administration* (written 1764, published 1775) that

> There is a source of instruction for the public and for the government . . . from which society can draw the greatest advantage: I mean conversation. . . . The manner in which another sees the object with which you are occupied, often being different from your own, makes you look at it under a new heading. The difficulties proposed to you make you know the weak point of your opinion, or, if you can resolve them, give it a new degree of solidity. Conversation gives us a lively and alert attention that sometimes proves to be more useful than meditation itself. The latter is sometimes fatiguing. After we have concentrated for a long time on a subject and no longer grasp anything new, then conversation comes to the aid of the exhausted mind. . . . The discussions of instructed persons then revolve around these important objects. One examines, one discusses, one defends; one sees enlightenment born from the shock of ideas and opinions. (Morellet 1814: 17–18, translated in Gordon 1994: 204)

He capped this extended recapitulation of the value of conversation by applying it directly to public discussions of policy: 'Or, l'effet des écrits publics sur l'administration est de tourner la conversation sur les matières d'économie politique' (Morellet 1814: 18).

Morellet took this public conversation to be a means by which to create a stable opinion:

> Now, I say that to give them [political views] the stability they need, they must be embraced after discussion, and consecrated by public opinion. Only then will they take on a certain consistency, just as spiritous liqueurs acquire the power to resist time after having passed through that state called *fermentation*. (Morellet 1814: 13–14, translated in Gordon 1994: 204)

But in a shift from the conversational model, this consecrated knowledge was no longer to be subject to debate; public opinion was meant to bring conversation to an end.

> When the public, instructed by writings and discussion, has adopted a truth, it becomes its faithful guardian. Opinion no longer changes because one cannot attack a truth that is well known except with sophistry, which cannot deceive a nation once it has been instructed in its true interests. (Morellet 1814: 14, translated in Gordon 1994: 205)

The Physiocrats, the better to justify the description of public opinion as infallible and unanimous, described it as following a reason so self-evident that understanding of that reason alone, without the need to resort to persuasion, would lead to universal assent in both the ruled and (*sotto voce*) the ruler. Pierre-Paul Le Mercier de la Rivière (1719–1801) put it in *L'ordre naturel et essentiel des sociétés politiques* (1767) that

> PAR-TOUT où la connoissance *évidente* de l'ordre naturel & essentiel des sociétés se trouvera tellement répandue, que chacun éclairé par cette lumìere, attache son bonheur au maintien religieux des loix, il doit régner un despotisme *personnel* & *légal*, qui est le seul & unique véritable despotisme, parce qu'il est le seul qui existe par lui-même, & qui ne puisse jamais être ébranlé. . . . EUCLIDE est un véritable despote; & les vérités géométriques qu'il nous a transmises, sont des loix véritablement despotiques: leur despotisme légal & le despotisme personnel de ce Législateur n'en sont qu'un, celui de la force irrésistible de l'évidence. (Le Mercier de la Rivière 1767: 185)

Princes were not submitting to enlightened men – not at all! The tribunal of public opinion to which they submitted, as every other man, was the internal tribunal of one's own reason as much as, or more than, it was a tribunal of other men's judgements. The enlightened's articulation of public opinion merely revealed the inarguable, direct and unmediated evidence of reason (Ozouf 1988: S11, S14–S15; see also Gunn 1995: 246–81).

Jacques Necker and Jacques Peuchet likewise took public opinion to be peaceful, consensual, stable and durable; Necker wrote in *De l'administration des finances de la France* (1785) that

> It is necessary to avoid confusing public opinion, as I have described it here, with those ephemeral movements that often pertain only to certain societies and certain circumstances. It is not before such judgments that the man capable of conducting a great administration should prostrate himself. On the contrary, it is necessary to know how to disdain them, in order to remain faithful to that public opinion whose characteristics

> are all authoritative [*imposants*] and which reason, time, and the universality of sentiments alone have the right to consecrate. (Necker 1785: 170–1, translated in Baker 1990: 194)

Necker also emphasised public opinion's aspect as sovereign reason:

> It reigns over all minds, and princes themselves respect it whenever they are not carried away by excessive passions: Some willingly take it into account, moved by their ambition for public favour, and others, less docile, are still unwittingly subject to it as a result of the influence of those around them. (Necker 1785: 166, translated in Baker 1990: 194; and see Necker 1785: 165, 168; Ozouf 1988: S10)

Peuchet, more adventurously, in his 'Discours préliminaire' (1789) located sovereignty in the enlightened elite that conducted the people towards a state of reason (Peuchet 1789: x, l–li , translated in Baker 1990: 195; 1990: 195). However defined, public opinion was becoming a sovereign that on the one hand displaced the king's authority, and on the other substituted itself for the divine tribunal whose judgements and retributions had been the previous counterbalance to the ills of the world. As Jacob-Nicolas Moreau (1717–1803) put it in the first volume of his *Principes de morale, de politique et de droit public* (1777),

> Mais voulez-vous savoir où il est, ce contre-poids redoubtable à la tyrannie? Il est dans la conscience publique, il est dans ce cri général de la raison, de la justice, de l'humanité, qui ne manque jamais de se faire entendre chez une Nation libre & instruite. (Moreau 1777: 59; Ozouf 1988: S10)

Throughout this rapid progression, public opinion was meant to control as much as to liberate: it opposed the uncontrolled multitude as much as the uncontrolled prince. Necker put it in *De l'administration des finances* that the

> spirit of society . . . reigns in all its force in the midst of a sensitive people, which loves equally to judge and be judged, which is neither distracted by political interests nor enfeebled by despotism nor dominated by too seething passions. (Necker 1785: 167, translated in Baker 1990: 196)

Peuchet wrote in 'Discours préliminaire' that

> Public opinion differs from both the spirit of obedience that must reign in a despotic state and the popular opinions that prevail in republican deliberations. It is composed of a mass of ideas that human experience

> and the progress of enlightenment have successively introduced into a state whose government does not permit expression of the energetic character of national liberty, but where the security of citizens is respected . . . It is the weapon that an enlightened people collectively opposes to the precipitous operations of an ambitious minister or a misguided administration. Its slow action would be little suited to a free people, and slaves would not have the force to direct it against the undertakings of an irascible and powerful master. (Peuchet 1789: ix–x, translated in Baker 1990: 196)

Necker and Peuchet took public opinion as treading a middle course between the arbitrary will of despotism and the uncontrolled and anarchic wills of (English) liberty, the two faces of rhetoric; partly because France was at the close of the *ancien régime* neither despotic nor free, and partly because they did not wish France to become either. The court of public opinion provided, instead of these too-passionate alternatives, a means towards (as Baker puts it) 'a politics of rational consensus' (Baker 1990: 196–7).

The reference to English liberty above is worth pursuing: the image in Enlightenment France of their neighbour to the north was not only one of liberty and public spirit to be emulated but also one of licence and popular passion to be eschewed. Montesquieu, for a notable example, shared in, and contributed to, a broader eighteenth-century French unease with England. France's neighbour to the north was the image of partisan division, unbridled political passions contrasted with the rule of reason, and a *terreur* derived both from the inflated fears by which factions justified their mutual opposition and, more deeply, from the instability consequent upon England's unpredictable state of liberty (Montesquieu 1989: 326 [3.19.27]; Baker 1990: 173–4, 176, 178–85; Ozouf 1988: S4–S5; and see Starobinski 1977). Such fears helped protect a free state's liberty; but Montesquieu noted their real costs.

Furthermore, and significantly, Montesquieu's classification of types of government substituted modern England, with its fear induced by unpredictable liberty, for the traditional despotism, where fear was induced by the arbitrary tyrant – and contrasted both with the virtuous republic and the stable monarchy (Baker 1990: 177). Indeed, Montesquieu, at least on occasion, took England as all too near to its counterpart of despotism:

> In order to favor liberty, the English have removed all the intermediary powers that formed their monarchy. They are quite right to preserve that liberty; if they were to lose it, they would be one of the most enslaved peoples on earth. (Montesquieu 1989: 18–19 [1.2.4]; Baker 1990: 178)

If Montesquieu himself did not use the word 'opinion' in reference to England, Henri Dubois de Launay (d. 1794) would in *Coup d'oeil sur le gouernement anglais* (1786), as he identified England's instability with opinion's mutability: 'a government established on so uncertain and shaky a basis . . . must necessarily totter and waver incessantly, bend before *every wind of doctrine*, and be as changeable as the empire of opinion' (Dubois de Launay 1786: 26, cited and translated in Baker 1990: 180). Gabriel Bonnot de Mably's comparison of ancient Athens and Sparta in *Observations sur l'histoire de la Grèce* (1766), invidious to Athens, had clear contemporary application:

> Thus to authorize the appeal of the sentences, decrees, and orders of all judges to the tumultuous public assembly – was this not to establish the ignorant and fickle multitude, jealous of the rich, always the dupe of some intriguer, and always governed by citizens who are both violent and adept at flattering their vices, as an all-powerful magistrate? Was this not to establish, in the name of democracy, a veritable anarchy? (Mably 1766: 75, translated in Johnson Wright 1997: 48)

Public opinion was formed against the licentious counter-image of English liberty. In its *philosophe* variant, the reason of public opinion was not meant to motivate the passions, but to suppress them – along with politics, and all its attendant compulsions and liberties.

The Minority Report of Mably and Peuchet

Mably and Peuchet[4] jointly presented a significant critique of the *philosophe* consensus, which preserved and extended aspects of the *salonnier* conception of public opinion. To begin with, Mably argued that individual opinion could not and should not dissolve itself and submit to a unified public opinion. He took (somewhat antiquatedly) all opinions to be irredeemably tainted by the passions, and did not believe that one could equate any opinion, even a public one, with evidential truth. Men had no great desire to assent to 'the truth of evidence'; instead, 'a passably reasonable opinion suffices us. For lack of a likely opinion, we will adopt a ridiculous one' (Mably 1768: 58, translated in Ozouf 1988: S16). *Contra* the Physiocrats, the identity of mankind consisted of their susceptibility to passion and interest, not to their reason, and not to the conclusions – the opinions – that could or would be drawn by that reason. As Mably put it, 'Il n'est donc pas vrai que l'homme soit toujours obligé de céder à l'évidence connue du bien public, puis-qu'il trouve dans son bien particulier un principle de résistance & de contradiction qui lui fait souhaiter que la Société soit sacrifiée' (Mably 1768: 191–2). Mankind's opinions would always be unreliable and divided (Mably 1768; Ozouf 1988: S16; cf. Shaftesbury 1999: 472–3 ['Miscellany V']).

Moreover, the Physiocratic belief that self-evident reason could operate in politics relied upon a belief that the end of politics consisted purely of material goods; Le Mercier had argued that, 'Humanly speaking, the greatest happiness consists for us *in the greatest possible abundance of objects that serve for our enjoyment, and the greatest possible liberty to profit from them*' (Le Mercier de la Rivière 1767: 27, translated in Johnson Wright 1997: 114). Mably, to the contrary, believed that, 'it is the cultivation of men, that is to say, it is the social virtues that serve as the basis for the happiness of society. That is the first object of politics; our fields will come later' (Mably 1768: 35, translated in Johnson Wright 1997: 114). Self-evident reason had no role in the achievement of this end.

What men called reason was nothing more than a vain and self-deluding description of their own ruling passions:

> This 'reason', whose uncertain commands we praise and of which we are so proud, is really nothing more than the product of our vanity. It is merely the name that we give to our prejudices, once they have been formed by accident and consecrated by education and habit. (Mably 1763: 22, translated in Johnson Wright 1997: 82)

Reason was weak, the passions ineradicable, and those ineradicable passions not benign in their influence: 'Nothing is sacred for the passions: wars, murders, treachery, violence, injustice, cowardice – such are their fruits' (Mably 1763: 24, translated in Johnson Wright 1997: 84). Men's passions must be controlled by reason. The task of politics was above all the regulation of those *moeurs domestiques*, those domestic virtues that concerned themselves with the governance of passion and led to the practice of political virtue: '*L'objet principal de la politique est de régler les moeurs*. . . . Ce n'est que par l'exercise des vertus domestiques qu'un peuple se prépare à la pratique des vertus publiques' (Mably 1763: 35, 43; Johnson Wright 1997: 84–6). Yet Mably had already established that individual reason, a frail and self-deluding vessel of the passions, was not capable of the task.

Mably's solution to this dilemma, most elaborated in *Doutes proposées aux philosophes economistes*, lay in the establishment of public deliberation attendant upon mixed government:

> It is thanks only to a tempered administration that all classes of citizens, brought together in a single place, can arrive at the truth by means of discussion, and grasp how important it is to them to strengthen the rule

> of law. I emphasize, monsieur, that in this way all of the orders of society balance each another, compel recognition, and hold each other in equilibrium; neither the people, the grandees, nor the prince possess enough authority to impose partial laws; and thus the nation, which has moved as close to the natural equality of men as is possible today, is truly the depository and protector of the laws. (Mably 1768: 85–6, translated in Johnson Wright 1997: 113; 1997: 113–14)

To these arguments we may add the (slightly retrospective) contention voiced by Dominique-Joseph Garat (1749–1833) in his *Mémoires historiques sur la vie de M. Suard* (1820), in a conversation between John Wilkes (1725–97) and Suard, that while the Physiocrats claimed that public opinion had some aggregative, hence democratic, authority, such a claim implied that public opinion had to have some relationship to individuals' opinions, and to the collective weight of those opinions. How, practically, could one either discover every individual's opinion or quantify how many individuals held any particular opinion, with an eye to the democratic legitimacy derived from majority support? The query in Garat was sharp: 'Compterez-vous les voix?' (Garat 1820: II, 92–8, esp. 96; Ozouf 1988: S16–S17). In the absence of such knowledge, the claim of enlightened men to articulate public opinion had to have a mediatory aspect as well as the asserted revelatory one. The only way truly to discern the will of the people was by direct representation – which way led towards the spectre of anarchic, divisive and passionate English liberty.

In a similar vein, Jacques Peuchet in his 'Discours préliminaire' took reason and the passions both to be ineradicable elements of human nature, promoted prudence and moderation in politics, and argued that philosophy and enlightenment could work with experience to improve the human lot, if not perfect it:

> L'homme a ses foiblesses, ses vices & ses vertus. Il est composé de raison & de passions. . . . On ne peut pas plus détruire l'un que l'autre. Mais l'experience peut apprendre & la philosophie enseigner ce qu'il faut faire pour rendre le mal moins puissant & le bien plus sensible. (Peuchet 1789: liv; Sheehan 2002: 940)

Peuchet took public opinion to arise from 'the opinion of enlightened men, whence it gains partisans and becomes the general conviction' (Peuchet 1789: x, translated in Sheehan 2002: 941). Following the Scots historian William Robertson, he gave 'l'invention de l'imprimerie' great credit for the progress in history of that mental climate that rendered public opinion possible: 'A ces grandes causes de civilisation inconnues au anciens peuples . . . Les unes ont multiplié les communications entre les hommes, on fait circuler les connoissances, attaqué les préjugés' (Peuchet 1789: viii). Peuchet particularly noted that public discussion and judgement properly pertained to local governments as well (Peuchet 1789: lxiv; Sheehan 2002: 941–3). Where Mably had associated public opinion with mixed government, Peuchet associated it with multiple levels of government. Both thinkers, by these innovations, changed the tack of the concept of public opinion decisively away from the parallel imperatives towards intellectual consensus and governmental unity.

In this joint critique of Mably and Peuchet, we may emphasise the continuingly conversational aspects: the ultimate superiority of passion over reason, and the scepticism of certain knowledge. To this we may add the more innovative reconfiguration of the polity precisely so as to preserve the conditions of public conversation – thus mixed government, multiple levels of government, and emphasis on the importance of the printing press as one of the prerequisites of public opinion. Where the *philosophes* sought to suppress the passions and end conversation, Mably and Peuchet posited a public opinion that both harmonised passion and reason and sustained continued conversation. In this minority report on public opinion, the spirit of *sermo* beat more strongly.

Rousseau's Harmony

To this joint critique by Mably and Peuchet of the main line of the French conception of public opinion, we may add the very different critique of Rousseau. Rousseau's rebellion against the mid-century championing of sociability and public opinion consisted centrally of a doubt that true dialogic equality of conversation could emerge from a condition of social and economic inequality. Where the *salon* tradition argued that unequals could speak as equals, Rousseau in *The Social Contract* (1750) implicitly harked back to the original Ciceronian definition of *sermo* in his insistence that proper communication took place between homogeneous equals.

> As long as several men together consider themselves to be a single body, they have only a single will, which relates to their common preservation and general welfare. Then all mechanisms of the State are vigorous and simple, its maxims are clear and luminous, it has no tangled, contradictory interests; the common good is clearly apparent everywhere, and requires only good sense to be perceived. Peace, union, and equality are enemies of political subtleties. (Rousseau 1994: 198 [4.1])

Rousseau's historical progression from equality to inequality, from intimate speech to interested speech, made the historical emergence of oratory into a decay rather than a civilising triumph. All men, in their various conditions, had, in a world of inequality, to persuade other men to their own advantage:

> He must therefore constantly try to interest them in his fate and to make them really or apparently find their own profit in working for his . . . [man is] under the necessity of deceiving all those he needs if he cannot get them to fear him and does not find it in his interest to make himself useful to them. (Rousseau 1997, esp. 170–1 [2.27])

Rousseau also parted from the *salonnières* in arguing that the realm of inequality inescapably corrupted the realm of conversation, of opinion:

> when private interests start to make themselves felt and small societies to influence the large one, the common interest changes and is faced with opponents; unanimity no longer prevails in the votes; the general will is no longer the will of all; contradictions and debates arise and the best advice is not accepted without disputes. (Rousseau 1994: 198 [4.1]; Shklar 1969: 76; see also Gunn 1995: 179–215)

Rousseau particularly emphasised that all intellectuals – the artists, the poets, the men of letters – took part in this corruption of opinion:

> the Sciences, Letters, and Arts . . . spread garlands of flowers over the iron chains with which they are laden, throttle in them the sentiment of that original freedom for which they seemed born, make them love their slavery, and fashion them into what is called civilized Peoples. Need raised up Thrones; the Sciences and Arts have made them strong. (Rousseau 1997: 6 [1])

The intellectuals' pretensions to autonomy and equality were just that – pretensions. They were courtiers masked, if not mere valets (Shklar 1969: 110–11).

Rousseau took the corollary of this argument to be that a radical alteration of corrupting society would be necessary to create the conditions for proper, uncorrupt communication. The public must become, if not absolutely homogeneous, sufficiently homogeneous that proper speech and public opinion would displace the realm of oratory and interest. So in the *Social Contract* he posited a communicative authority that would eschew rhetoric: 'Since the Legislator is therefore unable to use either force or reasoning, he must necessarily have recourse to another order of authority, whch can win over without violence and persuade without convincing' (Rousseau 1994: 156 [2.7]). The institution of the Censorship acted as a tribunal to articulate public opinion: 'Public opinion is the kind of law of which the Censor is the Minister . . . the censorial tribunal, far from being the arbiter of the people's opinion, merely declares it' (Rousseau 1994: 214–15 [4.7]). Without resort to force, properly articulated public opinion in turn would regulate society.

Rousseau's communicative ideal was not so much conversation as music. His desire for a language of music, of natural passions and sentiments communicated and persuaded directly without the distortions of mediatory language, not only informed his account of the descent of mankind from the state of nature but also fed into his conception of his ideal state, where the communication of the general will likewise avoided the distortions of mediatory language (Rousseau 1998: 331–2 [*Essay on the Origin of Languages*, Ch. 20]). The people was supposed to express the general will as an orchestra or a chorus produced tuneful music, the individual members cohering, with pleasurable sensuousness, as a passionate whole, without the resort to rationalising, linguistic coordination (Abizadeh 2001: 561; Kelly 1987; J. Scott 1998; Simon 2004; cf. Delehanty 2013: 73). Rousseau's ideal communicative articulation of public opinion was wordless, with as little place for conversation as for oratory.

The French Traditions

There were three traditions of public opinion in France in the last decades of the *ancien régime*. In the main line, the *philosophes* seized control of the concept of public opinion from the *salonnières*, and shifted public opinion from conversation to critique. The line indicated by Rousseau developed into the Marxist critique that sought a transformation of society so as to restore the proper conditions of communication – egalitarian as conversation had been originally, but in a consensual harmony rather than in a rational, linguistic conversation. In the tradition of Mably and Peuchet, many of the old *salonnière* and conversational assumptions persisted, most importantly the enduring conception that while truth was to be sought collectively, it could not ever be known certainly. Peuchet in particular also gave a hint as to a constitutional architecture that would best foster this conversational public opinion. This minority report from the French Enlightenment would find a new home across the Atlantic, in the new United States of America.

The Late and Limited Public Opinion of Britain

Britain was the site of another variant of public opinion. In the France of the *philosophes*, public opinion had oscillated towards a judgement informed more by critique than by conversation; in Britain, the oscillation was rather towards the realm of oratory, for a more traditional conception of opinion retained its currency. We should emphasise here an important distinction between Britain and France: in Britain, where the post-Revolutionary regime had institutionalised a remarkably wide range of freely oratorical speech both in Parliament and in the nation at large, polite conversation emerged as an adjunct to oratorical speech rather than as a replacement for it. Addison, for example, considered conversation as more a private affair among intimates than something to be extended to an ever-larger public (Bond 1965: I, 289 [No. 68, 18 May 1711]). Isaac Watts likewise still associated conversation with friendship: 'When we *converse* familiarly with a learned Friend, *we have his own Help at hand to explain to us every Word and Sentiment that seems obscure* in his discourse' (Watts 1743: 40; Mee 2011: 24–5). Watts also retained a Petrarchan conception of reading as a conversation between reader and writer, albeit put into a sentimental key: books conveyed to readers 'the Sentiments, Observations, Reasonings and Improvements of all the learned World, in the most remote Nations, and in former Ages, almost from the Beginning of Mankind' (Watts 1743: 32; Mee 2011: 24–5; see also Goring 2005). For all these writers, conversation was supposed to remain in its intimate channels, at a distance from the realm of oratory.

Now, conversation had a certain dynamic ambition that paralleled that in France. Consider Richard Steele's image of Augustus renouncing his princely power to engage in the world of conversation:

> *Augustus* lived amongst his Friends as if he had his Fortune to make in his own Court: Candour and Affability, accompanied with as much Power as ever Mortal was vested with, were what made him in the utmost Manner agreeable among a Set of admirable Men, who had Thoughts too high for Ambition, and Views too large to be gratified by what he could give them in the Disposal of an Empire, without the Pleasures of their mutual Conversation. A certain Unanimity of Taste and Judgment, which is natural to all of the same Order in the Species, was the Band of this Society; and the Emperour assumed no Figure in it but what he thought was his Due from his private Talents and Qualifications, as they contributed to advance the Pleasures and Sentiments of the Company. (Bond 1965: II, 592 [No. 280, 21 January 1712]; Mee 2011: 44)

This image in some ways paralleled that of Machiavelli's prince renouncing his power to become one of the citizens of a city in which all possess equal *virtù*, but transposed from the realm of virtue to the realm of manners. Likewise it paralleled the French ambition for the realm of conversation to set aside that of power – but here 'Unanimity of Taste and Judgment' substituted for the compelling reason of public opinion. While the French considered how public opinion was to be formed, the British instead considered how a unanimity of taste and judgement was to be constituted. The latter concern, ultimately, had diverted British interest in conversation towards the realms of philosophy and aesthetics.

Nevertheless, the British also made persisting reference to the importance of opinion in government. William Temple (1628–99) in his *Essay upon the original and nature of government* (1680 [written 1672]) wrote that,

> when vast numbers of men submit their lives and fortunes absolutely to the Will of one, it . . . must be force of custom, or opinion, the true ground and foundation of all Government, and that which subjects Power to Authority. *For Power, arising from Strength, is always in those that are governed, who are many: But Authority arising from opinion, is in those that Govern, who are few.* (Temple 1680: 53–4)

Temple took opinion and interest together to be the bulwarks of government:

> a Monarchy where the Prince governs by the affections, and according to the opinions and interests, of his people; or the bulk of them (that is, by many degrees the greatest or strongest part of them) makes of all others the safest and firmest Government. (Temple 1680: 85–6)

Locke likewise wrote of the power of opinion, and tied it to the (epideictic) judgement of virtue and vice (Locke 1997: 318–19, 321 [2.28.10–12]; see also Habermas 1991: 91–2). Locke thus tied together opinion and the judgement of morals; moral philosophy was thus based on the quite uncertain anchor of popular opinion. Hume likewise argued the power of opinion:

> as Force is always on the side of the governed, the governors have nothing to support them but opinion. It is, therefore, on opinion only that government is founded; and this maxim extends to the most despotic and most military governments, as well as to the most free and most popular. (Hume 1996: III, 28 ['Of the First Principles of Government'])

But these are references to the power of opinion, not to a concept such as 'public opinion'. In Britain, this scarcely manifested until late in the eighteenth century, and then frequently as a conservative idea, as in France, invoked to support the status quo (Gunn 1983: 260–315). Alexander Dalrymple's (1737–1808) *Parliamentary Reform* (1792) somewhat mischievously put it that

> *Our constitution*, although it may *not* be an *excellent one*, is truly, in its execution, an *happy one*, because *corruptions*, of *various kinds*, are so fortunately blended, as, in great measure, to correct each defect; and the whole is subjected to the *controul* of *publick opinion:* this, although no part of the nominal *constitution*, is *paramount to all!* and what makes the *government* of *this country* the best that *ever existed.* (*Monthly Review* 1793: 463; Gunn 1983: 289–90)

Burke made reference to a 'general opinion', but, while broadly similar to 'public opinion', it did not possess the latter's connotations as both unitary and thematically rational (E. Burke 1777: 48; Habermas 1991: 94–5).

For public opinion itself, we must look in mid-century to hints from Hume on how it was to be elicited:

> For though the people, collected in a body like the Roman tribes, be quite unfit for government, yet, when dispersed in small bodies, they are more susceptible both of reason and order; the force of popular currents and tides is in a great measure broken; and the public interests may be pursued with some method and constancy. (Hume 1996: III, 32 ['Of the First Principles of Government'])

Towards the end of the century, Jeremy Bentham (1748–1832) would articulate a liberal idea of public opinion (Bentham 1999: 29–34 ['An Essay on Political Tactics': Ch. II. Of Publicity. §1. Reasons for Publicity]; Fontana 1988: 149–57, 201–21; Cutler 1999). But this was more to adapt a pre-existing idea of public opinion into the new liberal order; to remark on Bentham is to remark how little he had in the way of predecessors. British thinkers recognised the importance of popular opinion, and they took part in the expansion of the concept of conversation, but they did not fear oratory as the French did. So the British contributed little to the development of the concept of public opinion, for the desire to bridle oratory had scant purchase upon them.

That said, Britain did witness the application of intimacy to political judgement. Hester Lynch Piozzi (1741–1821) wrote in *British*

Synonymy (1794), 'Let not princes flatter themselves therefore: they will be watched in private as much as in public life; and those who cannot pierce further, will judge of them by the appearances they shall exhibit in both' (Piozzi 1794: 151; Mee 2011: 11). Here the judgement of *sermo* now infiltrated into British political culture – and the application of the judgement of the private character of public figures would remain characteristic of this British variant of popular opinion.

America

As the culmination of this narrative, we may look to the United States of the era of the first generation after the American Revolution. We will look first to the well-known James Madison (1751–1836) – as always, the great innovator upon the rhetorical and republican traditions – and then to the lesser-known Tunis Wortman (d. 1822), whose thought aptly encapsulates the mental framework of early America. In the thought of these two figures, we may see how the minority report of Mably and Peuchet naturalised itself in America, and gave birth to the conversational variant of public opinion that would permeate the political thought and practice of the Great Republic.

The role of public opinion was not yet Madison's primary focus during the 1780s. Madison did pay some attention to the concept of public opinion during this decade: in the lead-up to the Constitutional Convention, he expressed a desire for 'some disinterested & dispassionate umpire in disputes between different passions & interests in the State' (Madison 1975: 384 [To George Washington, 16 April 1787]; Sheehan 2004: 417). He also took there to be a class of superior men relatively immune to the sway of passion, and hence capable of playing such a role (Madison 1975: 355 ['Vices of the Political System of the United States']; A. Gibson 2005b: 12). More abstractly, he wrote that 'it is the reason of the public alone, that ought to control and regulate the government' (Hamilton, Madison and Jay 1987: 260 [Essay #49]). His later judgement that '[e]nlightened statesmen will not always be at the helm' restricted the role of such arbiters, of the reason of the public, rather than eliminating it entirely (Hamilton, Madison and Jay 1987: 44 [Essay #10]). Yet ultimately, public opinion was peripheral to his thought during the years leading up to his co-authoring of the *Federalist*.

The concept of public opinion became more important to Madison in the late 1780s and early 1790s, as he continued to read and assimilate the latest French works on the subject. In part Madison focused on public opinion for tactical reasons, as his opposition to

Alexander Hamilton's (1755–1804) bank plan led him to search for a force with which to constrain the actions of the government (Matthews 2005; and note Sheehan 2004: 409–13). With the aid of Thomas Jefferson (1743–1826), who procured the latest wares in the Paris bookstores for his friend in far Virginny, Madison read the latest works by Necker, Mably, Mercier, etc., and thereby became conversant with the range of contemporary French thought on public opinion. Indeed, Sheehan notes that Madison's 'Notes on Government' and Party Press Essays 'incorporated ideas and even direct phraseology from some of these French sources Madison was studying' (Sheehan 2002: 932–3; and note 2005: 38–41).

Yet although he read the range of French thought upon public opinion, Madison followed the minority strand. Most French writers on the subject by the 1780s conceived of public opinion as articulated and directed by an enlightened elite, unitary and enduring, a compelling sovereign who could and should override the limitations provided by balances of power (Sheehan 2002: 934–40, 944–5). Madison drew most strongly on the minority report of Mably and Peuchet. From Mably, Madison assimilated the emphasis on the ruling power of the passions, the transitory coalescence of opinion, and the necessity for a balance of power within government so as to regulate mankind's unconquerable passions and interests (Sheehan 2002: 944). From Peuchet, he took the emphasis on the ineradicability of both reason and passion, the importance of prudence and moderation in politics, the ability of philosophy and enlightenment to ameliorate (if not perfect) the human condition, the importance of publicity – and most important of all, the mutual relationship of local government and public opinion (Sheehan 2002: 940–3; cf. Hume 1996: III, 127, 129 ['Of the Rise and Progress of the Arts and Sciences']). Madison also took Peuchet's lightly tossed-off phrase, 'l'empire de la raison', which would echo in English as the 'empire of reason' (Peuchet 1789: viii; Madison 1983: 139 ['Consolidation']; Sheehan 2002: 943). Mably and Peuchet, rather than the Physiocrats or Rousseau, were Madison's inspirations and models.

Immediately after the ratification of the Constitution, Madison justified his support for the Bill of Rights on the grounds that it would root the Constitution in public opinion:

> In proportion as government is influenced by opinion, it must be so, by whatever influences opinion. This decides the question concerning a *Constitutional Declaration of Rights*, which requires an influence on government, by becoming a part of the public opinion. (Madison 1983: 170 ['Public Opinion']; Sheehan 2002: 927; 2004: 417)

By the early 1790s, Madison had come to conceive of public opinion, correctly cultivated, as the medium by which society articulated its reasons and desires. Indeed, striking a Humean note, he stated generally that '[p]ublic opinion sets bounds to every government, and is the real sovereign in every free one' (Madison 1983: 170 ['Public Opinion']; Sheehan 2002: 926–7). In 1791, Madison concretely invoked public opinion during the debate on the Bank Bill: 'The public opinion hs been mentioned: If the appeal to the public opinion is suggested with sincerity, we ought to let our constituents have an opportunity to form an opinion on the subject' (Madison 1981: 387 [The Bank Bill]; Sheehan 2002: 927–8).

Madison elaborated his conception of public opinion at greater length in his 'Notes on Government' and his *National Gazette* Party Press Essays. In 'Government of the United States' and 'Public Opinion', he wrote that public opinion generally had the power to act in defence of popular liberty (Madison 1983: 218 ['Government of the United States']; 1983: 170 ['Public Opinion']; Matthews 1995: 215–17). Madison added in 'British Government', following Hume, that '[t]he boasted equilibrium of this government, (so far as it is a reality) is maintained less by the distribution of its powers, than by the force of public opinion' (Madison 1983: 201 ['British Government']; Sheehan 2002: 930; 2005: 38). In 'Public Opinion', as noted above, he emphasised public opinion's legitimating authority (Madison 1983: 170 ['Public Opinion']; Sheehan 2002: 931). In 'Spirit of Governments', Madison gave a more normative cast to this argument:

> A government, deriving its energy from the will of the society, and operating by the reason of its measures, on the understanding and interest of the society. Such is the government for which philosophy has been searching, and humanity been sighing, from the most remote ages. Such are republican governments which it is the glory of America to have invented, and her unrivalled happiness to possess. May her glory be compleated by every improvement on the theory which experience may teach; and her happiness be perpetuated by a system of administration corresponding with the purity of the theory. (Madison 1983: 234 ['Spirit of Governments']; Sheehan 2002: 931)

Public opinion, however, was not a matter of the whim of society's will. As Madison put it in 'Universal Peace', with generalisable implication,

> As wars of the first class were to be prevented by subjecting the will of the government to the will of the society, those of the second, can only be controuled by subjecting the will of the society to the reason of the

> society; by establishing permanent and constitutional maxims of conduct, which may prevail over occasional impressions, and inconsiderate pursuits. (Madison 1983: 207 ['Universal Peace']; Sheehan 2002: 948)

Public opinion was settled and enduring; hence Madison's stipulation above that the Bill of Rights would enter into public opinion over time (Madison 1983: 170 ['Public Opinion']; Sheehan 2004: 418). It was not, however, immutable: as any good conversation, the communication of sentiments that formed public opinion, and could overturn even the most settled public opinion, was a dynamic and ongoing process. An elected representative should not be immune from public judgement and censure; neither should an earlier articulation of public opinion be immune to overthrow by the continued communication of sentiments (Madison 1991: 238–9 ['Political Reflections']; Sheehan 2004: 422).

This much was general; in his specifics, Madison creatively refashioned the French notion of public opinion, with particular debt to Peuchet and Mably. Madison agreed with the mainstream of French thought in his conception of the role of the enlightened elite: 'The class of literati . . . are the cultivators of the human mind – the manufacturers of useful knowledge – the agents of the commerce of ideas – the censors of public manners – the teachers of the arts of life and the means of happiness' (Madison 1983: 168 ['Notes for Essays']). Yet Madison did not think this elite should dictate to the public. He retained his belief that faction, passion and interest were ineradicable, the checks and balances provided by the separation of powers indispensable, and the free expression and communication of belief (no matter how unenlightened) fundamental: 'man has a property in his opinions and the free communication of them' (Madison 1983: 217–18 ['Government of the United States'], 266 ['Property']; Sheehan 2002: 947, 949–50).

Contra Mably, Madison believed that the reason of public opinion was not helpless in the face of the passions. Public opinion could temper and refine the passions and the interests of the diverse factions, even if it could not eliminate them; checks and balances would minimise the ability of factions to act, and the very size of the nation, containing a myriad of factions, would likewise minimise the ability of any one faction to gain power. Alongside checks and balances, public opinion played the pre-eminent role in the control of faction and government. Against the (ventriloquised) charge that 'The people are stupid, suspicious, licentious. They cannot safely trust themselves', Madison could answer 'that the people ought to be enlightened, to be awakened, to be united, that after establishing a government they should watch over it, as well as obey it'. The question of how to forward as much as possible the enlightenment and the power of public opinion was therefore of vital importance (Hamilton, Madison and Jay 1987: 266–7 [Essay #51]; Madison 1983: 426 ['Who are the Best Keepers of the People's Liberties?']; Sheehan 2002: 950–4).

Madison's answer was to make size thematic in the relationship between public opinion and government. A large nation inhibited the power of a single faction, but it likewise inhibited the formation of public opinion (Madison 1983: 170 ['Public Opinion']; and see 1983: 137–9 ['Consolidation']; Matthews 1995: 81). Policy, therefore, should promote means by which to increase the number of enlightened citizens and to form such a public opinion across the nation's expanse. Madison consequently favoured improvements to transport systems and the fostering of newspapers, so as to increase the interchange of people, goods and ideas across the nation (Madison 1983: 170 ['Public Opinion']; Sheehan 2002: 952–3; see also Kobylka and Carter 1990). The spread of a common opinion would also counter the formation of local sentiments derived directly from local passions and interests – not least, since people prefer to express their beliefs in company rather than alone, because the knowledge that common sentiments were widely shared would serve to embolden those citizens who held them (Hamilton, Madison and Jay 1987: 258 [Essay #49]; A. Gibson 2005b: 14–15; and see Gabrielson 2009; cf. Temple 1680: 58–9; Hume 1996: III, 29 ['Of the First Principles of Government']; A. Smith 1978: 322; but for Smith, note Raphael 2007: 93).

Multiple levels of government were likewise meant to foster multiple communications of interest, opinion and (above all) sentiment: between the representatives of different regions, between government and the people (both influencing one another) and among the citizenry, the ultimate source of sovereign public opinion, as they considered, inspected, and when necessary provided the censorial rebuke intended to prompt their representatives and governments to reverse their policies (Madison 1983: 170 ['Public Opinion']; 1983: 192 ['Charters']; 1985: 391 [House Address to the President, 27 November 1794]; A. Gibson 2005b: 32–3; Sheehan 2002: 953–4; 2004: 417–18). The state and local governments especially anchored this public opinion:

> neither the voice nor the sense of ten or twenty millions of people, spread through so many latitudes as are comprehended within the United States, could ever be combined or called into effect, if deprived of those local organs, through which both can now be conveyed. (Madison 1983: 138 ['Consolidation'])

Sentiments could spread within their smaller realms more readily than they could at the national level, and so these levels of government provided a crucial forum for mobilising and articulating public opinion – not least, as in the state-level opposition Madison organised against the Federal government's Sedition Act (Madison 1991: 188–90 ['Virginia Resolutions']; 1991: 242 ['Political Reflections']; 1991: 341–7 ['The Report of 1800']; Sheehan 2004: 421). Public opinion provided the crucial mechanism that could unite a dispersed citizenry diverse in its passions and interests to unite effectively to oppose measures leading towards tyranny by a government, and/or by a factious majority temporarily in control of the government (Madison 1983: 138–9 ['Consolidation']; A. Gibson 2005b: 19–20). In the *Federalist*, however, Madison specified that enlightened opinion was supposed to complement the authority/reputation of tradition, and should not replace it:

> When the examples, which fortify opinion, are ancient, as well as numerous, they are known to have a double effect. In a nation of philosophers, this consideration ought to be disregarded. A reverence for the laws, would be sufficiently inculcated by the voice of an enlightened reason. But a nation of philosophers, is as little to be expected as the philosophical race of kings wished for by Plato. And in every other nation, the most rational government will not find it a superfluous advantage, to have the prejudices of the community on its side. (Hamilton, Madison and Jay 1987: 258 [Essay #49])

Madison shifted the emphasis of his thought towards public opinion in the 1790s, but there is no reason to believe that he rejected this basically complementary relationship, which was a translation of the traditional relationship between conversation and rhetoric.

Freedom of the press also became thematic, as a necessary means by which to allow public opinion to form. This point was particularly emphasised in Madison's 'Report of 1800', which opposed the Sedition Act's infringements on the freedom of the press not least because it was the effective means by which public opinion could both form and exercise its censorial function (Madison 1991: 341–2 ['The Report of 1800']; A. Gibson 2005b: 28–30; Sheehan 2004: 421). Freedom of the press was the means by which the public performed its mode of inquiry – a mode that retained a distinct relationship in Madison's conception to argument *in utramque partem*:

> Could it be so arranged that every newspaper, when printed on one side, should be handed over to the press of an adversary, to be printed on the other, thus presenting to every reader both sides of every question, truth

> would always have a fair chance. (Mattern 1997: 83 [James Madison to Nicholas P. Trist, 23 April 1828, Library of Congress, Trist Papers]; Matthews 2005: 64–5)

Sheehan summarises Madison's argument so: 'Public opinion is the sovereign authority in a genuine republic whose mild voice of reason is capable of transforming the will of a nation' (Sheehan 2004: 422). But that reason had that capacity precisely because it was a reason of the sentiments, working within the constitutional order. The ideal polity was to be established

> by eradicating local prejudices and mistaken rivalships, to consolidate the affairs of the states into one harmonious interest; and let it be the patriotic study of all, to maintain the various authorities established by our complicated system, each in its respective constitutional sphere; and to erect over the whole, one paramount Empire of reason, benevolence and brotherly affection. (Madison 1983: 139 ['Consolidation'])

The Madisonian project, in short, was the creation of the constitutional, political and social preconditions for the exercise of an enduringly conversational mode of public opinion, which sought to counsel rather than to rule the diverse passions of the American citizenry.

Tunis Wortman, author of *Treatise Concerning Political Enquiry, and the Liberty of the Press* (1800), articulated remarkably well the quasi-Madisonian conception of public opinion that was typical of the nascent United States, and that would become the almost-unconscious background of its theory and practice (R. Martin 2005). Tunis Wortman's thought complemented Madison's – and shows how generally the Madisonian conception of public opinion was coming to permeate the early Republic.

Wortman began by noting that while men were commonly subject to their passions, and susceptible to oratorical blandishments, the progress of science and knowledge – by which terms Wortman explicitly signified *judgement* – could control the passions:

> knowledge is the only preservative against the inordinate excitement of the passions. It is the genuine and incessant operation of judgment, to estimate the consequences of human action, and to decide upon its propriety, from the effects which are probable to result. (Wortman 1800: 38–9)

Wortman later defined *judgement*, quite traditionally, as the knowledge applied to morals and politics: '[t]he investigation of moral or political subjects, requires not the talent of invention; judgment and not genius is the faculty to be employed' (Wortman 1800: 41–2, 54–5). Such knowledge could and must be propagated:

> Knowledge is the only guardian principle, which can rescue us from the fatal despotism of irregular excitement. The extension of science, is the only rational method of establishing the universal empire of truth and virtue. . . . reason will become the universal standard of decision, and the empire of judgment will succeed to the pernicious dominion of the passions. (Wortman 1800: 41–3)

This broadening of judgement also constituted moral improvement: to act by passion was beastly or machine-like; to act from judgement distinctively and admirably human (Wortman 1800: 43).

As Wortman took knowledge to be the best method of societal improvement, so, as a corollary, he believed 'that freedom of investigation is one of the most important rights of a people' (Wortman 1800: 26, 45, 116, 133–4). Freedom of investigation – above all, the free exercise of political discussion – was a right grounded upon a capacity: 'whatever may be the abstract nature of truth, its evidences are capable of equal presentation to the percipient powers of all men' (Wortman 1800: 48–9, 55). As it was for Cicero, and all the conversational tradition that followed, that truth remained an indefinite proposition: '*Truth*, as an abstract term, is altogether insusceptible of definition' (Wortman 1800: 48; R. Martin 2005: 381–2). The knowledge of such truth certainly was not a prerogative of the republic's governors:

> When did infallibility become a distinguished attribute of the human legislator? At what happy aera were sovereigns and magistrates released from the prejudices, errors, and passions that are incident to their fellow-mortals? . . . it can never be contended, that it is the property of government to monopolize the wisdom of society. (Wortman 1800: 29–30, 55)

In a significant metaphor, Wortman remarked that truth 'is not a courtier whose residence is confined to palaces, nor is it always to be found in the solemn gravity of a deliberative assembly' (Wortman 1800: 49). Genius and invention might be highly variable capacities, but 'the attribute of *judgment* is more generally and impartially distributed . . . Whether it relates to principles or facts, it [truth] is to be discovered and ascertained by judgment; and judgment is a faculty possessed in common by mankind' (Wortman 1800: 49, 53–5, 63).

The subject matter of morality and politics was also well within the range of ordinary human judgement:

> Whatever constitutes despotism or cruelty, will be continually the same. Considerations of rank and power, can never alter the genuine character of human action: if the scymeter is stained with innocent blood, it matters nothing whether the fatal blow was struck by a monarch or a robber. Oppression and crime are the same in every quarter of the globe; the experience of mankind, with respect to their characteristics, will be constant and uniform; upon those subjects, therefore, the sentence of human understanding, will be ever steady and correspondent.
>
> He who can form a proper estimate of individual conduct and morality, will be also enabled to form a tolerably correct opinion of the measures and morality of the cabinet. (Wortman 1800: 60)

The actions of government generally were within the capacity of ordinary human judgement; and indeed,

> [i]t is the duty of Science to review the art of Legislation, to correct its imperfections, and remove its deformities. It is the province of Wisdom to erect the political edifice agreeably to the rules of solid and rational Architecture. (Wortman 1800: 62–3, 65–7, 113)

In sum, Wortman, like Madison, took public opinion to be sovereign:

> With relation to government, public opinion is omnipotent. It is the general will or acquiescence that supports every species of political institution, or rather, to speak more correctly, it is impossible that any government should exist in direct contravention of the general will. . . . It is true at Petersburgh and Constantinople, as well as at Philadelphia. (Wortman 1800: 24)

Wortman stipulated that judgement, as all knowledge, might be improved by those overlapping preceptors, education and experience (Wortman 1800: 53, 57–8). Discussion was the means by which mankind improved its power of judgement: '[b]y the frequent habits of discussion, his discriminating powers will be rendered more acute, and his decisions will improve in accuracy; upon most questions his judgment will be competent to distinguish' (Wortman 1800: 60, 160–1). Freedom of discussion improved this education of the judgement: 'the principal requisite will be to furnish him with the necessary means of information, and to present the case with copiousness and perspicuity to his view' (Wortman 1800: 60; cf. Kobylka and Carter 1990: 40–50).

Government should not take on this educative function: '[i]t is better qualified to exercise the office of an Executioner, than to assume the province of an Instructor', and, moreover, it was all too liable to abuse such powers (Wortman 1800: 130). Society was in any case sovereign, and so public opinion must remain independent of government, so as to retain society's superiority (Wortman 1800: 118, 130, 175–6). But Wortman stipulated that society was not a monist conception:

> Society does not constitute an intellectual unity; it cannot resolve itself into one single organized percipient, in which the rays of Intelligence are concentrated and personified: each of its members necessarily retains his personal identity and his individual understanding. By Public Opinion we are, therefore, to imply an aggregation of individual sentiment.
>
> It is the individual who is to reflect and decide. By Public Opinion we are to understand that general determination of private understandings which is most extensively predominant. When a sufficient number of the members of a community have established a coincidence of sentiment upon any particular subject, such agreement of their personal judgments may be correctly termed the general or Public Opinion. When they have concurred in volition upon any given point, that concurrent volition may be denominated the public or general will. (Wortman 1800: 118–19)

The language of the 'general will' was Rousseauian, but the rest of the intellectual context was not. The conception of public opinion as an aggregate of individual sentiments meant that it could not easily be measured, and had in many cases, where 'express declarations of the people' were not available, to 'be implied from their silent acquiescence' (Wortman 1800: 119). In such cases, a Burkean presumption applied:

> the current of public opinion must always be presumed to pursue a direction in favour of established institutions. The general acquiescence which is paid to the laws, and the uniform submission and obedience observed towards the government, must be received as conclusive testimony that they are supported by public opinion. (Wortman 1800: 120)

Furthermore, where public opinion was defined as an aggregate of individual sentiments, dissent was to be expected, and 'public opinion' resolved into a reliance upon the majority: 'It is probable, that upon most subjects some dissenting voices would be found. Perfect unanimity is seldom to be expected. But in a true practical sense the opinion of the majority is to be deemed the general opinion' (Wortman 1800: 120).

While Wortman stipulated that '[t]here are some topics upon which an uniformity in sentiment is pretty generally established', his emphasis was on those subjects where public opinion was not yet settled (Wortman 1800: 120–1). Here public opinion's reliance on individual opinions created an imperative for freedom of discussion:

> The formation of general opinion upon correct and salutary principles, requires the unbiassed exercise of individual intellect; neither prejudice, authority, or terror, should be suffered to impede the liberty of discussion; no undue influence should tyrannize over mind; every man should be left to the independent exercise of his reflection; all should be permitted to communicate their ideas with the energy and ingenuousness of truth. (Wortman 1800: 121)

This freedom was the necessary means by which society could progress towards the truth: '[e]xposed to the incessant attack of Argument, the existence of Error would be fleeting and transitory; while Truth would be seated upon a basis of adamant, and receive a perpetual accession to the number of her votaries' (Wortman 1800: 121). Moreover, this process of inquiry not only habituated mankind to seek the truth but also (unlike the Physiocrats) universalised the realisation that judgement might err, as it 'habituates us to a frequent revisal of our sentiments' (Wortman 1800: 123). The discovery of truth proceeded from a root in mankind's 'diversity of sentiment', which was not to be overridden, but to be brought into alignment by the very process of discovery: '[i]n proportion as investigation continues free and unrestricted, the mass or error will be subject to continual diminution, and the determinations of distinct understandings will gradually harmonize' (Wortman 1800: 121–3). Wortman was as optimistic as any devotee of reason that *magna est veritas et praevalebit* – '[i]t cannot surely be visionary to predict the ultimate triumph of Truth' – yet he did not seem to believe that it would imminently prevail:

> Whatever may be the oscillation of principles, the pendulum is finally destined to rest at the salutary point of Rectitude. Many are the considerations which may accelerate, and numberless the causes that may retard the melioration of society. In the midst of every obstacle that presents itself to be encountered by Fortitude, it is a source of never-failing consolation, that Mind has already proceeded too far to retrograde. (Wortman 1800: 122–4)

While the eschaton tarried, enlightenment was the responsibility and property of individuals: '[a]ll our prospects of improvement must therefore depend upon the industry and exertion of individuals' (Wortman 1800: 128–9). That exertion, in effect, was to be in constant conversation.

Wortman also specified that mankind could not reliably distinguish the exercise of judgement from the exercise of passion and interest. To discriminate between the two required a judgement as to whether human motivation derived from seeking personal advantage or the general good. Even were humans capable of looking into other people's hearts, their motivations were generally 'a complicated mixture' of self-interest and benevolence, and the pleasure they took from doing good could never be disentangled from their self-regard (Wortman 1800: 104). Furthermore, an enlightened self-interest generally aligned with the general good: 'Justice and Policy, however they may differ in the motives by which they are actuated, will pronounce the same decision whenever the same question is presented under identical circumstances' (Wortman 1800: 104–5). To attempt to suppress the passions in these circumstances would be both vain and pernicious.

Wortman further stated that society must have 'a species of censorial jurisdiction over its political institutions' (Wortman 1800: 125, 181). But, surely with a glance at Revolutionary France, this censorship was to be gentle in form. The nation's censorship should not act directly, for that 'would destroy the necessity, and therefore undermine the whole theory of delegation: for why should we appoint organs for the transaction of affairs to which their constituents are sufficiently competent?' (Wortman 1800: 126). Neither should society delegate its censorial powers to a representative body empowered to override the normally constituted government:

> It would be impossible to imagine a more flagitious and terrible expedient. No device could be more dangerous, or pregnant with such complicated calamity. It would be the establishment of an *imperium in imperio:* it would unite in one tremendous engine all the dreadful powers of Despotism and all the direful evils of Anarchy. (Wortman 1800: 126–7)

The censorship must be exercised only by the gentle medium of public opinion: 'Society has no other resource for the melioration of its condition, and the improvement of its political institutions, except what is derived from the reciprocal communication of Thought, and the increasing energy and correctness of individual Understanding' (Wortman 1800: 128). Wortman also argued, undoubtedly with an eye to France, that the exercise of public opinion fostered gradual reform, and allowed society to avoid the passionate violence of revolution, which as like as not proceeded to a new despotism (Wortman 1800: 183–92). Such reform must be slow and peaceful: 'Rashness is not her attribute, nor physical Force her weapon. Her province is to enlighten Society by candid and argumentative addresses to the understanding' (Wortman 1800: 191). This censorship also retained an individual cast: 'Society cannot delegate its revisionary powers to any special organized assembly: those powers can only be exercised through the medium of personal deliberation' (Wortman 1800: 138).

The exercise of public opinion would conduce to the stability of government – a government properly attentive to the wishes of society – by mobilising the sentiments of the people in support of the government (Wortman 1800: 134). Publicity also enlightened and improved government: 'Confidence is mutually reciprocated between the Government and the People. In proportion as the public mind becomes habituated to discussion, it is rendered more enlightened and informed' (Wortman 1800: 155–6). Finally, the press was the ideal medium for communicating rational sentiments:

> As a vehicle of information the Press is possessed of peculiar advantages. The rapidity of oral addresses – the declamatory stile, impassioned manner, and intemperate gesture of the Orator – may arrest the Imagination and enlist the Passions: but whatever is presented to us in Print is less alloyed with any circumstance unconnected with its merits. Reason has time to operate, and Truth an opportunity to be enforced. We have leisure to meditate and examine. If our attention has been diverted from the speaker, or we have mistaken his sentiments, our loss in the one case, and our error in the other, is not to be repaired: but the printed volume is ever open to our view; we can ponder upon its contents at leisure, and remove our hasty impressions. The latter, therefore, is more favorable to the propagation of Truth, and less liable to become converted into a pernicious engine of Design. . . . There is no vehicle better adapted for the circulation of reasoning, or the communication of sentiment, than the Press. There is none which is better qualified for acquiring an ascendancy over Morals and Conduct. (Wortman 1800: 245, 247; cf. Rapin 1672: 40–1)

The defence of the press was now a political principle of the first order. And we may note that this was also the culmination of the entire conversational project. Castiglione had written,

> although the potentiality for these virtues is rooted within our souls, it often fails to develop unless helped by education. For if it is to pass to actuality and to its full realization, it cannot, as I said, rely on Nature

> alone but needs the assistance of skillful practice and reason to purify and enlighten the soul by removing from it the dark veil of ignorance, which is the cause of most human errors. (Castiglione 1976: 291–2 [Bk 4])

By the press mankind now would practise its reason; by public opinion mankind would enlighten its several souls; from these enlightened souls would come that epideictic exercise of judgement and taste that constituted the knowledge of good and evil, of virtue and vice, and guide mankind to act accordingly. The old idea of conversation as both the suture between knowledge of the world and knowledge of the theoretical good, and the means by which to nudge the world towards the hazily perceived future of Utopia, here received an exact translation into Tunis Wortman's American idiom of public opinion.

Conclusion

In Madison and Wortman we find jointly an American conclusion that included public opinion both as the communication of rational sentiments and as the provision only of the moral role of a censor upon the passions of the multitude; freedom of the press as a necessary corollary to the establishment of public opinion; conversational freedom of inquiry in pursuit of the irresoluble and the expectation of persistent dissent as linked parts of the conception of public opinion; and the design of government architecture to include multiple levels of government in an extensive republic so as to foster the spread of enlightening public opinion. *Conversatio*'s orientation towards the eternal good, and *sermo*'s orientation towards worldly good, fused in a conversation meant to determine how worldly good could best lead towards eternal good, or at least the secular progress of mankind. The *philosophe* French precedent played a role – the conception of the press as radical tribune was an inheritance of this tradition. Yet British philosophy, and the minority report of the French Enlightenment, gave this conception of public opinion a more deferential mien, one calculated to defer to the free passions of the multitude. An aspiration to reason, to conversation, coexisted with a sense of its limitations, and of the enduring power of passion, of oratory. Here we find a conception of the public sphere translated into actual practice – and the ancestor of the actual practice of our own day. The theoretical aspirations of the other traditions of the Enlightenment have never yet come to pass; the variant of Madison and Wortman has endured in the world until the present moment, and long yet may endure.

Notes

1. For an overview and critique of the historiography of public opinion in eighteenth-century France, see Chisick 2002.
2. I am indebted to Andrew Stevens for reminding me of Lady Philosophy, and of the broader complicating point that such abstractions are often gendered feminine.
3. I am grateful to my father, Francis Ballard Randall, for the insight that the image of the tribunal in eighteenth-century France must hark back explicitly to the history of Rome.
4. I cite Peuchet above where his conception of public opinion aligned with the *philosophes*. I cite for the minority report the more interesting aspects of his thought, where he differed from the *philosophes*.

Conclusion

The conversational Enlightenment included *salon* society, the culture of politeness, the theoretical integration of women into historiographical analysis, the university seminar in Germany, and the pedagogy of England and Scotland. In the realm of the fine arts it included paintings by Hogarth and Watteau, architectural theory by Boffrand and landscape theory by Whately, string quartets by Haydn and Mozart, ballets by Noverre and novels by Defoe and Austen. In the realm of philosophy, conversation animated the thought of the Earl of Shaftesbury, David Hume, Adam Smith and George Campbell. In the world of French political thought, conversation turned opinion into public opinion – and when challenged at home by the *philosophes*, the conversational conception of the *philosophes* fled across the ocean to America, to habituate itself via thinkers such as James Madison and Tunis Wortman, in the constitutional architecture and political practice of the United States. The conversational Enlightenment was large, and very influential indeed.

These first two books have been history, following in Habermas' footsteps and providing a substitute historical narrative for the one he provided. The final book will be partly intellectual history as well, as it sketches the oratorical half of the rhetorical public sphere. It will also follow Habermas in his leap from history to theory – for although he did indeed continue his narrative of intellectual history from Kant down to himself, his crucial claim was that the Enlightenment provided a transcendent moment within history that allowed the transmutation from historical example to universalising theory. I will conclude my historical narratives – of prudence, economics, violence, law and historiography – with an outline of the theory of the rhetorical public sphere.

Bibliography

A., D. 1683. *The Whole Art of Converse*. London: Joseph Hindmarsh.

Abbott, Don. 1998. 'Blair "Abroad": The European Reception of the *Lectures on Rhetoric and Belles Lettres*.' In *Scottish Rhetoric and Its Influences*, ed. Lynee Gaillet. Mahwah: Hermagoras Press. 67–77.

Abizadeh, Arash. 2001. 'Banishing the Particular: Rousseau on Rhetoric, *Patrie*, and the Passions.' *Political Theory* 29, 4: 556–82.

Adorno, Theodor W. 2002. *Essays on Music*, ed. Richard Leppert, trans. Susan H. Gillespie. Berkeley and Los Angeles: University of California Press.

Agnew, Jean-Christophe. 1986. *Worlds Apart: The Market and the Theater in Anglo-American Thought, 1550–1750*. Cambridge and New York: Cambridge University Press.

Agnew, Lois. 1998. 'Rhetorical Style and the Formation of Character: Ciceronian Ethos in Thomas Wilson's *Arte of Rhetorique*.' *Rhetoric Review* 17, 1: 93–106.

Alberti, Leon Battista. 1966. *On Painting*, trans. John R. Spencer. New Haven and London: Yale University Press.

—. 1988. *On the Art of Building in Ten Books*, trans. Joseph Rykwert, Neil Leach, and Robert Tavernor. Cambridge, MA: MIT Press.

Albertus, Magnus. 1893. *B. Alberti Magni Opera omnia*, vol. XVIII, ed. Auguste Borgnet. Paris: Vives.

Alighieri, Dante. 1912. *The Convivio of Dante Alighieri*, trans. Philip Wicksteed. London: Dent.

—. 1966. *Dantis Alagherii Epistolae: The Letters of Dante*, trans. Paget Toynbee. Oxford: Clarendon Press.

—. 1969. *A Translation of the Latin Works of Dante*, trans. A. G. Ferrers Howell. New York: New York.

Alison, Archibald. 1790. *Essays on the Nature and Principles of Taste*. Edinburgh: J. J. G. and G. Robinson.

Allanbrook, W. J. 1983. *Rhythmic Gesture in Mozart: Le nozze di Figaro and Don Giovanni*. Chicago: University of Chicago Press.

Anderson, Christy. 2000. 'Monstrous Babels: Language and Architectural Style in the English Renaissance.' In *Architecture and Language: Constructing Identity in European Architecture, c. 1000–c. 1650*, ed. Georgia Clarke and Paul Crossley. Cambridge: Cambridge University Press. 148–61.

Anselment, Raymond. 1970. 'Rhetoric and the Dramatic Satire of Martin Marprelate.' *Studies in English Literature, 1500–1900* 10, 1: 103–19.

Arbeau, Thoinot. 1967. *Orchesography*, trans. Mary Stewart Evans. New York: Dover.

Archer, John. 1979. 'Character in English Architectural Design.' *Eighteenth-Century Studies* 12, 3: 339–71.

Aretino, Pietro. 1957. *Lettere sull'arte*, vol. 1, ed. Ettore Camesasca. Milan: Edizioni del Milione.

Aristophanes. 1978. *The Wasps*, trans. Benjamin Rogers. In *Aristophanes*, vol. I. London and Cambridge, MA: William Heinemann and Harvard University Press.

Aristotle. 1962. *On Interpretation*, trans. Harold Cook. London and Cambridge, MA: William Heinemann and Harvard University Press.

—. 1984. *The Complete Works of Aristotle*, 2 vols, ed. Jonathan Barnes. Princeton: Princeton University Press.

—. 1996. *Poetics*, trans. Malcolm Heath. London and New York: Penguin.

—. 2004. *Rhetoric*, trans. W. Rhys Roberts. Mineola, NY: Dover.

Armenini, Giovanni Battista. 1977. *On the True Precepts of the Art of Painting*, trans. Edward J. Olszewski. New York: Burt Franklin.

Arnauld, Antoine and Pierre Nicole. 1662. *La Logique ou L'Art de Penser.* Paris: Guignart, Savreux, Lavnay.

Ascoli, Albert. 1989. 'The Vowels of Authority (Dante's *Convivio* IV.vi.3–4).' In *Discourses of Authority in Medieval and Renaissance Literature*, ed. Kevin Brownlee and Walter Stephens. Hanover and London: University Press of New England. 23–46.

Astell, Mary. 1697. *A Serious Proposal to the Ladies for the Advancement of Their True and Greatest Interest.* London: Richard Wilkin.

Auerbach, Erich. 1953. *Mimesis: The Representation of Reality in Western Literature*, trans. Willard R. Trask. Princeton: Princeton University Press.

Augustine. 1937. *De beata vita. Happiness: A Study*, ed. and trans. Francis E. Tourscher. Philadelphia: Peter Reilly.

Austen, Jane. 2013. *Persuasion.* New York and London: W. W. Norton.

Avison, Charles. 1760. *Six Sonatas for the Harpsichord, with Accompanyments for two Violins and a Violincello*, op. 7. Newcastle: Johnson.

Bacilly, Bénigne de. 1679. *L'Art de bien chanter de M. de Bacilly. Augmenté d'un Discours qui sert de Réponse à la Critique de ce Traité.* Paris: Chez l'Autheur.

—. 1968. *A Commentary upon the Art of Proper Singing*, trans. and ed. Austin B. Caswell. Brooklyn: Institute of Medieval Music.

Bacon, Francis. 1909. *Essays: Civil and Moral.* In *The Harvard Classics*, ed. Charles Eliot, vol. 3. New York: P. F. Collier.

Baier, Annette. 1988. 'Hume's Account of Social Artifice: Its Origins and Originality.' *Ethics* 98, 4: 757–78.

Baker, Keith Michael. 1990. 'Public Opinion as Political Invention.' In *Inventing the French Revolution: Essays on French Political Culture in the Eighteenth Century.* Cambridge: Cambridge University Press. 167–99.

Balbi, Giovanni. 1506. *Catholicon*. Venice: Liechtenstein.

Baldinucci, Filippo. 1682. *Vita del Cavaliere Gio: Lorenzo Bernino*. Florence: Vangelisti.

Le Ballet de Monseigneur le duc de Vandosme. 1610. Paris: Heuqueville.

Barbaro, Daniele. 1567. *I Dieci Libri dell'architectura*. Venice: Senese and Chrieger.

Baridon, Michel. 2008. *A History of the Gardens of Versailles*, trans. Adrienne Mason. Philadelphia: University of Pennsylvania Press.

Barker, Emma. 2007. 'Mme Geoffrin, Painting and Galanterie: Carle Van Loo's "Conversation Espagnole" and "Lecture Espagnole".' *Eighteenth Century Studies* 40, 4: 587–614.

Barros, Ricardo. 2010. *Dance as a Discourse: The Rhetorical Expression of the Passions in French Baroque Dance*. Saarbrucken: Lambert Academic.

Bartel, Dietrich. 1997. *Musica Poetica: Musical-Rhetorical Figures in German Baroque Music*. Lincoln: University of Nebraska Press.

Barth, George. 1992. *The Pianist as Orator: Beethoven and the Transformation of Keyboard Style*. Ithaca: Cornell University Press.

Barthes, Roland. 1977. 'The Death of the Author', trans. Stephen Heath. In *Image – Music – Text*. New York Noonday Press. 142–8.

Bartolomeo, Joseph. 1994. *A New Species of Criticism: Eighteenth-Century Discourse on the Novel*. Newark: University of Delaware Press.

Bates, David William. 2012. *States of War: Enlightenment Origins of the Political*. New York: Columbia University Press.

Batey, Mavis. 2005. 'The Pleasures of the Imagination: Joseph Addison's Influence on Early Landscape Gardens.' *Garden History* 33, 2: 189–209.

Batteux, Charles. 1747. *Les beaux arts réduits à un même principe*. Paris: Durand.

—. 1981. *Les beaux-arts réduits à un même principe*. In *Music and Aesthetics in the Eighteenth and Early-Nineteenth Centuries*, ed. Peter le Huray and James Day. Cambridge: Cambridge University Press. 40–56.

Baumgarten, Alexander Gottlieb. 1954. *Reflections on Poetry: Alexander Gottlieb Baumgarten's Meditationes philosophicae de nonnullis ad poema pertinentibus*, trans. Karl Aschenbrenner and William B. Holther. Berkeley: University of California Press.

Baxandall, Michael. 1971. *Giotto and the Orators: Humanist Observers of Painting in Italy and the Discovery of Pictorial Composition 1350–1450*. Oxford: Clarendon Press.

Bayle, Pierre. 1735. *The Dictionary Historical and Critical of Mr Peter Bayle. The Second Edition. Volume the Second*. London: Knapton, et al.

Beal, Peter. 1998. *In Praise of Scribes: Manuscripts and their Makers in Seventeenth Century England*. Oxford: Clarendon Press.

Beasley, Faith E. 2006. *Salons, History, and the Creation of Seventeenth-Century France: Mastering Memory*. Aldershot: Ashgate.

Bédard, Jean-François. 2003. *The Architect as Honnête Homme: The Domestic Architecture and Decoration of Gilles-Marie Oppenord (1672–1742). Volume I: Text*. PhD diss., Columbia University.

—. 2011. *Decorative Games: Ornament, Rhetoric, and Noble Culture in the Work of Gilles-Marie Oppenord (1672–1742)*. Newark: University of Delaware Press.

Beghin, Tom. 1997. 'Haydn as Orator.' In *Joseph Haydn and his World*, ed. Elaine Sisman. Princeton: Princeton University Press. 201–54.

Beghin, Tom and Sander M. Goldberg, eds. 2007. *Haydn and the Performance of Rhetoric*. Chicago and London: University of Chicago Press.

Bellegarde, Jean-Baptiste Morvan de. 1688. *Réflexions sur ce qui peut plaire ou déplaire dans le commerce du monde*. Paris: Seneuze.

—. 1697. *Reflexions sur le ridicule et sur les moyens de l'éviter*. Paris: Guignard.

—. 1702. *Lettres curieuses de littérature et de morale*. Paris: Guignard.

—. 1707. *Reflexions upon the Politeness of Manners; with Maxims for Civil Society*. London: Newborough, et al.

Belting, Hans. 1994. *Likeness and Presence: A History of the Image before the Era of Art*, trans. Edmund Jephcott. Chicago and London: University of Chicago Press.

Bembo, Pietro. 1525. *Prose nelle quali si ragiona della volgar lingua*. Venice: Tacuino.

—. 1954. *Gli Asolani*, trans. Rudolf B. Gottfried. Bloomington: Indiana University Press.

Bending, Stephen. 2006. 'Mrs. Montagu's Contemplative Bench: Bluestocking Gardens and Female Retirement.' *Huntington Library Quarterly* 69, 4: 555–80.

Bennett, Tony. 1996. 'Really Useless 'Knowledge': A Political Critique of Aesthetics.' In *Design and Aesthetics: A Reader*, ed. Jerry Palmer and Mo Dodson. London and New York: Routledge. 33–48.

Bent, Margaret. 2010. 'Grammar and Rhetoric in Late Medieval Polyphony: Modern Metaphor or Old Simile?' In *Rhetoric Beyond Words: Delight and Persuasion in the Arts of the Middle Ages*, ed. Mary Carruthers. Cambridge: Cambridge University Press. 52–71.

Bentham, Jeremy. 1999. *Political Tactics*, ed. Michael James, Cyprian Blamires and Cathereine Pease-Watkin. Oxford: Clarendon Press.

Berger, Carol. 1981. 'The Hand and the Art of Memory.' *Musica Disciplina* 35: 87–120.

Bergeron, David. 2006. *Textual Patronage in English Drama, 1570–1640*. Aldershot: Ashgate.

Berkeley, George. 1996. *Principles of Human Knowledge*. Oxford: Oxford University Press.

Bermingham, Ann. 1995. 'Elegant Females and Gentlemen Connoisseurs: The Commerce in Culture and Self-Image in Eighteenth-Century England.' In *The Consumption of Culture 1600–1800: Image, Object, Text*, ed. Ann Bermingham and John Brewer. London and New York: Routledge. 489–513.

Bernstein, Richard. 1983. *Beyond Objectivism and Relativism: Science, Hermeneutics, and Praxis*. Philadelphia: University of Pennsylvania Press.

Berry, Christopher J. 2013. *The Idea of Commercial Society in the Scottish Enlightenment*. Edinburgh: Edinburgh University Press.

Bertucci, Paola. 2008. 'Domestic Spectacles: Electrical Instruments between Business and Conversation.' In *Science and Spectacle in the European Enlightenment*, ed. Bernadette Bensaude-Vincent and Christine Blondel. Aldershot: Ashgate. 75–87.

Betri, Maria Luisa and Elena Brambilla, eds. 2004. *Salotti e ruolo femminile in Italia: Tra fine Seicento e primo Novecento*. Venice: Marsilio.

Biagioli, Mario. 1993. *Galileo, Courtier: The Practice of Science in the Culture of Absolutism*. Chicago and London: University of Chicago Press.

—. 1996. 'Etiquette, Interdependence, and Sociability in Seventeenth-Century Science.' *Critical Inquiry* 22, 2: 193–238.

Bitzer, Lloyd. 1969. 'Hume's Philosophy in Campbell.' *Philosophy and Rhetoric* 2: 139–66.

Blainville, Charles Henri. 1767. *Histoire générale, critique et philologique de la musique*. Paris: Pissot.

Blair, Hugh. 2005. *Lectures on Rhetoric and Belles Lettres*, ed. Linda Ferreira Buckley and S. Michael Halloran. Carbondale: Southern Illinois University Press.

Blondel, Jacques-François. 1771. *Cours d'architecture. Tome Premier.* Paris: Desaint.

Bloom, Rori. 2009. *Man of Quality, Man of Letters: The Abbé Prévost Between Novel and Newspaper.* Lewisburg: Bucknell University Press.

Boffrand, Germain. 2002. *Book of Architecture*, trans. David Britt. Aldershot: Ashgate.

Boileau-Despréaux, Nicolas. 1966. *Oeuvres complètes*. Paris: Gallimard.

Bond, Donald F., ed. 1965. *The Spectator*, 5 vols. Oxford: Clarendon Press.

—. ed. 1987. *The Tatler*, 3 vols. Oxford: Clarendon Press.

Bonds, Mark Evan. 1991. *Wordless Rhetoric: Musical Form and the Metaphor of the Oration*. Cambridge, MA, and London: Harvard University Press.

Booth, Wayne. 1961. *The Rhetoric of Fiction*. Chicago: University of Chicago Press.

Borsay, Peter. 1989. *The English Urban Renaissance: Culture and Society in the Provincial Town 1660–1770*. Oxford: Clarendon Press.

—. 2013. 'Pleasure Gardens and Urban Culture in the Long Eighteenth Century.' In *The Pleasure Garden, from Vauxhall to Coney Island*, ed. Jonathan Conlin. Philadelphia: University of Pennsylvania Press. 49–77.

Bose, Mishtooni. 1996. 'Humanism, English Music and the Rhetoric of Criticism.' *Music & Letters* 77, 1: 1–21.

Botero, Giovanni. 1606. *Maximes d'estat militaires et politiques*, trans. Pierre de Deimier. Paris: Du Bray. [*Aggiunte alla sua ragion di Stato* (1598).]

Bouhours, Dominique. 1682. *Les Entretiens d'Ariste et d'Eugène*. Amsterdam: Le Jeune.

—. 1705. *The Art of Criticism: or, The Method of Making a Right Judgment Upon Subjects of Wit and Learning*. London: Brown and Roper.

—. 1743. *La Manière de bien Penser dans les Ouvrages d'Esprit*. Paris: Desprez and Cavelier.

Boullée, Étienne-Louis. 1968. *Architecture: Essai sur l'art*, ed. Jean-Marie Pérouse de Montclos. Paris: Hermann.

Bourdieu, Pierre. 1993. *The Field of Cultural Production*. New York: Columbia University Press.

Box, M. A. 1990. *The Suasive Art of David Hume*. Princeton: Princeton University Press.

Boyer, Abel. 1702. *The English Theophrastus: or, the Manners of the Age*. London: Turner and Chantry.

Bracciolini, Poggio. 1978. 'On Nobility', trans. David Marsh and Renée Neu Watkins. In *Humanism & Liberty: Writings on Freedom from Fifteenth-Century Florence*, ed. Renée Neu Watkins. Columbia: University of South Carolina Press. 121–48.

Brainard, Ingrid. 2016. 'The Speaking Body: Gaspero Angiolini's *Rhétorique Muette* and the *Ballet d'Action* in the Eighteenth Century.' In *Critica Musica: Essays in Honour of Paul Brainard*, ed. John Knowles. New York and London: Routledge. 15–56.

Brewer, John. 1995. '"The Most Polite Age and the Most Vicious": Attitudes towards Culture as a Commodity, 1660–1800.' In *The Consumption of Culture 1600–1800: Image, Object, Text*, ed. Ann Bermingham and John Brewer. London and New York: Routledge. 341–61.

Brillon, Pierre-Jacques. 1701. *Apologie de monsieur de La Bruyère, ou réponse à la critique des caractères de Theophraste*. Paris: Delespine.

Brinton, Alan. 1983. 'Quintilian, Plato, and the *vir bonus*.' *Philosophy and Rhetoric* 16, 3: 167–84.

Broman, Thomas. 1998. 'The Habermasian Public Sphere and Science in the Enlightenment.' *History of Science* 36, 2: 123–49.

Brooke, Henry. 1767. *The Fool of Quality; or, the History of Henry Earl of Moreland*, 4 vols. London: W. Johnston.

Brooke, Humphrey. 1681. *The durable legacy*. London: M. White.

Brooks, Jeanice. 2000. *Courtly Song in Late Sixteenth-Century France*. Chicago and London: University of Chicago Press.

Brossard, Sébastien de. 1703. *Dictionaire de Musique*. Paris: Ballard.

Brothers, Cammy. 2000. 'Architecture, Texts, and Imitation in Late-Fifteenth- and Early-Sixteenth-Century Rome.' In *Architecture and Language: Constructing Identity in European Architecture, c. 1000–c. 1650*, ed. Georgia Clarke and Paul Crossley. Cambridge: Cambridge University Press. 82–101.

Brown, Howard Mayer. 1980. 'Words and Music: Willaert, the Chanson and the Madrigal about 1540.' In *Florence and Venice: Comparisons and Relations. Volume II: Cinquecento*, ed. Sergio Bertelli, Nicolai Rubinstein and Craig Hugh Smith. Florence: La Nuova Italia Editrice. 217–66.

—. 1982. 'Emulation, Competition, and Homage: Imitation and Theories of Imitation in the Renaissance.' *Journal of the American Musicological Society* 35: 1–48.

Brown, Leslie Ellen. 1980. 'Oratorical Thought and the *Tragédie Lyrique*: A Consideration of Musical-Rhetorical Figures.' *College Music Symposium* 20, 2: 99–116.

—. 1995. 'The Idea of Life as a Work of Art in Scottish Enlightenment Discourse.' In *Studies in Eighteenth-Century Culture*, vol. 24, ed. Carla H. Hay and Syndy M. Conger. Baltimore and London: Johns Hopkins University Press. 51–67.

Brubaker, Leslie. 2003. 'Text and Picture in Manuscripts: What's Rhetoric Got To Do With It?' In *Rhetoric in Byzantium*, ed. Elizabeth Jeffreys. Aldershot: Ashgate. 255–65.

Bruford, W. H. 2010. *The German Tradition of Self-Cultivation: 'Bildung' from Humboldt to Thomas Mann*. Cambridge: Cambridge University Press.

Bruni, Leonardo. 1987. 'The Dialogues.' In *The Humanism of Leonardo Bruni: Selected Texts*, trans. and ed. Gordon Griffiths, James Hankins and David Thompson. Binghamton, NY: Medieval and Renaissance Texts and Studies. 63–84.

Buchenau, Stefanie. 2013. *The Founding of Aesthetics in the German Enlightenment: The Art of Invention and the Invention of Art*. Cambridge: Cambridge University Press.

Buelow, George J. 1966. 'The *Loci Topici* and Affect in Late Baroque Music: Heinichen's Practical Demonstration.' *The Music Review* 27: 161–76.

—. 1983. 'Johann Mattheson and the Invention of the *Affektenlehre*.' In *New Mattheson Studies*, ed. George J. Buelow and Hans Joachim Marx. Cambridge: Cambridge University Press. 393–407.

Buelow, George J., Peter A. Hoyt and Blake Wilson. 2001. 'Rhetoric and Music.' In *The New Grove Dictionary of Music and Musicians*, vol. 21, 2nd edn, ed. Stanley Sadie. London: Macmillan. 260–75.

Burke, Edmund. 1777. *A Letter from Edmund Burke, Esq; One of the Representatives in Parliament for the City of Bristol, to John Farr and John Harris, Esqrs. Sheriffs of that City, on the Affairs of America*. London: Dodsley.

—. 1958. *A Philosophical Inquiry into the Origin of Our Ideas of the Sublime and Beautiful*, ed. J. T. Boulton. London: Routledge and Kegan Paul.

Burke, Peter. 1993. *The Art of Conversation*. Ithaca: Cornell University Press.

Burkholder, J. Peter. 1985. 'Johannes Martini and the Imitation Mass of the Late Fifteenth Century.' *Journal of the American Musicological Society* 38, 3: 470–523.

Burmeister, Joachim. 1993. *Musical Poetics*, trans. Benito V. Rivera, ed. Claude V. Palisca. New Haven: Yale University Press.

Bushnell, Rebecca W. 1996. *A Culture of Teaching: Early Modern Humanism in Theory and Practice*. Ithaca and London: Cornell University Press.

Bussels, Stijn. 2012. *The Animated Image: Roman Theory on Naturalism, Vividness and Divine Power*. Berlin: Akademie.

Buszin, Walter E. 1946 'Luther on Music.' *The Musical Quarterly* 32, 1: 80–97.

Butler, Gregory G. 1977. 'Fugue and Rhetoric.' *Journal of Music Theory* 21, 1: 49–109.

Bygrave, Stephen. 2009. *Uses of Education: Readings in Enlightenment in England*. Lewisburg: Bucknell University Press.

C., S. 1673. *The Art of Complaisance or the Means to Oblige in Conversation*. London: John Starkey; revising Eustache du Refuge, *Traité de la cour*, Paris, 1616.

Calvin, Jean. 1542. *La forme des prières et chantz ecclésiastiques*. Geneva.

—. 2001. *John Calvin: Writings on Pastoral Piety*, ed. and trans. Elsie Anne McKee. New York: Paulist Press.

Campanella, Tommaso. 1638. *Rationalis philosophiae pars quarta, videlicet Poeticorum liber unus, iuxta propria principia*. Paris: Du Bray.

Campbell, George. 1963. *The Philosophy of Rhetoric*, ed. Lloyd Bitzer. Carbondale: Southern Illinois University Press.

Carpani, Gisueppe. 1823. *Le Haydine, ovvero lettere su la vita e le opere del celebre maestro Giuseppe Haydn, Edizione Seconda*. Padua: Tipografia della Minerva.

Carr, Rosalind. 2014. *Gender and Enlightenment Culture in Eighteenth-Century Scotland*. Edinburgh: Edinburgh University Press.

Carruthers, Mary, ed. 2010. *Rhetoric Beyond Words: Delight and Persuasion in the Arts of the Middle Ages*. Cambridge: Cambridge University Press.

Cassirer, Ernst. 1951. *The Philosophy of the Enlightenment*, trans. Fritz C. A. Koelln and J. P. Pettegrove. Princeton: Princeton University Press.

Castiglione, Baldesar. 1976. *The Book of the Courtier*, trans. George Bull. New York: Penguin.

Caussin, Nicolas. 1678. *The Holy Court, in Five Books*, trans. Sir Thomas Hawkins. London: John Williams.

Cave, Terence. 1979. *The Cornucopian Text: Problems of Writing in the French Renaissance*. Oxford: Clarendon Press.

Cellauro, Louis. 2004. 'Daniele Barbaro and Vitruvius: The Architectural Theory of a Renaissance Humanist and Patron.' *Papers of the British School at Rome* 72: 293–329.

[Chaillou, Pierre-Louis.] 1766. *Des commissions extraordinaires en matière criminelle*. n.p.

Chancy, François de. 2006. *2nd Livre d'Airs de cour*, vol. 2. Paris: Éditions du Centre de Musique Baroque de Versailles.

Charron, Pierre. n.d. [after 1612]. *Of Wisdome*, trans. Samson Lennard. London: Printed [at Eliot's Court Press] for Edward Blount & Will: Aspley.

Chartier, Roger. 1991. *The Cultural Origins of the French Revolution*, trans. Lydia G. Cochrane. Durham, NC, and London: Duke University Press.

—. 1997. 'The Man of Letters.' In *Enlightenment Portraits*, ed. Michael Vovelle, trans. Lydia Cochrane. Chicago and London: University of Chicago Press.

Chisick, Harvey. 2002. 'Public Opinion and Political Culture in France during the Second Half of the Eighteenth Century.' *The English Historical Review* 117, 470: 48–77.

Cholières, Nicolas de. 1587. *Les Après disnées*. Paris: Richer.

Christout, Marie-Françoise. 1987. *The Ballet de Cour in the 17th Century*. Geneva: Minkoff.

Cibber, Colley. 1826. *An Apology for the Life of Mr. Colley Cibber*. [*Autobiography. A Collection of the most instructive and amusing lives ever published, written by the parties themselves. Volume I. – Colley Cibber*.] London: Hunt and Clarke.

Cicero. 1960. *Cicero: De inventione. De optimo genere oratorum. Topica*, trans. H. M. Hubbell. London and Cambridge, MA: William Heinemann and Harvard University Press.

—. 1967. *De oratore*, vols I–II, trans. H. Rackham. London and Cambridge, MA: William Heinemann and Harvard University Press.

—. 1971. *Cicero: Brutus, Orator*, trans. H. M. Hubbell. London and Cambridge, MA: Harvard University Press.

—. 1979. *Pro Archia Poeta*, trans. N. H. Watts. In *Cicero. XI: The Speeches*. London and Cambridge, MA: William Heinemann and Harvard University Press.

—. 1988. *De re publica*. In *De re publica. De Legibus*, trans. Clinton Walker Keyes. London and Cambridge, MA: William Heinemann and Harvard University Press.

—. 1989. *Tusculan Disputations*, trans. J. E. King. Cambridge, MA, and London: Harvard University Press.

Clark, Henry C. 1992. 'Conversation and Moderate Virtue in Adam Smith's "Theory of Moral Sentiments".' *The Review of Politics* 54, 2: 185–210.

—. 1993. 'Women and Humanity in Scottish Enlightenment Social Thought: The Case of Adam Smith.' *Historical Reflections/Réflexions Historiques* 19, 3: 335–61.

Cohen, Michèle. 2008. "A Proper Exercise for the Mind': Conversation and Education in the Long Eighteenth Century.' In *The Concept and Practice of Conversation in the Long Eighteenth Century, 1688–1848*, ed. Katie Halsey and Jane Slinn. Newcastle: Cambridge Scholars. 103–27.

Colclough, David. 2005. *Freedom of Speech in Early Stuart England*. Cambridge: Cambridge University Press.

Coleman, Joyce. 1996. *Public Reading and the Reading Public in Late Medieval England and France*. Cambridge: Cambridge University Press.

Collins, Amanda. 2002. *Greater than Emperor: Cola di Rienzo (ca. 1313–54) and the World of Fourteenth Century Rome*. Ann Arbor: University of Michigan Press.

Collins, Nancy W. 2006. *The Problem of the Enlightenment Salon: European History of Post-Revolutionary Politics 1755–1850*. PhD diss., University of London.

Colomby, Sieur de, François de Cauvigny. 1631. *De l'autorité des roys*. Paris: Du Bray.

Comsa, Maria Teodora, et al. 2016. 'The French Enlightenment Network.' *The Journal of Modern History* 88: 495–534.

Conan, Michel. 2005. 'Friendship and Imagination in French Baroque Gardens before 1661.' In *Baroque Garden Cultures: Emulation, Sublimation, Subversion*, ed. Michel Conan. Washington, DC: Dumbarton Oaks Research Library and Collection. 323–83.

—. 2007. 'Royal Gardens, Fashionable Promenades, and Public Opinion in Seventeenth- and Eighteenth-Century Paris.' In *Performance and Appropriation: Profane Rituals in Gardens and Landscapes*, ed. Michel Conan. Washington, DC: Dumbarton Oaks Research Library and Collection. 43–57.

Constable, John. 1738. *The conversation of gentlemen considered in most of the ways, that make their mutual company agreeable, or disagreeable*. London: Printed by J. Hoyles: and sold by the booksellers of London and Westminster.

Copley, Stephen. 1995. 'Commerce, Conversation and Politeness in the Early Eighteenth-Century Periodical.' *British Journal for Eighteenth-Century Studies* 18: 63–77.

Cormack, Robin. 2003. '"Living Painting".' In *Rhetoric in Byzantium*, ed. Elizabeth Jeffreys. Aldershot: Ashgate. 235–47.

Costelloe, Timothy. 2003. 'Hume, Kant, and the "Antinomy of Taste".' *Journal of the History of Philosophy* 41, 2: 165–85.

—. 2004. 'Hume's Aesthetics: The Literature and Directions for Future Research.' *Hume Studies* 30, 1: 87–126.

—. 2007. *Aesthetics and Morals: Philosophy of David Hume*. New York and London: Routledge.

Cowan, Brian. 2004. 'The Rise of the Coffee House Reconsidered.' *Historical Journal* 47, 1: 21–46.

—. 2005. *The Social Life of Coffee: The Emergence of the British Coffeehouse*. New Haven and London: Yale University Press.

Cowart, Georgia J. 2008. *The Triumph of Pleasure: Louis XIV & the Politics of Spectacle*. Chicago and London: University of Chicago Press.

Cowper, William. 1994. *The Task and Selected other Poems*, ed. James Sambrook. New York: Routledge.

Cox, Leonard. 1532. *The art or crafte of rhetoryke*. London: Robert Redman.

Crane, Mary Thomas. 2009. 'Illicit Privacy and Outdoor Spaces in Early Modern England.' *Journal for Early Modern Cultural Studies* 9, 1: 4–22.

Craveri, Benedetta. 2005. *The Age of Conversation*, trans. Teresa Waugh. New York: New York Review Books.

Cressy, David. 1980. *Literacy and the Social Order: Reading and Writing in Tudor and Stuart England*. Cambridge: Cambridge University Press.

Croce, Benedetto. 1968. *Aesthetic as Science of Expression and General Linguistic*, trans. Douglas Ainslie. New York: Noonday Press.

Crousaz, Jean Pierre de. 1715. *Traité du beau*. Amsterdam: L'Honoré.

—. 1722. *Traité de l'éducation des enfans*, 2 vols. La Haye: Vaillant and Prevost.

Crow, Thomas E. 1985. *Painters and Public Life in Eighteenth-Century Paris*. New Haven: Yale University Press.

Curtius, Ernst Robert. 1963. *European Literature and the Latin Middle Ages*, trans. Willard Trask. New York: Harper & Row.

Cutler, Fred. 1999. 'Jeremy Bentham and the Public Opinion Tribunal.' *The Public Opinion Quarterly* 63, 3: 321–46.

Dacier, Anne Lefévre. 1714. *Des causes de la corruption du goût*. Paris: Rigaud.

D'Alembert, Jean-Baptiste le Rond. 1822. *Oeuvres de D'Alembert. Tome Quatrième*. Paris: Belin.

D'Alton, J. F. 1962. *Roman Literary Theory and Criticism: A Study in Tendencies*. New York: Russell & Russell.

Dalton, Susan. 2003. *Engendering the Republic of Letters: Reconnecting Public and Private Spheres in Eighteenth-Century Europe*. Montreal and Kingston: McGill-Queens University Press.

—. 2009. 'Giustina Renier Michiel and Conflicting Ideas of Gender in Late Eighteenth-Century Venice.' In *Italy's Eighteenth Century: Gender and Culture in the Age of the Grand Tour*, ed. Paula Findlen, Wendy Wassyng Roworth and Catherine M. Sama. Stanford: Stanford University Press. 79–100.

Darnton, Robert. 1995. *The Forbidden Best-Sellers of Pre-Revolutionary France*. New York: W. W. Norton.

David, Hans T., Arthur Mendel and Christoph Wolff, eds. 1998. *The New Bach Reader: A Life of Johann Sebastian Bach in Letters and Documents*. New York: W. W. Norton.

Davidson, Hugh M. 1965. *Audience, Words, and Art: Studies in Seventeenth Century French Rhetoric*. Columbus: Ohio State University Press.

Davidson, Jenny. 2004. *Hypocrisy and the Politics of Politeness: Manners and Morals from Locke to Austen*. Cambridge: Cambridge University Press.

Davies, Paul and David Hemsoll. 2000. 'Sanmicheli's Architecture and Literary Theory.' In *Architecture and Language: Constructing Identity in European Architecture, c. 1000–c. 1650*, ed. Georgia Clarke and Paul Crossley. Cambridge: Cambridge University Press. 102–17.

Davis, Herbert. 1964. *Jonathan Swift: Essays on his Satire and Other Studies*. New York: Oxford University Press.

De Bolla, Peter. 2008. 'Portraiture as Conversation.' In *The Concept and Practice of Conversation in the Long Eighteenth Century, 1688–1848*, ed. Katie Halsey and Jane Slinn. Newcastle: Cambridge Scholars. 170–82.

[De Brosses, Charles and Maleteste de Villey.] 1762. *Nouvelles remontrances du parlement de Bourgone au Roi*. n.p.

De Jong, Erik A. 2007. 'Taking Fresh Air: Walking in Hollland, 1600–1750.' In *Performance and Appropriation: Profane Rituals in Gardens and Landscapes*, ed. Michel Conan. Washington, DC: Dumbarton Oaks Research Library and Collection. 19–40.

De Pure, Michel. 1668. *Idée des Spectacles Anciens et Nouveaux*. Paris: Brunet.
Defoe, Daniel. 1699. *The Compleat Mendicant*. London: E. Harris.
—. 1881a. *Dickory Cronke*, ed. Walter Scott. In *The Novels and Miscellaneous Works of Daniel De Foe*, vol. II. London: Y. Tegg.
—. 1881b. *Memoirs of a Cavalier*, ed. Walter Scott. In *The Novels and Miscellaneous Works of Daniel De Foe*, vol. II. London: Y. Tegg.
—. 1881c. *Roxana*, ed. Walter Scott. In *The Novels and Miscellaneous Works of Daniel De Foe*, vol. IV. London: Y. Tegg.
—. 1950. *Moll Flanders*. New York: Modern Library.
—. 1965. *Colonel Jack*. London: Oxford University Press.
Dejean, Joan. 1997. *Ancients Against Moderns: Culture Wars and the Making of a Fin de Siècle*. Chicago and London: University of Chicago Press.
Delehanty, Ann T. 2013. *Literary Knowing in Neoclassical France: From Poetics to Aesthetics*. Lewisburg: Bucknell University Press.
Delon, Michel. 1981. 'La marquise et le philosophe.' *Revue des Science Humaines* 54, 182: 65–78.
Démoris, René. 1971. 'Les fêtes galantes chez Watteau et dans le roman contemporain.' *Le Dix-Huitième Siècle* 3: 337–57.
Dennis, Michael. 1986. *Court and Garden: From the French Hôtel to the City of Modern Architecture*. Cambridge, MA: MIT Press.
Des Périers, Bonaventure. 1972. *Novel Pastimes and Merry Tales*, trans. Raymond C. La Charité and Virginia A. La Charité. Lexington: University Press of Kentucky.
Descartes, René. 1644. *Specimina philosophiae: seu Dissertatio de Methodo*, trans. Etienne de Courcelles. Amsterdam: Elzevir.
—. 1961. *Compendium of Music (Compendium musicae)*, trans. Walter Robert. Rome: American Institute of Musicology.
—. 1985. *The Philosophical Writings of Descartes*, vols I–II, trans. John Cottingham, Robert Stoothoff and Dugald Murdoch. Cambridge: Cambridge University Press.
—. 2006. *A Discourse on the Method of Correctly Conducting One's Reason and Seeking Truth in the Sciences*, trans. Ian Maclean. Oxford: Oxford University Press.
D'Ezio, Marianna. 2011. 'Literary and Cultural Intersections between British and Italian Women Writers and *Salonnières* during the Eighteenth Century.' In *Readers, Writers, Salonnières: Female Networks in Europe, 1700–1900*, ed. Hilary Brown and Gillian Dow. Bern: Peter Lang. 11–29.
—. 2014. 'Isabella Teotochi Albrizzi's Venetian Salon: A Transcultural and Transnational Example of Sociability and Cosmopolitanism in Late Eighteenth- and Early Nineteenth-Century Europe.' In *Social Networks in the Long Eighteenth Century: Clubs, Literary Salons, Textual Coteries*, ed. Ileana Baird. Newcastle: Cambridge Scholars. 175–98.
Dickins, Amanda. 2008. 'An "Intercourse of Sentiments" and the Seductions of Virtue: The Role of Conversation in David Hume's Philosophy.'

In *The Concept and Practice of Conversation in the Long Eighteenth Century, 1688–1848*, ed. Katie Halsey and Jane Slinn. Newcastle: Cambridge Scholars. 20–39.

Dictionnaire universel. 1701. 3 vols, ed. Antoine Furetière and Basnage de Bauval. Rotterdam: Leers.

Dictionnaire universel. Tome Septieme. 1771. Paris: Compagnie des Libraires Associés.

Diderot, Denis, ed. 1782. *Encyclopédie. Tome XVI.* Lausanne and Berne: Sociétés Typographiques.

—. 1975. *Salons. Vol. I: 1759, 1761, 1763*, 2nd edn, ed. Jean Seznec and Jean Adhémar. Oxford: Clarendon Press.

—. 1995. *Héros et martyrs: Salons de 1769, 1771, 1775, 1781*, ed. Else Marie Bukdahl, et al. Paris: Hermann.

Dijn, Annelien de. 2012. 'The Politics of Enlightenment: From Peter Gay to Jonathan Israel.' *The Historical Journal* 55, 3: 785–805.

Dolce, Lodovico. 1960. *Dialogo della Pittura.* In *Trattati d'arte del Cinquecento fra Manierismo e Controriforma*, vol. 1, ed. Parola Barocchi. Bari: Laterza & Figli. 141–206.

—. 2015. *Dialogo della instituzion delle donne, secondo li tre stati che cadono nella vita umana*, ed. Helena Sanson. Cambridge: Modern Humanities Research Association.

Dominik, William, ed. 1997. *Roman Eloquence: Rhetoric in Society and Literature.* London and New York: Routledge.

Donato, Maria Pia. 2009. 'Female Self-Affirmation in the Roman Salon of the Grand Tour', trans. Matthew Sneider. In *Italy's Eighteenth Century: Gender and Culture in the Age of the Grand Tour*, ed. Paula Findlen, Wendy Wassyng Roworth and Catherine M. Sama. Stanford: Stanford University Press. 59–78.

Donatus, Tiberius Claudius. 1905–6. *Tiberi Claudi Donati ad Tiberium Claudium Maximum Donatianum filium suum Interpretationes Vergilianae*, 2 vols, ed. Heinrich Georges. Leipzig: Teubner.

Donawerth, Jane. 1998. 'Conversation and the Boundaries of Public Discourse in Rhetorical Theory by Renaissance Women.' *Rhetorica* 16, 2: 181–99.

—, ed. 2002. *Rhetorical Theory by Women before 1900: An Anthology.* Lanham: Rowman & Littlefield.

Doni, Anton Francesco. 1549. *Disegno del Doni.* Venice: Gioliti.

Doran, Madeleine. 1963. *Endeavors of Art: A Study of Form in Elizabethan Drama.* Madison: University of Wisconsin Press.

Dostal, Robert. 1980. 'Kant and Rhetoric.' *Philosophy and Rhetoric* 13, 4: 223–44.

Drake, Judith [?]. 1696. *An Essay in defense of the Female Sex.* London: Roper, Wilkinson, and Clavel.

Dreyfus, Laurence. 1996. *Bach and the Patterns of Invention.* Cambridge, MA, and London: Harvard University Press.

Drummond, George. 1740. 'Rules of Conversation.' Edinburgh University Library, Special Collections Department, Dc.4.54/17.

Dubois de Launay, Henri. 1786. *Coup d'oeil sur le gouernement anglais*.n.p.

Dubois de St Gelais, Louis-François. 1728. *Description des tableaux du Palais Royal*. Paris: D'Houry.

Dubos, Jean-Baptiste. 1748. *Critical Reflections on Poetry, Painting and Music*, 3 vols, trans. Thomas Nugent, 5th edn. London: Nourse.

Duclos, Charles Pinot. 1751. *Considérations sur les moeurs de ce siècle*. n.p.

—. 1772. *Considérations sur les moeurs de ce siècle*, 6th edn. Paris: n.p.

Dufresny, Charles Rivière. 1699. *Amusements sérieux et comiques*. Amsterdam: Desbordes.

Dumarsais, César Chesnau. 1757. *Traité des Tropes*. Leipzig: Fritsch.

Duncan, David Allen. 1989. 'Persuading the Affections: Rhetorical Theory and Mersenne's Advice to Harmonic Orators.' In *French Musical Thought, 1600–1800*, ed. Georgia Cowart. Ann Arbor and London: UMI Research Press. 149–75.

Dunn, John. 1983. 'From Applied Theology to Social Analysis: The Break between John Locke and the Scottish Enlightenment.' In *Wealth and Virtue*, ed. Istvan Hont and Michael Ignatieff. Cambridge: Cambridge University Press. 119–35.

Dunn, Kevin. 1994. *Pretexts of Authority: The Rhetoric of Authorship in the Renaissance Preface*. Stanford: Stanford University Press.

Duvenage, Pieter. 2003. *Habermas and Aesthetics: The Limits of Communicative Reason*. Cambridge: Polity.

Dwyer, John. 1987. *Virtuous Discourse: Sensibility and Community in Late Eighteenth-Century Scotland*. Edinburgh: John Donald.

—. 1990. 'The Imperative of Sociability.' *British Journal for Eighteenth-Century Studies* 13: 169–84.

—. 1998. *The Age of Passions: An Interpretation of Adam Smith and Scottish Enlightenment Culture*. East Linton: Tuckwell Press.

Edmondson, Chloe. Forthcoming. 'Julie de Lespinasse and the "Philosophical" Salon.' In *Networks of Enlightenment: Digital Approaches to the Republic of Letters*, ed. Chloe Edmondson and Dan Edelstein. Liverpool: Oxford Studies in the Enlightenment.

Eger von Kalkar, Heinrich. 1952. *Das Cantuagium*, ed. Heinrich Hüschen. Cologne: Staufen.

Eisenstein, Elizabeth. 1983. *The Printing Revolution in Early Modern Europe*. Cambridge: Cambridge University Press.

Elias, Norbert. 2000. *The Civilizing Process*, trans. Edmund Jephcott. Oxford: Blackwell.

Elsner, Jaś and Michel Meyer, eds. 2014. *Art and Rhetoric in Roman Culture*. Cambridge: Cambridge University Press.

Elyot, Thomas. 1962. *The Book named The Governor*, ed. S. E. Lehmberg. London and New York: Dent and Dutton.

Enders, Jody. 1992. 'Music, Delivery, and the Rhetoric of Memory in Guillaume de Machaut's *Remède de Fortune*.' *PMLA* 107, 3: 450–64.

Erasmus, Desiderius. 1908. *Ciceronianus or A Dialogue on the Best Style of Speaking*, trans. Izora Scott. New York: New York City Teachers College, Columbia University.

—. 1965. *The Colloquies of Erasmus*, trans. Craig R. Thompson. Chicago and London: University of Chicago Press.

Fader, Don. 2003. 'The *Honnête homme* as Music Critic: Taste, Rhetoric, and Politesse in the 17th-Century French Reception of Italian Music.' *The Journal of Musicology* 20, 1: 3–44.

Fairclough, Mary. 2013. *The Romantic Crowd: Sympathy, Controversy and Print Culture*. Cambridge: Cambridge University Press.

Fairfax, Edmund. 2003. *The Styles of Eighteenth-Century Ballet*. Lanham and Oxford: Scarecrow Press.

Faret, Nicholas. 1632. *The Honest Man: or The Art to Please in Court*, trans. Edward Grimstone. London: Printed by Thomas Harper, for Edward Blount.

Farnsworth, Rodney. 1990. 'How the Other Half Sounds: An Historical Survey of Musical Rhetoric during the Baroque and After.' *Rhetoric Society Quarterly* 20, 3: 207–24.

Fawcett, Trevor. 1985. 'Self-Improvement Societies: The Early "Lit. and Phils.".' In *Life in the Georgian Town: Papers Given at the Georgian Group Symposium*. London: Georgian Group. 15–25.

Félibien, André. 1705. *Entretiens sur les vies et sur les ouvrages des plus excellens peintres anciens et modernes*, 2 vols. London: Mortier.

Fénelon, François. 1722. *Dialogues Concerning Eloquence*. London: Printed by T. Wood for J. Walthoe.

Ferrone, Vincenzo. 2015. *The Enlightenment: History of an Idea*, trans. Elisabetta Tarantino. Princeton and Oxford: Princeton University Press.

Fielding, Henry. 1972. 'An Essay on Conversation.' In *The Miscellanies*, I, ed. Henry Knight Miller. In *The Wesleyan Edition of the Works of Henry Fielding*, gen. ed. W. B. Coley, 5 vols. Middletown: Wesleyan University Press, 1967–75. 119–52.

Filarete (Antonio di Piero Averlino). 1965. *Treatise on Architecture: Being the Treatise by Antonio di Piero Aberlino, Known as Filarete*, 2 vols, trans. John R. Spencer. New Haven and London: Yale University Press.

Finscher, Ludwig. 1974. *Studien zur Geschichte des Streichquartetts. 1: Die Entstehung des klassischen Streichquartetts. Von den Vorformen zur Grundlegung durch Joseph Haydns*. Kassel: Bärenreiter.

Firenzuola, Agnolo. 1802. *Opere di messer Agnolo Firenzuola, Fiorentino*. Milan: Dalla Società Tipografica de' Classici Italiani.

Fleury, Claude. 1686. *Traité du choix et de la method des études*. Paris: Aubouin, Emery, and Clousier.

Fontana, Biancamaria, ed. 1988. *Benjamin Constant: Political Writings*. Cambridge: Cambridge University Press.

Fonte, Moderata [Modesta Pozzo]. 1997. *The Worth of Women*, ed. and trans. Virginia Cox. Chicago: University of Chicago Press.

Fontenelle, Bernard le Bovier de. 1990. *Conversations on the Plurality of Worlds*, trans. H. A. Hargreaves. Berkeley and Los Angeles: University of California Press.

Forbes, Duncan. 1975. *Hume's Philosophical Politics*. Cambridge: Cambridge University Press.

—. 1982. 'Natural Law and the Scottish Enlightenment.' In *The Origins and Nature of the Scottish Enlightenment*, ed. R. H. Campbell and Andrew S. Skinner. Edinburgh: John Donald. 186–204.

Fordyce, David. 1757. *Dialogues Concerning Education*, vol. II, 3rd edn. London: Dilly.

—. 1758. *The Elements of Moral Philosophy*, 3rd edn. London: Dodsley and Dodsley.

Fordyce, James. 1777. *Addresses to Young Men*, vol. I. London: Cadell.

—. 1809. *Sermons to Young Women*, vol. I, 13th edn. London: Cadell and Davies.

Foster, David. 1994. 'Taming the Father: John Locke's Critique of Patriarchal Fatherhood.' *Review of Politics* 56, 4: 641–70.

Foucault, Michel. 1979. 'What is an Author?' In *Textual Strategies: Perspectives in Post-Structuralist Criticism*, ed. Josué Harari. Ithaca: Cornell University Press. 141–60.

Fox, Adam. 2000. *Oral and Literate Culture in England 1500–1700*. Oxford: Oxford University Press.

France, Peter. 1972. *Rhetoric and Truth in France: Descartes to Diderot*. Oxford: Clarendon Press.

—. 1992. *Politeness and Its Discontents: Problems in French Classical Culture*. Cambridge: Cambridge University Press.

Franko, Mark. 1993. *Dance as Text: Ideologies of the Baroque Body*. Cambridge: Cambridge University Press.

Fumaroli, Marc. 1983. 'Rhetoric, Politics, and Society: From Italian Ciceronianism to French Classicism.' In *Renaissance Eloquence: Studies in the Theory and Practice of Renaissance Rhetoric*, ed. James J. Murphy. Berkeley, Los Angeles and London: University of California Press. 253–73.

—. 1988. 'The Republic of Letters', trans. R. Scott Walker. *Diogenes* 143: 129–52.

—. 2011. *When the World Spoke French*, trans. Richard Howard. New York: New York Review Books.

Fusée de Voisenon, Claude Henri de [?]. 1753. *Réponse du Coin du Roi au Coin de la Reine*. Paris: n.p.

Gabrielson, Teena. 2009. 'James Madison's Psychology of Public Opinion.' *Political Research Quarterly* 62, 3: 431–44.

Gaffurius, Franchinus. 1968. *Practica musicae*, ed. and trans. Clement A. Miller. Dallas: American Institute of Musicology.

Galilei, Vincenzo. 2003. *Dialogue on Ancient and Modern Music*, trans. Claude V. Palisca. New Haven: Yale University Press.

Gallet, Michel and Jörg Garms. 1986. *Germain Boffrand 1667–1754: L'aventure d'un architecte indépendant*. Paris: Herscher

Garat, Dominique-Joseph. 1820. *Mémoires historiques sur la vie de M. Suard, sur ses écrits et sur le XVIIIe siècle*, 2 vols. Paris: Belin.

Garver, Eugene. 1987. *Machiavelli and the History of Prudence*. Madison: University of Wisconsin Press.

—. 2004. *For the Sake of Argument: Practical Reasoning, Character, and the Ethics of Belief*. Chicago: University of Chicago Press.

Gay, Peter. 1995. *The Enlightenment: An Interpretation. The Rise of Modern Paganism*, vol. 1. New York and London: W. W. Norton.

—. 1996. *The Enlightenment: An Interpretation. The Science of Freedom*, vol. 2. New York and London: W. W. Norton.

Gehrke, Pat. 2002. 'Turning Kant Against the Priority of Autonomy: Communication Ethics and the Duty to Community.' *Philosophy and Rhetoric* 35, 1: 1–21.

Genlis, Stéphanie-Félicité, Comtesse de. 1825. *Memoirs of the Countess de Genlis, illustrative of the history of the eighteenth and nineteenth centuries*, vol. II, trans. unknown. New York: Wilder & Campbell.

Gerbino, Anthony. 2010. *François Blondel: Architecture, Erudition, and the Scientific Revolution*. London and New York: Routledge.

Germann, Georg. 1972. *Gothic Revival in Europe and Britain: Sources, Influences, and Ideas*, trans. Gerald Onn. London: Lund Humphries with the Architectural Association.

Gibbon, Edward. 1776. *The History of the Decline and Fall of the Roman Empire*, vol. 1. London: Strahan and Cadell.

Gibson, Alan. 2005a. 'Madison on Democracy, Property, and Civic Education: A Reply to Matthews and Sheehan.' *The Review of Politics* 67, 1: 69–76.

—. 2005b. 'Veneration and Vigilance: James Madison and Public Opinion, 1785–1800.' *The Review of Politics* 67, 1: 5–35.

Gibson, Jonathan. 2008. '"A Kind of Eloquence Even in Music": Embracing Different Rhetorics in Late Seventeenth-Century France.' *The Journal of Musicology* 25, 4: 394–433.

Giesecke, Annette Lucia. 2007. *The Epic City: Urbanism, Utopia, and the Garden in Ancient Greece and Rome*. Washington, DC: Center for Hellenic Studies.

Giles, Jeffrey. 1981. 'Dance and the French Enlightenment.' *Dance Chronicle* 4, 3: 245–63.

Gill, Christopher. 1984. 'The Ethos/Pathos Distinction in Rhetorical and Literary Criticism.' *The Classical Quarterly*, n.s. 34, 1: 149–66.

Gill, Natasha. 2010. *Educational Philosophy in the French Enlightenment: From Nature to Second Nature*. Farnham: Ashgate.

Girouard, Mark. 1978. *Life in the English Country House: A Social and Architectural History*. New Haven and London: Yale University Press.

Gleadle, Kathryn. 2003. '"Opinions Deliver'd in Conversation": Conversation, Politics, and Gender in the Late Eighteenth Century.' In *Civil Society in British History: Ideas, Identities, Institutions*, ed. Jose Harris. Oxford: Oxford University Press. 61–78.

Glidden, Hope. 1981. 'Recouping the Text: The Theory and the Practice of Reading.' *L'Esprit Créateur* 21, 2: 25–36.

Goldgar, Anne. 1995. *Impolite Learning: Conduct and Community in the Republic of Letters 1680–1750*. New Haven and London: Yale University Press.

Golinski, Jan. 1986. 'Science in the Enlightenment.' *History of Science* 24, 2: 411–24.

—. 2011. 'Science in the Enlightenment, Revisited.' *History of Science* 49, 2: 217–31.

Goodman, Dena. 1992. 'Public Sphere and Private Life: Toward a Synthesis of Current Historiographical Approaches to the Old Regime.' *History and Theory* 31, 1: 1992: 1–20.

—. 1994. *The Republic of Letters: A Cultural History of the French Enlightenment*. Ithaca and London: Cornell University Press.

—. 2017. Review of *The World of the Salons* by Antoine Lilti. *English Historical Review* 132, 555: 406–9.

Goodman, Elise. 1982. 'Rubens's *Conversatie à la Mode*: Garden of Leisure, Fashion, and Gallantry.' *The Art Bulletin* 64, 2: 247–59.

Goozé, Marjanne E. 2011. 'Mimicry and Influence: The "French" Connection and the Berlin Jewish Salon.' In *Readers, Writers, Salonnières: Female Networks in Europe, 1700–1900*, ed. Hilary Brown and Gillian Dow. Bern: Peter Lang. 49–71.

Gordon, Daniel. 1992. 'Philosophy, Sociology, and Gender in the Enlightenment Conception of Public Opinion.' *French Historical Studies* 17, 4: 882–911.

—. 1994. *Citizens Without Sovereignty: Equality and Sociability in French Thought, 1670–1789*. Princeton: Princeton University Press.

—. 2002. 'The Canonization of Norbert Elias in France: A Critical Perspective.' *French Politics, Culture & Society* 20, 1: 68–94.

Goring, Paul. 2005. *The Rhetoric of Sensibility in Eighteenth-Century Culture*. Cambridge: Cambridge University Press.

Gracián, Baltasar. 1945. *The Art of Worldly Wisdom*, trans. Joseph Jacobs. New York: Macmillan.

Grafton, Anthony and Lisa Jardine. 1986. *From Humanism to the Humanities: Education and the Liberal Arts in Fifteenth- and Sixteenth-Century Europe*. Cambridge, MA: Harvard University Press.

Grant, Mary and George Fiske. 1924. 'Cicero's "Orator" and Horace's "Ars Poetica".' *Harvard Studies in Classical Philology* 35: 1–74.

Grassi, Ernesto. 1990. *Vico and Humanism: Essays on Vico, Heidegger, and Rhetoric*. New York: Peter Lang.

Greenfield, Concetta. 1981. *Humanist and Scholastic Poetics, 1250–1500*. London and Toronto: Associated University Presses.

Greig, Hannah. 2012. '"All Together and All Distinct": Public Sociability and Social Exclusivity in London's Pleasure Gardens, c. 1740–1800.' *Journal of British Studies* 51, 1: 50–75.

Grignon, Marc and Juliana Maxim. 1995. 'Covenance, Caractère, and the Public Sphere.' *Journal of Architectural Education* 49, 1: 29–37.

Grotius, Hugo. 1738. *The Rights of War and Peace*, ed. Jean Barbeyrac, trans. anon. London: Innis, et al.

Guazzo, Stefano. 1967. *The Civile Conversation of M. Steeven Guazzo*, trans. George Pettie and Bartholomew Young, 2 vols. London: Constable 1925; repr. New York: AMS Press.

Guest, Ivor. 1996. *The Ballet of the Enlightenment: The Establishment of the Ballet d'Action in France, 1770–1793*. London: Dance Books.

Guez de Balzac, Jean-Louis. 1638. *New epistles of monsieur de Balzac*, trans. Sir Richard Baker. London: Cotes, et al.

—. 1652. 'A Discourse of the Conversation of the Romans.' In *The Roman: The Conversation of the Romans and Maecenas*, trans. unknown. London: Printed by T. N. for J. Holden. 41–109.

Guichard, Charlotte. 2012. 'Taste Communities: The Rise of the "Amateur" in Eighteenth-Century Paris.' *Eighteenth-Century Studies* 45, 4: 519–47.

Guido da Pisa. 1974. *Expositiones et glose super Comediam Dantis or Commentary on Dante's Inferno*, ed. Vincenzo Cioffari. Albany: State University of New York Press.

Gunn, J. A. W. 1983. *Beyond Liberty and Property: The Process of Self-Recognition in Eighteenth-Century Political Thought*. Kingston and Montreal: McGill-Queen's University Press.

—. 1993. 'Opinion in Eighteenth-Century Thought: What did the Concept Purport to Explain?' *Utilitas* 5, 1: 17–33.

—. 1995. *Queen of the World: Opinion in the Public Life of France from the Renaissance to the Revolution*. Oxford: Voltaire Foundation.

Gurstein, Rochelle. 2000. 'Taste and "the Conversible World" in the Eighteenth Century.' *Journal of the History of Ideas* 61, 2: 203–21.

Habermas, Jürgen. 1973. *Theory and Practice*, trans. John Viertel. Boston: Beacon Press.

—. 1979. 'What is Universal Pragmatics?' In *Communication and the Evolution of Society*, trans. Thomas McCarthy. Boston: Beacon Press. 1–68.

—. 1984–7. *The Theory of Communicative Action*, vols 1–2, trans. Thomas McCarthy. Boston: Beacon Press.

—. 1991. *The Structural Transformation of the Public Sphere: An Inquiry into a Category of Bourgeois Society*, trans. Thomas Burger and Frederick Lawrence. Cambridge, MA: MIT Press.

—. 1998. *On the Pragmatics of Communication*, ed. Maeve Cooke. Cambridge, MA: MIT Press.

Hamerton, Katherine J. 2002. *Women's Taste in the French Enlightenment: From the Honnête Model to the Domestic Paradigm, 1674–1762, Volume One*. PhD diss., University of Chicago.

—. 2010. 'A Feminist voice in the Enlightenment Salon: Madame de Lambert on Taste, Sensibility, and the Feminine Mind.' *Modern Intellectual History* 7, 2: 209–38.

Hamilton, Alexander, James Madison and John Jay. 1987. *The Federalist: Or, the New Constitution*, 2nd edn, ed. Max Beloff. Oxford: Blackwell.

Hampton, Timothy. 1991. 'Unreadable Signs: Montaigne, Virtue, and the Interpretation of History.' In *Humanism in Crisis: The Decline of the French Renaissance*, ed. Philippe Desan. Ann Arbor: University of Michigan Press. 85–106.

Hanley, Ryan Patrick. 2011. 'Educational Theory and the Social Vision of the Scottish Enlightenment.' *Oxford Review of Education* 37, 5: 587–602.

Hanning, Barbara R. 1989. 'Conversation and Musical Style in the Late Eighteenth-Century Parisian Salon.' *Eighteenth-Century Studies* 22, 4: 512–28.

Hanvelt, Marc. 2012. *The Politics of Eloquence: David Hume's Polite Rhetoric*. Toronto: University of Toronto Press.

Hardison, Osborne Bennett, Jr. 1962. *The Enduring Monument: A Study of the Idea of Praise in Renaissance Literary Theory and Practice*. Chapel Hill: University of North Carolina Press.

Harrán, Don. 1986. *Word–Tone Relations in Musical Thought: From Antiquity to the Seventeenth Century*. Stuttgart: American Institute of Musicology and Hänssler.

—. 1988. 'Elegance as a Concept in Sixteenth-Century Music Criticism.' *Renaissance Quarterly* 41, 3: 413–38.

Harrington, Dana. 2001. 'Gender, Commerce, and the Transformation of Virtue in Eighteenth-Century Britain.' *Rhetoric Society Quarterly* 31, 3: 33–52.

Harth, Erica. 1992. *Cartesian Women: Versions and Subversions of Rational Discourse in the Old Regime*. Ithaca and London: Cornell University Press.

Hauthal, Ferdinand, ed. 1866. *Acronis et Porphyrionis comentarii in Q. Horatium Flaccum*, vol. II. Berlin: Springer.

Haywood, Eliza. 1723. *The Injur'd Husband; or, the Mistaken Resentment*. London: Brown, et al.

Head, Richard. 1675. *Proteus Redivivus: or the Art of Wheedling, or Insinuation, Obtain'd by General Conversation*. London: W. D.

Heller, Deborah. 1998. 'Bluestocking Salons and the Public Sphere.' *Eighteenth-Century Life* 22, 2: 59–82.

Hellgouarch'h, Jacqueline. 2000. *L'Esprit de société: Cercles et 'salons' parisiens au XVIIIe siècle*. Paris: Garnier.

Hermogenes. 1987. *On Types of Style*, trans. Cecil W. Wooten. Chapel Hill and London: University of North Carolina Press.

Herrick, Marvin. 1946. *The Fusion of Horatian and Aristotelian Literary Criticism, 1531–1555*. Urbana: University of Illinois Press.

Hertz, Deborah. 1988. *Jewish High Society in Old Regime Berlin*. New Haven and London: Yale University Press.

Hesse, Carla Alison. 2001. *The Other Enlightenment: How French Women Became Modern*. Princeton: Princeton University Press.

Heyden, Sebald. 1972. *De arte canendi*, ed. and trans. Clement A. Miller. Dallas: American Institute of Musicology.

Hill, John. 1753. *The Inspector*, vol. 1. London: Griffiths, et al.

Hirschman, Albert. 1977. *The Passions and the Interests: Political Arguments for Capitalism before Its Triumph*. Princeton: Princeton University Press.
Hobbes, Thomas. 1972. *On Man*. In *Man and Citizen*, ed. Bernard Gert. Garden City: Anchor Books. 33–85.
Hochstrasser, T. J. 2000. *Natural Law Theories in the Early Enlightenment*. Cambridge: Cambridge University Press.
Holbach, Paul Henri Thiry, baron d'. 1770. *Essai sur les préjugés: ou, De l'influence des opinions sur les moeurs et sur le bonheur des Hommes*. London [Amsterdam]: n.p.
Horace. 1482. *Opera*, ed. Cristoforo Landino. Florence: Miscomini.
—. 1536. *Horatius cum quinque commentis. Quin. Horatii Flacci poemata omnia*. Venice: Tacuini.
—. 1977. *Horace's Satires and Epistles*, trans. Jacob Fuchs. New York: W. W. Norton.
Hosler, Bellamy. 1981. *Changing Aesthetic Views of Instrumental Music in 18th-Century Germany*. Ann Arbor: UMI Research Press.
Hotman, Antoine. 1616. *Deux paradoxes de l'amitié et de l'avarice*. In *Opuscules françoises des Hotmans*, Jean Hotman, François Hotman and Antoine Hotman. Paris: Veuve M. Guillemot.
Howard, Deborah. 2000. 'Languages and Architecture in Scotland, 1500–1660.' In *Architecture and Language: Constructing Identity in European Architecture, c. 1000–c. 1650*, ed. Georgia Clarke and Paul Crossley. Cambridge: Cambridge University Press. 162–72.
Howell, Wilbur Samuel. 1961. *Logic and Rhetoric in England, 1500–1700*. New York: Russell & Russell.
—. 1971. *Eighteenth-Century British Logic and Rhetoric*. Princeton: Princeton University Press.
Huet, Pierre-Daniel. 1722. *Huetiana, ou Pensées diverses de M. Huet*. Paris: Estienne.
Humboldt, Wilhelm von. 1854. *The Sphere and Duties of Government*, trans. Joseph Coulthard. London: John Chapman.
Hume, David. 1996. *The Philosophical Works of David Hume*, vols I–IV. Bristol: Thoemmes Press.
—. 1998. *Selected Essays*, ed. Stephen Copley and Andrew Edgar. Oxford: Oxford University Press.
—. 2013. *David Hume: 'Dialogues Concerning Natural Religion' in Focus*, ed. Stanley Tweyman. London: Routledge.
Hunt, John Dixon and Peter Willis, eds. 1988. *The Genius of the Place: The English Landscape Garden 1620–1820*. Cambridge, MA, and London: MIT Press.
Hunt, Margaret R. 2010. *Women in Eighteenth-Century Europe*. London and New York: Routledge.
Hunt, Tony. 1970. 'The Rhetorical Background to the Arthurian Prologue: Tradition and the Old French Vernacular Prologues.' *Forum for Modern Language Studies* 6, 1: 1–23.

—. 1972. 'Tradition and Originality in the Prologues of Chrestien de Troyes.' *Forum for Modern Language Studies* 8, 4: 320–44.

Hurley, Alison E. 2010. 'Peculiar Christians, Circumstantial Courtiers, and the Making of Conversation in Seventeenth-Century England.' *Representations* 111, 1: 33–59.

Hutcheson, Francis. 1753. *An Inquiry into the Original of our Ideas of Beauty and Virtue*. London: Ware, et al.

—. 1756. *An Essay on the Nature and Conduct of the Passions and Affections: With Illustrations on the Moral Sense*. London: Innys, et al.

Isherwood, Robert M. 1989. 'The Conciliatory Partisan of Musical Liberty: Jean Le Rond d'Alembert, 1717–1783.' In *French Musical Thought, 1600–1800*, ed. Georgia Cowart. Ann Arbor and London: UMI Research Press. 95–119.

Isidore of Seville. 2006. *The Etymologies of Isidore of Seville*, trans. Stephen A. Barney, et al. Cambridge: Cambridge University Press.

Israel, Jonathan I. 2001. *Radical Enlightenment: Philosophy and the Making of Modernity*. Oxford: Oxford University Press.

—. 2006. *Enlightenment Contested: Philosophy, Modernity, and the Emancipation of Man 1670–1752*. Oxford: Oxford University Press.

—. 2011. *Democratic Enlightenment: Philosophy, Revolution, and Human Rights 1750–1790*. Oxford: Oxford University Press.

Jacob, Margaret C. 1981. *The Radical Enlightenment: Pantheists, Freemasons, and Republicans*. London and Boston: Allen & Unwin.

—. 1991. 'The Enlightenment Redefined: The Formation of Modern Civil Society.' *Social Research* 58, 2: 475–95.

—. 1994. 'The Mental Landscape of the Public Sphere: A European Perspective.' *Eighteenth-Century Studies* 28, 1: 95–113.

Jacob, Margaret C. and Dorothée Sturkenboom. 2003. 'A Women's Scientific Society in the West: The Late Eighteenth-Century Assimilation of Science.' *Isis* 94, 2: 217–52.

James, Carolyn and Bill Kent. 2009. 'Renaissance Friendships: Traditional Truths, New and Dissenting Voices.' In *Friendship: A History*, ed. Barbara Caine. London: Equinox. 111–64.

Jamyn, Amadis. 1887. 'Discours de l'honneur et de l'ambition.' In *L'Académie des derniers Valois, 1570–1585*, Edouard Fremy. Paris: Leroux. 306–12.

Jensen, H. James. 1976. *The Muses' Concord: Literature, Music, and the Visual Arts in the Baroque Age*. Bloomington and London: Indiana University Press.

Johns, Adrian. 1998. *The Nature of the Book. Print and Knowledge in the Making*. Chicago and London: University of Chicago Press.

Jones, Peter. 1976. 'Cause, Reason, and Objectivity in Hume's Aesthetics.' In *Hume: A Re-Evaluation*, ed. Donald W. Livingston and James T. King. New York: Fordham University Press. 323–42.

Jones, William. 1784. *Treatise of the Art of Music*. Colchester: Printed for the Author, by W. Keymer.

Jonsson, Ritva and Leo Treitler. 1983. 'Medieval Music and Language: A Reconsideration of the Relationship.' *Studies in the History of Music. Vol. 1: Music and Language*. New York: Broude Brothers. 1–23.

Junius, Franciscus. 1638. *The Painting of the Ancients*, trans. by the author. London: Richard Hodgkinsonne.

Kahn, Victoria. 1985. *Rhetoric, Prudence, and Skepticism in the Renaissance*. Ithaca and London: Cornell University Press.

—. 1994. *Machiavellian Rhetoric: From the Counter-Reformation to Milton*. Princeton: Princeton University Press.

Kaiser, T. E. 1989–90. 'Rhetoric in the Service of the King: The Abbé Du Bos and the Concept of Public Judgment.' *Eighteenth-Century Studies* 23, 2: 182–99.

Kale, Steven D. 2002. 'Women, the Public Sphere, and the Persistence of Salons.' *French Historical Studies* 25, 1: 115–48.

—. 2004. *French Salons: High Society and Political Sociability from the Old Regime to the Revolution of 1848*. Baltimore: Johns Hopkins University Press.

Kames, Henry Homes, Lord. 1967. *Elements of Criticism*, vols I–III. Edinburgh and London: Millar, Kincaid, and Bell, 1762; repr. New York: Johnson Reprint Corporation.

—. 2007. *Sketches of the History of Man Considerably Enlarged by the Last Additions and Corrections of the Author. Book I: Progress of Men Independent of Society*, ed. James A. Harris. Indianapolis: Liberty Fund.

Kant, Immanuel. 1952. *The Critique of Judgment*, trans. James Meredith. Oxford: Clarendon Press.

—. 1996. *Critique of Pure Reason: Unified Edition*, trans Werner Pluhar. Indianapolis and Cambridge: Hackett.

Keefe, Simon P. 2001. *Mozart's Piano Concertos: Dramatic Dialogue in the Age of Enlightenment*. Woodbridge: Boydell Press.

Kelly, Christopher. 1987. '"To Persuade without Convincing": The Language of Rousseau's Legislator.' *American Journal of Political Science* 31, 2: 321–35.

Kennedy, George A. 1963. *The Art of Persuasion in Greece*. Princeton: Princeton University Press.

—. 1999. *Classical Rhetoric and its Christian and Secular Tradition*. Chapel Hill: University of North Carolina Press.

—. 2008. *The Art of Rhetoric in the Roman World 300 B.C.–300 A.D.* Eugene: Wipf & Stock.

Kennedy, William. 1978. *Rhetorical Norms in Renaissance Literature*. New Haven and London: Yale University Press.

Kerry, Paul E. 2008. 'Heinrich von Kleist and the Transformation of Conversation in Germany.' In *The Concept and Practice of Conversation in the Long Eighteenth Century, 1688–1848*, ed. Katie Halsey and Jane Slinn. Newcastle: Cambridge Scholars. 65–86.

Kim, Hyun-Ah. 2008. *Humanism and the Reform of Sacred Music in Early Modern England: John Merbecke the Orator and The Booke of Common Praier Noted (1550)*. Aldershot: Ashgate.

Kircher, Athanasius. 1650. *Musurgia universalis, sive ars magna consoni et dissoni*, 2 vols. Rome: Franciscus Corbelletti's heirs.

Kirkendale, Ursula. 1980. 'The Source for Bach's *Musical Offering*: The *Institutio oratoria* of Quintilian.' *Journal of the American Musicological Society* 33, 1: 88–141.

Kirkendale, Warren. 1979. 'Ciceronians versus Aristotelians on the Ricercar as Exordium, from Bembo to Bach.' *Journal of the American Musicological Society* 32, 1: 1–44.

—. 1997. 'On the Rhetorical Interpretation of the Ricercar and J. S. Bach's *Musical Offering*.' *Studi Musicali* 26: 331–76.

Kivy, Peter. 1967. 'Hume's Standard of Taste: Breaking the Circle.' *British Journal of Aesthetics* 7, 1: 57–66.

—. 1976. *The Seventh Sense: A Study of Francis Hutcheson's Aesthetics and its Influence in Eighteenth-Century Britain*. New York: Burt Franklin.

—. 1983. 'Hume's Neighbour's Wife: An Essay on the Evolution of Hume's Aesthetics.' *The British Journal of Aesthetics* 23, 3: 195–208.

Klein, Lawrence E. 1984–5. 'The Third Earl of Shaftesbury and the Progress of Politeness.' *Eighteenth-Century Studies* 18, 2: 186–214.

—. 1989. 'Liberty, Manners, and Politeness in Early Eighteenth-Century England.' *The Historical Journal* 32, 3: 583–605.

—. 1993. 'Gender, Conversation and the Public Sphere in Early Eighteenth-Century England.' In *Textuality and Sexuality: Reading Theories and Practices*, ed. Judith Still and Michael Worton. Manchester and New York: Manchester University Press. 100–15.

—. 1994. *Shaftesbury and the Culture of Politeness: Moral Discourse and Cultural Politics in Early Eighteenth-Century England*. Cambridge: Cambridge University Press.

—. 1995. 'Politeness for Plebes: Consumption and Social Identity in Early Eighteenth-Century England.' In *The Consumption of Culture 1600–1800: Image, Object, Text*, ed. Ann Bermingham and John Brewer. London and New York: Routledge. 362–82.

—. 1996. 'Coffeehouse Civility, 1660–1714: An Aspect of Post-Courtly Culture in England.' *Huntington Library Quarterly* 59, 1: 30–51.

—. 1997a. 'The Figure of France: The Politics of Sociability in England, 1660–1715.' In *Exploring the Conversible World: Text and Sociability from the Classical Age to the Enlightenment*, ed. Elena Russo. Yale French Studies, No. 92. 3–45.

—. 1997b. 'Sociability, Solitude, and Enthusiasm.' *Huntington Library Quarterly* 60, 1/2: 153–77.

—. 2001. 'Enlightenment as Conversation.' In *What's Left of Enlightenment? A Postmodern Question*, ed. Keith Michael Baker and Peter Hanns Reill. Stanford: Stanford University Press. 148–66, 188–92.

—. 2002. 'Politeness and the Interpretation of the British Eighteenth Century.' *The Historical Journal* 45, 4: 869–98.

Klein, Robert. 1979. 'Judgment and Taste in Cinquecento Art Theory.' In *Form and Meaning: Essays on the Renaissance and Modern Art*, trans. Madeline Jay and Leon Wieseltier. New York: Viking Press. 161–9.

Kloek, Joost and Wijnand Mijnhardt. 2004. *Dutch Culture in a European Perspective. Vol. 2: 1800: Blueprints for a National Community*, trans. Beverley Jackson. Houndsmill: Palgrave Macmillan.

Knox-Shaw, Peter. 2004. *Jane Austen and the Enlightenment*. Cambridge: Cambridge University Press.

Kobylka, Joseph F. and Bradley Kent Carter. 1990. 'The Dialogic Community: Education, Leadership, and Participation in James Madison's Thought.' *The Review of Politics* 52, 1: 32–63.

Kors, Alan Charles. 1976. *D'Holbach's Coterie: An Enlightenment in Paris*. Princeton: Princeton University Press.

Koselleck, Reinhart. 1988. *Critique and Crisis: Enlightenment and the Pathogenesis of Modern Society*, trans. unknown. Cambridge, MA: MIT Press.

Krause, Sharon R. 2008a. *Civil Passions: Moral Sentiment and Democratic Deliberation*. Princeton and Oxford: Princeton University Press.

—. 2008b. 'Passion, Power, and Impartiality in Hume.' In *Bringing the Passions Back In: The Emotions in Political Philosophy*, ed. Rebecca Kingston and Leonard Ferry. Vancouver: University of British Columbia Press. 126–44.

Kristeller, Paul Oskar. 1961. *Renaissance Thought: The Classic, Scholastic and Humanist Strains*. New York: Harper & Row.

—. 1965. *Renaissance Thought II: Papers on Humanism and the Arts*. New York: Harper & Row.

Kruft, Hanno-Walter. 1994. *A History of Architectural Theory from Vitruvius to the Present*, trans. Ronald Taylor, Elsie Callander and Antony Wood. New York and London: Princeton Architectural Press and Zwemmer.

Kulenkampf, Jens. 1990. 'The Objectivity of Taste: Kant and Hume.' *Noûs* 24, 1: 93–110.

Lacépède, Étienne de. 1970. *La poétique de la musique*, 2 vols. Geneva: Slatkine Reprints.

La Croix, Phérotée de. 1694. *L'art de la Poësie françoise et latine avec une idée de la musique sous une nouvelle méthode*. Lyon: Thomas Amaulry.

La Mothe Le Vayer, François de. 1671. *Cincq dialogues faits à l'imitation des anciens, par Oratius Tubero*. Mons: La Fleche.

La Motte, Antoine Houdar de. 1716. *Réflexions sur la critique*. Paris: Du Puis.

La Vopa, Anthony J. 2009. 'A New Intellectual History? Jonathan Israel's Enlightenment.' *The Historical Journal* 52, 3: 717–38.

Lamp, Kathleen S. 2013. *A City of Marble: The Rhetoric of Augustan Rome*. Columbia: University of South Carolina Press.

Lampron, Eve Marie. 2011. 'From Venice to Paris: Fame, Gender and National Sensibilities in Late Eighteenth- and Early Nineteenth-Century Female Literary Networks.' In *Readers, Writers, Salonnières: Female Networks in Europe, 1700–1900*, ed. Hilary Brown and Gillian Dow. Bern: Peter Lang. 31–47.

Lamy, Bernard. 1676. *The Art of Speaking*, trans. unknown. London: Godbid and Pitt.

Landes, Joan B. 1988. *Women and the Public Sphere in the Age of the French Revolution*. Ithaca and London: Cornell University Press.

Langer, Ullrich. 1990. *Divine and Poetic Freedom in the Renaissance: Nominalist Theology and Literature in France and Italy*. Princeton: Princeton University Press.

—. 1994. *Perfect Freedom: Studies in Literature and Moral Philosophy from Boccaccio to Corneille*. Geneva: Droz.

Langford, Paul. 1997. 'British Politeness and the Progress of Western Manners: An Eighteenth-Century Engima.' *Transactions of the Royal Historical Society* 7: 53–72.

—. 2002. 'The Uses of Eighteenth-Century Politeness.' *Transactions of the Royal Historical Society* 12: 311–31.

Lanson, Gustave. 1891. *Choix de lettres du XVIIIe siècle*. Paris: Hachette.

Law, Jules. 1993. *The Rhetoric of Empiricism: Language and Perception from Locke to I. A. Richards*. Ithaca and London: Cornell University Press.

Lawson, John. 1758. *Lectures Concerning Oratory*. Dublin: George Faulkner.

Le Camus de Mézières, Nicolas. 1992. *The Genius of Architecture; or, the Analogy of that Art with our Sensations*, trans. David Britt. Santa Monica: Getty Center for the History of Art and the Humanities.

Le Cerf de la Viéville, Jean-Laurent. 1972. *Comparaison de la musique italienne et de la musique française*, 2 vols. Geneva: Minkoff Reprint.

Le Club des dames, ou le retour de Descartes. 1784. Paris: Bureau de la Bibliotheque des Romans.

Le Faucheur, Michel. 1680. *An Essay upon the Action of an Orator, as to his pronunciation and gesture*, trans. unknown. London: Nich. Cox.

Le Mercier de la Rivière, Pierre-Paul. 1767. *L'ordre naturel et essentiel des sociétés politiques*. London: Nourse.

Le Moyne, Pierre. 1640. *Les Peintures Morales*. Paris: Cramoisy.

Le Roy, Adrian. 1571. *Livre d'Airs de Cour miz sur le luth*. Paris: Le Roy and Ballard.

Ledbetter, David. 2002. *Bach's Well-Tempered Clavier: The 48 Preludes and Fugues*. New Haven: Yale University Press.

Lespinasse, Julie de. 1887. *Lettres inédites de Mademoiselle de Lespinasse*, ed. Charles Henry. Paris: Libraire de las Société des Gens de Lettres.

*Lettre de M. *** à Mlle *** sur l'Origine de la Musique*. 1734. In *Mercure de France* (May): 861–70.

Lichtenstein, Jacqueline. 1993. *The Eloquence of Color: Rhetoric and Painting in the French Classical Age*, trans. Emily McVarish. Berkeley: University of California Press.

Lilti, Antoine. 2015. *The World of the Salons: Sociability and Worldliness in Eighteenth-Century Paris*, trans. Lydis G. Cochrane. Oxford: Oxford University Press.

Lipsius, Justus. 1594. *Two Bookes of Constancie*, trans. John Stradling. London: Richard Johns.

Locke, John. 1693. *Some Thoughts Concerning Education*. London: A. and J. Churchill.

—. 1720. *A Collection of Several Pieces of Mr. John Locke*. London: Bettenham and Francklin.

—. 1966. *Of the Conduct of the Understanding*, ed. Francis Garforth. New York: Teachers College Press.

—. 1997. *An Essay Concerning Human Understanding*, ed. Roger Woolhouse. London: Penguin.

—. 2003. *Two Treatises of Government and A Letter Concerning Toleration*, ed. Ian Shapiro. New Haven and London: Yale University Press.

Loewenstein, Karl. 1973. *The Governance of Rome*. The Hague: Martinus Nijhoff.

Logan, George M. 1983. *The Meaning of More's Utopia*. Princeton: Princeton University Press.

Lomazzo, Giovanni Paolo. 1590. *Idea del tempio della pittura*. Milan: Ponto.

—. 2013. *Idea of the Temple of Painting*, trans. Jean Julia Chai. University Park: Pennsylvania State University Press.

Lombardi, Carmela, ed. 1998. *Il ballo pantomimo: lettere, saggi e libelli sulla danza (1773–1785)*. Turin: Scriptorium.

Long, R. James. 1972. 'The Science of Theology According to Richard Fishacre: An Edition of the Prologue to his *Commentary on the Sentences*.' *Modern Studies* 34: 71–98.

Longinus. 2000. *On the Sublime*, trans. T. S. Dorsch. In *Classical Literary Criticism*. New York: Penguin. 113–66.

Losse, Deborah. 1994. *Sampling the Book: Renaissance Prologues and the French Conteurs*. London and Toronto: Associated University Presses.

Lougee, Carolyn C. 1976. *Le Paradis des Femmes: Women, Salons, and Social Stratification in Seventeenth Century France*. Princeton: Princeton University Press.

Love, Harold. 1993. *Scribal Publication in Seventeenth-Century England*. Oxford: Clarendon Press.

Luther, Martin. 1873. *D. Martini Lutheri Opera Latina*, vol. VII, ed. Heinrich Schmidt. Frankfurt: Heyder and Zimmer.

Lyly, John. 1578. *Euphues: The Anatomy of Wit*. London: Cawood.

—. 1580. *Euphues and his England*. London: Cawood.

—. [1589.] *Pappe with an hatchet*. [London: T. Orwin].

Lynn, Michael R. 1999. 'Enlightenment in the Public Sphere: The Musée de Monsieur and Scientific Culture in Late-Eighteenth-Century Paris.' *Eighteenth Century Studies* 32, 4: 463–76.

—. 2006. *Popular Science and Public Opinion in Eighteenth-Century France*. Manchester and New York: Manchester University Press.

Lyons, John D. 1999. *Kingdom of Disorder: The Theory of Tragedy in Classical France*. West Lafayette: Purdue University Press.

Mabillon, Jean. 1691. *Traité des études monastiques*. Paris: Robustel.

Mably, Gabriel Bonnot de. 1763. *Entretiens de Phocion, sur le rapport de la morale avec la politique*. Zurich: Heidegger.

—. 1766. *Observations sur l'histoire de la Grèce*. Geneva: Compagnie des Libraires.

—. 1768. *Doutes proposés aux philosophes économistes sur l'ordre naturel et essentiel des sociétés politiques*. The Hague and Paris: Nyon and Durand.

MacClintock, Carol. 1959. 'Molinet, Music, and Medieval Rhetoric.' *Musica Disciplina* 13: 109–21.

Mace, Dean T. 1969. 'Pietro Bembo and the Literary Origins of the Italian Madrigal.' *The Musical Quarterly* 55, 1: 65–86.

Mace, Thomas. 1676. *Musick's Monument*. London: Ratcliffe and Thompson.

Machiavelli, Niccolò. 2003. *Discourses on Livy*, trans. Julia Conaway Bondanella and Peter Bondanella. Oxford: Oxford University Press.

MacIntyre, Alasdair. 1959. 'Hume on "Is" and "Ought".' *Philosophical Review* 68, 4: 451–68.

Mackenzie, Henry. 1773. *The Man of the World*, vol. I. London: Strahan and Cadell.

Macrobius. 2011. *Saturnalia*, 3 vols, ed. and trans. Robert A. Kaster. Cambridge, MA, and London: Harvard University Press.

Madison, James. 1975. *The Papers of James Madison. Vol. 9: 9 April 1786–24 May 1787 and Supplement 1781–1784*, ed. Robert A. Rutland and William M. E. Rachal. Chicago and London: University of Chicago Press.

—. 1981. *The Papers of James Madison. Vol. 13: 20 January 1790–31 March 1791*, ed. Charles F. Hobson and Robert A. Rutland. Charlottesville: University Press of Virginia.

—. 1983. *The Papers of James Madison. Vol. 14: 6 April 1791–16 March 1793*, ed. Robert A. Rutland and Thomas A. Mason. Charlottesville: University Press of Virginia.

—. 1985. *The Papers of James Madison. Vol. 15: 24 March 1793–20 April 1795*, ed. Thomas A. Mason, Robert A. Rutland and Jeanne K. Sisson. Charlottesville: University Press of Virginia.

—. 1991. *The Papers of James Madison. Vol. 17: 31 March 1797–3 March 1801, with a Supplement 22 January 1778–9 August 1795*, ed. David B. Mattern, J. C. A. Stagg, Jeanne K. Cross and Susan Holbrook Perdue. Charlottesville: University Press of Virginia.

Maguire, Henry. 1994. *Art and Eloquence in Byzantium*. Princeton: Princeton University Press.

Maland, David. 1970. *Culture and Society in Seventeenth-Century France*. New York: Charles Scribner's Sons.

Malesherbes, Chrétien-Guillaume de Lamoignon de. 1808. *Oeuvres inédites*, ed. N. L. Pissot. Paris: Buisson, et al.

Malvezzi, Virgilio. 1650. *Considerations upon the lives of Alcibiades and Corialanus*, trans. Robert Gentiles. London: Wilson and Moseley.

Mancini, Giulio. 1956. *Considerazioni sulla pittura*, vol. I, ed. Adriana Marucchi and Luigi Salerno. Rome: Accademia Nazionale dei Lincei.

Mandeville, Bernard. 1988. *The Fable of the Bees: or Private Vices, Publick Benefits*, vol. 2, ed. F. B. Kaye. Indianapolis: Liberty Fund.

Maniates, Maria Rika. 1969. '"Sonate, que me veux-tu?": The Enigma of French Musical Aesthetics in the 18th Century.' *Current Musicology* 9: 117–40.

—. 1983. 'Music and Rhetoric: Facets of Cultural History in the Renaissance and Baroque.' *Israel Studies in Musicology* 3: 44–69.

Manley, Mary de la Rivière. 1705. *The Secret History of Queen Zarah, and the Zarazians*. Albigion [i.e., London]: n.p..

Map, Walter. 1983. *De nugis curialium: Courtiers' Trifles*, ed. and trans. M. R. James, rev. C. N. L. Brooke and R. A. B. Mynors. Oxford: Clarendon Press.

Marchal, Roger. 1991. *Madame de Lambert et son milieu*. Oxford: Voltaire Foundation.

Marchetto of Padua. 1961. *Pomerium*, ed. Joseph Vecchi. Rome: American Institute of Musicology.

Marivaux, Pierre Carlet de Chamblain de. 1714. *La Voiture embourbée*. Paris: Huet.

Marmontel, Jean-François. 1786. 'Critique.' In *Encyclopédie Methodique. Tome Premier Seconde Partie*. Padua: Del Negro. 551–61.

—. 1827. *Memoirs of Marmontel*, vol. II. London: Hunt and Clarke.

[Marprelate, Martin.] [1588.] *The Epistle*. [East Molesey: Robert Waldegrave].

Marpurg, Friedrich Wilhelm. 1753–4. *Die Abhandlung von der Fuge*, vols I-II. Berlin: Haude und Spener.

Marsh, David. 1980. *Quattrocentro Dialogue: Classical Tradition and Humanist Innovation*. Cambridge, MA, and London: Harvard University Press.

Marshall, David L. 2010. *Vico and the Transformation of Rhetoric in Early Modern Europe*. Cambridge: Cambridge University Press.

Martianus Capella. 1977. *Martianus Capella and the Seven Liberal Arts. Vol. II: The Marriage of Philology and Mercury*, trans. William Harris Stahl and Richard Johnson with E. L. Burge. New York: Columbia University Press.

Martin, John. 1997. 'Inventing Sincerity, Refashioning Prudence: The Discovery of the Individual in Renaissance Europe.' *The American Historical Review* 102, 5: 1309–42.

Martin, John Rupert. 1977. *Baroque*. New York: Harper & Row.

Martin, Meredith. 2010. 'The Ascendancy of the Interior in Eighteenth-Century French Architectural Theory.' In *Architectural Space in Eighteenth-Century Europe: Constructing Identities and Interiors*, ed. Denise Amy Baxter and Meredith Martin. Aldershot: Ashgate. 15–34.

Martin, Robert W. T. 2005. 'Between Consensus and Conflict: Habermas, Post-Modern Agonism, and the Early American Public Sphere.' *Polity* 37, 3: 365–88.

Massini, Filippo. 1588. *Lettioni Dell'Estatico Insensato*. Perugia: Petrucci.

Masson, Charles. 1699. *Nouveau traité des regles pour la composition de la musique*,2nd edn. Paris: Ballard.

Mattern, David B., ed. 1997. *James Madison's 'Advice to my Country'*. Charlottesville: University Press of Virginia.

Mattheson, Johann. 1964. *Critica Musica*. Amsterdam: Knuf.

—. 1981. *Der vollkommene Capellmeister: A Revised Translation with Critical Commentary*, trans. and ed. Ernest C. Harriss. Ann Arbor: UMI Research Press.

Matthews, Richard K. 1995. *If Men Were Angels: James Madison and the Heartless Empire of Reason*. Lawrence: University Press of Kansas.

—. 2005. 'James Madison's Political Theory: Hostage to Democratic Fortune.' *The Review of Politics* 67, 1: 49–67.

Maxwell, Alexander. 2014. *Patriots Against Fashion: Clothing and Nationalism in Europe's Age of Revolutions*. Houndsmill: Palgrave Macmillan.

May, James. 1988. *Trials of Character: The Eloquence of Ciceronian Ethos*. Chapel Hill and London: University of North Carolina Press.

May, Steven. 1980. 'Tudor Aristocrats and the Mythical "Stigma of Print".' *Renaissance Papers* 10 (Spain: The Southeastern Renaissance Conference): 11–18.

Mazzotti, Massimo. 2004. 'Newton for Ladies: Gentility, Gender and Radical Culture.' *The British Journal for the History of Science* 37, 2: 119–46.

McClellan, James E., III. 1985. *Science Reorganized: Scientific Societies in the Eighteenth Century*. New York: Columbia University Press.

McClelland, Charles E. 1980. *State, Society, and University in Germany 1700–1914*. Cambridge: Cambridge University Press.

McKenna, Stephen J. 2006. *Adam Smith: The Rhetoric of Propriety*. Albany: State University of New York Press.

—. 2011. 'Adam Smith's Rhetorical Art of Character.' In *Character, Self, and Sociability in the Scottish Enlightenment*, ed. Thomas Ahnert and Susan Manning. New York: Palgrave Macmillan. 49–65.

McKeon, Zahava. 1982. *Novels and Arguments: Inventing Rhetorical Criticism*. Chicago and London: University of Chicago Press.

Meconi, Honey. 1994. 'Does *Imitatio* Exist?' *The Journal of Musicology* 12, 2: 152–78.

Mee, Jon. 2011. *Conversable Worlds: Literature, Contention, and Community 1762 to 1830*. Oxford: Oxford University Press.

Melton, James Van Horn. 2001. *The Rise of the Public in Enlightenment Europe*. Cambridge: Cambridge University Press.

—. 2007. 'School, Stage, Salon: Musical Cultures in Haydn's Vienna.' In *Haydn and the Performance of Rhetoric*, ed. Tom Beghin and Sander M. Goldberg. Chicago: University of Chicago Press. 80–108.

Ménestrier, Claude-François. 1681. *Des Représentations en musique anciennes et modernes*. Paris, René Guignard.

—. 1682. *Des Ballets anciens et modernes selon les regles du theatre*. Paris: Guignard.

Merbecke, John. 1574. *The Lyues of Holy Sainctes*. London: Denham and Watkins.

—. 1582. *Examples Drawen Out of Holy Scripture*. London: East.

Mercier, Louis-Sébastien. 1773. *Du Théâtre ou Nouvel essai sur l'art dramatique*. Amsterdam: Van Harrevelt.

—. 1782–8. *Tableau de Paris*, 12 vols. Amsterdam.

Mersenne, Marin. 1627. *Traité de l'harmonie universelle*. Paris: Baudry.

—. 1636. *Harmonie universelle*. Paris: Cramoisy.

—. 1637. *Seconde partie de l'harmonie universelle*. Paris: Ballard.

Milano, Ronit. 2015. *The Portrait Bust and French Cultural Politics in the Eighteenth Century*. Leiden: Brill.

Millar, Fergus. 1977. *The Emperor in the Roman World (31 B.C.–A.D. 337)*. Ithaca: Cornell University Press.

Millar, John. 1803. *An Historical View of the English Government*, vol. IV. London: Mawman.

—. 1960. *The Origin of the Distinction of Ranks*. In William C. Lehmann, *John Millar of Glasgow 1735–1801: His Life and Thought and his Contributions to Sociological Analysis*. Cambridge: Cambridge University Press. 175–322.

Miller, Asher Ethan. 2013. *The Path of Nature: French Paintings from the Wheelock Whitney Collection 1785–1850*. New York: Metropolitan Musem of Art.

Miller, Perry. 1961. *The New England Mind: The Seventeenth Century*. Boston: Beacon Press.

Minnis, Alastair. 1984. *Medieval Theory of Authorship: Scholastic Literary Attitudes in the Later Middle Ages*. London: Scolar Press.

Minor, Vernon Hyde. 2006. *The Death of Baroque and the Rhetoric of Good Taste*. Cambridge: Cambridge University Press.

Minturno, Antonio Sebastiano. 1559. *De poeta*. Venice.

Monk, Samuel Holt. 1944. 'A Grace Beyond the Reach of Art.' *Journal of the History of Ideas* 5, 2: 131–50.

Montaigne, Michel de. 2003. *The Complete Works*, trans. Donald Frame. New York and Toronto: A. A. Knopf.

Montes, Leonidas. 2004. *Adam Smith in Context: A Critical Reassessment of Some Central Components of His Thought*. New York: Palgrave Macmillan.

Montesquieu, Charles-Louis de Secondat, baron de. 1989. *The Spirit of the Laws*, ed. and trans. Anne M. Cohler, Basia Carolyn Miller and Harold Samuel Stone. Cambridge: Cambridge University Press.

Monteverdi, Claudio. 1973. *Lettere, dediche, e prefazioni*, ed. Domenico De' Paoli. Rome: De Santis.

—. 1992. *The Operas of Monteverdi*. London and New York: Calder and Riverrun Press.

Montgomery, Robert L. 1992. *Terms of Response: Language and Audience in Seventeenth- and Eighteenth-Century Theory*. University Park: Pennsylvania State University Press.

The Monthly Review; or, Literary Journal, Enlarged: From January to April, inclusive. 1793. Vol. X. London: Griffiths.

Moore, James. 1976. 'Hume's Theory of Justice and Property.' *Political Studies* 24: 103–19.

Moran, Bruce T. 2006. 'Courts and Academies.' In *Cambridge History of Science. Vol. 3: Early Modern Science*, ed. Katherine Park and Lorraine Daston. Cambridge: Cambridge University Press. 251–71.

Moran, Mary Catherine. 2000. '"The Commerce of the Sexes": Gender and the Social Sphere in Scottish Enlightenment Accounts of Civil Society.' In *Paradoxes of Civil Society: New Perspectives on Modern German and British History*, ed. Frank Trentmann. New York and Oxford: Bergahn Books. 61–84.

More, Hannah. 1799. *Strictures on the Modern System of Female Education*, vol. II. London: Cadell and Davies.

More, Thomas. 2003. *Utopia*, trans. Paul Turner. London: Penguin.

Moreau, Jacob-Nicolas. 1777. *Principes de morale, de politique et de droit public. Tome Premier*. Paris: De L'imprimerie royale.

Morellet, André. 1770. *Réfutation de l'ouvrage qui a pour titre 'Dialogues sur le commerce des bléds'*. London.

—. ed. 1812. *Eloges de Madame Geoffrin*. Paris: Nicole.

—. 1814. *Réflexions sur les avantages de la liberté d'écrire et d'imprimer sur les matières de l'administration*. Paris: Magimel and Delaunay.

—. 1988. *Mémoires de l'Abbé Morellet de l'Académie française sur le dix-huitième siècle et sur la révolution*, ed. Jean-Pierre Guicciardi. Paris: Mercure de France.

—. 1991. *Lettres d'André Morellet. Vol. 1: 1759–1785*, ed. Dorothy Medlin, Jean-Claude David and Paul Leclerc. Oxford: Voltaire Foundation.

Mori, Maria Teresa. 2000. *Salotti: La sociabilità delle élite nell'Italia dell'Ottocento*. Rome: Carocci.

Morris, Robert. 1734. *Lectures on Architecture*. London: Brindley.

—. 1757. *Select Architecture*, 2nd edn. London: Sayer.

Morrow, Mary Sue. 1997. *German Music Criticism in the Late Eighteenth Century: Aesthetic Issues in Instrumental Music*. Cambridge: Cambridge University Press.

Motley, Mark. 1990. *Becoming a French Aristocrat: The Education of the Court Nobility, 1580–1715*. Princeton: Princeton University Press.

Mousourakis, George. 2007. *A Legal History of Rome*. London and New York: Routledge.

Moyes, Craig. 2011. 'Seventeenth-Century Prose Narrative.' In *The Cambridge History of French Literature*, ed. William Burgwinkle, Nicholas Hammond and Emma Wilson. Cambridge: Cambridge University Press. 323–32.

Mullan, John. 1988. *Sentiment and Sociability: The Language of Feeling in the Eighteenth Century*. Oxford: Clarendon Press.

Nardin, Jane. 1973. *Those Elegant Decorums: The Concept of Propriety in Jane Austen's Novels*. Albany: State University of New York Press.

Nashe, Thomas. 1589a. *Mar-Martine*. [London?: n.p.]

—. 1589b. *Martins Months Minde*. [London : Printed by Thomas Orwin].

Naudé, Gabriel. 1667. *Considérations politiques sur les coups d'estat*. n.p.

Necker, Jacques. 1785. *Oeuvres de M. Necker. Tome 1*. London: Hookham.

Nelson, N. E. 1933. 'Cicero's *De Officiis* in Christian Thought: 300–1300.' In *Essays and Studies in English and Comparative Literature*. Ann Arbor: University of Michigan Press. 59–160.

Neubauer, John. 1986. *The Emancipation of Music from Language: Departure from Mimesis in Eighteenth-Century Aesthetics*. New Haven: Yale University Press.

Neve, Richard. 1726. *The City and Country Purchaser, and Builder's Dictionary*. London: Browne, et al.

Nevile, Jennifer. 2004. *The Eloquent Body: Dance and Humanist Culture in Fifteenth-Century Italy*. Bloomington and Indianapolis: Indiana University Press.

Nicholas of Lyre. 1545. *Bibliorum sacrorum tomus tertius, cum Glossa Ordinaria, & Nicolai Lyrani Postilla, moralitatibus, Additionibus & Replicis*. Lyons: Trechsel.

Nicole, Pierre. 1677. *Moral Essays*, vols 1–2, trans. unknown. London: Magnus and Bentley.

Nolan, Barbara. 1986. '"A Poet Ther Was": Chaucer's Voices in the General Prologue to the Canterbury Tales.' *PMLA* 101, 2: 154–69.

North, Marcy. 1999. 'Anonymity's Revelations in "The Arte of English Poesie".' *Studies in English Literature, 1500–1900* 39, 1: 1–18.

—. 2003. *Anonymous Renaissance: Cultures of Discretion in Tudor–Stuart England*. Chicago and London: University of Chicago Press.

Nourse, Timothy. 1700. *Campania Foelix*. London: Bennet.

Noverre, Jean Georges. 1760. *Lettres sur la danse, et sur les ballets*. Lyons: Delaroche.

Nye, Edward. 2008. '"Choreography" Is Narrative: The Programmes of the Eighteenth-Century "Ballet d'Action".' *Dance Research: The Journal of the Society for Dance Research* 26, 1: 42–59.

—. 2011. *Mime, Music and Drama on the Eighteenth-Century Stage: The Ballet d'Action*. Cambridge: Cambridge University Press.

Ollier, Marie-Louise. 1974. 'The Author in the Text: The Prologues of Chrétien de Troyes.' *Yale French Studies* 51: 26–41.

Ong, Walter J. 1968. 'Tudor Writings on Rhetoric.' *Studies in the Renaissance* 15: 39–69.

—. 1975. 'The Writer's Audience Is Always a Fiction.' *PMLA* 90, 1: 9–21.

—. 2004. *Ramus, Method, and the Decay of Dialogue: From the Art of Discourse to the Art of Reason*. Chicago and London: University of Chicago Press.

Ozouf, Mona. 1988. '"Public Opinion" at the End of the Old Regime.' *The Journal of Modern History* 60, Supplement: S1–S21.

Palisca, Claude V. 1972. '*Ut oratoria musica*: The Rhetorical Basis of Musical Mannerism.' In *The Meaning of Mannerism*, ed. Franklin W. Robinson and Stephen G. Nichols, Jr. Hanover: University Press of New England. 37–65.

—. 1989. '"Baroque" as a Music-Critical Term.' In *French Musical Thought, 1600–1800*, ed. Georgia Cowart. Ann Arbor and London: UMI Research Press. 7–21.

Pallavicino, Sforza. 1831. *Del bene. Libri Quattro. Volume Secondo*. Milan: Silvestri.

Parker, Mara. 2002. *The String Quartet, 1750–1797: Four Types of Musical Conversation*. Aldershot: Ashgate.

Pascal, Blaise. 1846. *Thoughts of Blaise Pascal*. Andover and New York: Allen, Morrill and Wardwell, and Newman.

Pask, Kevin. 1996. *The Emergence of the English Author: Scripting the Life of the Poet in Early Modern England*. Cambridge: Cambridge University Press.

Paulson, Ronald. 1975. *Emblem and Expression: Meaning in English Art of the Eighteenth Century*. Cambridge, MA: Harvard University Press.

Pauwels, Yves. 2000. 'The Rhetorical Model in the Formation of French Architectural Language in the Sixteenth Century: The Triumphal Arch as Commonplace.' In *Architecture and Language: Constructing Identity in European Architecture, c. 1000–c. 1650*, ed. Georgia Clarke and Paul Crossley. Cambridge: Cambridge University Press. 134–47.

Payne, Alina A. 2000. 'Architects and Academies: Architectural Theories of *Imitatio* and the Literary Debates on Language and Style.' In *Architecture and Language: Constructing Identity in European Architecture, c. 1000–c. 1650*, ed. Georgia Clarke and Paul Crossley. Cambridge: Cambridge University Press. 118–33.

Peacham, Henry, the Younger. 1622. *The Compleat Gentleman*. London: Constable.

Pekacz, Jolanta T. 1999a. *Conservative Tradition in Pre-Revolutionary France: Parisian Salon Women*. New York: Peter Lang.

—. 1999b. 'The *Salonnières* and the *Philosophes* in Old Regime France: The Authority of Aesthetic Judgment.' *Journal of the History of Ideas* 60, 2: 277–97.

Pelletier, Louise. 2006. *Architecture in Words: Theatre, Language and the Sensuous Space of Architecture*. London and New York: Routledge.

Pellisson, Paul. 1656. 'Discours sur les oeuvres de M. Sarasin.' In *Les Oeuvres de Monsieur Sarasin*. Paris: Courbé. 1–72.

Peregrini, Matteo. 1639. *Delle acutezze*. Genoa: Farroni, et al.

Perkins, Leeman L. 1984. 'The *L'Homme Armé* Masses of Busnoys and Okeghem: A Comparison.' *The Journal of Musicology* 3, 4: 363–96.

Perrault, Claude, ed. 1684. *Les dix livres d'architecture de Vitruve*. Paris: Coignard.

Peterman, Larry. 1993. 'Privacy's Background.' *The Review of Politics* 55, 2: 217–46.

Petrarca, Francesco. 2003. *The Secret, by Francesco Petrarch, with Related Documents*, trans. and ed. Carol E. Quillen. Boston and New York: Bedford/St. Martin's.

Peuchet, Jacques. 1789. 'Discours préliminaire.' In *Encyclopedie méthodique: Jurisprudence. Vol. 9: Police et municipalités*. Paris and Liège: Panckoucke and Plomteux.

Pfeffer, Jacqueline L. 2001. 'The Family in Locke's Political Thought.' *Polity* 33, 4: 593–618.

Phillipson, Nicholas. 2010. *Adam Smith: An Enlightened Life*. New Haven and London: Yale University Press.

Piles, Roger de. 1677. *Conversations sur la connoissance de la peinture*. Paris: Langlois.

—. 1708. *Cours de peinture par principes*. Paris: Estienne.

Pincus, Steve. 1995. '"Coffee Politicians Does Create": Coffeehouses and Restoration Political Culture.' *Journal of Modern History* 67, 4: 807–34.

Pino, Paolo. 1960. *Dialogo di pittura*. In *Trattati d'arte del Cinquecento fra Manierismo e Controriforma*, vol. 1, ed. Parola Barocchi. Bari: Laterza & Figli. 93–139.

Piozzi, Hester Lynch. 1794. *British Synonymy; or, An Attempt at Regulating the Choice of Words in Familiar Conversation*, vol. 1. London: Robinson and Robinson.

Plato. 1945. *The Republic of Plato*, trans. Francis Cornford. London: Oxford University Press.

Plett, Heinrich. 2004. *Rhetoric and Renaissance Culture*. Berlin and New York: De Gruyter.

—. 2012. *Enargeia in Classical Antiquity and the Early Modern Age: The Aesthetics of Evidence*. Leiden: Brill.

Plutarch. 1972. *Moralia*, vol. IV, trans. Frank Cole Babbitt. London and Cambridge, MA: William Heinemann and Harvard University Press.

Pocock, J. G. A. 1983. 'Cambridge Paradigms and Scotch Philosophers: A Study of the Relations between the Civic Humanist and the Civil Jurisprudential Interpretation of Eighteenth-Century Social Thought.' In *Wealth and Virtue*, ed. Istvan Hont and Michael Ignatieff. Cambridge: Cambridge University Press. 235–52.

—. 1985. *Virtue, Commerce, and History: Essays on Political Thought and History, Chiefly in the Eighteenth Century*. Cambridge: Cambridge University Press.

—. 1999–2015. *Barbarism and Religion*, 6 vols. Cambridge: Cambridge University Press.

Pohl, Nicole. 2006. '"Perfect Reciprocity": Salon Culture and Epistolary Conversations.' *Women's Writing* 13, 1: 139–59.

Polleross, Friedrich. 1998. 'Architecture and Rhetoric in the Work of Johann Bernhard Fischer von Erlach', trans. Peter Ian Waugh. In *Infinite Boundaries:*

Order, Disorder and Reorder in Early Modern German Culture, ed. Max Reinhart. Kirksville: Sixteenth Century Journal. 121–46.

Pope, Alexander. 1963. *The Poems of Alexander Pope*, ed. John Butt. New Haven: Yale University Press.

Popkin, Richard. 1979. *The History of Scepticism from Erasmus to Spinoza*. Berkeley: University of California Press.

Porter, Roy. 2000. *The Creation of the Modern World: The Untold Story of the British Enlightenment*. New Yufse)ork: W. W. Norton.

Porter, Roy and Mikulás Teich, eds. 1981. *The Enlightenment in National Context*. Cambridge: Cambridge University Press.

Potkay, Adam. 1994. *The Fate of Eloquence in the Age of Hume*. Ithaca and London: Cornell University Press.

Poulakos, John. 2007. 'From the Depths of Rhetoric: The Emergence of Aesthetics as a Discipline.' *Philosophy and Rhetoric* 40, 4: 335–52.

Poussin, Nicolas. 1964. *Lettres et propos sur l'art*, ed. Anthony Blunt. Paris: Hermann.

Praz, Mario. 1971. *Conversation Pieces: A Survey of the Informal Group Portrait in Europe and America*. University Park and London: Pennsylvania State University Press.

Prendergast, Amy. 2015. *Literary Salons Across Britain and Ireland in the Long Eighteenth Century*. New York: Palgrave Macmillan.

Prévost, Antoine François. 1967. *Le Pour et Contre. Tome I, comprenant les volumes 1 à 5*. Geneva: Slatkine Reprints.

Priezac, Daniel de. 1652. *Discours politiques*. Paris: Rocolet.

Prill, Paul. 1987. 'Rhetoric and Poetics in the Early Middle Ages.' *Rhetorica* 5, 2: 129–47.

Prince, Michael. 1996. *Philosophical Dialogue in the British Enlightenment: Theology, Aesthetics, and the Novel*. Cambridge: Cambridge University Press.

Prostko, Jack. 1989. '"Natural Conversation Set in View": Shaftesbury and Moral Speech.' *Eighteenth-Century Studies* 23, 1: 42–61.

Pufendorf, Samuel. 1729. *Of the Law of Nature and Nations*, 4th edn, ed. Jean Barbeyrac, trans. Basil Kennett. London: Walthoe, et al.

Pujol, Stéphane. 2001. 'Conversation.' In *Encyclopedia of the Enlightenment*, ed. Michel Delon. Chicago and London: Fitzroy Dearborn. 313–17.

Puppi, Lionello. 1972. 'The Villa Garden of the Veneto from the Fifteenth to the Eighteenth Century.' In *The Italian Garden*, ed. David R. Coffin. Washington, DC: Dumbarton Oaks. 81–114.

Quatremère de Quincy, Antoine-Chrysostome. 1788. *Encyclopédie méthodique. Architecture. Tome Premier.* 1788. Paris: Panckoucke.

—. 1825. *Encyclopédie méthodique. Architecture. Tome Troisième*. 1825. Paris: Agasse.

Quintilian. 1920–2. *Institutio oratoria*, 4 vols, ed. and trans. H. E. Butler. London and New York: William Heinemann and G. P. Putnam's Sons.

Racine, Jean. 1987. *Phaedra*, trans. Richard Wilbur. New York: Harcourt.

Rameau, Jean-Philippe. 1722. *Traité de l'harmonie*. Paris: Ballard.
Ramus, Petrus. 1546. *Dialectici commentarii tres authore Audomaro Talaeo editi*. Paris: Grandin.
—. 1555. *Dialectique de Pierre de la Ramee*. Paris: Wechel.
Randall, David. 2008. 'Ethos, Poetics, and the Literary Public Sphere.' *Modern Language Quarterly* 69, 2: 221–43.
—. 2011a. 'Empiricism, the New Rhetoric, and the Public Sphere.' *Telos* 154: 51–73.
—. 2011b. 'Humean Aesthetics and the Rhetorical Public Sphere.' *Telos* 157: 148–63.
—. 2011c. 'The Prudential Public Sphere.' *Philosophy & Rhetoric* 44, 3: 205–26.
—. 2016a. 'The Rhetoric of Violence, the Public Sphere, and the Second Amendment.' *Philosophy & Rhetoric* 49, 2: 125–48.
—. 2016b. 'Adam Smith's Mixed Prudence and the Economy of the Public Sphere.' *Political Studies* 64, 2: 335–50.
—. 2018. *The Concept of Conversation: From Cicero's* Sermo *to the* Grand Siècle*'s* Conversation. Edinburgh: Edinburgh University Press.
Randall, John Herman, Jr. 1960. *Aristotle*. New York and London: Columbia University Press.
Ranum, Patricia M. 2001. *The Harmonic Orator: The Phrasing and Rhetoric of the Melody in French Baroque Airs*. Hillsdale: Pendragon Press.
Raphael, D. D. 2007. *The Impartial Spectator: Adam Smith's Moral Philosopy*. Oxford: Clarendon Press.
Raphael, D. D. and A. L. Macfie. 1976. 'Introduction.' In *The Theory of Moral Sentiments*, Adam Smith, ed. D. D. Raphael and A. L. Macfie. Oxford: Oxford University Press. 1–52.
Rapin, René. 1672. *Reflections Upon the Use of the Eloquence of These Times*, trans. unknown. Oxford: Printed and sold by the booksellers there.
—. 1675. *Réflexions sur la poétique de ce temps et sour les ouvrages des poetes anciens y modernes*. Paris: Barbin.
—. 1706. *The Whole Critical Works of Monsieur Rapin*, vols I–II, 2nd edn, trans. Basil Kennet. London: Bonwicke, et al.
Rault, de Roüen. 1680. 'De L'Origine de La Danse'. In *Extraordinaire du Mercure Galant: Quartier d'Avril 1680. Tome X*. Lyon: Amaulry. 186–208.
Ray, William. 2004. 'Talking About Art: The French Royal Academy Salons and the Discursive Citizen.' *Eighteenth-Century Studies* 37, 4: 527–52.
Raymond, Joad. 1999. 'The Newspaper, Public Opinion, and the Public Sphere in the Seventeenth Century.' In *News, Newspapers, and Society in Early Modern Britain*, ed. Joad Raymond. London: Frank Cass. 109–40.
—. 2003. *Pamphlets and Pamphleteering in Early Modern Britain*. Cambridge: Cambridge University Press.
Rebhorn, Wayne A. 1993. 'Baldesar Castiglione, Thomas Wilson, and the Courtly Body of Renaissance Rhetoric.' *Rhetorica* 11, 3: 241–74.

—. 1995. *The Emperor of Men's Minds: Literature and the Renaissance Discourse of Rhetoric*. Ithaca and London: Cornell University Press.

Recueil de pièces concernant les différends des pairs de France avec les présidens à mortier du Parlement de Paris. 1716. Paris: Coustelier.

Rée, Jonathan. 1978. 'Philosophy and the History of Philosophy.' In *Philosophy and its Past*, Jonathan Rée, Michael Ayers and Adam Westoby. Hassocks: Harvester Press. 1–39.

Reicha, Antoine. 2000. *Treatise on Melody*, trans. Peter M. Landey. Hillsdale: Pendragon Press.

Relihan, Constance. 1994. *Fashioning Authority: The Development of Elizabethan Novelistic Discourse*. Kent and London: Kent State University Press.

Repton, Humphry. 1805. *Observations on the Theory and Practice of Landscape Gardening*. London: Taylor.

Retford, Kate. 2006. *The Art of Domestic Life: Family Portraiture in Eighteenth-Century England*. New Haven and London: Paul Mellon Cenre for Studies in British Art.

Reynolds, Christopher A. 1995. *Papal Patronage and the Music of St. Peter's, 1380–1513*. Berkeley and Los Angeles: University of California Press.

Reynolds, Joshua. 1959. *Discourses on Art*, ed. Robert Wark. San Marino: Huntington Library.

Richardson, Jonathan. 1725. *An Essay on the Theory of Painting*, 2nd edn enlarged. London: Printed for A. C.

Richardson, Samuel. 1928. *Familiar Letters on Important Occasions*, ed. Brian W. Downs. New York: Dodd, Mead.

Richetti, John. 1983. *Philosophical Writing: Locke, Berkeley, Hume*. Cambridge, MA, and London: Harvard University Press.

Rigberg, Lynn. 1999. *Jane Austen's Discourse with New Rhetoric*. New York: Peter Lang.

Ripa, Cesare and Cesare Orlandi. 1765. *Iconologia*, vol. II. Perugia: Costantini.

Ritzarev, Marina. 2006. *Eighteenth-Century Russian Music*. London and New York: Routledge.

Robespierre, Maximilien de. 1828. *Papiers inédits trouvès chez Robespierre, Saint-Just, Payan, etc. Tome Second*. Paris: Baudouin Frères.

Robortello, Francesco. 1548. *Utinensis in librum Aristotelis de arte poeticae explicationes*. Florence: n.p.

Roche, Daniel. 1978. *Le siècle des lumières en province: Académies et académiciens provinciaux, 1680–1789. Tome I*. Paris: Mouton.

Rohan, Henri, Duc de. 1641. *Treatise of the interest of the princes and states of Christendom*, trans. Henry Hunt. London: Hodgkinsonne.

Rollin, Charles. 1734. *The Method of Teaching and Studying the Belles Lettres*, 4 vols, trans. unknown. London: Bettesworth and Hitch.

—. 1737. *The Method of Teaching and Studying the Belles Lettres. The Second Edition*, 4 vols, trans. unknown. London: Bettesworth and Hitch.

Ronsard, Pierre. 1563. *Discours des Miseres de ce Temps*. Paris: Buon.

Roos, Merethe. 2009. 'The Salon as an Arena of Secularization: Music Performed on Intimate Stages in the Last Decades of the 18 [*sic*] Century. New Perspectives on the Function of the Salon.' *Theatrum Historiae* 4: 155–68.

Rosen, David and Aaron Santesso. 2013. *The Watchmen in Pieces: Surveillance, Literature, and Liberal Personhood*. New Haven and London: Yale University Press.

Rothschild, Jeffrey. 1990. 'Renaissance Voices Echoed: The Emergence of the Narrator in English Prose.' *College English* 52, 1: 21–35.

Rousseau, Jean-Jacques. 1994. *On the Social Contract*. In *Collected Writings of Rousseau. Vol. 4: Social Contract, Discourse on the Virtue Most Necessary for a Hero, Political Fragments, and Geneva Mansucript*, trans. Judith R. Bush, Roger D. Masters and Christopher Kelly, ed. Roger D. Masters and Christopher Kelly. Hanover and London: University Press of New England.

—. 1997. *Discourse on Inequality, Part II*. In *The Discourses and Other Early Political Writings*, ed. Victor Gourevitch. Cambridge: Cambridge University Press. 164–94.

—. 1998. *Essay on the Origin of Languages and Writings Related to Music*, trans. and ed. John T. Scott. Hanover: University Press of New England.

—. 2004. *Letter to d'Alembert*. In *The Collected Writings of Rousseau. Vol. 10: Letter to D'Alembert and Writings for the Theater*, ed. and trans. Allan Bloom, Charles Butterworth and Christopher Kelly. Hanover and London: University Press of New England.

Rowe, Greg. 2002. *Princes and Political Cultures: The New Tiberian Senatorial Decrees*. Ann Arbor: University of Michigan Press.

Russo, Elena. 2001. 'From *Précieuse* to Mother Figure: Sentiment, Authority, and the Eighteenth-Century *Salonnière*.' *Studies on Voltaire and the Eighteenth Century* 12: 179–98.

—. 2007. *Styles of Enlightenment: Taste, Politics, and Authorship in Eighteenth-Century France*. Baltimore: Johns Hopkins University Press.

—. 2017. Review of *The World of the Salons* by Antoine Lilti. *Reviews in History*. http://www.history.ac.uk/reviews/review/2041.

Rygg, Kristin. 2000. *Masqued Mysteries Unmasked: Early Modern Music Theater and Its Pythagorean Subtext*. Hillsdale: Pendragon Press.

Sabbatini, Luigi Antonio. 1802. *Trattati sopra le Fughe Musicali*. Venice: Valle.

Sabl, Andrew. 2002. *Ruling Passions: Political Offices and Democratic Ethics*. Princeton: Princeton University Press.

Sacy, Louis de. 1715. *Traité de la gloire*. Paris: Huet.

Saint-Évremond, Charles de Marguetel de Saint Denis, Sieur de. 1700. *The Works of Mr. de St. Evremont*. London: Printed for Awnsham and John Churchill.

Saint-Lambert, Michel de. 1984. *Principles of the Harpsichord*, trans. and ed. Rebecca Harris-Warrick. Cambridge: Cambridge University Press.

Salutati, Coluccio. 1951. *De laboribus Herculis*, 2 vols, ed. B. L. Ullman. Zurich: Thesaurus Mundi.

Saunders, J. W. 1951. 'The Stigma of Print: A Note on the Social Bases of Tudor Poetry.' *Essays in Criticism* 1, 2: 139–64.

Schaeffer, John D. 1990. *Vico, Rhetoric, and the Limits of Relativism*. Durham, NC, and London: Duke University Press.

Schaeffer, Peter. 1986. 'Humanism on Display: The Epistles Dedicatory of Georg von Logan.' *Sixteenth Century Journal* 17, 2: 215–23.

Schama, Simon. 1990. *Citizens: A Chronicle of the French Revolution*. New York: Vintage.

Schmitter, Amy M. 2012. 'Family Trees: Sympathy, Comparison, and the Proliferation of the Passions in Hume and his Predecessors.' In *Emotion and Cognitive Life in Medieval and Early Modern Philosophy*, ed. Martin Pickavé and Lisa Shapiro. Oxford: Oxford University Press. 255–78.

Schochet, Gordon J. 1988. *The Authoritarian Family and Political Attitudes in 17th-Century England: Patriarchalism in Political Thought*. New Brunswick: Transaction Books.

Scholes Robert and Robert Kellogg. 1966. *The Nature of Narrative*. New York: Oxford University Press.

Schulenberg, David. 1992. 'Musical Expression and Musical Rhetoric in the Keyboard Works of J. S. Bach.' In *Johann Sebastian: A Tercentenary Celebration*, ed. Seymour L. Benstock. Westport: Greenwood Press. 95–109.

Schultz, James. 1984. 'Classical Rhetoric, Medieval Poetics, and the Medieval Vernacular Prologue.' *Speculum* 59, 1: 1–15.

Schulz, Johann Abraham Peter. 1774. 'Trio.' In *Allgemeine Theorie der schönen Künste*, Johann Georg Sulzer. Leipzig: Weidmann. 1180–1.

Scott, John T. 1998. 'The Harmony Between Rousseau's Musical Theory and His Philosophy.' *Journal of the History of Ideas* 59, 2: 287–308.

Scott, Katie. 1995. *The Rococo Interior: Decoration and Social Spaces in Early Eighteenth-Century Paris*. New Haven and London: Yale University Press.

Scudéry, Madeleine de. 1680. *Conversations sur divers sujets. Tome Premier*. Lyon: Amaulry.

—. 2002. 'On Conversation', trans. Jane Donawerth. In *Rhetorical Theory by Women before 1900: An Anthology*, ed. Jane Donawerth. Lanham: Rowman & Littlefield. 84–90.

Secord, James. 1985. 'Newton in the Nursery: Tom Telescope and the Philosophy of Tops and Balls, 1761–1838.' *History of Science* 23, 2: 127–51.

Shaftesbury, Anthony Ashley Cooper, Third Earl of. 1699. *An Inquiry Concerning Virtue, In Two Discourses*. London: Bell, Castle, and Buckley.

—. 1732. *Characteristics of Men, Manners, Opinions, Times*, vol. III. London: John Darby.

—. 1900. *The Life, Unpublished Letters, and Philosophical Regimen of Anthony, Earl of Shaftesbury*, ed. Benjamin Rand. London and New York: Swan Sonnenschein and Macmillan.

—. 1999. *Characteristics of Men, Manners, Opinions, Times*, ed. Lawrence E. Klein. Cambridge: Cambridge University Press.

Shanks, Torrey. 2015. *Authority Figures: Rhetoric and Experience in John Locke's Political Thought*. University Park: Pennsylvania State University Press.

Shapin, Steven. 1994. *A Social History of Truth: Civility and Science in Seventeenth-Century England*. Chicago and London: University of Chicago Press.

Sheehan, Colleen A. 2002. 'Madison and the French Enlightenment: The Authority of Public Opinion.' *The William and Mary Quarterly*, 3rd series 59, 4: 925–56.

—. 2004. 'Madison v. Hamilton: The Battle over Republicanism and the Role of Public Opinion.' *American Political Science Review* 98, 3: 405–24.

—. 2005. 'Public Opinion and the Formation of Civic Character in Madison's Republican Theory.' *The Review of Politics* 67, 1: 37–48.

Shields, David S. 1997. *Civil Tongues & Polite Letters in British America*. Chapel Hill and London: University of North Carolina Press.

Shklar, Judith. 1969. *Men and Citizens: A Study of Rousseau's Social Theory*. Cambridge: Cambridge University Press.

Shusternan, Richard. 1989. 'Of the Scandal of Taste: Social Privilege as Nature in the Aesthetic Theories of Hume and Kant.' *Philosophical Forum* 20, 3: 211–29.

Sidney, Philip. 2002. *An Apology for Poetry or The Defence of Poetry*, ed. Geoffrey Shepherd and R. W. Maslen. Manchester and New York: Manchester University Press.

Silhon, Jean de. 1643. *Le Ministre d'estat, seconde partie, avec le veritable vsage de la politique moderne*. Paris: Iouxte la Copie Imprimée.

—. 1661. *De la certitude des connoissances humaines, où sont particulièrement expliquez les principes de la morale et de la politique*. Paris: De l'imprimerie royale.

Simon, Julia. 2004. 'Singing Democracy: Music and Politics in Jean-Jacques Rousseau's Thought.' *Journal of the History of Ideas* 65, 3: 433–54.

Sisman, Elaine R. 1993. *Haydn and the Classical Variation*. Cambridge, MA: Harvard University Press.

Skinner, Quentin. 1987. 'Sir Thomas More's *Utopia* and the Language of Renaissance Humanism.' In *The Languages of Political Theory in Early-Modern Europe*, ed. Anthony Pagden. Cambridge: Cambridge University Press. 123–57.

—. 1996. *Reason and Rhetoric in the Philosophy of Hobbes*. Cambridge: Cambridge University Press.

Sloan, Lucinda Heck. 1990. *The Influence of Rhetoric on Jean-Philippe Rameau's Solo Vocal Cantatas and Treatise of 1722*. New York: Peter Lang.

Sloboda, Stacey. 2010. 'Fashioning Bluestocking Conversation: Elizabeth Montagu's Chinese Room.' In *Architectural Space in Eighteenth-Century Europe: Constructing Identities and Interiors*, ed. Denise Amy Baxter and Meredith Martin. Aldershot: Ashgate. 129–48.

Smarr, Janet Levarie. 2005. *Joining the Conversation: Dialogues by Renaissance Women*. Ann Arbor: University of Michigan Press.

Smith, Adam. 1978. *Lectures on Jurisprudence*, ed. R. L. Meek, D. D. Raphael and P. G. Stein. Oxford: Clarendon Press.

—. 1985. *Lectures on Rhetoric and Belles Lettres*, ed. J. C. Bryce. Indianapolis: Liberty Fund.

—. 2002. *The Theory of Moral Sentiments*, ed. Knud Haakonssen. Cambridge: Cambridge University Press.

—. 2003. *The Wealth of Nations*. New York: Bantam.

Smith, A. William, ed. and trans. 1995. *Fifteenth-Century Dance and Music: Twelve Transcribed Italian Treatises and Collections in the Tradition of Domenico da Piacenza. Vol. I: Treatises and Music*. Stuyvesant: Pendragon Press.

Smith, Christine. 1992. *Architecture in the Culture of Early Humanism: Ethics, Aesthetics, and Eloquence 1400–1470*. Oxford: Oxford University Press.

Smith, Theresa Ann. 2006. *The Emerging Female Citizen: Gender and Enlightenment in Spain*. Berkeley and Los Angeles: University of California Press.

Solkin, David H. 1993. *Painting for Money: The Visual Arts and the Public Sphere in Eighteenth-Century England*. New Haven and London: Paul Mellon Centre for Studies in British Art.

Spacks, Patricia Meyer. 2003. *Privacy: Concealing the Eighteenth-Century Self*. Chicago and London: University of Chicago Press.

Stamp, John. 2002. *Slander and Censorship in Late Sixteenth Century Literature*. PhD diss., University of California.

Starobinski, Jean. 1977. 'Eloquence and Liberty.' *Journal of the History of Ideas* 38, 2: 195–210.

Staves, Susan. 1982. 'A Few Kind Words for the Fop.' *Studies in English Literature, 1500–1900* 22: 413–28.

Stein, Peter. 1980. *Legal Evolution: The Story of an Idea*. Cambridge: Cambridge University Press.

Sterne, Laurence. 1980. *Tristram Shandy*. New York and London: W. W. Norton.

Stevens, Jane R. 1989. 'The Meaning and Uses of *Caractère* in Eighteenth Century France.' In *French Musical Thought, 1600–1800*, ed. Georgia Cowart. Ann Arbor and London: UMI Research Press. 23–52.

Stevens, John. 1992. 'Music, Number and Rhetoric in the Early Middle Ages.' In *Companion to Contemporary Musical Thought*, vol. 2, ed. John Paynter, Tim Howell, Richard Orton and Peter Seymour. London and New York: Routledge. 885–910.

Stolnitz, Jerome. 1963. 'Locke and the Category of Value in Eighteenth-Century British Aesthetic Theory.' *Philosophy* 38, 143: 40–51.

Strassburg, Gottfried von. 1960. *Tristan*, trans. A. T. Hatto. Edinburgh: Penguin.

Street, Alan. 1987. 'The Rhetorico-Musical Structure of the "Goldberg" Variations: Bach's *Clavier-Übung* IV and the *Institutio oratoria* of Quintilian.' *Music Analysis* 6, 1/2: 89–131.

Stroud, Scott. 2005. 'Rhetoric and Moral Progress in Kant's Ethical Community.' *Philosophy and Rhetoric* 38, 4: 328–54.

—. 2006. 'Kant on Community: A Reply to Gehrke.' *Philosophy and Rhetoric* 39, 2: 157–65.

Struever, Nancy S. 1970. *The Language of History in the Renaissance: Rhetoric and Historical Consciousness in Florentine Humanism*. Princeton: Princeton University Press.

—. 1985. 'The Conversable World: Eighteenth-Century Transformations of the Relation of Rhetoric and Truth.' In *Rhetoric and the Pursuit of Truth: Language Change in the Seventeenth and Eighteenth Centuries*, Brian Vickers and Nancy Struever. Los Angeles: William Andrews Clark Memorial Library. 79–119.

—. 1989. 'Machiavelli, Montaigne, and the Problem of External Address in Renaissance Ethics.' In *Discourses of Authority in Medieval and Renaissance Literature*, ed. Kevin Brownlee and Walter Stephens. Hanover and London: University Press of New England. 236–53.

Suard, Jean-Baptiste. 1774. *Discours prononcés dans l'Académie française, le jeudi 4 août à la réception de M. Suard*. Paris: Demonville.

Sulzer, Johann Georg. 1995. *General Theory of the Fine Arts*, trans. Thomas Christensen. In *Aesthetics and the Art of Musical Composition in the German Enlightenment: Selected Writings of Johann Georg Sulzer and Heinrich Christoph Koch*, ed. and trans. Nancy Kovaleff Baker and Thomas Christensen. Cambridge: Cambridge University Press.

Summers, David. 1987. *The Judgment of Sense: Renaissance Naturalism and the Rise of Aesthetics*. Cambridge: Cambridge University Press.

Sutton, Geoffrey V. 1995. *Science for a Polite Society: Gender, Culture, and the Demonstration of Enlightenment*. Boulder: Westview Press.

Sutton, John L., Jr. 1984. 'The Source of Mrs. Manley's Preface to "Queen Zarah".' *Modern Philology* 82: 167–72.

Swanson, Janice. 1981. 'Toward a Rhetoric of Self: The Art of *Persuasion*.' *Nineteenth-Century Fiction* 36, 1: 1–21.

Sweet, R. H. 2002. 'Topographies of Politeness.' *Transactions of the Royal Historical Society* 12: 355–74.

Swift, Jonathan. 1704. *A Tale of a Tub*. London: Nutt.

—. 1957. *A Proposal for Correcting the English Tongue, Polite Conversation, Etc.*, ed. Herbert Davis and Louis Landa. Oxford: Blackwell. Vol. 4 of *The Prose Works of Jonathan Swift*, Herbert Davis, gen. ed., 14 vols. Oxford: Blackwell, 1935–1968.

—. 2013. *Parodies, Hoaxes, Mock Treatises: Polite Conversation, Directions to Servants and Other Works*, ed. Valerie Rumbold. Cambridge: Cambridge University Press.

Szambien, Werner. 1986. *Symétrie, goût, caractère: Théorie et terminologie de l'architecture à l'âge classique 1550–1800*. Paris: Picard.

Tacitus. 1925. *Dialogus. Agricola. Germania*, trans. William Peterson. London and New York: William Heinemann and G. P. Putnam's Sons.

Talon, Omer. 1577. *Petri Rami Professoris Regii, et Audomari Talaei Collectanae. Praefationes, Epistolae, Orationes*. Paris: Apud Dionysium Vallensem.

Tasso, Torquato. 1633. *De la noblesse*, trans. J. Baudoin. Paris: Courbé.

—. 1858. *I Dialoghi di Torquato Tasso*, ed. Cesare Guasti. Florence: Felice Le Monnier.

Tave, Stuart. 1973. *Some Words of Jane Austen*. Chicago and London: University of Chicago Press.

Temple, William. 1680. *Essay upon the original and nature of government*. In *Miscellanea*. London: Printed by A. M. and R. R. for Ed. Gellibrand. 45–95.

—. 1814. *The Works of Sir William Temple*, 4 vols. London: F. C. and J. Rivington [etc.].

Terence. 2001. *Terence I: The Woman of Andros. The Self-Tormenter. The Eunuch*, trans. John Barsby. Cambridge, MA, and London: Harvard University Press.

Terrall, Mary. 1995. 'Émilie du Châtelet and the Gendering of Science.' *History of Science* 33, 3: 283–310.

—. 1996. 'Salon, Academy, and Boudoir: Generation and Desire in Maupertuis's Science of Life.' *Isis* 87, 2: 217–29.

Tesauro, Emanuele. 1670. *Connoccchiale aristotelico*. Turin: Zavatta.

Theobald, Lewis. 1717. *The Censor*, vol. II. London: Brown.

Thom, Martin. 1995. *Republics, Nations, and Tribes*. London and New York: Verso.

Thomas, Antoine Léonard. 1819. *Oeuvres de Thomas. Tome Premier*. Paris: Belin.

Thomas, Downing A. 1995. *Music and the Origins of Language: Theories from the French Enlightenment*. Cambridge: Cambridge University Press.

Thomas, Edmund. 2014. 'On the Sublime in Architecture.' In *Art and Rhetoric in Roman Culture*, ed. Jaś Elsner and Michel Meyer. Cambridge: Cambridge University Press. 37–88.

Thweatt, Vivien. 1980. *La Rochefoucuald and the Seventeenth-Century Concept of the Self*. Geneva: Droz.

Tinkler, John F. 1988. 'Humanism and Dialogue.' *Parergon: Bulletin of the Australian and New Zealand Association for Medieval and Renaissance Studies* 6: 197–214.

—. 1991. 'Erasmus' Conversation with Luther.' *Archiv für Reformationsgeschichte* 82: 59–81.

Toft, Robert. 1984. 'Musicke a Sister to Poetrie: Rhetorical Artifice in the Passionate Airs of John Dowland.' *Early Music* 12, 2: 191–7, 199.

Townsend, Dabney. 1987. 'From Shaftesbury to Kant: The Development of the Concept of Aesthetic Experience.' *Journal of the History of Ideas* 48, 2: 287–305.

—. 1991. 'Lockean Aesthetics.' *The Journal of Aesthetics and Art Criticism* 49, 4: 349–61.

—. 2001. *Hume's Aesthetic Theory: Taste and Sentiment*. London and New York: Routledge.

Tribby, Jay. 1992. 'Body/Building: Living the Museum Life in Early Modern Europe.' *Rhetorica* 10, 2: 139–63.

Troyes, Chrétien de. 1987. *Arthurian Romances*, trans. D. D. R. Owen. London: Dent.

Tuck, Richard. 1987. 'The "Modern" Theory of Natural Law.' In *The Langauges of Political Theory in Early-Modern Europe*, ed. Anthony Pagden. Cambridge: Cambridge University Press. 99–119.

Tuveson, Ernest. 1974. *The Imagination as a Means of Grace: Locke and the Aesthetics of Romanticism*. New York: Gordian Press.

'Ueber Musik, ihre Wirkung und Anwendung.' 1792. *Flensburgsches Wochenblat für Jedermann* V/11 (12 September), 85–8, and V/12 (19 September), 89–95.

Valenza, Robin. 2009. *Literature, Language, and the Rise of the Intellectual Disciplines in Britain, 1680–1820*. Cambridge: Cambridge University Press.

Van Deusen, Nancy. 1985. 'Origins of a Significant Medieval Genre: The Musical "Trope" up to the Twelfth Century.' *Rhetorica* 3, 4: 245–67.

Van Eck, Caroline. 1995. '*Par le Style on Atteint au Sublime*: The Meaning of the Term "Style" in French Architectural Theory of the Late Eighteenth Century.' In *The Question of Style in Philosophy and the Arts*, ed. Caroline Van Eck, James McAllister and Renée Van De Vall. Cambridge: Cambridge University Press. 89–107.

—. 1998. 'The Structure of "De re aedificatoria" Reconsidered.' *Journal of the Society of Architectural Historians* 57, 3: 280–97.

—. 2000. 'Architecture, Language, and Rhetoric in Alberti's *De re aedificatoria*.' In *Architecture and Language: Constructing Identity in European Architecture, c. 1000–c. 1650*, ed. Georgia Clarke and Paul Crossley. Cambridge: Cambridge University Press. 72–81.

—. 2007. *Classical Rhetoric and the Visual Arts in Early Modern Europe*. Cambridge: Cambridge University Press.

Van Orden, Kate. 2005. *Music, Discipline, and Arms in Early Modern France*. Chicago and London: University of Chicago Press.

Vasari, Giorgio. 1881. *Le vite de' più eccelenti pittori scultori ed architettori. Tomo VII*, ed. Gaetano Milanesi. Florence: Sansoni.

Vaumorière, Pierre d'Ortigue, Sieur de. 1691. *L'Art de plaire dans la conversation* (Paris, 1690), trans. unknown, *The Art of Pleasing in Conversation*. London: R. Bentley.

Vial, Stephanie D. 2008. *The Art of Musical Phrasing in the Eighteenth Century: Punctuating the Classical 'Period'*. Rochester: University of Rochester Press.

Vianey, Joseph. 1903. 'L'Arioste et les discours de Ronsard.' *Revue Universitaire* 12: 473–5.

Vicentino, Nicola. 1996. *Ancient Music Adapted to Modern Practice*, trans. Maria Rika Maniates, ed. Claude V. Palisca. New Haven and London: Yale University Press.

Vickers, Brian. 1983. 'Epideictic and Epic in the Renaissance.' *New Literary History* 14, 3: 497–537.

—. 1984. 'Figures of Rhetoric/Figures of Music?' *Rhetorica* 2, 1: 1–44.

—. 1988. *In Defence of Rhetoric*. Oxford: Clarendon Press.

Vidal, Mary. 1992. *Watteau's Painted Conversations: Art Literature, and Talk in Seventeenth- and Eighteenth-Century France*. New Haven and London: Yale University Press.

—. 2006. 'Style as Subject in Watteau's Images of Conversation.' In *Antoine Watteau: Perspectives on the Artist and the Culture of his Time*, ed. Mary D. Sheriff. Cranbury: Associated University Presses. 76–93.

Vidler, Anthony. 1987. *The Writing of the Walls: Architectural Theory in the Late Enlightenment*. Princeton: Princeton Architectural Press.

Vitruvius. 1960. *The Ten Books on Architecture*, trans. Morris Hicky Morgan. New York: Dover.

Vivenza, Gloria. 2001. *Adam Smith and the Classics: The Classical Heritage in Adam Smith's Thought*. Oxford: Oxford University Press.

Voltaire (François-Marie Arouet). 1750. *La Voix du sage et du people*. Amsterdam: Le Sincere.

—. 1786. *Oeuvres Completes de Voltaire. Tome Quarante-Troisieme*. Gotha: Ettinger.

Vulson, Marc de, Sieur de la Colombière. 1648. *Le Vray théâtre d'honneur et de chevalerie*, 2 vols. Paris: Courbé.

Wahl, Elizabeth Susan. 1999. *Invisible Relations: Representations of Female Intimacy in the Age of Enlightenment*. Stanford: Stanford University Press.

Walker, Jeffrey. 1996. 'Before the Beginnings of "Poetry" and "Rhetoric": Hesiod on Eloquence.' *Rhetorica* 14, 3: 243–64.

—. 2000. *Rhetoric and Poetics in Antiquity*. Oxford: Oxford University Press.

Walker, Obadiah. 1673. *Of education, especially of young gentlemen*. Oxford: At the Theater.

Walker, Paul. 1995. 'Rhetoric, the Ricercar, and J. S. Bach's *Musical Offering*.' In *Bach Studies 2*, ed. Daniel R. Melamed. Cambridge, Cambridge University Press. 175–91.

Walker, William. 1994. *Locke, Literary Criticism, and Philosophy*. Cambridge: Cambridge University Press.

Walters, Alice N. 1997. 'Conversation Pieces: Science and Politeness in Eighteenth-Century England.' *History of Science* 35, 2: 121–54.

Ward, Lee. 2010. *John Locke and Modern Life*. Cambridge: Cambridge University Press.

Ware, Isaac. 1768. *A Complete Body of Architecture*. London: Rivington, et al.

Warner, Michael. 2002. *Publics and Counterpublics*. New York: Zone Books.

Warnick, Barbara. 1985. 'Charles Rollin's *Traité* and the Rhetorical Theories of Smith, Campbell, and Blair.' *Rhetorica* 3, 1: 45–65.

—. 1993. *The Sixth Canon: Belletristic Rhetorical Theory and its French Antecedents*. Columbia: University of South Carolina Press.

Warren, Leland E. 1983. 'Turning Reality Round Together: Guides to Conversation in Eighteenth-Century England.' *Eighteenth Century Life* 8: 65–87.

Watson, Peter. 2010. *The German Genius: Europe's Third Renaissance, the Second Scientific Revolution, and the Twentieth Century*. New York: HarperCollins.

Watts, Isaac. 1743. *The Improvement of the Mind: or, a Supplement to the Art of Logick*, 2nd edn. London: Brackstone and Long.

Weaver, John. 1721. *Anatomical and Mechanical Lectures upon Dancing*. London: Brotherton, et al.

Weber, William. 1980. 'Learned and General Musical Taste in Eighteenth-Century France.' *Past and Present* 89: 58–85.

Weckel, Ulrike. 2000. 'A Lost Paradise of a Female Culture? Some Critical Questions Regarding the Scholarship on Late Eighteenth- and Early Nineteenth-Century German Salons', trans. Pamela E. Selwyn. *German History* 18, 3: 310–36.

Weimann, Robert. 1996. *Authority and Representation in Early Modern Discourse*. Baltimore and London: Johns Hopkins University Press.

Weinberg, Bernard. 1952. 'Robortello on the Poetics.' In *Critics and Criticism: Ancient and Modern*, ed. R. S. Crane. Chicago: University of Chicago Press. 319–48.

—. 1961. *A History of Literary Criticism in the Italian Renaissance*, vols I–II. Chicago: University of Chicago Press.

Whately, Thomas. 1770. *Observations on Modern Gardening*. London: Payne.

Wheelock, Gretchen A. 1992. *Haydn's Ingenious Jesting With Art: Contexts of Musical Wit and Humor*. New York: Schirmer Books.

White, Daniel E. 2006. *Early Romanticism and Religious Dissent*. Cambridge: Cambridge University Press.

Williams, Peter. 1983. 'The Snares and Delusions of Musical Rhetoric: Some Examples from Recent Writings on J. S. Bach.' In *Alte Musik: Praxis und Reflexion*, ed. Peter Reidemeister and Veronika Gutmann. Winterthur: Amadeus. 230–40.

Williamson, Tom. 1995. *Polite Landscapes: Gardens and Society in Eighteenth-Century England*. Baltimore: Johns Hopkins University Press.

Wilson, Blake McDowell. 1995. '*Ut Oratoria Musica* in the Writings of Renaissance Music Theorists.' In *Festa Musicologica: Essays in Honor of George J. Buelow*, ed. Thomas J. Mathiesen and Benito V. Rivera. Stuyvesant: Pendragon Press. 341–68.

Wilson, Kenneth Jay. 1985. *Incomplete Fictions: The Formation of English Renaissance Dialogue*. Washington, DC: Catholic University of America Press.

Wilson, Thomas. 1553. *The Arte of Rhetorique*. London: Richard Grafton.

Winn, James Anderson. 1981. *Unsuspected Eloquence: A History of the Relations between Poetry and Music*. New Haven and London: Yale University Press.

Witt, Ronald. 2011. *The Two Latin Cultures and the Foundation of Renaissance Humanism in Medieval Italy*. Cambridge: Cambridge University Press.

Wood, Paul. 1994. 'Science, the Universities, and the Public Sphere in Eighteenth-Century Scotland.' *History of Universities* 13: 99–135.

Wortman, Tunis. 1800. *Treatise Concerning Political Enquiry, and the Liberty of the Press*. New York: Printed by George Forman for the Author.

Wren, Christopher. 1750. *Parentalia; or, Memoirs of the family of the Wrens*. London: Osborn.

Wright, James. 1693. *The Humours, and Conversations of the Town, Expos'd in Two Dialogues: The First, of the Men; The Second, of the Women*. London: Bentley and Tonson.

Wright, Johnson Kent. 1997. *A Classical Republican in Eighteenth-Century France: The Political Thought of Mably*. Stanford: Stanford University Press.

Xanthakis-Karamanos, Georgia. 1979. 'The Influence of Rhetoric on Fourth-Century Tragedy.' *The Classical Quarterly*, n.s. 29, 1: 66–76.

Young, Benjamin C. 2013. *Eloquence and Music: The Querelle des Bouffons in Rhetorical Context*. PhD diss., Columbia University.

Index

Works, when not anonymous or collaborative, are listed together with their authors or creators.

CPSIA information can be obtained
at www.ICGtesting.com
Printed in the USA
JSHW030346041120
9291JS00002B/41

9 781474 448673